Spatiality, Sovereignty and Carl Schmitt

The writings of Carl Schmitt are indissociable from both an historical period and a contemporary moment. He will forever be remembered for his association with the National Socialists of 1930s Germany, and as the figure whose writings on sovereignty, politics and the law provided justification for authoritarian, decisional states. Yet at the same time, the post-September 11th 2001 world is one in which a wide range of scholars have increasingly turned to Schmitt to understand a world of 'with us or against us' Manichaeism, spaces of exception that seem to be placed outside the law by legal mechanisms themselves, and the contestation of a unipolar, post-1989 world. This attention marks out Schmitt as one of the foremost emerging thinkers in critical theory and assures his work a large and growing audience.

This work brings together geographers, and Schmitt scholars who are attuned to the spatial dimensions of his work, to discuss his 1950 book *The Nomos of the Earth in the International Law of the* Jus Publicum Europaeum. This broad range of contributors examine the *Nomos* in relation to broader debates about enmity and war, the production of space, the work of Michel Foucault and Giorgio Agamben, and the (non-)recuperability of such an intellect tainted by his anti-Semitism and links to the Nazi party.

Of particular interest, the book contains new translations by Matthew Hannah of Schmitt's (1933) 'Forms of Modern Imperialism in International Law' and his (1939) 'Großraum versus Universalism: The International Legal Struggle over the Monroe Doctrine'. This work will be of great interest to researchers in political theory, socio-legal studies, geopolitics and critical IR theory.

Stephen Legg is Associate Professor in Geography at the University of Nottingham. He researches twentieth-century colonial India, deploying theoretical insights from literatures addressing governmentality, memory and scale.

Interventions
Edited by: Jenny Edkins, *Aberystwyth University* and
Nick Vaughan-Williams, *University of Warwick*

As Michel Foucault has famously stated, 'knowledge is not made for understanding; it is made for cutting.' In this spirit the Edkins–Vaughan–Williams Interventions series solicits cutting-edge, critical works that challenge mainstream understandings in international relations. It is the best place to contribute post-disciplinary works that think rather than merely recognise and affirm the world recycled in IR's traditional geopolitical imaginary.

Michael J. Shapiro, University of Hawai'i at Mãnoa, USA

The series aims to advance understanding of the key areas in which scholars working within broad critical post-structural and postcolonial traditions have chosen to make their interventions, and to present innovative analyses of important topics.

Titles in the series engage with critical thinkers in philosophy, sociology, politics and other disciplines and provide situated historical, empirical and textual studies in international politics.

Critical Theorists and International Relations
Edited by Jenny Edkins and Nick Vaughan-Williams

Ethics as Foreign Policy
Britain, the EU and the Other
Dan Bulley

Universality, Ethics and International Relations
A grammatical reading
Véronique Pin-Fat

The Time of the City
Politics, philosophy, and genre
Michael J. Shapiro

Governing Sustainable Development
Partnership, protest and power at the World Summit
Carl Death

Insuring Security
Biopolitics, security and risk
Luis Lobo-Guerrero

Foucault and International Relations
New critical engagements
Edited by Nicholas J. Kiersey and Doug Stokes

International Relations and Non-Western Thought
Imperialism, colonialism and investigations of global modernity
Edited by Robbie Shilliam

Autobiographical International Relations
I, IR
Edited by Naeem Inayatullah

War and Rape
Law, memory and justice
Nicola Henry

Madness in International Relations
Psychology, security and the global governance of mental health
Alison Howell

Spatiality, Sovereignty and Carl Schmitt
Geographies of the nomos
Edited by Stephen Legg

Spatiality, Sovereignty and Carl Schmitt
Geographies of the nomos

Edited by Stephen Legg

LONDON AND NEW YORK

First published 2011
by Routledge
2 Park Square, Milton Park, Abingdon, Oxon, OX14 4RN

Simultaneously published in the USA and Canada
by Routledge
711 Third Avenue, New York, NY 10017

Routledge is an imprint of the Taylor & Francis Group, an informa business

First issued in paperback 2011

© 2011 Selection and editorial matter, Stephen Legg;
individual chapters, the contributors.

The right of Stephen Legg to be identified as editor of this
work has been asserted by him in accordance with the
Copyright, Designs and Patent Act 1988.

All rights reserved. No part of this book may be reprinted or
reproduced or utilised in any form or by any electronic, mechanical,
or other means, now known or hereafter invented, including photocopying
and recording, or in any information storage or retrieval system,
without permission in writing from the publishers.

Trademark notice: Product or corporate names may be trademarks or
registered trademarks, and are used only for identification and
explanation without intent to infringe.

British Library Cataloguing in Publication Data
A catalogue record for this book is available from the British Library

Library of Congress Cataloging in Publication Data
Spatiality, sovereignty and Carl Schmitt: geographies of the Nomos/
  [edited by] Stephen Legg.
  p. cm. – (Interventions)
  Includes bibliographical references and index.
  1. International relations. 2. Schmitt, Carl, 1888–1985.
  3. Schmitt, Carl, 1888–1985. Nomos der Erde im Völkerrecht
  des Jus Publicum Europaeum. English   4. Political science –
  Philosophy. 5. Geopolitics. I. Legg, Stephen.
  JZ1305.S695 2011
  327.101 – dc22   2010048529

ISBN: 978-0-415-60067-5 (hbk)
ISBN: 978-0-415-52286-1 (pbk)

Typeset in Times New Roman
by Florence Production Ltd, Stoodleigh, Devon

Contents

List of contributors		viii
Acknowledgements		xiii

1 **Introduction: geographies of the nomos**   1
STEPHEN LEGG AND ALEXANDER VASUDEVAN

PART I
Positions and concepts: Schmitt translations   25

    Note on translations   27
    MATTHEW HANNAH

2 **Forms of modern imperialism in international law**   29
CARL SCHMITT 1933, TRANS. MATTHEW HANNAH

3 ***Großraum* versus universalism: the international legal struggle over the Monroe Doctrine**   46
CARL SCHMITT 1939, TRANS. MATTHEW HANNAH

PART II
Historical geographies of the nomos   55

4 **Appropriating, distributing, and producing space after 9/11: the newest nomos of the Earth?**   57
TIMOTHY W. LUKE

5 **Echoes of Carl Schmitt among the ideologists of the new American Empire**   74
GERRY KEARNS

6 **Reading Schmitt geopolitically: nomos, territory and *Großraum***   91
STUART ELDEN

7 **Interwar spatial chaos? Imperialism, internationalism
    and the League of Nations**   106
    STEPHEN LEGG

PART III
Analytical geographies of the nomos   125

8 **Colonial war: Carl Schmitt's deterritorialization of enmity**   127
    MATHEW COLEMAN

9 **A new nomos of post-nomos? Multipolarity, space,
    and constituent power**   143
    RORY ROWAN

10 **Carl Schmitt and the question of spatial ontology**   163
    CLAUDIO MINCA

11 **Between nomos and everyday life: securing the spatial
    order of Foucault and Schmitt**   182
    PETER ROGERS

PART IV
Responses to the *Nomos*   199

12 **Remembering Nazi intellectuals**   201
    DAVID ATKINSON

13 **Partisan space**   211
    DANIEL CLAYTON

14 **The virtual nomos?**   220
    FRANÇOIS DEBRIX

15 **Pastoral power**   227
    MATTHEW HANNAH

16 **Mapping Schmitt**   234
    MICHAEL HEFFERNAN

17 **Air power**   244
    NASSER HUSSAIN

18 **Postcolonialism**   251
    JULIA LOSSAU

19	*Land and Sea* EDUARDO MENDIETA	260
20	Free sea PHILIP E. STEINBERG	268
21	No peace beyond the line PETER STIRK	276
22	The border NICK VAUGHAN-WILLIAMS	284
23	*Ordnung* und *Ortung*/order and localisation THALIN ZARMANIAN	291
	Index	298

Contributors

David Atkinson is a Reader in Cultural and Historical Geography at the University of Hull. His research addresses the histories of geographical knowledge, especially under fascisms. He also works on modern Italy with foci concerning the geographies of colonialism in North Africa and the roles of monuments and memory in the Italian city. He has co-edited *Geopolitical Traditions: A Century of Geopolitical Thought* (with Klaus Dodds, Routledge, 2000) and *Cultural Geography: A Critical Dictionary of Key Concepts* (with David Sibley, Peter Jackson and Neil Washbourne, IB Taurus, 2005).

Daniel Clayton is a Lecturer in the School of Geography and Geosciences at the University of St Andrews. His specialities include colonial, tropical and socialist geographies and his publications include *Islands of Truth: The Imperial Fashioning of Vancouver Island* (University of British Columbia Press, 2000) and papers in *French Historical Studies*, the *Journal of Historical Geography* and *L'Espace Géographique*.

Mathew Coleman is Assistant Professor of Geography and a Fellow at the Center for Interdisciplinary Law and Policy Studies at Ohio State University. He has research and teaching interests in political and economic geography, with a special emphasis on critical geopolitics and the politics of security. His current research explores local-federal immigration policing partnerships in the US in light of the way in which immigration policing has been made central to the war on terror. He has published in leading journals, such as *Antipode*, *Political Geography*, the *Annals of the Association of American Geographers*, *Environment and Planning D: Society and Space* and *Geopolitics*.

François Debrix is Director of ASPECT (Alliance for Social, Political, Ethical and Cultural Thought) and Professor of Political Science at Virginia Tech. He is the author of *Beyond Biopolitics: Theory, Violence, and Horror in World Politics* (with Alexander Barder, forthcoming Routledge, 2011), *Tabloid Terror* (Routledge, 2008) and *Re-Envisioning Peacekeeping* (University of Minnesota Press, 1999). He is also the co-editor of *Rituals of Mediation* (with Cynthia Weber, University of

Minnesota Press, 2003) and *The Geopolitics of American Insecurity* (with Mark Lacy, Routledge, 2009), and editor of *Language, Agency, and Politics in a Constructed World* (M.E. Sharpe, 2003).

Stuart Elden is a Professor of Political Geography at Durham University, and is the editor of *Environment and Planning D: Society and Space*. He works on social/spatial theory and the concept of territory, with publications including *Mapping the Present: Heidegger, Foucault and the Project of a Spatial History* (Continuum, 2001), *Understanding Henri Lefebvre: Theory and the Possible* (Continuum, 2004), *Speaking Against Number: Heidegger, Language and the Politics of Calculation* (Edinburgh University Press, 2006), and *Terror and Territory: The Spatial Extent of Sovereignty* (University of Minnesota Press, 2009).

Matthew Hannah is Professor of Human Geography at Aberystwyth University. His research interests include continental political and social theory, and genealogies of modern calculable territory in the US and Germany. His publications include *Governmentality and the Mastery of Territory in Nineteenth-century America* (Cambridge University Press, 2000) and *Dark Territory in the Information Age: Learning from the West German Census Controversies of the 1980s* (Ashgate, 2010).

Michael Heffernan is Professor of Geography at the University of Nottingham. His publications include *The Meaning of Europe: Geography and Geopolitics* (Hodder, 2003) and *The European Geographical Imagination* (Franz Steiner, 2007). He is currently working on, among other things, a history of geography and cartography during and after the First World War.

Nasser Hussain is Associate Professor of Law, Jurisprudence and Social Thought at Amherst College. He is the author of *The Jurisprudence of Emergency: Colonialism and the Rule of Law* (University of Michigan Press, 2003). He has published in journals such as *Critical Inquiry*, *Stanford Law Review* and *Boston Review*. He is currently completing a manuscript entitled *War by Every Other Name: Colonial Occupation, Air Power, Counterinsurgency*.

Gerry Kearns is Professor in Government and International Affairs and is Director of the School of Public and International Affairs at Virginia Tech. He writes on historical aspects of political and medical geography and has completed *Geopolitics and Empire: The Legacy of Mackinder* (Oxford University Press, 2009). A forthcoming volume is entitled *Young Ireland: Colonialism, Violence, Nationalism* (Manchester University Press). He has published in journals such as *Political Geography*, the *Journal of Historical Geography*, *New Formations* and the *Annals of the Association of American Geographers*.

Stephen Legg is Associate Professor in Cultural and Historical Geography at the University of Nottingham. His research focuses on colonial India, drawing upon theories of postcolonialism, memory and the political. His first book, *Spaces of Colonialism: Delhi's Urban Governmentalities* (Blackwell, 2007), examined the racial, disciplinary and biopolitical ordering of the capital of colonial India. His other research, concerning the nationalist movement in Delhi, and the impact of internationalist networks, such as the League of Nations, on the politics of interwar India, has been published in journals such as *Gender, Place and Culture*, *Environment and Planning A* and *D: Society and Space* and the *Transactions of the Institute of British Geographers*.

Julia Lossau is Assistant Professor of Cultural Geography at the Geographical Institute at Humboldt University, Berlin. She works on the relationship between cultural theory and geography with a special interest in (the histories of) political geography and geopolitics, in questions of postcolonialism and memory as well as in contemporary forms of public art and discourses of aesthetics. Her publications include *Die Politik der Verortung. Eine postkoloniale Reise zu einer anderen Geographie der Welt* (transcript, 2002) and *Themenorte* (co-edited with M. Flitner, LIT, 2005). She has published in journals such as *Erdkunde*, *Géographie et Cultures* and *Cultural Geographies*.

Timothy W. Luke is University Distinguished Professor, Political Science, and Program Chair, Government and International Affairs, at Virginia Polytechnic Institute and State University. His areas of specialisation include environmental and cultural studies as well as comparative politics, international political economy, and modern critical social and political theory. He serves on the editorial boards of *Capitalism Nature Socialism*, *New Political Science*, *Current Perspectives in Social Theory*, *Telos*, *Critical Social Policy* and *Fast Capitalism*. His most recent books include *There is a Gunman on Campus: Terror and Tragedy at Virginia Tech* (with Ben Agger, Rowman & Littlefield, 2008), *Museum Politics: Power Plays at the Exhibition* (University of Minnesota Press, 2002) and *Capitalism, Democracy, and Ecology: Departing from Marx* (University of Illinois Press, 1999).

Eduardo Mendieta is Professor in the Philosophy Department at Stonybrook University and co-editor of *Environment and Planning D: Society and Space*. His research interests include the history of ethics, biophilosophy, European philosophy and critical theory as reflected in his publications, which include *Global Fragments: Critical Theory, Latin America and Globalizations* (SUNY Press, 2007) and *Adventures of Transcendental Philosophy: Karl-Otto Apel's Semiotics and Discourse Ethics* (Rowman & Littlefield, 2002).

Claudio Minca is Professor and Head of the Socio-Spatial Analysis Group at Wageningen University, the Netherlands and Professor of Geography at Royal Holloway, University of London and Visiting Professor at the

College of Tourism, Rikkyo University, Tokyo. His current research centres on three major themes: the spatialisation of (bio)politics; tourism and travel theories of modernity; and the relationship between modern knowledge, space and landscape in postcolonial geography. His most recent books are *Social Capital and Urban Networks of Trust* (with J. Hakli, Ashgate, 2009) and *Travels in Paradox: Remapping Tourism* (with T. Oakes, Rowman & Littlefield, 2006).

Peter Rogers is a Lecturer in the Sociology of Law and Director of the Bachelor of Social Science in the Faculty of Arts at Macquarie University (Sydney). Peter's research into urban regeneration and the social exclusion of young people fostered his keen interest in the sociology of space and the operations of democratic governance. This has developed further through work on the New Security Challenges programme, culminating in a recent book co-authored with Jon Coaffee and David Murakami-Wood entitled *Everyday Resilience of the City* (Palgrave Macmillan, 2008). *Cities under Siege: The Rhythms of Security in the Democratic City* (Ashgate) is in press.

Rory Rowan is a doctoral candidate at the Department of Geography at Royal Holloway, University of London. His research project focuses on the relationship between political ontology and spatial concepts in Carl Schmitt's thought and how it impacts on the value and limitations of his work for geopolitical analysis and democratic theory. He is co-author, with Eva Kenny, of 'Ghostlike Abstractions: Enmity, Sovereignty, and the Discourse of the "War on Terror"' in Petersen and Riou (eds), *Zeichen des Krieges in Literatur, Film und den Medien 3: Terror* (Ludwig Verlag, 2008).

Philip E. Steinberg is a Professor in the Department of Geography at Florida State University and Reviews Editor of *Political Geography*. He researches the governance and representation of spaces that stretch the conceptual boundaries of the state system, especially the ocean, the Internet and the Arctic. His publications include *The Social Construction of the Ocean* (Cambridge University Press, 2001), *What Is a City? Rethinking the Urban after Hurricane Katrina* (with Rob Shields, University of Georgia Press, 2008), and *Managing the Infosphere: Governance, Technology, and Cultural Practice in Motion* (with Stephen McDowell and Tami Tomasello, Temple University Press, 2008).

Peter Stirk is a Senior Lecturer in the School of Government and International Affairs, Durham University. His research focuses on the politics of military occupation, political thought and international relations, and German political thought. His publications include *Critical Theory: Politics and Society* (Pinter, 2000), *Carl Schmitt, Crown Jurist of the Third Reich on Preemptive War, Military Occupation and World Empire* (Edwin Mellen Press, 2005), *Twentieth-Century German Political Thought*

xii *List of contributors*

(Edinburgh University Press, 2006) and *The Politics of Military Occupation* (Edinburgh University Press, 2009).

Alexander Vasudevan is a Lecturer in Cultural and Historical Geography at the University of Nottingham. His research focuses on the cultural geographies of Weimar Germany as well as the politics of housing in contemporary Berlin. He has published in *Cultural Geographies*, *Environment and Planning A* and *D*, *Geopolitics* and *Geoforum*. He is currently working on a book project that explores the historical and political geographies of the squatter movement in Berlin.

Nick Vaughan-Williams is Assistant Professor of International Security at the Department of Politics and International Studies, University of Warwick. He is co-author of *Critical Security Studies: An Introduction* (with Columba Peoples, Routledge, 2010), author of *Border Politics: The Limits of Sovereign Power* (Edinburgh University Press, 2009) and co-editor of *Critical Theorists and International Relations* (with Jenny Edkins, Routledge, 2009) and co-editor of *Terrorism and the Politics of Response* (with Angharad Closs Stephens, Routledge, 2008). He is co-editor (with Jenny Edkins) of the Routledge book series 'Interventions'.

Thalin Zarmanian has recently completed her doctorate in International Relations and Security Studies at the Graduate School for Social, Economic and Political Sciences at the Università degli Studi di Milano, Italy. She also holds a degree in law. In 2006 she published an article about Schmitt's treatment of problems of political order, both domestic and international, in the *Leiden Journal of International Law*.

Acknowledgements

This edited collection emerged from two sessions I convened at the 2009 Annual Meeting of the Association of American Geographers, entitled 'Geographies of Schmitt's Nomos of the Earth'. From this incongruous location (Las Vegas) emerged a strikingly coherent and stimulating series of view- and debating-points regarding the *Nomos* and Schmitt's work more broadly. Many of the contributors have papers here (Atkinson, Coleman, Debrix, Kearns, Luke, Minca, Rogers, Rowan) but the sessions also benefitted from the contributions (as audience member or chair) of Simon Dalby, Phil Steinberg and Gerard Toal. The selection of original papers, further contributors and the coming together of the volume has been a genuinely collaborative venture, but has benefitted especially from the contributions of Mathew Coleman, Stuart Elden, Gerry Kearns and Rory Rowan. The volume is especially indebted to Matthew Hannah not just for his response piece, but also for his generous translations of Schmitt's work.

In a self-consciously non-decisionistic and conversationalist move, as editor I have encouraged no line or perspective on Schmitt's work, although the co-authored introduction sets the critical but respectful tone for the volume as a whole. It has been a privilege to share in such different attempts to engage with a thinker who many of the contributors believe to be both at fault and phenomenally intelligent. Dissociating Schmitt's insights into the modern and historical world from the insidious effects of his authoritarian anti-liberalism has been profoundly challenging, although I hope the insights presented here into the geographies of his nomos works will be sufficiently rewarding to justify the risks here taken.

I would like to thank Nicola Parkin at Routledge for her help in putting together this collection, and Nick Vaughan-Williams and Jenny Edkins for welcoming us to the 'Interventions' series. Alice Schubert at Duncker & Humblot publishers in Berlin helped secure the copyright to present Matthew Hannah's translation of the Schmitt articles, from the following:

'Völkerrechtliche Formen des modernen Imperialismus' in *Positionen und Begriffe: im Kampf mit Weimar–Genf–Versailles, 1923–1939*. Berlin: Duncker und Humblot (1988) pp. 162–80.

'Großraum gegen Universalismus: der völkerrechtliche Kampf um die Monroedoktrin' in *Positionen und Begriffe: im Kampf mit Weimar–Genf–Versailles, 1923–1939*. Berlin: Duncker und Humblot (1988) pp. 295–302.

Permission to use the cover image (Guillaume de Lisle's 1722 *Carte d'Amerique*) has been provided by the David Rumsey Map Collection; my thanks to Mike Heffernan for suggesting it. Robert Richardson at Telos Press kindly supplied permission for the use of the abridged table of contents from their version of *The* Nomos *of the Earth*. Stuart Elden's article is a reworked version of a paper first published in, and reproduced with the permission of, Radical Philosophy:

Elden, S. (2010) 'Reading Schmitt Geopolitically: Nomos, Territory and Großraum', *Radical Philosophy*, 161: 18–26.

Stephen Legg
University of Nottingham
August 2010

1 Introduction

Geographies of the nomos

Stephen Legg and Alexander Vasudevan

> This is a moment to seize. The kaleidoscope has been shaken. The pieces are in flux. Soon they will settle again. Before they do, let us re-order this world around us.
>
> (Tony Blair, Prime Minister, 2 December 2001)[1]

> There should be no doubt that the decision of whether or not armed force is to be used is a decision for the executive. Formal constraints, in statute or convention, do not work when faced with the reality of planning and deployment.
>
> (Lord Falconer, Lord Chancellor, 7 April 2006)[2]

The writings of Carl Schmitt are now indissociable from both an historical period and a twenty-first-century moment. He will forever be remembered for his association with the National Socialists of 1930s Germany, and as the figure whose writings on sovereignty, politics and the law provided justification for authoritarian, decisional states. Yet at the same time, the post-September 11th 2001 world is one in which a wide range of scholars have turned to Schmitt to understand the enmity of a new century of conflict characterised by the emergence of spaces of exception placed outside the law *by and through* the law and the wider contestations of a global American *imperium* through which such legal geographies owe their provenance. Such analyses have been applied to representatives of sovereignty at the centre of political hierarchies, such as Lord Falconer's defence, above, of the decision-making power of the executive to decide on the use of force in concrete, material situations. George W. Bush and his advisors ape Schmitt's doctrines to an extent that would be comic had their consequences not been so tragic: the friend–enemy distinction of warning Iran that 'Our nation and our fight against terror will uphold the doctrine: either you're with us or against us'[3]; the lawful yet exceptional spaces of Guantánamo Bay (Hussain, 2007); the empire-denying logic of America's absent-presentism in Donald Rumsfeld's insistence in April 2003 that 'We're not imperialistic. We never have been' (cited in Ferguson, 2003); and Bush's (2010) autobiographical meditation on his *Decision Points* (also see Kearns, this volume). Others, under the guidance of the philosopher Giorgio Agamben (1998, 2005), have blended Schmitt's work on sovereignty with Walter Benjamin's suggestion that the exception becomes the norm, to examine the 'petty sovereigns' (Butler, 2006, 56) of exception who divide, profile and insecure us in the spaces of the airport, the mall, the passport office or the Internet.

Yet, these Schmittean analyses can lapse into caricature. They can simply become too easy; and this is the very thing Schmitt is not. Chantal Mouffe (2007, 148) has stressed how opposed the Bush regime's slack conflation of aesthetic, moral and economic categories in the 'war on terror' has been to Schmitt's (1996 [1932]) insistence on a purely political distinction between friends and enemies based on a public, existential threat. But she also points out that Bush embodies the messianic humanitarian universalism that Schmitt so loathed. The world vision he promoted was not one of a global friend–enemy divide, but of a more ambiguous with–against division that instituted geographically complex processes of incorporation and integration (see Elden, 2009, 27–31). As the Blair quotation with which we began shows, one of the responses to the September 2001 attacks was to seize an opportunity to forge a new world order out of the kaleidoscopic disordering of . . . what? No territorial boundaries had shifted and state-based sovereignty remained ostensibly intact at that point. What, many people argue, had been shattered by the aerial partisans on September 11th was what Schmitt termed the 'nomos'.

Nomos conventionally referred to the law, or the 'principles governing human conduct' (Oxford English Dictionary, 2009). But Schmitt reinterpreted nomos, drawing upon its Greek etymology, as referring to something both more concrete, and transcendental, than the law. In terms of the latter, the nomos was described as *prior* to every legal, economic and social order. Rather, it was constituted by three processes: of appropriation, distribution and production (Schmitt, 2003 [1950], 329). But these processes were applied to and through the *land*, and thus gave each nomos a grounded and specific nature. In *The* Nomos *of the Earth in the International Law of the* Jus Publicum Europaeum, published in 1950, Schmitt used these concepts to consider how the Earth had been apportioned (Schmitt, 2003 [1950], 79). After tracing the history of the term *nomos* from antiquity, Schmitt then traced the historical geographical appropriation, distribution and production of the globe through colonisation and jurisprudence (see the appendix to this introduction for the contents of *The* Nomos *of the Earth*). This took place through 'global lines', the first of which were the *rayas* that orchestrated the claims of Catholic colonial land claims. Pope Alexander VI's 1494 edict set a pole to pole line 100 miles west of the meridian of the Azores and Cape Verde (marked on Guillaume de Lisle's 1722 map on the cover to this volume), which was superseded by another line drawn 370 miles west of Cape Verde by the Spanish-Portuguese Treaty of Tordesillas (1494), and sanctioned by Pope Julius II. All newly discovered territories east of the line went to Portugal, while Spain took those lands to the west. These lines internally dividing European conquests were later supplemented by amity lines, beyond which force and violence, not law and treaty, would govern land appropriation in an historical move, and one reproduced entirely in Schmitt's world-view, which considered native people and their territories as 'free space' (see the division of North America between French, Spanish and English empires in de Lisle's map). This instituted the beginning of a comprehensive world spatial order, devised, administered and enforced by Europe, which allowed its state system to function stably by exporting war to the rest of the world between 1713 and 1914. Anticipating recent attempts to express the interdependence of the imperial 'core and periphery' (Hall and Rose, 2006), Schmitt recognised (and celebrated) that the entire European state system was dependent upon colonialism and imperialism. Only with the emergence of American informal economic imperialism and the 'spatial sovereignty' of its Monroe Doctrine did the European nomos crumble. Although Schmitt refused to predict the coming nomos, his work provides endlessly provocative ways for considering the contemporary world.

To be sure, as Timothy Luke argues in this volume, the Cold War bipolar order collapsed between 1989 and 1991, while the global recession has further forestalled any calcification of a new global order. But in attempting to analyse this twenty-year period, it ironically remains the case that most commentators use Schmitt's 1920s–30s work on decisionism, legality, jurisprudence, constitutionalism and exceptions, rather than his 1930s–50s works on America's absent-present global sovereignty, the relationships of politics and law to the land, and the collapse of the ordering nomos of the *Jus Publicum Europaeum*. While Schmitt's (2003 [1950]) *The Nomos of the Earth* has started to receive serious attention in international relations and international law (Hooker, 2009; Odysseos and Petito, 2007), there has been no detailed analyses of the complex geographies which, this volume will argue, were central to Schmitt's biographical context, his analysis of the world around him, his appreciation of global order, and also to the very ontological orientation of his work. This introduction will consider the necessity and dangers of reading and periodising Schmitt before summarising his pre-nomos works, and their inherent spatiality. It will then summarise existing discussions of Schmitt and the nomos, within geography and beyond, before introducing some of the key features of the *Nomos* and associated works to emerge in this volume.

Reading Schmitt

Just as the use of Schmitt in the contemporary demands careful consideration, so must any appreciation of his biography. The tag of 'Nazi legal theorist' simplifies consideration of the fact that his 1921 writing on *Die Diktatur* explicitly advocated 'commissarial' dictatorships that dealt with extraordinary circumstances so as to restore, or create, a 'normal' situation, rather than a sovereign, unlimited dictatorship (Müller, 2003, 21). If Schmitt became a full and official member of the Nazi party in 1933, he also remained committed to concepts of the state and of jurisprudence which it became increasingly apparent were being undermined by the party and the movement to which he was tethered, but from which he was cut free in 1936 (Müller, 2003, 41). The SS openly attacked Schmitt, recalling suspicions about his Catholic background and former Jewish acquaintances, forcing him to resign from almost all his party positions. But before, and after, this brief period of official party duties, Schmitt worked to curry the favour of Nazi officials, just as he cultivated a deeply conservative, anti-liberal and anti-Jewish corpus of works. This presents us with the much broader dilemma of how to deal with 'Nazi intellectuals', as discussed by David Atkinson in this volume. Howard Williams (2005, xi) proffered the Aristotelian adage that wisdom and intelligence need not make one decent and just; William Rasch (2005, 180) argued that we do not have to sympathise with Schmitt to benefit from his insights; Andrew Neal (2010, 136) chose to treat Schmitt as symptomatic of those practices he claimed to diagnose; while Paul Piccone and Gary Ulmen (1987, 4) asked why shouldn't we learn from our opponents, reading them, as Walter Benjamin had done, against the grain? This is, indeed, the route adopted by an astonishing range of thinkers and activists in the twentieth century. Jan-Werner Müller (2003) has tracked Schmitt's influence through thinkers such as Hannah Arendt and Hans Morgenthau, to the lawyers of the Franco and Salazar regimes, to West German constitutional debates and 1968 student revolutionaries. Each of these interpreters has drawn on a particular phase of Schmitt's writing, and has chosen to remember or actively forget parts of his biographical narrative. His is not a life that can be adequately summarised here (see Balakrishnan, 2000; Bendersky, 1983; Müller, 2003, 14–47). But it is important to address the ways his life has been narrated, and the periodisations these narratives have bequeathed us.

As suggested above, Schmitt's engagement with the National Socialists will forever brand his writings. At the same time, recent scholarship has traced the complex genealogy of Schmitt's writings from early experiments in literary expressionism to Weimar-era monographs on jurisprudence and legal decisionism (Müller, 2003). Mika Ojakangas (2004) breaks Schmitt's work into three periods or phases: decisionism (Weimar); movement (Nazism); and finally concrete order thinking (nomos). This roughly corresponds with Jean-François Kervégan's (1999, 55) suggestion that Schmitt's writings form two bodies, of pre- and post-National Socialism, with a period of change precipitated by his joining the party in 1933, when he started to question his theories of the state and to consider the international, which ended in 1943 with his turn to historical and philosophical meditations on world order. Yet tied to this narrative is one of the most emotive approaches to Schmitt's life, concerning his relationship to the 'Jewish Question'. Raphael Gross (2007) divides Schmitt's life into three phases of anti-Semitism: a structural phase before 1933 expressed in his legal and political writings; an explicit phase between 1933 and 1945 during his collaboration with the Nazi party; and a post-war period of reinterpretation and disowning of his more radically anti-

Semitic activities. The ongoing publications of Schmitt's letters and diaries (see Bendersky, 2009) adds further richness to the contrasts between his early Jewish friendships and the intellectual engagements that spanned his long life, and the conference he organised in 1936 to discuss the influence of 'Judaism in Legal Studies', or the continual strain of anti-Jewish sentiment in his writings. Much of this writing merged with the broader scapegoating of Jews for the undermining of state sovereignty and economy. But more persistent was Schmitt's aligning of Jewish thought with placeless liberal positivism, which posited norms that could be applied anywhere, with no attachment to locality. Schmitt firmly argued in 1940 that Jewish (diasporic) existence had no natural relationship with concrete land or ground, thus emptying out the concept of territory (Carty, 2001, 36, citing Schmitt's *Völkerrechtliche Grossraumordnung*, as discussed by Elden in this volume). He remained committed to this point, repeating during his interrogation at Nuremberg in April 1947 that, although he had little to do with the Jewish Question: 'I wrote only once that Jewish theorists have no understanding of this territorial theory' (Schmitt in Bendersky (trans.), 1987, 99). His work more broadly shifts blame away from Germany for the two World Wars and shifts it to those parties who undermined a nomos that allowed bracketed wars. While the Holocaust is painfully silent from Schmitt's work, in one audacious passage he comes close to hinting that it was humanism that provided the underpinning for this total dehumanisation:

> The expulsion of the inhuman from the human was followed in the 19th century by an even deeper division, between the *superhuman* and the *subhuman*. Just as the human presupposed the inhuman, so, with dialectical necessity, the superhuman entered history with its hostile twin: the subhuman.
>
> (Schmitt, 2003 [1950], 104)

What the above indicates are the complex underpinnings to Schmitt's thought and his positioning regarding the Nazi party. But what it also suggests is how deeply influenced his opinions were by his ongoing, lifelong campaign against liberalism. This was the obverse face of his obsession with sovereignty. He posited the two as locked in battle; not just in juridical or philosophical realms, but in the material and political world. Here, liberalism was corroding state sovereignty from within, by promoting discussion over decision, and from without, by promoting landless universalism over land-based territorial statehood (Axtmann, 2007, 541). Running subjacent to Schmitt's shift from domestic to international law, and throughout his party affiliations and anti-Semitism, was this profound anti-liberalism. As discussed below, Schmitt's *Political Theology* (2005 [1922]) and *The Concept of the Political* (1996 [1932]) articulated a now (in)famous attack on the quantitative, neutralising state, paralysed by liberal constitutionalism: 'that is, governmentality, the constitutional and institutional guarantee of limited government and individual rights; culturally, the emphasis on compromise over conflict, and the individual over the group' (McCormick, 1997, 6).

But from the mid-1930s onwards Schmitt also railed against liberal *internationalism*, the trans-state belief in rules or norms that could determine the free relationship of individual subjects (Carty, 2001, 26). Just as Schmitt objected to the placeless spatiality of legal positivism, so he objected to the universalism of the war- and politics-oppressing peace of 1919 (Kelly, 2003, 196). As Carlo Galli (2008, 2) has argued:

> Universalism, then, is the representation of the international scene as a smooth and homogenous space which is morally and legally malleable; but for Schmitt, this space is actually functional for those in power (the Anglo-Saxons and their economic potential) who act politically by way of the moral disqualification of their enemies.

What Galli also recognised was the different dimensions of the shift in Schmitt's *geographical* thinking. This was, in one sense, a scalar shift, having realised that his writings on state and sovereignty had lost purchase with the National Socialists, Schmitt set out to propose an alternative vision of world ordering to that of geopolitics. Yet this also marked a shift to a much more explicitly spatial politics in Schmitt's work. While the first phase emphasised concrete order, through research into the decision, exception, sovereignty and political theology of the state, the second foregrounded space and politics explicitly. The following section will sketch out in more detail Schmitt's earlier works, and their germane geographies, before moving on to the *Nomos* and its interpretations to date.

From domestic to international sovereignty

A more obviously literary categorisation of Schmitt's life differentiates his career by his most influential published works, listed by Marramao (2000) as *Political Theology*, *The Concept of the Political* and *The Nomos of the Earth* (although the publication in English of *Constitutional Theory*, Schmitt, 2008 [1928], may see this list amended). In the former, Schmitt sought to further clarify Bodin's definition of the sovereign as the absolute and perpetual power of a commonwealth, through his more Hobbesian and restrictive opening definition: 'Sovereign is he who decides on the exception' (Schmitt, 2005 [1922], 4). This 'borderline concept' showed how the sovereign was both revealed *by* and *in* the decision on a state of emergency, through creating a condition *beyond* the law *through* the law. Schmitt insisted such exceptions were more interesting than the rule, but that they also created the norm (Kelly, 2003, 182, and Schmitt's writing on commissarial dictatorships from the year before). He argued that this sovereignty was at the core of the state, but that its form was a product of the secularisation of theological concepts, in which the decision replicated the miracle, and the sovereign made the laws of the kingdom, just as God made the laws of nature. While Schmitt's allusions to secularised religious concepts would decline in the 1930s, in part due to National Socialist scepticism over religion in general and Catholicism in particular, they forcefully re-emerged in his nomos phase, especially through the theologically and imperially restraining concept of the *katechon* (see Hell, 2009). Within this grand theorising there is, however, a commitment to the 'concrete application' of the decision by a sovereign who decides *in* a situation of conflict (Schmitt, 2005 [1922], 6). This concreteness of law was necessary because the exceptional threat could not be anticipated in advance; the decision was, for Schmitt, absolute purity. As such,

> All law is 'situational law'. The sovereign produced and guarantees the situation in its totality. He has the monopoly of this last decision ... Precisely a philosophy of concrete life must not withdraw from the exception and the extreme case, but must be interested in it to the highest degree.
>
> (Schmitt, 2005 [1922], 13, 15)

This argument went beyond the moment of exception, however, to establish Schmitt's geographical critique of liberal, norm-based legal theory. He argued that, against positivistic, spaceless legal theory, *all* legal perception was based on a series of decisions that added to legal concepts a condition or element from the 'circumstance' of the decision that remains an '... independently determining moment' (Schmitt, 2005 [1922], 30).

Both the attacks on liberalism, and the commitment to situational law, were carried forward to *The Concept of the Political* (first published in 1927, revised as Schmitt, 1996 [1932]). Here Schmitt dissociated politics from the state and, reversing many popular conceptions, argued that politics actually predated and was the condition for the state, and nationalism. He argued that liberal society had penetrated the state, bringing with it previously non-state debates and categories of religion, culture, education and economy. This was creating a total, quantitative state that tried to do everything but was neutralised from doing anything politically. Free of the state, the political could only be defined in its own terms, and the core purpose of these terms was to distinguish between friend and enemy (Schmitt, 1996 [1932], 26). This binary could draw on other distinctions (such as the moral division of good and evil or the aesthetic division of beautiful or ugly) but was ultimately autonomous and primary. The enemy had to pose an existential and public threat to a way of life in a manner that was not predictable, and thus still demanded a sovereign decision on the nature of the enemy. The attack on liberal neutrality is laid bare here, but in so doing, so is the very political nature of Schmitt's definitions (Axtmann, 2007, 537). In Weimar Germany at the time politics was exactly *not* this (Slomp, 2009, 27). While the Weimar constitution was lauded as a triumph of liberal democracy, for many, including Schmitt, it remained the product of 'an aborted civil war and a complete political stalemate' (Müller, 2003, 24).

Liberal parliamentarianism and legal positivism only served to mask, for Schmitt, a deeper crisis in the very exercise of the political (see Jacobson and Schlink, 2002). The *Concept of the Political* is, therefore, as much manifesto as analysis, as was the *The Prince* by the exiled Machiavelli, with whom the post-Nuremburg Schmitt would melancholically compare himself.

Within this oddly normative anti-normativistic text a more complex geography of politics emerges. First, politics, like the sovereign decision, is situational: only participants can judge a conflict and decide on the friend–enemy distinction. This is not an intellectual choice, but one concerned with the 'inherent reality' and 'real possibilities' of a situation (Schmitt, 1996 [1932], 27–8). This would evolve into Schmitt's focus on *Ordnung* and *Ortung* (order and localisation/orientation, see Zarmanian in this volume). But the non-predictable decisionism at the heart of politics surely makes it less localisable than a state of exception? Marramao (2000, 1577–8), for instance, argues that while the spatial dimension of Schmitt's politics is central, it cannot be circumscribed, confined or topologically delimited, but can be temporarily localised; like the decision and its borderline, the political works not by founding or composing, but by settling and dividing. Slomp (2009, 9) likewise argues that the political cannot be associated with a stable location, but only exists when security is at stake. This political spatialisation has been taken up by Agamben (1998, 19–20) who insists that while one may be able to locate states of exception (Agamben, 2005), exceptionalism is inherently unlocalisable. The second geography at play in this book, however, returns to the scalar dimensions of liberalism, and hints at the global level of Schmitt's future concerns. Running throughout the book is a barely concealed rage against the League of Nations and the peace Treaty of Versailles (see Legg in this volume). While this was common among conservative mandarins in Weimar Germany, Schmitt's target was liberal 'humanism' that did not distinguish between states, friends or enemies, but spoke of mankind. Both the League's failure to allow bracketed wars, and its conflation of moral (evil) and political (enemy) categories into 'wars for humanity' ultimately made violence and war *more* likely for Schmitt (1996 [1932], 53). As Galli commented of the functionalism of this supposedly smooth international space, however, this humanism simply masked imperialist expansion. While Schmitt was writing about external forces in Germany, this insight would later be expanded to the globe in his 1930s writings.

These writings were published in a variety of media, most of which are still unavailable in English. Some, as discussed later, were collected as *Völkerrechtliche Großraumordnung mit Interventionsverbot für raumfremde Mächte: Ein Beitrag zum Reichsbegriff im Völkerrecht* (Schmitt, 1991 [1941]), which Elden (this volume) translates as *International Law of* Großraum-*Ordering with a Prohibition on Intervention for Extra-Regional Powers: A Contribution to the Concept of* Reich *in International Law*. Others have since appeared in the 1991 volume *Staat, Großraum, Nomos: Arbeiten aus den Jahren 1916–1969* (Schmitt, 1995, *State,* Großraum, Nomos: *Works from the*

Years 1916–1969) which includes a cluster of texts that further explore the spatial dimensions of the *Großraum* concept, from essays on 'Die Auflösung der europäische Ordnung in "International Law", 1890–1939' ('The Resolution of the European Order in "International Law", 1890–1939') to 'Die Raumrevolution: Durch den totalen Krieg zu einem totalen Frieden' ('The Spatial Revolution: From Total War to Total Peace'). Taken together, they offer a further point of purchase on the evolution of Schmitt's complex geographical imaginary and, as such, append a corrective to the textual history of key concepts from earlier work on sovereign exceptionalism to his postwar engagement with the nature of the nomos (see Ojakangas, 2004). Matthew Hannah has provided translations of two key texts from this period, which initially appeared in Schmitt's (1988 [1940]) collection *Positionen und Begriffe: im Kampf mit Weimar–Genf–Versailles: 1923–1939* (*Positions and Concepts: Struggles with Weimar–Geneva–Versailles: 1923–1939*). The first, 'Forms of modern imperialism in international law' from 1932 sets out an analysis that would be carried to its fullest fruition in *The Nomos of the Earth* (and is described by Mouffe, 2007, 149, as extremely relevant for the present moment). Here Schmitt suggests that the American Monroe Doctrine has surpassed previous imperial divisions of the world population into non-/Christians or un-/civilised with that of creditor/debtor nations. Previously confined to South America, this policy of official absence but effective presence had been stretched worldwide, making America the new 'arbiter of the world'. The following 1939 text '*Großraum* versus universalism: the international legal struggle over the Monroe Doctrine' sees Schmitt more critically denounce the Monroe Doctrine's' expansion beyond a territorially delimited space, through dollar diplomacy, into a universal ideology that had the potential to turn the whole world into a battlefield.

The boldness with which Schmitt insisted that principles of space (such as spheres of influence, back country, contiguity or propinquity) had been neglected in international law was commented on the following year in *The American Political Science Review* (Kruszewski, 1940, 974). These articles are vital framings for the *Nomos* book, which was largely finished by the end of the War, but was published (with expurgations) in 1950 (Carty, 2001, 56). His passionate advocacy of *Großraum* politics was toned down, although he still castigated the League of Nations for its failings on this front and proposed *Großräume* as one of the few legitimate solutions in the search for the new nomos (Schmitt, 2003 [1950], 247, 354). The *Nomos* also drew on the mythico-poetical *Land and Sea*, which is discussed in this volume by Mendieta. Here, implicitly building on his commitment to territorial (and *Großraum*) bases for both law and mankind, Schmitt described England's collective embracing of a sea-based imperialism as 'A revolution of sweeping scope, that of planetary space' (Schmitt, 1997 [1942], 28) (see Steinberg's response to the concept of the 'free sea', this volume). This saw Schmitt at his mostly explicitly geographical before the *Nomos* book, declaring that every basic order was a *spatial* order, and describing how non-European spaces were viewed as 'abandoned property' (Schmitt, 1997 [1942], 37, 38).

Before going on to examine the geographies of the nomos, and geographers' use of Schmitt, we must acknowledge the growing critical commentary accruing around the *Nomos* work. Some of this has taken up Schmitt's core continental interest to consider the construction of Europe as a political space post-1950 (Burgess, 2009), while others have drawn on Schmitt to consider Europe as a security space, though largely from the perspective of exceptionalism rather than the nomos (for instance, Huysmans, 2008). Gilroy (2004, 21, also see Lossau in this volume) has used Schmitt's early comments on imperialism and humanitarianism to reflect upon postcolonial Europe, although he criticised Schmitt's lack of interest in the political mechanics of empire or colonialism, which a reading of the *Nomos* might do a little to qualify. Scholars of imperialism and postcolonialism have also engaged with Schmitt's work, although the post-Agamben emphasis on exceptionalism has by far outweighed any consideration of the *Nomos* as a unique way of exploring the spread of imperialism through the lens of international law, rather than political-economy or cultural representation (see Hansen and Stepputat, 2005; Mbembe, 2003). There are exceptions, however, such as Lauren Benton's (2010) excellent study of the legal geographies of imperialism, which concludes with a critical discussion of the *Nomos* as a frame for understanding the varied and contingent experiments with imperial sovereignty.

As suggested above, the *Nomos* has been deployed more intently in analysing contemporary American 'imperialism', or the capillary workings of a decentred, but still heavily American, 'Empire'. William Rasch (also editor of a substantial collection of papers on the *Nomos* in *The South Atlantic Quarterly*, see Rasch, 2005) has analysed 'American supremacy' using works from Schmitt's domestic and internationalist phases, picking up on America's history of denying its conquests and the exclusions inherent to human rights (Rasch, 2003). The war on terror has, however, seen the *Nomos* deployed to offer understanding of the contemporary world beyond that simply of exceptionalism, although these analyses do still carry great weight (see Neal, 2010). Such analyses have considered what contemporary violence means for the current nomos (see Shapiro, 2008, and Kearns and Rowan in this volume) or for understandings of the partisan (drawing on Schmitt, 2007 [1963], also see Hooker, 2009, and Clayton in this book). This draws upon a broader reappraisal of Schmitt among the political left. These works include those of: Susan Buck-Morss (2008) who values Schmitt's consideration of the *political* nature of global power; Chantal Mouffe's (2007) use of Schmitt to warn against a unipolar world (see Rowan's critical commentary in this volume); Levinson's (2005) appreciation of the *Nomos* as simultaneously reactionary and progressive; and the linking of Schmitt's concepts to iconic Marxist concepts such as primitive (juridical) accumulation (Stepputat, 2008, 338) or enclosure (Shapiro, 2008, 70). This literature follows an older Italian school of *Marxist Schmittiani*, but is also heavily influenced by contemporary

Italian theorists Giorgio Agamben and Antonio Negri, writing with Michael Hardt (Müller, 2003, 229).

Indeed, Hardt and Negri's *Empire* (2000) and its successor volumes, *Multitude* (2004) and *Commonwealth* (2009), may be seen, in this context, as setting out a project predicated on the articulation of a *deterritorialising* counter-nomos (Coleman and Grove, 2009). The conceptual arc of Agamben's own work has, in turn, followed the contours and contradictions of both Schmitt's earlier and later writings. In one of his most recent books, *Il Regno e la Gloria* (2007), Agamben even goes so far as to invert Schmitt's definition of political theology. What is at stake here for Agamben are the very origins of modern governmentality that he traces back to an older Christian dispositif organised around the concept of *oiknomia* (Minca, 2009).

While Schmitt has been pushed and experimented with in these lines of critical theory, such explorations have not been universally well received in international relations, the discipline to which the *Nomos* is perhaps most obviously aligned. Chandler (2008), for instance, accuses critical international relations theorists of idealising Schmitt, and of rhetorically using him, whether in a cosmopolitan or post-structuralist vein, to deflect criticisms from their own ethical positions or their problematic relation to liberalism (the *Nomos* is also dismissed as irrelevant today). Others, however, have engaged with the book more seriously. Louiza Odysseos and Fabio Petito's (2007) edited volume on Schmitt's international political thought provided a sustained series of arguments for placing Schmitt among the pantheon of classical realist scholars, and situated the *Nomos* as an historical account of international relations (see Coleman, this volume). Rasch (2003, 128) used Schmitt to relate the classic dates 1648 (establishing the plurality of states) and 1713 (establishing their relative balance) to the exporting of violence beyond Europe. Galli (2008, 7) has drawn on Schmitt's comments (or lack of) on the Cold War to reflect that it offered no nomos; capitalists and communists were simply 'brothers' in universalism, divided by the contradictions of political economy, but sharing a 'naval' society of limitless technology. Hooker's (2009) impressive work links the two phases of Schmitt's work, drawing in detail on his theories of sovereignty, histories of space and the partisan, to reflect on Schmitt's contribution to international thought.

In this work, Hooker (2009, 78) drew parallels between the sovereign decision on the exception and the role of the 'spatial act of puncture', or discovery, on the spatial order. His reading of the *Nomos* suggests that European state organisation did not evolve smoothly but was marked by radical shifts in spatial consciousness. This brings to the fore one of the key questions in discussing Schmitt's later works: what happens to Schmitt's theory of the decision and the exception in the *Nomos*? Claudia Aradau (2007, 493) reinforces Hooker's reading, stressing that the sovereign decision on the enemy is 'brushed aside' in the *Nomos* in favour of the spatial division of the Earth; this does, however, represent another exception, rooted in geopolitics, technology and discoveries rather than a sovereign *decision* (also see Jameson,

2005; Ojakangas, 2004, 116). The ultimate expression of this exception is the naming of the New World as 'free space' (for a detailed and critical reading of Schmitt 'beyond the line', see Stirk, this volume). Galli (2008, 4; also see Hooker, 2009, 90) labels Schmitt's internationalist period as openly 'post-decisionist', although he later talks of the English 'decision for the sea', which transformed their island from an out-posting of Europe to something of and for the oceans themselves (Schmitt, 1997 [1942], 50). There is also further evidence of decisionistic thinking in the *Nomos*; European sovereign states solved the problem of *justa causa*: 'Who decides? (the great *Quis judicabit*?). Only the sovereign could decide this question, both within the state and between states' (Schmitt, 2003 [1950], 157). Likewise, Stirk (2005, 94) has shown that Schmitt was reluctant to define a *nation's* enemy (see Coleman, this volume, on the spatiality of enmity). In part, this was so as to not be caught out by developments in international relations, but it was also consonant with Schmitt's insistence that decisions could only be made in concrete situations (although he happily identified foreign law as the enemy of any people).

Schmitt's geographies

> As scientific, mathematical, or technical disciplines, geography and cartography certainly are neutral. However, as every geographer knows, they can be instrumentalized in ways both immediately relevant and highly political. This is particularly evident with respect to the concept of the Western Hemisphere. Despite the neutrality of geography as a science, purely geographical concepts can generate a political struggle, which sometimes justifies Thomas Hobbes' pessimistic maxim that even arithmetic and geometric certainties become problematic if they fall within the sphere of the political: the intense friend–enemy distinction.
>
> (Schmitt, 2003 [1950], 88)

> I am much indebted to geographers, most of all to Mackinder. Nevertheless, a juridical way of thinking is far different from geography. Jurists have not learned their science of matter and soil, reality and territoriality from geographers.
>
> (Schmitt, 2003 [1950], 37)

> Geojurisprudence is thus neither law, not geography, nor politics. It is the projection of National Socialist power dreams and wishful spatial thinking into the sphere of jurisprudence.
>
> (Gyorgy, 1943, 686)

The geographical antecedents to Schmitt's theory on the nomos were clearly set out by the author himself and were further adumbrated by early commentators who already distinguished Schmitt's work from the epistemological assumptions that had come to characterise the German school of *Geopolitik* (see Gyorgy, 1943; for a more recent reappraisal, see Minca, 2006). While Schmitt acknowledged the work of various geographers in *The Nomos of the Earth*, only recently have the spatial dimensions of his work been explored within the discipline itself.

The growing interest in reading Schmitt geographically draws inspiration, in no small part, from the work of Giorgio Agamben whose own ideas owe their provenance to Schmitt most notably as the theorist of the exception (for alternative readings see Barnett, 2004 and Pratt, 2005). Geographical approaches to Agamben have thus focused on Agamben's (1998, 2005) recasting of Schmitt's original notion of the sovereign exception. What this has meant in practical terms is a further spatialisation of the exception and the attempt to map distinct 'socio-geographical phenomena' in which the exception is understood to operate (Belcher *et al.*, 2008, 499). It is in such punctiform sites, so it is argued, that the ban is located, bare life is produced and sovereign power exercised (Ek, 2006; Gregory, 2006; Kearns, 2006; Landzelius, 2006; Minca, 2005, 2006; Reid-Henry, 2007). If Agamben's own theorisings pre-date the events of September 11th, 2001, the 'progressive normalisation' of new geographies of the exception is widely understood to have intensified within Western democracies as both a product and symptom of an ongoing global war on terror and a new regime of biopolitical security (Minca, 2006, 388). Within this framework, Schmitt's early work on the relationship between sovereignty and the exception, most notably set out in *Political Theology* (1922) and *The Concept of the Political* (1932), is simply adopted as something of an unstated point of departure for rethinking the complex geography at the heart of Agamben's project.

And yet, Agamben's theoretical apparatus cannot be reduced to a 'static geometry' as a number of commentators have rightly argued (Belcher *et al.*, 2008: 499; Debrix, 2009; Minca, 2006, 2007). Central, after all, to Agamben's argument is what he describes as the 'paradox of sovereignty' (1998: 15). According to Agamben, this paradox is contingent on the fact that the sovereign is simultaneously 'outside and inside the juridical order' (1998, 15). For Agamben, the state of exception is thus 'essentially unlocalizable'. But more than this and, as he goes on to suggest in a key passage in *Homo Sacer*,

> one of the theses of the present inquiry is that in our age, the state of exception comes more and more to the foreground as the fundamental political structure and ultimately begins to become the rule. When our age tried to grant the unlocalizable a permanent and visible localization, the result was the concentration camp.
>
> (1998, 20)

Seen in this context, it is perhaps not surprising that geographers have attempted to map a determinate geography of exceptional and unspecified spaces from the camp and the airport to the border and the police checkpoint (see Adey, 2009; Gregory, 2006; Paglen, 2006; Reid-Henry, 2007). At the same time, as Derek Gregory (2006) reminds us, 'sites like Guantánamo Bay need to be seen not as paradigmatic spaces of political modernity . . . but rather as *potential* spaces whose realization is an occasion for political struggle' (405; emphasis added). What is, in other words, crucial here is less a question of retracing the durable materialisations of the exception than attending to the very conditions of possibility that grant the exception its '*potential* as a geopolitical construct' (Debrix, 2009, 7; original emphasis).

Adopting this posture has prompted a more critical parsing of the spatial ontology that subtends Agamben's work (Minca, 2007). This has, on the one hand, prompted greater engagement with the *topological* dimensions of the exception and in which the exception is understood as a dynamic and fluid set of power relations (Belcher *et al.*, 2008; see Gregory, 2004). On the other hand, a number of scholars have also seized on Agamben's (1998) assertion that 'we are all virtually *homines sacri*' to insist on the *virtuality* of an exception that 'reveals a far more complex, and less spatially and temporally fixed, relation between juridical-political order and spatial orientation' (Vaughan-Williams, 2010, 1081). Both Nick Vaughan-Williams and François Debrix tease out, for example, the virtual spatiality present in Agamben's analyses. For Vaughan-Williams (2009, 16), 'Agamben's diagnosis is highly suggestive of a new kind of *nomos* of the earth' while Debrix aligns our contemporary geopolitical condition with 'a *nomos* of exception' (2009). The reference to nomos is of particular salience and not only refers back to the work of Schmitt but to the chapters in *Homo Sacer* where Agamben runs together Schmitt's earlier work on the exception with his later work on the 'nomos of the Earth'.

In those chapters, Agamben describes the sovereign exception as a fundamental localisation, or *Ortung* to use the Schmittian appellation. Agamben understands Schmitt to have aligned such an 'ordering of space' with the 'determination of a juridical and a territorial ordering' (of an *Ordnung* and an *Ortung*). To Agamben, it is the very link between localisation (*Ortung*) and ordering (*Ordnung*) that constitutes the nomos of the Earth. Such a link also implies the delineation of a space or zone that is 'excluded from the law'. In Agamben's re-reading of Schmitt, the 'state of exception . . . is not external to the *nomos* but rather, even in its clear delimitation, included in the *nomos* as a moment that is in every sense fundamental' (Agamben, 1998, 36, 37). It is, moreover, Agamben's wager that an older nomos as set out by Schmitt in *The Nomos of the Earth* has broken down and that the contours of a new global nomos have only now begun to take shape. This is a (geo)-political system, however, that 'no longer orders forms of life and juridical rules in a determinate place but, instead, contains at its very centre [. . .] a "dislocating localization" that exceeds it and into which every form of life and every norm can be virtually taken' (Agamben, 1998, 175).

It is against this backdrop that geographers and other scholars have explored to great analytical effect the relationship between the sovereign exception and both older forms of colonial power (Gregory, 2005; Kearns, 2006; Nally, 2008) and new forms of global biopolitics (Amoore, 2006; Doty, 2007; Minca, 2006, 2007; Vaughan-Williams, 2010). In so doing, it has also become clear that the very antinomies that underpin Agamben's spatial ontology are themselves a product of the complex geographical imaginary that is at the centre of Schmitt's own project. One of the main aims of this book is to therefore work backwards from Agamben and re-examine the complex affinities and discontinuities between Schmitt's work on sovereign exceptionalism and his later work on spatial appropriation and ordering as set out in *The* Nomos *of the Earth*.

This edited volume brings together a host of academics from within and beyond the geographical discipline who have an interest in, and expertise to offer on, these geographies of the nomos, and nomic geographies. Their exceptional range and quality, through the translated texts, the longer chapter pieces, to the shorter responses, defy summary, and their relevance to existing debates is testified by the number of citations made above. In the remainder of this introduction we would simply like to briefly draw attention to some recurrent geographies of the nomos that the contributors have addressed. These include questions of order and orientation, geopolitics and *Großraum*, performative spaces and spatial ontology, and the potentially compatible Foucauldian approach to sovereignty, spatiality and liberalism.

Thalin Zarmanian (this volume) explores the central relationship between *Ordnung* and *Ortung* (order and orientation/localisation) in the *Nomos*. The relationship between these two forces is central to Schmitt's conception of the nomos (and will be familiar to many geographers as a unique retelling of the society-space dialectic), and allows him to navigate both the traps of materialism and idealism. This was a dialectic that remained fundamentally unresolved, as with other dialectics in Schmitt's spatial ontology (see below). While stressing the power of the nomos, it was always an idiosyncratic combination of orderings and orientations, such as empires, aerial spaces, *Großraum* and the *Jus Publicum Europaeum* (Hooker, 2009, 13, 72). The latter itself was more of a grammar of international hostility than a strict code of conduct, that insisted upon the state as key actor, the suppression of civil war and promotion of non-discriminatory war, freedom of the seas and the management of territorial change (Schmitt, 2003 [1950], Part III).

Schmitt's advocation of a *Großraum* world-view, as demonstrated in the second of the translated texts in this volume, grew out of his admiration for the origins of America's Monroe Doctrine, when it was a territorially delimited, hemispherical order. From economic origins, it had found continental coherence, but had then been distorted into a liberal, universal, spaceless policy of (non-)intervention. Reviving this sense of place-bound larger spaces of sovereign coherence was central to Schmitt's attempt to regain favour and currency with the National Socialists after 1936. Though obviously similar in many respects, Schmitt's vision was explicitly not a geopolitical one. Though he drew from, and was categorised with, theorists of geojurisprudence (Gyorgy,

1943), there were important differences, namely Schmitt's rejection of maritime power in favour of land-based sovereignty (Hooker, 2009, 99; for broader discussion, see Elden, this volume). His view of land was not that of colonialists (population and land), or of geopolitics (space and politics), but of *Großraum* (land, people and idea) in opposition to liberal internationalism (Carty, 2001, 36). Schmitt failed, however, to detail the organisation of *Reich* (empire) and *Volk* (people) within these *Großraum*, as was commented upon at the time (Gyorgy, 1943, 683). While still attracting discussion in some quarters as a viable counter-imaginary to a unipolar world (Mouffe, 2007), the incoherence and anti-democratic dangers of this world-view can be equally well argued for (Rowan, this volume).

The disappointment of Schmitt's spatial world-view in terms of *Großraum* is perhaps made starker by comparison to his occasional writings on space that stress its aliveness and mutability. Indeed, elsewhere in the *Völkerrechtliche Grossraumordnung*, Schmitt advocated a biological over a mathematical approach to thinking state space. This would stress that movement made, rather than happened in, space, leading to the conclusion: '*Der Raum wird zum Leistungsraum*' ('the space becomes a space of performance') (Schmitt, 1941, cited in Carty, 2001, 45). This was an abiding interest in Schmitt's thought. For instance, sixteen years before, as Schmitt railed against the League of Nation's defence of the status quo, he had claimed that: 'It is strange that the age whose thinking is dominated by the idea of eternal becoming, eternal flow, and substanceless functioning would like to stabilize an existing state of affairs within the political domain' (Schmitt, 1925, 293). This sense of movement, change and space was central to Schmitt's ability to reconcile order and orientation; as Draghici (1997, viii) put it, to incorporate '. . . oppositions, structural as well as ideational, reconciling them, and so rendering tolerable experiences that otherwise are incoherent' into a relational approach to space.

This brings us to the vexed question of Schmitt's spatial ontology, which is characterised by a radical indeterminacy. This is down, in part, to his subjects of study, which bridge the statuses of ontological conditions and grounded orders. But, as Rory Rowan makes clear in his contribution to this volume, it is also a recurrent feature in all of Schmitt's work. The dialectic between open indeterminism and closed order plays out in the borderline question of the sovereign decision that establishes order, the enemy threat that creates political unity, the decision of the people that creates a constitution, or the appropriation of land that creates the nomos. This is far from a Hegelian dialectic in that there is no moment of synthesis because the two parts are never felt to be separate: the exception and the norm are *of* each other; just as the nomos is both powerful and perpetually on the point of collapse. Borders are both stable and containing yet are defined by the very movement across them (Vaughan-Williams, this volume) and by the memories of the nomadism that makes them necessary (Debrix, this volume), as well as by the dubious myths that are constructed around them (see Stirk, this volume, on 'amity lines'). All orders, thus, need and are made by an outside, even if it is a virtual or materially negligible one (see Debrix, this volume). Minca's chapter dwells extensively on this question of ontology, and describes the 'horror vacui' Schmitt felt regarding the opening of empty space within global politics. But he also addresses, via the work of Andrea Cavalletti, the spatial politics of population in Schmitt, or his 'biopolitics'. This is a reading much inspired by Agamben's argument that the sovereign *always* had an interest in the politics of life. While providing new ways of thinking about the normalisation of the exception, this raises interesting questions about Schmitt's utility for examining a process he openly loathed; namely, the quantitative expansion of the state through the process of liberal governmentalisation, as the McCormick (1997, 6) quote above suggests.

This links into the broader question of how to think Schmitt alongside other thinkers who have criticised the liberal project. Schmitt is not lacking company as an anti-liberalist (Holmes, 1996). But there are also critical theories on liberalism that can complement, and possibly offer an 'antidote' (Neal, 2010, 143) to Schmitt's thought. One such thinker is Foucault, whose theories would also benefit from Schmitt's global outlook and attempts to rethink the spatiality of modern sovereignty (rather than attempt juridical regicide). There is also a need to situate the governmentalities Foucault describes within a more global *Jus Publicum Europaeum* (Dean, 2004) that goes beyond the European 'balance of Europe' (Foucault, 2007, chapter 11) and the economic geography of the world market (Foucault, 2008, chapter three). The contributors to this volume suggest several ways of doing this. Stephen Legg considers the mobile intersections of sovereign powers and governmental rationalities through the operation of the League of Nations in the concrete situations Schmitt spoke of but rarely evidenced. Matthew Hannah's innovative response examines pastoralism as a shared genealogy of Foucault and Schmitt, while Peter Rogers dwells at length on the nomos and everyday life. At this spatial and temporal scale many sites of convergence between the two thinkers emerge: both value space, although Schmitt pays more attention to land and territory. Foucault himself began his theorisation of biopolitics with an inversion of Clausewitz that suggested politics was war pursued by other means. While over the following years Foucault presented ever-changing contexts for the birth of biopolitics, his first attempt described the collapse of pyramidial descriptions of society that became replaced by a binary structure. Within the context of enmity and societies that must be defended, he (Foucault, 2003, 51, cited in Rogers, this volume) portentously claimed that:

> ... we have to interpret the war that is going on beneath peace; peace itself is a coded war. We are therefore at war with one another; a battlefront runs through the whole of society, continuously and permanently, and it is this battlefield that puts us all on one side or the other. There is no such thing as a neutral subject. We are all inevitably someone's adversary.

The debate about Foucault and Schmitt may ultimately remind us of the incredibly fertile nature of the latter's thinking, but it also speaks to the philosophical and empirical restraints within which he operated. While keen to mine the potential of the geographies within Schmitt's *Nomos*, the contributors to this volume remain acutely aware of the shortcomings of his spatial imagination (see, especially, Heffernan and Lossau's contributions) and the dangers of reading such a controversial figure out of context. The authors variously draw attention to the confusion with which Schmitt used terms such as 'territory' (Elden), his failure to consider the bordering and enclosing, everyday, measures he hinted at (Rogers), and his neglect of geographical dimensions such as environment (Heffernan). His dismissal of internationalist institutions, the rights of colonised peoples, and his continued advocacy of a *Großraum* world-view must be read as explicitly political, anti-liberal sentiments. Running throughout these commentaries is, then, a healthy scepticism about the nomos as a concept. Its empirical accuracy has been challenged (Scheuerman, 2004), while others have questioned whether the nomos itself is the latest in a long line of colonial mythologies (Aravamudan, 2005; Dean, 2006). This is a possibility raised by the romantic language that Schmitt condemned in others, but which has drawn so many to his nomos writings. Whether this prose is 'illuminating' or simply 'dazzling' remains to be seen, as does whether we can extract useful insights from a body of work purposefully constructed, in the words of Ernst Jünger, as a '. . . mine that explodes silently' within liberal thought (Müller, 2003, 8–9).

Notes

1   Cited in Mann, Nyta (4 January 2002) 'Blair returns to new world order' *BBC News Website*. Accessed on 8 July 2010 at http://news.bbc.co.uk/1/hi/uk_politics/1742954.stm.
2   Cited in Wintour, Patrick (8 April 2006) 'Falconer spurns campaign to give MPs vote on going to war' *The Guardian*. Accessed on 8 July 2010 at www.guardian.co.uk/politics/2006/apr/08/uk.houseofcommons/print.
3   Cited in Arifa, Akbar (11 January 2002) 'Bush tells Iran: You are either with us or against us' *The Independent*. Accessed on 8 July 2010 at www.independent.co.uk/news/world/americas/bush-tells-iran-you-are-either-with-us-or-against-us-662879.html.

Appendix: Contents of *The* Nomos *of the Earth*

Part I: Five Introductory Corollaries

1 Law as a unity of order and orientation
2 Pre-global international law
3 International law in the Christian Middle Ages
4 On the meaning of the word *nomos*
5 Land-appropriation as a constitutive process of international law

Part II: The Land-Appropriation of the World

1 The first global lines
2 Justification of the land-appropriation of a New World: Francisco de Vitoria
3 Legal title to the land-appropriation of a New World: discovery and occupation

Part III: The Jus Publicum Europaeum

1 The state as the agency of a new, interstate, Eurocentric, spatial order of the Earth
2 The transformation of medieval wars (duels or feuds) into non-discriminatory state wars
3 Freedom of the sea
4 Territorial changes
5 Reference to possibilities and elements of international law unrelated to the state

Part IV: The Question of a New Nomos *of the Earth*

1 The last pan-European land-appropriation: the Congo Conference of 1885
2 Dissolution of the *Jus Publicum Europeum* (1890–1918)
3 The League of Nations and the problem of the spatial order of the Earth
4 Transformation of the meaning of war
5 The Western Hemisphere
6 Transformation of the meaning of recognition in international law
7 War with modern means of destruction

Part V: Appendix: Three Concluding Corollaries

1 Appropriation/distribution/production: an attempt to determine from *Nomos* the basic questions of every social and economic order (1953)
2 *Nomos – Nahme –* Name (1957)
3 The new *Nomos* of the Earth (1955)

References

Adey, P. (2009) Facing Airport Security: Affect, Biopolitics, and the Preemptive Securitisation of the Mobile Body, *Environment and Planning D: Society and Space* 27, 274–95.

Agamben, G. (1998) *Homo Sacer: Sovereign Power and Bare Life*. Stanford University Press: Stanford, CA.

—— (2005) *State of Exception*. University of Chicago Press: Chicago; London.

—— (2007) *Il Regno et la Gloria*. Neri Pozza: Vincenza.

Amoore, L. (2006) Biometric Borders: Governing Mobilities in the War on Terror, *Political Geography* 25, 336–51.

Aradau, C. (2007) Law Transformed: Guantanamo and the 'Other' Exception, *Third World Quarterly* 28, 489–501.

Aravamudan, S. (2005) Carl Schmitt's The Nomos of the Earth: Four Corollaries, *South Atlantic Quarterly* 104, 227–36.

Axtmann, R. (2007) Humanity or Enmity? Carl Schmitt on International Politics, *International Politics* 44, 531–51.

Balakrishnan, G. (2000) *The Enemy: An Intellectual Portrait of Carl Schmitt*. Verso: London; New York.

Barnett, C. (2004) Deconstructing Radical Democracy: Articulation, Representation and Being-with-Others, *Political Geography* 23, 503–28.

Belcher, O., Martin, L., Secor, A., Simon, S. and Wilson, T. (2008) Everywhere and Nowhere: The Exception and the Topological Challenge to Geography, *Antipode* 40, 499–503.

Bendersky, J. W. (1983) *Carl Schmitt, Theorist for the Reich*. Princeton University Press: Princeton, NJ.

—— (trans.) (1987) Interrogation of Carl Schmitt by Robert Kempner (I), *Telos* 72, 97–107.

—— (2009) Love, Law, and War: Carl Schmitt's Angst, *Telos* 147, 171–91.

Benton, L. (2010) *A Search for Sovereignty: Law and Geography in European Empires 1400–1900*. Cambridge University Press: Cambridge.

Buck-Morss, S. (2008) Sovereign Right and the Global Left, *Cultural Critique* 69, 145–71.

Burgess, J. P. (2009) The New *Nomos* of Europe, *Geopolitics* 14, 135–60.

Bush, G. W. (2010) *Decision Points*. Crown Publishing Group: New York.

Butler, J. (2006) *Precarious Life: The Powers of Mourning and Violence*. Verso: London.

Carty, A. (2001) Carl Schmitt's Critique of Liberal International Legal Order between 1933 and 1945, *Leiden Journal of International Law* 14, 25–76.

Chandler, D. (2008) The Revival of Carl Schmitt in International Relations: The Last Refuge of Critical Theorists? *Millennium – Journal of International Studies* 37, 27–48.

Coleman, M. and Grove, K. (2009) Biopoltics, Biopower and the Return to Sovereignty, *Environment and Planning D: Society and Space* 27, 489–507.

Dean, M. (2004) *Nomos* and the Politics of World Order. In *Global Governmentality: Governing International Spaces* (eds W. Larner and W. Walters). Routledge: New York; London, pp. 40–58.

—— (2006) A Political Mythology of World Order Theory, *Culture & Society* 23, 1–22.

Debrix, F. (2009) The Nomos of Exception and the Virtuality of Political Space in Schmitt and Agamben, Paper presented at the 2009 Annual Meeting of the American Political Science Association, Toronto, 3–7 September.
Doty, R. (2007) States of Exception on the Mexico-US Border: Security, 'Decisions' and Civilian Border Patrols, *International Political Sociology* 1, 113–37.
Draghici, S. (1997) Foreword. In *Land and Sea* (ed. C. Schmitt, trans. S. Draghici). Plutarch Press: Washington, DC, pp. vii–xv.
Ek, R. (2006) Giorgio Agamben and the Spatialities of the Camp, *Geografiska Annaler Series B: Human Geography* 88B, 363–86.
Elden, S. (2009) *Terror and Territory: The Spatial Extent of Sovereignty*. University of Minnesota Press: Minneapolis.
Ferguson, N. (2003) Hegemony or Empire? *Foreign Affairs* 82, 154–61.
Foucault, M. (2003) *Society Must Be Defended: Lectures at the Collège De France 1975–76*. Penguin: London.
—— (2007) *Security, Territory, Population: Lectures at the Collège De France 1977–78*. Palgrave Macmillan: Basingstoke; New York.
—— (2008) *The Birth of Biopolitics: Lectures at the Collège De France, 1978–79*. Palgrave Macmillan: Basingstoke.
Jacobson, A. J. and Schlink, B. (eds) (2002) *Weimar: A Jurisprudence of Crisis*. University of California Press: Berkeley.
Galli, C. (2008) Carl Schmitt and the Global Age. Presented at *Buffalo Conference on Political Philosophy 'New Paths in Political Philosophy'*.
Gilroy, P. (2004) *After Empire: Melancholia or Convivial Culture?* Routledge: London.
Gregory, D. (2004) *The Colonial Present: Afghanistan, Palestine, Iraq*. Blackwell: Oxford.
—— (2005) Colonial Precedents and Sovereign Powers: A Response, *Progress in Human Geography* 29(3): 367–79.
—— (2006) The Black Flag: Guantánamo Bay and the Space of Exception, *Geografiska Annaler: Series B, Human Geography* 88(4): 405–27.
Gross, R. (2007) *Carl Schmitt and the Jews: The 'Jewish Question,' The Holocaust, and German Legal Theory*. University of Wisconsin Press: Madison.
Gyorgy, A. (1943) The Application of German Geopolitics: Geo-Sciences, *The American Political Science Review* 37, 677–86.
Hall, C. and Rose, S. O. (2006) Introduction: Being at Home with the Empire. In *At Home with the Empire: Metropolitan Culture and the Imperial World* (eds C. Hall and S. O. Rose). Cambridge University Press: Cambridge, pp. 1–31.
Hansen, T. B. and Stepputat, F. (eds) (2005) *Sovereign Bodies: Citizens, Migrants, and States in the Postcolonial World*. Princeton University Press: Princeton, NJ; Oxford.
Hardt, M. and Negri, A. (2000) *Empire*. Harvard University Press: Cambridge, MA.
—— (2004) *Multitude*. Penguin Books: London.
—— (2009) *Commonwealth*. Belknap Press: Cambridge, MA.
Hell, J. (2009) Katechon: Carl Schmitt's Imperial Theology and the Ruins of the Future, *The Germanic Review* 84, 283–326.
Holmes, S. (1996) *The Anatomy of Antiliberalism*. Harvard University Press: Harvard, MA.
Hooker, W. (2009) *Carl Schmitt's International Thought*. Cambridge University Press: Cambridge.

Hussain, N. (2007) Beyond Norm and Exception: Guantánamo, *Critical Inquiry* 33, 734–53.
Huysmans, J. (2008) The Jargon of Exception – On Schmitt, Agamben and the Absence of Political Society, *International Political Sociology* 2, 165–83.
Jameson, F. (2005) Notes on the Nomos, *South Atlantic Quarterly* 104, 199–204.
Kearns, G. (2006) Bare Life, Political Violence and the Territorial Structure of Britain and Ireland. In *Violent Geographies: Fear, Terror and Political Violence* (eds D. Gregory and A. Pred). Routledge: London, pp. 9–34.
Kelly, D. (2003) *The State of the Political: Conceptions of Politics and the State in the Thought of Max Weber, Carl Schmitt and Franz Newman*. Oxford University Press: Oxford.
Kervégan, J.-F. (1999) Carl Schmitt and 'World Unity'. In *The Challenge of Carl Schmitt* (ed. C. Mouffe). Verso: London, pp. 54–74.
Kruszewski, C. (1940) International Affairs: Germany's Lebensraum, *The American Political Science Review* 34, 964–75.
Landzelius, M. (2006) 'Homo Sacer' out of Left Field: Communist 'Slime' as Bare Life in 1930s and Second World War Sweden, *Geografiska Annaler Series B: Human Geography*, 88B, 453–75.
Levinson, B. (2005) The Coming Nomos; or, the Decline of Other Orders in Schmitt, *South Atlantic Quarterly* 104, 205–15.
Marramao, G. (2000) The Exile of the *Nomos*: For a Critical Profile of Carl Schmitt, *Cardozo Law Review* 5–6, 1567–87.
Mbembe, A. (2003) Necropolitics, *Public Culture* 15, 11–40.
McCormick, J. P. (1997) *Carl Schmitt's Critique of Liberalism: Against Politics as Technology*. Cambridge University Press: Cambridge.
Minca, C. (2005) The Return of the Camp, *Progress in Human Geography*, 29, 405–12.
—— (2006) Giorgio Agamben and the New Biopolitical Nomos, *Geografiska Annaler, Series B: Human Geography*, 88B, 387–403.
—— (2007) Agamben's Geographies of Modernity, *Political Geography* 26, 78–97.
—— (2009) The Reign and Glory: or Reflections on the Theological Foundations of the Credit Crunch, *Environment and Planning D: Society and Space* 27, 177–82.
Mouffe, C. (2007) Carl Schmitt's Warnings on the Dangers of a Unipolar World. In *The International Political Thought of Carl Schmitt: Terror, Liberal War and the Crisis of Global Order* (eds L. Odysseos and F. Petito). Routledge: London, pp. 147–53.
Müller, J.-W. (2003) *A Dangerous Mind: Carl Schmitt in Post-War European Thought*. Yale University Press: New Haven, CT.
Nally, D. P. (2008) 'That Coming Storm': The Irish Poor Law, Colonial Biopolitics, and the Great Irish Famine, *Annals of the Association of American Geographers* 98, 714–41.
Neal, A. W. (2010) *Exceptionalism and the Politics of Counter-Terrorism: Liberty, Security and the War on Terror*. Routledge: London.
Odysseos, L. and Petito, F. (eds) (2007) *The International Political Thought of Carl Schmitt: Terror, Liberal War and the Crisis of Global Order*. Routledge: London.
Ojakangas, M. (2004) *A Philosophy of Concrete Life: Carl Schmitt and the Political Thought of Late Modernity*. Sophi: Jyväskylä.
Paglen, T. (2006) Groom Lake and the Imperial Production of Nowhere. In *Violent Geographies: Fear, Terror and Political Violence* (eds D. Gregory and A. Pred). Routledge: London, pp. 237–54.

Piccone, P. and Ulmen, G. (1987) Introduction to Carl Schmitt, *Telos* 72, 3–14.
Pratt, G. (2005) Abandoned Women and Spaces of Exception, *Antipode* 37, 1053–78.
Rasch, W. (2003) Human Rights as Geopolitics: Carl Schmitt and the Legal Form of American Supremacy, *Cultural Critique* 54, 120–47.
—— (2005) Introduction: Carl Schmitt and the New World Order, *South Atlantic Quarterly* 104, 177–83.
Reid-Henry, S. (2007) Exceptional Sovereignty? Guantánamo Bay and the Re-colonial Present, *Antipode* 39, 627–48.
Scheuerman, W. E. (2004) International Law as Historical Myth, *Constellations* 11, 537–50.
Schmitt, C. (1925) The Status Quo and the Peace. In *Weimar: A Jurisprudence of Crisis* (eds A. J. Jacobson and B. Schlink). University of California Press: Berkeley, pp. 290–93.
—— (1988 [1940]) *Positionen Und Begriffe: im Kampf mit Weimar–Genf–Versailles: 1923–1939* (ed. C. Schmitt). Duncker & Humblot: Berlin.
—— (1991 [1941]) *Völkerrechtliche Großraumordnung mit Interventionsverbot für Raumfremde Mächte: Ein Beitrag zum Reichsbegriff im Völkerrecht*. Duncker & Humblot: Berlin.
—— (1995) *Staat, Großraum, Nomos: Arbeiten aus den Jahren 1916–1969*. Duncker & Humblot: Berlin.
—— (1996 [1932]) *The Concept of the Political*. University of Chicago Press: Chicago.
—— (1997 [1942]) *Land and Sea*. Plutarch Press: Washington, DC.
—— (2003 [1950]) *The Nomos of the Earth in the International Law of the Jus Publicum Europaeum*. Telos Press: New York.
—— (2005 [1922]) *Political Theology: Four Chapters on the Concept of Sovereignty*. University of Chicago Press: Chicago.
—— (2007 [1963]) *Theory of the Partisan: Intermediate Commentary on the Concept of the Political*. Telos Press Publishing: New York.
—— (2008 [1928]) *Constitutional Theory*. Duke University Press: Durham, NC.
Shapiro, K. (2008) *Carl Schmitt and the Intensification of Politics*. Rowman & Littlefield: Lanham, MD.
Slomp, G. (2009) *Carl Schmitt and the Politics of Hostility, Violence and Terror*. Palgrave Macmillan: Basingstoke.
Stepputat, F. (2008) Forced Migration, Land and Sovereignty, *Government and Opposition* 43, 337–57.
Stirk, P. M. R. (ed.) (2005) *Carl Schmitt, Crown Jurist of the Third Reich: On Pre-Emptive War, Military Occupation, and World Empire*. Edwin Mellen Press: Lampeter.
Vaughan-Williams, N. (2009) Virtual Border (In)security. Paper presented at the 2009 annual meeting of the International Studies Association, New York, February.
—— (2010) The UK Border Security Continuum: Virtual Biopolitics and the Simulation of the Sovereign Ban, *Environment and Planning D: Society and Space*, 28(6), 1071–83.
Williams, H. (2005) Preface. In *Carl Schmitt, Crown Jurist of the Third Reich: On Pre-Emptive War, Military Occupation, and World Empire* (ed. P. M. R. Stirk). Edwin Mellen Press: Lampeter, pp. vii–xii.

Part I

Positions and concepts

Schmitt translations

Note on translations

Matthew Hannah

Few substantive explanatory notes have been provided for references Schmitt makes to events, treaties, concepts, etc. that may be unknown to some readers (the Little Entente, the Memel conflict, etc.). This omission is partly in the interest of keeping the translations as short as possible. In addition, however, many of the chapters in this volume help fill in the contextual picture, and reliable information on all historical references is in any case now instantly accessible online for the curious reader.

A few translation issues reappear throughout both essays, so it is worth explaining here how they have been handled. First, *Politik* is translated generally as 'politics' although there are one or two passages in which 'policy' is more appropriate. This general preference is in line with Schmitt's overarching focus on 'politics' and his insistence on recognizing 'the political' as excessive with respect to any of the more technical and limited terms used to describe political institutions and processes (Schmitt, 1996 [1932]). *Völkerrecht* is translated as the 'law of nations' where Schmitt is taking a longer historical view, and as 'international law' when his subject is the period from the nineteenth century to the present, the period in which something like a modern academic corpus of legal writings acquires clearer contours. The adjective *völkerrechtlich* is rendered as 'international legal' throughout.

Two patterns of geographical usage in Schmitt's writing have also required decisions worth mentioning here. First Schmitt usually identifies the League of Nations geographically as the 'Geneva League of Nations'. This specification places the League of Nations not only in a particular city but expressly in the context of Swiss political neutrality (established in 1815). In view of Schmitt's long-term project of challenging the sufficiency of claims, projects and institutions of purported 'neutrality' wherever they arise in political discourse, the repeated identification of the League with Geneva is also in effect a rhetorical insistence upon its specific positionality, and by extension, a challenge to its claim to represent universal interests (see McCormick, 1997). This thrust becomes clearer in the latter parts of the longer essay, where Geneva is contrasted with the 'real' decision-making centre of Washington, DC. Thus the 'Geneva' will be preserved wherever Schmitt uses it, despite the inevitable strangeness of the practice to English readers. However, the 'League of

Nations' or the 'League of Nations Covenant', both of which are usually given their full names by Schmitt, will sometimes be identified with the shortened 'League' or 'Covenant', or omitted altogether where doing so does not obscure Schmitt's meaning, to avoid what reads in English as excessive repetitiveness.

Second, some aspects of Schmitt's usage of terms relating to the United States and other states of the Western Hemisphere would be confusing to English readers if translated directly from the German. It is usually clear that by 'American states' he means states of the Americas, not the constituent states of the United States, and thus I have translated the German directly in such cases. However, Schmitt sometimes refers to 'the American Continent', by which he means what in English would be termed 'the Americas'. The latter term, or in one instance, 'the Western Hemisphere', will thus be used throughout.

I am grateful to Stephen Legg for initial comments on earlier drafts of the translations, to Peter Stirk for detailed suggestions regarding accurate rendition of Schmitt's German, and to Gerry Kearns for a substantial investment of time in helping to smooth out the English of the final versions. All surviving mistakes are mine.

References

McCormick, J. P. (1997) *Carl Schmitt's Critique of Liberalism: Against Politics as Technology*. Cambridge University Press: Cambridge.

Schmitt, C. (1996 [1932]) *The Concept of the Political*. University of Chicago Press: Chicago.

2 Forms of modern imperialism in international law[1]

Carl Schmitt 1933, trans. Matthew Hannah

The imperialism of the United States of America, above all, counts in current thought and usage [*in der heute üblichen Vorstellungs- und Redeweise*] as the most modern imperialism, because it is principally an economic imperialism, and thus appears to distinguish itself from other forms, especially from every military imperialism. The economic stands in the foreground to such a degree that it is sometimes even used to deny the fact of imperialism at all, in that economy and politics are opposed to one another on the basis of an inherited nineteenth-century antithesis, and the economic is situated as something essentially non-political, the political as something essentially non-economic. In this way a famous political economist and sociologist, Joseph Schumpeter, could still express the view, in the year 1919, that what the Anglo-Saxons do, in contrast to what the Prussians and other militarists have done, is 'by definition' [*'begriffsnotwendig'*] never imperialism but something essentially different, because it signifies only economic and therefore peaceful expansion.

This highly political denial of the political character of economic processes and concepts will be discussed further here. It belongs in any case to the uniqueness of American imperialism that from the very beginning, from the first second of its existence, it has worked with the antithesis 'economic versus political'. The formula of Washington's famous farewell speech from the year 1796 has been quoted endlessly: as much trade as possible, as little politics as possible. Trade and 'economy' appear again here as the *eo ipso* non-political. Until near the end of the nineteenth century, that is, until around the time when one begins, in America as well, to speak of imperialism and to describe the massive extension of power of the United States as 'imperialistic', this opposition of trade and politics appears repeatedly in official statements. For example, in the many statements on the Monroe Doctrine it is asserted that a European state may engage in as much trade as it wishes in the Americas, but it may not do anything political. [Exactly] when the moment arrives at which the pursuit of trade becomes political is naturally decided by the United States of America. American imperialism is indeed an economic imperialism, but not for that reason any less intensively imperialistic.

It is among the residues of the nineteenth century that one understands the contrast between 'economic' and 'political' as if economic expansion and exploitation were inherently 'non-political' and as a result also 'peaceful'. Yet it is furthermore characteristic of every extension of power – whether or not it represents itself primarily as economic – that it produces a specific justification. It requires a principle of legitimacy, an entire inventory of legal concepts and formulae, of modes of speech, of slogans[. T]hese are not merely 'ideological' pretences, and do not serve merely propagandistic ends, but rather are just one instance of the simple truth that all human activities have some intellectual character; politics, imperialistic as much as any other historically significant politics, is likewise never non-intellectual 'by nature'. Never in the history of humankind have such justifications and principles of legitimacy been lacking; there has also never been a law of nations [*Völkerrecht*] in the absence of such justifications.

The international principles of legitimacy and legal forms of modern imperialism – if we think of the modern age as beginning roughly with the European sixteenth century – can be represented in their sequence at least with a few sentences, so that what is characteristic of the American forms stands out more clearly. The law of nations, [as presented] in schoolbooks and popular accounts even into the nineteenth century, meant the law of nations of Christian peoples. It was seen as an important *novum* when in 1856 at the Paris Conference Turkey was taken up into the 'family of nations' although it was a non-Christian state. From the Christian–non-Christian antithesis emerged particular, quite precise and not merely ideological forms of international legal relations, for example the practice of 'capitulations' between Christian and non-Christian states, exemptions from foreign jurisdiction, extraterritoriality of Europeans in 'exotic' lands, etc.

In the course of the nineteenth century the distinction between Christian and non-Christian peoples was secularized into the distinction between civilized, half-civilized and uncivilized peoples. To this [latter] distinction [. . .] [there then] correspond the international legal concepts and methods of nineteenth-century European imperialism, notably the development of protectorates and colonies[. W]ith respect to half-civilized peoples, for the purposes of imperial rule, use is made of the form of the protectorate, while uncivilized [peoples] are dealt with as colonies. On the basis of the distinction between protectorate and colony, a series of additional forms of international legal relations characteristic of the nineteenth century are constructed. One still finds a highly typical relic [*Rest*] of this distinction between civilized, uncivilized and half-civilized peoples in the Covenant of the Geneva League of Nations from 1919, Article 22, in the rules governing mandates, that is, where the victors [in the First World War] take as spoils previously Turkish regions and the German colonies. There one reads, in a conspicuously pathetic form otherwise unknown to the League of Nations Covenant, that there are peoples not yet able – the 'yet' should be noted here – to govern [*leiten*] themselves 'under the strenuous conditions of the modern world', and that it is a 'sacred trust' of civilization to educate these peoples so that they may govern themselves.[2] This Article 22 of the League of Nations Covenant is perhaps the most compromised example of the legitimizing function of the distinction between civilized and uncivilized peoples on the basis of which the civilized peoples assign themselves the right to 'educate', that is, to rule, the less civilized in the form of mandates, protectorates and colonies. The Article is the last and, as often in history, at the same time the classic summary expression of an entire epoch. On its basis rested what can be called the imperialism of European peoples in the nineteenth century. Most would feel today that this kind of justification of rule over other peoples has become very problematic at the least.

What is of concern here, in view of the imperialism of the United States, is that the United States has long since [moved] beyond this stage. It naturally also has colonies, such as the Philippines, and does not disdain to make use of the vocabulary and methods of 'civilization'[. B]ut above and beyond that, entirely different concepts and different methods have emerged. If I may bring to a close this short overview, which began with the distinction between Christian and non-Christian peoples and led to the distinction between civilized and uncivilized peoples, it can be said that the new distinction at the root of the American forms comes down to the distinction between creditors and debtors. Whether this new division of peoples and states is more peaceful than those of previous centuries would be a question unto itself. In any case the development of imperialistic argumentation tends toward the view that now [it is] creditor- and debtor-peoples [who] confront one another. For this division, which has a fateful currency for us Germans, the imperialism of the United States has, over more than a generation, developed an entire world of concepts, institutions, formulae and methods, of which we in Germany had little idea before the war although they were already present in finished form and [although] the specific idiom of this imperialism had already sounded often from the lips of [*im Munde ... häufig ertönt ist*] a man like Wilson before the year 1918.

At the core of all arguments brought forth defensively or offensively in justification by the United States in international law or foreign policy for a hundred years stands the Monroe Doctrine from the year 1823. It has been treated many times. I must mention it here although in my opinion it has already essentially fulfilled its function. It is characteristic of the first great stage of development of American imperialism. The Monroe Doctrine has accompanied the foreign policy of the United States since 1823, in fact already earlier, though the customary date is that of the address of President Monroe. Alongside the development of the American state itself [there] moves like a shadow the ongoing development of the Monroe Doctrine. It begins, at least apparently, in a purely defensive manner. It is oriented in the year 1823 against the Europe of that time and its contemporary 'League of Nations', that is, against the Holy Alliance and its interventions in South America; also against Russia, which had established itself on the North Coast of Alaska[. It] was in short the defensive stance of a still very weak colonial state in a peripheral position. The Great Powers of the year 1823 did not take this Monroe Doctrine very seriously. The English government took part in [its] proclamation because England's interests were in conflict with that European continental league that called itself 'Holy Alliance'. From this defensive *pronunciamento* of a small colonial state in the year 1823 there subsequently emerged an international legal instrument of hegemony of this state over the Americas in their entirety.

In the meantime the United States has become far more than a hegemonic power restricted to the Americas. Initially the famous sentence, 'America for the Americans', and the rejection of any European 'interference', seemed to suffice. The Monroe Doctrine at first sight says something quite modest: no European state may interfere in [inter-]American relations, and in turn the United States will not interfere in European relations; existing European possessions [in the Americas] in 1823 are recognized but may not be extended. These simple sentences then unfold into the basis for a great 'doctrine', whose content changes and adapts continuously, and whose practical significance is sometimes very great, sometimes recedes again [into the background].

There is a large literature about the Monroe Doctrine, [in which] the development from a means of defence to an instrument of hegemony over the American continent has also often been traced. [This development] began with the inadmissibility in principle of any intervention, with the solemnly emphasized 'basic principle of non-intervention', and ended up finding in the very same doctrine the justification for interventions by the United States in the affairs of other American states. A remarkable development into the opposite. This dialectical unfolding of a political principle, however, runs through the entire history of the Monroe Doctrine, and lies not only in the development from defensive posture to imperialistic expansion, but also from the principle of non-intervention to an instrument of an ongoing policy of intervention, from protest against the legitimating principle of the Holy Alliance to the current basic operating principle [*gehandhabten Grundsatz*] by which the United States – Wilson, too, announced this – recognizes no American government that has come to power by revolutionary means, and tolerates only legal governments in the Americas.

A new international legal principle of legitimacy develops, beginning with the struggle against the previous principle of legitimacy and with the political self-isolation of the United States of America, and ending with the United States exercising influence upon other powers that encompasses all of humanity. The individual dates of this development will not be recounted here; this short overview aims merely to emphasize one point [*es kommt . . . auf eins an*]: the Monroe Doctrine, which served at first to secure the Americas for the United States against the European Great Powers, then to submit all other states in the Americas to the hegemony of the United States, then to justify the interference, the control, the international policing of the United States in the Americas, this Monroe Doctrine appears today to have completed its service. It has in the meantime generated a series of special doctrines, for example the so-called Caribbean Doctrine, which perform specific tasks.

There are, as noted, apart from the many books and treatises, a large number of official statements by the United States government referring to the Monroe Doctrine. In all of this it becomes ever clearer that this Monroe Doctrine is a very general, very broad 'doctrine', capable of justifying the most contradictory forms of activity. The United States has, for example, invoked the Monroe Doctrine in refusing to get involved in any [intra-] European issues; it nevertheless entered the war in 1917 against Germany, but at the same time signalled its special status in contrast to its European comrades-in-arms as a merely 'associated' (not allied) power, through a peace with Germany separate from the Versailles Treaty.

Twenty-five years ago [the United States] permitted European states, in this instance the creditor states that sought satisfaction of claims [*ihre Recht suchten*] from Venezuela and other South American states, to blockade an American coast; in other cases, however, it has forbidden the same measures by appealing to the same Monroe Doctrine. [The United States] has declared that it is not a contravention of the Monroe Doctrine when a European state pursues its rightful claims, and that the Monroe Doctrine does not stand in the way of American states that have not paid their debts being forced to do so[. B]ut on the other hand it takes the view that the question of whether an American state has committed an injustice, and whether the pursuit of justice by the non-American state as injured party is permissible or not under international law, is to be decided by the United States of America. In other words, what exactly the concrete content of this ever more ambiguous, highly changeable Monroe Doctrine is, is decided by the United States alone. It alone determines what the Monroe Doctrine really means in any concrete case. On some occasions interventions are rejected and justified; on others the United States declares itself disinterested regarding some action of non-American states against American states. Always, however, it holds fast to one [principle]: that nobody is entitled to demand from the United States any action, interference, intervention, assistance, negotiation or anything else on the basis of the Monroe Doctrine; while on the other hand the United States may, if it considers it a proper application of the Monroe Doctrine to do so, interfere, intervene, negotiate, coerce [*oktroyieren*], step in with weapons at the ready [*mit bewaffneter Hand einschreiten*] at any time.

With these discussions I did not intend historically to narrate [*schildern*] the development of a highly complicated principle with examples from the foregoing century, but rather to highlight a particular principle of imperialism. When we pose the question, what is the Monroe Doctrine actually, with its many unclarities, contradictions, its peculiar entitlements and non-entitlements of the United States, it is first necessary to observe that the Monroe Doctrine is a unilateral declaration of the United States, an address of the President from the year 1823. It is not a treaty: it was not agreed with other states. The United States, as Wilson emphasized in 1916, proclaimed it on the basis of its own authority, and lays great value on the fact that it did so. For from this it follows that the definition and interpretation of the Monroe Doctrine is exclusively a matter for the United States. The United States nevertheless signs no treaty and commits to no international legal relations without the proviso, if not always explicit, of the Monroe Doctrine. What the Monroe Doctrine then means *in concreto*, this, as noted, [the United States] itself interprets, defines and determines. The Monroe Doctrine is not a treaty, but rather a unilateral declaration of the United States. It is in addition only an official statement; value is laid upon the fact that the legislative bodies never expressly enacted the Monroe Doctrine. It is possible then at any time to disavow it. It is crucial properly to perceive and to interpret the elasticity of such a principle.

A further question arises: Is the Monroe Doctrine something that has anything at all to do with international law? It figures in every textbook on international law, there are numerous international legal dissertations, treatises [and] essays about it, but is it really international law or 'merely' a political maxim? In official statements of the American government and of the various Secretaries of State one can find indications for the one as well as for the other [view]. Here, too, there are open contradictions. Secretary of State Olney says in 1895, for example [that] this Monroe Doctrine is a part of American public law ['public law' in English in original], [that] it is soundly based upon general legal principles (for example that of self-defence) and richly sanctioned by innumerable precedents. Accordingly it would thus be law and not merely politics. On the other hand Secretary of State Knox says in 1911 [that] the Monroe Doctrine has nothing at all to do with law in the technical sense, [that] it rests only upon politics and power. The primary conclusion that must be drawn from this is that nobody may assert legal claims against the United States on the basis of the Monroe Doctrine.

Yet the entire question, [namely], is the Monroe Doctrine a matter of international law or rather a political matter, a legal principle or only a principle of political action for the United States?, suffers from an alternative between law and politics that cannot consistently be made to hold up [*sich ... nicht ... konsequent durchführen lässt*] in international law. It would be wrong to believe that it is simply a Machiavellian trick of the United States if it holds to such an ambiguous and 'elastic' maxim. International law as well as constitutional law is itself political law. It is not possible to say, the Monroe Doctrine is 'purely political' and thus does not belong in international law (thus, for example, K. Strupp in his 'Dictionary of International Law' [*Wörterbuch des Völkerrechts*]). Scholars of international law discuss it nevertheless, even if they come to the conclusion that it is 'not law but politics'. It is, despite all claims to the contrary [*eben doch*], an essential part of international law, for one thing, insofar as it purports concretely to apply certain general principles such as the right of self-defence, for another, because it is recognized at least as a proviso in all treaties of the United States.

With the growing power of the United States all states have silently submitted themselves to the Monroe Doctrine. A very interesting symptom of this recognition is Article 21 of the Geneva League of Nations Covenant. There it is expressly stated that the Monroe Doctrine does not stand in contradiction to the Covenant of the League of Nations.[3] More will be said momentarily about this Article 21 of the Covenant. But if the League of Nations Covenant itself labels the Monroe Doctrine an 'understanding' or, as Article 21 can also be interpreted, as an *'entente'*, it is already clear in these expressions that one may not approach a unique phenomenon like the Monroe Doctrine with the primitive alternative: not international law but politics. The Monroe Doctrine is naturally a political instrument. But every legal concept of international law is likewise such a political instrument. It is a prodigious achievement of the United States that it succeeded in making such a 'doctrine' stick and in forcing the rest of the world, all other states and peoples, to recognize an extremely unclear, ambiguous, often contradictory principle that in any case may only be interpreted and authentically construed by the United States[. T]he [end] result of this [achievement] is that nobody may demand anything of the United States that is not in accord with the Monroe Doctrine, while the United States may at any time demand respect for the Monroe Doctrine, whereby it is simultaneously recognized that in case of doubt only the United States may determine exactly what the content of the Monroe Doctrine is.

This remarkable elasticity and extensibility, this holding open of all possibilities, this holding open above all of the alternative law or politics is in my opinion typical of every true and great imperialism. It is unthinkable that a Great Power, and still less, that an imperialistic world power, would commit itself to a codex of firm norms and concepts that an externally situated foreigner could turn against it. Hughes summarized the essential [point] thus in the year 1923: the definition, interpretation and application of the Monroe Doctrine is a matter for the United States. Every party that enters into international relationships with it must know that the United States holds fast to it; every party that concludes a treaty with the United States knows that the treaty involves this proviso.

Today, however, the United States hardly need appeal to the Monroe Doctrine any longer. Once a debtor state, it has become a creditor state. The Monroe Doctrine has done its duty, it has subordinated the Americas to the hegemony of the United States. Now there emerges a divergence in two directions: on the one hand the United States has to consolidate its hegemonic position [*sich ... in ihrer Hegemonie einrichten*] within the Americas, naturally according to new principles. Here the old Monroe Doctrine is no longer adequate; more intensive and more narrowly juridical forms are needed, for the broad elasticity of the Monroe Doctrine is only useful so long as matters have not been decided in favour of the United States. On the other hand the United States has relations outside the Americas with the entire rest of the world, it is close to becoming the world's arbiter. From both of these [developments] – from concentration within the Americas on the one hand and from world expansion on the other – there emerge again a series of characteristic international legal practices [*Vorgänge*] and new constructions.

Concentration and consolidation of hegemony have led to new methods of rule over Central American states, to new international legal forms of imperialism. If constructions such as protectorates and colonies were characteristic of the colonial imperialism of the European peoples in the nineteenth century, so it is the achievement of the United States of America to have invented the intervention treaty and related forms of legal title to intervention. [This course of] development began with the principle of non-intervention, with the purportedly sacred principle of non-intervention – that was the basis of the Monroe Doctrine of 1823; it ended in a praxis that not only justifies intervention but even generates a special and characteristic category of intervention treaties. In truth intervention into the affairs of dependent states belongs to every imperialism, because imperialism always also means hegemony.

The forms and methods of intervention are, however, quite variable. The intervention of France in the affairs of states of the Little Entente makes use of other forms and means than the intervention of England in the affairs of Egypt. Yet the intervention treaty per se, that is, a juristically formulated agreement allowing a state, under specific preconditions [and] with specific means, to intervene in the affairs of another state, was first established [*gefunden*] by the United States. It extended the system of intervention treaties especially to the states of Central America, to Cuba, Haiti, Santo Domingo, Panama, Nicaragua, etc. All of these states are bound and subordinated to the United States through a characteristic form of treaty, but they officially remain 'sovereign' states. Little remains of the old forms of protectorates and colonies. These states have their own governments, their own representation in international legal matters, their own emissaries, but they stand nevertheless under a very effective 'supervision' [*'Kontrolle'*] by the United States.

A very clear example of such an intervention treaty is the treaty Cuba was forced to enter into as compensation for the fact that it had to accept its independence from Spain from the hand of the United States. The United States declared war on Spain in 1898 in order to free Cuba and to make it a sovereign, independent and free state. The world was initially astounded at the generosity with which a great people went to war for the freedom of another people and solemnly guaranteed the freedom of the Cuban Republic. The new Cuban Republic found itself immediately required, however, while American soldiers were on the island, to conclude a treaty with the United States, the content of which came directly from the so-called Platt Amendment[. Accordingly], Cuba gave the United States the right to intervene – the expression 'to intervene' is [actually] used – for the preservation of Cuba's independence; further, to secure a Cuban government in a position to protect life, property and personal freedom and to maintain public security and order in Cuba; and finally in order to ensure the fulfilment [*zur Sicherung*] of certain financial requirements. Above all it is a matter of protecting life, property and freedom.

This means that American capital invested in Cuba is under the protection of the United States of America, and the United States decides on its own whether a Cuban government is able to provide adequate protection and to maintain public security and order. Cuba explicitly concedes to the United States the right, under these preconditions (upon whose satisfaction the United States decides), to intervene in the domestic affairs of Cuba. The treaty stipulates that particular naval bases, coal and oil stations on Cuba are left under the control of the United States, so that any intervention can immediately be carried out with the requisite military and naval firmness [*Nachdrücklichkeit*]. The United States has repeatedly landed troops on Cuba. Not only in 1900, 1901 and 1902 but also later, American troops have regularly appeared on Cuba[. A] landing of American Marines forced the resignation of a Cuban president and the installation of a Cuban government prepared to offer American corporations new concessions, or [was intended in another instance] to restore financial order. The landing of 1912 was expressly declared not to be an intervention, on the grounds that the treaty gave the United States the right to intervene. The year 1919 saw the interesting case of a landing to secure independent elections.

This intervention treaty with Cuba – herein lies the new, and especially in juristic terms the most interesting [aspect] – is founded in a double manner. The treaty is namely on the one hand an international legal treaty between the new, sovereign Republic of Cuba and the United States. On the other hand, however, in 1901 the United States forced the Cuban National Assembly and government to incorporate the content of the intervention treaty into the Cuban constitution, with the full force of a constitutional law, so that the content of the intervention treaty is secured both in international law and in domestic legal terms as part of the Cuban constitution. The Cuban National Assembly charged with drafting the constitution [*verfassungsgebende Nationalversammlung*], which attempted to resist this, was forced to yield to the pressure of American warships and troops.

The consummation of this system consists then in the further stipulation that the sovereign state of Cuba obligates itself not to conclude any treaty that could endanger its independence, that the United States has a monopoly on protection of this independence and – without being obligated to take over the international legal representation of Cuba externally – may nevertheless supervise the entire [range of] foreign policy dealings and all international legal arrangements of the Cubans[. This is purportedly justified] because [the United States] must see to it that the Cubans do not bind themselves to a third state, whether American or non-American, in a way such that the United States perceives an endangerment of Cuban independence.

We recall the discussions of the summer of 1931 about the concept of 'independence' on the occasion of plans for a customs union between Austria and Germany. At that time the question was raised whether such a customs union between Austria and Germany would endanger the independence of Austria. In the case of Cuba an analogous question would not even pose a juristic problem, but rather would be decided in favour of imperialistic interests [*im imperialistischen Sinne*] juristically as well. A dialectical reversal can take place that quickly in political relations, and the party that protects the freedom and independence of another state is naturally and logically also the party whose protection suspends [*aufhebt*] the freedom and independence of the protected.

It is necessary, for a number of good reasons, some of which will be discussed below, to keep in view the fact that [*Es wird . . . daran festgehalten, daß*] the United States does not enjoy a 'protectorate' over Cuba in the obsolete sense of the nineteenth century; that would be an international legal form developed for relations between civilized and half-civilized peoples. Both states are instead assumed to [*sollen*] be at the same stage in terms of civilization. But the one [state] is unfortunately not always able to uphold public security and order or to protect private property, to hold unbiased elections, to elect the right president, etc., and so is supervised and corrected by the other [state] with the best of intentions, without this officially constituting a form of subordination. On the basis of formal international legal equality there emerge here strange forms of rule, of supervision, of intervention, which are perhaps too elastic for our continental European thinking, [but] which belong to political reality and also have their international legal peculiarities.

There is an entire system of such intervention treaties between the United States and other Latin American states. Particularly the military protection of the Panama Canal and with it political rule over this canal are matters for the United States. The Republic of Panama, which was founded especially for this purpose and which had to conclude the typical intervention treaty, ceded to the United States the land necessary for military and naval control, and entered into additional treaties that likewise occasion the periodic landing of troops[. A]mong [these], one treaty in particular stands out because it is noteworthy in connection with the Kellogg-Briand Pact,[4] namely, the treaty of 28 July 1926. Through [this treaty] Panama has obligated itself, whenever the United States goes to war, [and] regardless of which part of the world is the scene of hostilities, to consider itself, Panama, a party at war on the side of the United States. Independently, that is, of whether there has been an attack on Panama, independently of whether the canal has been attacked, the Republic of Panama is obligated to see itself as a warring party as soon as the United States enters hostilities anywhere on Earth.

This method of intervention treaties leads to [what is] in effect an especially intensive form of subordination of another state, but the juristic form is so 'legal' and based upon 'coordination', so inconspicuous and elastic, that, within the room for manoeuvre available to them, the dependent states may conduct their foreign policy intercourse, maintain their foreign relations like any other sovereign state[. A]bove all, they are [able to be] members of the Geneva League of Nations, although the Covenant of the League stipulates that only free and self-governing states may be members. All of these states that stand under intervention treaties and must put up with repeated troop landings, even a state like Panama, which concluded the [aforementioned] treaty with the United States in 1926, count [officially] as free, sovereign states, are fully entitled members of the League of Nations. Panama is presently (February 1932) even a member of the League of Nations Council.

The American method of intervention treaties has until now remained essentially limited to the Americas. The United States has no interest, at least for the moment, in extending such a practice to other continents. It has in addition a second, very effective means of carrying through its hegemony in the Americas: its practice of recognition of new governments. In the Latin American states in which revolutions, coups and putsches are relatively frequent, everything depends for the regime of the moment, financially and politically, upon being recognized by the United States. Here the United States has a very simple principle: it does not recognize revolutionary governments and allows only legal governments to count as legitimate. We in Germany unfortunately know from experience that it is in some circumstances extremely difficult to distinguish precisely between legality and illegality, namely if [matters have reached the point of] armed civil war. Such questions are in large part decided for American states by the United States. It is thus today in a position to determine the fate of the government of practically every American state. In addition, many American states have concluded treaties among themselves in which they obligate themselves to recognize only 'legal' governments. Above all, in practice all of this means that in the ongoing revolutions and putsches the United States determines which government is legal or not.

Beyond the foregoing, general international legal principles, of which the United States makes use, naturally also continue to be of great significance. For example, the proposition has been put forward, not officially by the United States but by theorists and practitioners of international law in the United States, that private property is 'sacred'[. According to this view,] a state, even if it dispossesses its own citizens, may nevertheless not dispossess foreigners, at least not without full compensation. It is understandable that such a theory finds its advocates in a state that is creditor of the entire world and whose capitalists have invested gigantic sums in other states. For the past two years or so, however, it has been advocated in Germany as well by numerous authors. I do not consider it correct, but can understand that it is championed from an American standpoint. It is a typical American theory, a theory belonging to a state whose imperialistic expansion consists in the expansion of its possibilities for capital investment and exploitation.

The distinctiveness with which the United States sets itself up as hegemonic power in the Americas already stands out in the practice of intervention treaties and the recognition of new governments. On the other hand, in relation to the non-American world, a series of other methods of securing influence has emerged. For in fact the United States is to a great degree the arbiter of the world. It alone decided the World War to the detriment of Germany through its intervention in 1917; it in fact turned a war that until then was essentially a European war into a world war; thereupon it pulled out again in a curious way directly after the war. This should not be understood as though the United

States preys upon the whole world [*sich ... auf die ganze Welt stürzten*] out of some imperialistic presumption; it is rather interesting to note how often it is pressed, half against its will, to play a role where it does not wish to interfere. Thus it entered the world war; thus it was actually [the United States] that forced the European powers, especially France, to establish the Geneva League of Nations; and thus it was the United States of all nations who then did not join this selfsame League, while nevertheless allowing the American states dependent upon it, controlled by it and bound to it, such as Cuba, Panama and so on, to become members of the Geneva League of Nations.

Eighteen American states, a third of the membership of the League, now take part in decisions on all European or Asian affairs[. B]ut the American Monroe Doctrine, whose primacy is, as noted, recognized in Article 21 of the Covenant of the League of Nations, has precedence over the League Covenant and prevents the interference of the Geneva League in American affairs. Panama and Guatemala are members of the League of Nations. If a difference were to arise between Panama and Guatemala, the Geneva League would not have the right to interfere, although both states are members. Or if American troops land there with a major military or naval presence, and if they are active in Nicaragua, Panama or Haiti, it is not a matter for Geneva, while in turn these American states, all fully entitled members of the League of Nations, take part in all decisions in Geneva regarding European affairs. The situation is such that American states controlled by the United States participate in deciding on European issues, whereas on the other hand any interference by the Geneva League of Nations can be declared inadmissible on the basis of the Monroe Doctrine.

The League of Nations is, then, if I may put it this way, lame in the American leg, though the Americans enjoy full participation in European affairs, for example in questions of minorities, the Memel conflict, Austrian-German customs union, etc. This is a very interesting system. There is in fact system in it, not deliberate planning [*bewuste Planmäßigkeit*] in the Machiavellian sense; rather, what is characteristic of these unique methods of American politics rests simply upon the fact that the United States, in European matters, can be officially absent but effectively present. It is present, for neither Cuba nor Panama can take significant political steps without the express or tacit approval of the United States; nevertheless, [the latter] is officially absent. Yet this unique and highly elastic connection of official absence with effective presence functions beyond the affairs of the Geneva League of Nations as well. Suffice it to mention the Dawes Plan of 1924: an American, a 'citizen of the United States' [English in original] carries it out, makes the essential decision, but it is officially not the government, rather merely a citizen of the United States who decides.

Wilson, as noted, forced the French government to take part in the founding of the League of Nations; when the League of Nations was established, the United States pulled back. Wilson forced through Article 21 of the Covenant, against which the French jurist Larnaude had expressed very sensible reservations. When Wilson demanded that the recognition of the Monroe Doctrine be written into the text of the League of Nations Covenant, that the Monroe Doctrine be given precedence over any such Covenant, Larnaude posed a series of counter-questions, namely about the content of the Monroe Doctrine, which, as discussed above, is not easy to determine but rather leaves everything essential to the decision and interpretation of the United States. At that point Wilson, after a few general phrases, simply demanded apodictically that the recognition of the Monroe Doctrine be incorporated into the Covenant of the League of Nations in the suggested form, because otherwise the United States would be forced to withhold its further cooperation. Thus the subordination was taken up and stands in Article 21 of the Covenant as a fully valid constituent part, though the United States did not join the League and did not become a member. The Geneva League of Nations has thus subordinated itself to the Monroe Doctrine and has even enshrined [*manifestiert*] the superior [claims] of American principles and of American politics in the text of its Covenant. The League of Nations Council avoids any clear interpretation of or position regarding this Article 21.

In December of 1928, when the Council of the League met on the occasion of a conflict between Bolivia and Paraguay, it in fact came to pass that the Council sent three telegrams to the governments of these states, in which it admonished the parties to the conflict to settle their differences in a peaceful manner. When the Council Chair Briand was asked a week later how the situation had developed it turned out that both American members of the League of Nations had come to an agreement in Washington. The Geneva League of Nations Council was kept informed on the further course of the matter neither by Washington nor by the Bolivian government nor by the government of Paraguay, although it could have been, at least out of politeness. In the Americas the Geneva League of Nations is only in a position to exert such influence as is tolerated by the United States. The military occupation of American states by the troops of the United States is a regular occurrence. Today [US troops] remain in Haiti, in 1921 they were in Paraguay, in 1924 in Panama, in 1926 in Nicaragua to restore order, etc. All of these states are members of the Geneva League of Nations. Yet the Geneva League does not perceive such activities and ignores them. In Geneva it would be considered tactless even to steer conversation toward this question.

The United States is also the only power until now to have delivered [*herbeigeführt*] a ratified treaty on the question of disarmament. From among the many suggestions for disarmament that have been made, up to now only the Washington Accord of 1921 has emerged as a finished disarmament treaty. It was concluded not in Geneva but in Washington.

The Kellogg-Briand Pact places the final seal upon this development, so to speak. It was signed in Paris on 27 August 1928 and carries the name of the American Secretary of State Kellogg. The solemn 'renunciation of war', as well, emanated from Washington and not from Geneva. This important event deserves a brief discussion, for here it is a matter of the crucial question, who establishes peace on Earth? We all wish for peace, but questions unfortunately also arise [regarding] who decides what peace is, who [decides] what constitutes order and security, who [decides] what is a tolerable and what is an intolerable state of affairs. And this decision about peace on Earth has been taken out of the hands of the Geneva *société des nations* [French in original] by the United States through the Kellogg-Briand Pact. The Kellogg-Briand Pact contains, as is well known, a 'renunciation of war'; almost all states on Earth have joined this [renunciation], including Soviet Russia, Turkey and other states who are not members of the League of Nations. War is, at least 'formally', renounced not by the Geneva League of Nations but by means of the Kellogg-Briand Pact.

Let us look more carefully at what this means. It says in the very brief Pact that war is *'verdammt'* (to condemn) [English translation in original]. But it is never utterly 'censured' [*'verurteilt'*] and in no way 'abolished' [*'abgeschafft'*]. 'Never again war' is not found in the Kellogg-Briand Pact[, b]ut rather war is condemned only as an 'instrument of national politics'. Now we would naturally need to pose the question, when are wars an instrument of national politics and how are we to understand those that are not [*was sind die andern Kriege*]? There are wars that are 'renounced' as an instrument of national policy and may not ever occur again, and there are other wars of which nothing is said, which, in other words, in juristic terms, are *e contrario* permitted. Briand, in his correspondence with Kellogg, gave the following classic commentary: a war is an instrument of national politics if it is prosecuted on the basis of arbitrariness, self-interest and injustice. It is emphasized as well that wars that are an instrument of international politics are *eo ipso* just. You see here very typical forms of different imperialisms. Imperialism prosecutes no national wars, these are renounced; it engages at most in wars that serve an international politics; it engages in no unjust wars, only just wars[. I]ndeed we will see that it does not go to war at all, even when it does things with armed masses of troops, tanks and armoured vehicles, which would of course be considered war if anyone else did them.

From the German standpoint one could now raise the further question of which sort of war is in reality the more just, the imperialistic-international or the national[. B]ut it would already be an error, according to the clear wording of the Kellogg-Briand Pact, to believe that the Pact contains in its wording, at least *pro forma*, a renunciation of all conceivable wars. After the experiences of the post-war years we need to pose rather a different question: If war is really renounced and condemned, even if only as [an] 'instrument of national politics', then what exactly is war? I do not need to recall events in China in order to make [the reader] aware that such a question is unfortunately quite pressing [*sehr nahe liegt*]. We have lived through major landings of troops year after year. We have experienced great battles, bombardments of coasts, landings of Italian ships in Corfu, landings of American Marines in Panama, Nicaragua, and so on, invasions of French and Belgians into the German *Ruhrgebiet*, etc. All of this did not count as war and was thus not 'renounced'.

What then exactly is war? We receive a characteristic answer from an essay by a well-known pacifist and professor in Geneva, Hans Wehberg, in the journal 'Peace Watch' [*'Der Friedenswarte'*] (January 1932). There one reads,

> according to laws in force, one can speak in the case of the Chinese-Japanese conflict only of a military occupation, not of a war. This conclusion is in no way altered by the fact that the so-called 'peaceful occupation' (*occupatio pacifica*), whether justified as a matter of the protection of life and property of Japanese citizens or as a reprisal for Chinese violations of international law, was accompanied by bombardments, even by battles of greater or lesser scope.

It is thus a matter only of peaceful occupation, not war.

How is a jurisprudence possible that in view of bloody struggles, in view of tens of thousands of casualties, dares still to speak of 'peaceful occupation' and thereby delivers up the concept of 'peace' to scorn and ridicule? The thought process runs as follows: either something is war or it is peace. What is war? Whatever is not peaceful means. What are peaceful means? Whatever is not war. There is no intermediate phenomenon [*Zwischending*]. Now, however, a peaceful occupation, even if accompanied by battles of greater or lesser scope, is not war, *ergo* it is a peaceful means, *ergo* the affair also has nothing to do with the Kellogg-Briand Pact.

The Geneva League of Nations apparently sees its function [*Leistung*] in the juridification of international relations, that is, in effecting this kind of conceptual construction. For [the League] the issue is juristically in good order, and will always remain so. Thus atrocious reprisals are possible, murderous shellings, even bloody struggles and battles: all of this is not war in the juristic sense, and the peace, for which suffering humanity waits with yearning, has already long been granted to it; [humanity] has only, for lack of juristic perspicacity, failed to notice. The objects of such peaceful measures would thus do well to take note: first, war is only renounced as a means of national politics, and second, it turns out that the popular perception whereby 'battles of greater or lesser scope' have something to do with war is false.

There is something else to observe as well: the Kellogg-Briand Pact includes numerous reservations, tacked on by the signing powers in various addenda, for example the reservation of self-defence against an attack, according to which every state decides for itself whether it is under attack[. F]or example, as H. Wehberg reports, a resolution of the Japanese League of Nations Society [*Völkerbundliga*] of 16 November 1931 labelled steps presently being taken by Japan against China as 'self-defence measures'. England, alone among states, interestingly registered a reservation for 'national honour'. The others did not find the courage to make this reservation openly; most content themselves with reservations in the case of self-defence or the violation of existing treaties, and with excepting themselves from the renunciation of war.

As far as the reservation of the Monroe Doctrine goes, it can be assumed to rise above any practically effective doubt.

As the Monroe Doctrine lies in the hand of the United States, the latter can [*Wie die Monroedoktrin in der Hand der Vereinigten Staaten liegt, so können sie*] take the standpoint, with respect to the Kellogg-Briand Pact as well, that is only proper to a world power, namely, that it itself defines, interprets and applies. It decides when something is war or rather a peaceful means of international politics, a peaceful means of upholding order and security in a state which itself is not able to do so, [a peaceful means] of protection of life and private property, or in general of pacifying the Earth. If it really comes to that, the Kellogg-Briand Pact could have a similar function for the Earth to that which the Monroe Doctrine had for the Americas. All attempts to incorporate the Kellogg-Briand Pact into the League of Nations Covenant have not succeeded and cannot succeed. One reads in the commentary on the League of Nations Covenant by Schücking-Wehberg (third edition 1931, p. 180) that the incorporation of the Kellogg-Briand Pact in the Covenant is difficult because the Kellogg-Briand Pact knows 'no sanction, no organization and no definition'. Exactly this is the point, and the great superiority, the astounding political accomplishment of the United States reveals itself ever anew in the fact that it makes use of general, open concepts.

I would like to caution against the opinion that what is at issue here is a low form of craftiness and Machiavellianism. Such an elasticity, such an ability to operate with broad terms and to force the peoples of the Earth to respect them, is a phenomenon of world-historical significance. With those decisive political concepts the issue is who interprets, defines and applies them; who says, by means of concrete decision, what is peace, what [is] disarmament, what intervention, what public order and security. It is one of the most important phenomena in the entire legal and intellectual life of humanity that whoever has real power is also able to appropriate and determine concepts and words. *Caesar dominus et supra grammaticam*: the emperor is ruler over grammar as well. Imperialism forges for itself its own concepts, and a false normativism and formalism only leads to a situation in which in the end nobody knows what is war and what is peace.

I would like once again to caution against the misunderstanding according to which we are dealing with things here that [a people] can simply decide to do [*die man beliebig machen könne*]. It is an expression of true political power if a great people [can] determine on its own the forms of speech and even the mode of thought of other peoples, the vocabulary, the terminology and the concepts. We as Germans are obviously in a miserable political [state of] powerlessness, not only in the world but also within Europe, and as a German I can only feel in these discussions of American imperialism like a beggar in rags [might feel] speaking of the riches and treasures of others.

We must, however, if we are permitted, finally, to consider our own German fate, attend to one implication of knowledge of the essence of imperialistic methods. For an historically significant imperialism, not only military and naval armament is essential, not only economic and financial wealth, but also this capability to determine the content of political and legal concepts. This side of imperialism – I speak here not specifically of the American [version] – is very dangerous for a people, like the Germans, [who are] on the defensive, perhaps even more dangerous than military repression and economic exploitation. A people is only conquered when it subordinates itself to the foreign vocabulary, the foreign construction [*Vorstellung*] of what law, especially international law, is. Then in addition to the surrender of weapons there is the surrender of one's own law. In the situation in Germany today everything depends upon seeing through the veil of words and concepts, of juridifications and moralizations, not in derisive critique but also not in fawning [*dienstfertiger*] subordination to foreign terms and demands for 'moral disarmament' that are nothing other than instruments of foreign power. This form of consciousness, this sensibility for the fact that concepts and forms of thinking as well can be matters for political decision, is necessary and must remain vigilant. For we subordinate ourselves to no imperialism, neither to the American, which is not immediately proximate [*benachbart*] and dangerous to us, nor to a far more dangerous and proximate imperialism, and we will [*wollen . . . uns*] subordinate ourselves neither legally nor morally and intellectually.

Notes

1 ['Völkerrechtliche Formen des modernen Imperialismus', *Könisberger Auslandsstudien* 8 (1933) 117–42. Translation based upon version reprinted in C. Schmitt (1940), *Positionen und Begriffe: im Kampf mit Weimar–Genf–Versailles, 1923–1939*, Hamburg-Wandsbek: Hanseatische Verlagsanstalt, 162–80. New printing (1988): Berlin: Duncker und Humblot. Translator's notes appear in square brackets in the text (if brief) or in longer explanatory footnotes. Schmitt has no footnotes in the version of the text on which this translation is based. (Trans.)]
2 [Passages from the League of Nations Covenant are taken from the English text rather than translated from Schmitt's citation of the German. The version used is that of Yale University Law School's Avalon Project: http://avalon.law.yale.edu/20th_century/leagcov.asp, accessed 10 April 2010. (Trans.)]
3 [The English text of Article 21 reads as follows: 'Nothing in this Covenant shall be deemed to affect the validity of international engagements, such as treaties of arbitration or regional understandings like the Monroe doctrine, for securing the maintenance of peace.' (Yale University Law School, Avalon Project: Documents in Law, History and Diplomacy, http://avalon.law.yale.edu/20th_century/leagcov.asp#art21, accessed 6 August 2009) (Trans.)]
4 [The pact was known in Germany simply as the *Kelloggpakt*. Briand's name has been added throughout the translation to conform to English convention. (Trans.)]

3 *Großraum* versus universalism
The international legal struggle over the Monroe Doctrine[1]

Carl Schmitt 1939, trans. Matthew Hannah

The true, original Monroe Doctrine, as the brainchild of John Quincy Adams and as articulated in the address of President Monroe on 2 December 1823, contains three simple thoughts: independence of states in the Americas; non-colonization in this space; non-interference of extra-American powers in this space, coupled with non-interference of America in non-American space. In the course of time, many adaptations to changing political circumstances, many exegeses and extensions have naturally been made. The details of this development are not of interest here.[2] What is essential is that the Monroe Doctrine remains true and un-falsified as long as the idea of a concrete, specific *Großraum* is accepted, [a space] in which extra-regional [*raumfremde*] powers may not interfere.

The opposite of such a principle grounded in concrete space is a universalistic world-principle encompassing the entire Earth and all of humanity. This leads naturally to the interference of everyone in everything. While the spatial idea involves a perspective of delimitation and distribution and thus constructs a legal ordering principle [*ordnendes Rechtsprinzip*], the universalistic claim to world-interference [*Welt-Einmischungsanspruch*] obliterates any reasonable delimitation and distinction. Where such space-disregarding universalizations lead has been demonstrated in many instances by the practice of the Geneva League of Nations. I need only recall that on the question of whether what was then Austria should be permitted to enter into a customs union with the German *Reich* (1931), ultimately the vote of a Cuban, [Antonio Sánchez] Bustamante, could prove decisive for the opinion of the Permanent Court of International Justice.[3] In all important European issues, not least in the so-called right of protection for minorities, one can identify the disorienting and destructive effect of universalistic methods, whose real harm lies in the fact that they continue to justify interference by extra-regional powers. One may say without exaggeration that the Geneva League of Nations perished on the disparity between its universalistic construction and the objective necessity of an internal self-ordering of the European *Großraum*. All references to this disparity have counted for nothing.[4] The universalists were not to be convinced, because they were unable to free themselves from the ideology of the liberal democratic Western powers.

The economic-imperialistic policy of President Theodore Roosevelt that began near the end of the nineteenth century signified a turning point in the history of the American Monroe Doctrine. Roosevelt misused the Monroe Doctrine as a pretext for particularly ruthless methods of liberal-capitalist 'Dollar Diplomacy'. These methods provoked a thorough critique, the validity of which has been recognized in principle in the qualifying and ameliorating explanations put forward since 1928. A strong Ibero-American school of thought [*Richtung*] is working to [re-]establish the specifically Western-Hemispheric and [purely] defensive character of the Monroe Doctrine against such imperialistic abuses, and thus to salvage its original meaning.[5] In fact the original American Monroe Doctrine had nothing to do with the basic principles and methods of modern liberal capitalist imperialism. As a true spatial doctrine [the original Monroe Doctrine] stands in express contradiction to any space-disregarding transformation of the Earth into an abstract world- and capital-market. This entire developmental stage inaugurated by Roosevelt can thus be apostrophized with the formula Monroe versus Roosevelt.

That such a distortion [*Umfälschung*] of the Monroe Doctrine into an imperialistic principle of world trade was possible will remain for all time a distressing example of the deafening effect of empty slogans. The distortion reached its high point when President Woodrow Wilson formally announced on 22 January 1917 that the Monroe Doctrine must become a doctrine for the world. He meant by this not a sensible transference of the non-interventionist spatial thinking contained in the true Monroe Doctrine to other regions, but, quite to the contrary, a spatially undifferentiated [*raumlose*] and borderless extension of liberal democratic principles to the entire Earth and all of humanity.[6] In this way he sought a justification for his massive interference in non-European areas completely foreign to him and in military conflicts between the European powers.

For anyone accustomed to clear concepts, the statement that the Monroe Doctrine must become a world doctrine, in the sense that Wilson gave it in 1917, will at first be completely unintelligible. How can a basic principle whose specific meaning and legal logic [*Rechtsgedanke*] lies in its restriction to a specific hemisphere and at whose core [lies] the basic principle of non-intervention of extra-regional powers, become a general, spatially undifferentiated and borderless world doctrine and the justification for interference in a war fought on a distant continent? What does Monroe's protest from the year 1823, which was directed against the interference of Russia and the Holy Alliance in intra-American relations, have to do with the interests of the capitalist world market in Europe or Asia? Indeed the methods and interests of this world capitalism suspend the very spatial borders and distinctions that give concepts and images of interference and non-interference any intelligible content in the first place.

The transformation of a spatially conceived principle of non-interference into a spatially undifferentiated general system of interference was made possible by the fact that Woodrow Wilson substituted for the original and true Monroe principle the ideological idea of liberal democracy and its associated images, especially those of 'free' world trade and [a] 'free' world market. Thus began a bitter struggle over the Monroe Doctrine. Theodore Roosevelt, Woodrow Wilson and the current President Franklin D. Roosevelt, in transforming a specifically American spatial conception into a transnational and trans-ethnic world ideology, have attempted to use the Monroe Doctrine as an instrument for the domination of the world market by Anglo-Saxon capital. After the World War the Monroe Doctrine was applied to China in such a way as to sustain the basic principle of the 'open door' and of free capitalistic competition, as against the political claims of Japan. It will be especially difficult for the positivistically oriented jurist to see through the peculiar reinterpretation laid out here. The positivist,[7] disgusted by the noise of slogans, prefers to turn away from such operations, only, of course, to function all the more eagerly in their service once the slogans have hit their mark. Let us direct our attention to the intellectual struggle that has been fought for years now over the so-called 'East Asian' or 'Japanese Monroe Doctrine'.

This already deserves our special attention because almost all of the legal evidence brought forward by the American and English side against the Japanese encroachment has also been brought into play in the same or similar form against the legitimate claims of Germany. The English-American claim to [the mantle of] global judge [*Weltenrichters*] is expressed for example in the Stimson Doctrine,[8] which reserves [for these powers] the 'recognition' or 'non-recognition' of territorial alterations. The book by the same Secretary of State Stimson on the crisis in the Far East[9] makes plain not only the basic liberal democratic *Weltanschauung* but also the taken-for-granted identification of Anglo-Saxon interests with international law as such. Both are accordingly directed also against the German *Reich* and Italy. The appeal made in various formulations, on the German, Italian and Japanese side, to political and economic *Lebensrecht* ['Right to Live'] and *Lebensraum* ['Living-Space'], always run up against the same entitlement to interference claimed by the Western democracies.

A large literature has also emerged regarding the Asian or Japanese Monroe model, the 'Asia Monroe-shugi'. Actually, as far as I am able to establish, there are no government statements that officially claim for Japan the word [or] the formula 'Monroe Doctrine'. Nevertheless the formula and its use in numerous unofficial pronouncements has already sufficed to provoke a series of critical publications. These advocate with great energy the position [*Tendenz*] that the Monroe Doctrine is a monopoly of the United States of America, and that it cannot be transferred to other political and geopolitical situations, or can only be so transferred with the permission and approval of the United States. This literature is today, after the statements [made] in the *Führer*'s address of 28 April 1939, of particular interest to German guardians of the law [*Rechtswahrer*]. [The literature] will be discussed briefly here, not in order exhaustively to review all of its many individual pieces of evidence,[10] but rather to highlight its core international legal argument. It rests upon a peculiar connection between simple argumentation from ownership and [from] the nature of treaties currently in force [*Vertragslage*] (*pacta sunt servanda*), that is, [from] a bald treaty-positivism[, on the one hand,] and [on the other] the basic ideological principles of a liberal democratic and liberal-capitalist *Weltanschauung*.

As long as Russia was England's enemy, there were nevertheless no objections to the deployment of an Asian Monroe Doctrine by Japan. As early as 1905 [US] President, Theodore Roosevelt, is supposed to have encouraged the Japanese Viscount Kaneko to transfer the Monroe Doctrine to Asia. Roosevelt obviously based [this suggestion] on the idea that such a transference would ensure the economic development of East Asia by American capital, that is, the application of the world-economic methods of Anglo-Saxon imperialism to East Asia, especially to China. An East Asian Monroe Doctrine with this sense and content would thus have been nothing other than the opening of China for exploitation by Anglo-Saxon capital, that is, the transformation of China into an American-English colony. This was perfectly acceptable [*Damit war man natürlich einverstanden*]. Yet no sooner did it become evident that there was an essential difference between this Anglo-Saxon capital interest in China, on the one hand, and Japan's political claims upon Manchuria and [interest in] a reform and reorganization of China, on the other, than the aforementioned literature took up the cause [*setzte sich ein*] and attempted in various ways to cast doubt upon the transferability of the Monroe Doctrine and the admissibility of a 'Japanese Monroe Doctrine'.

A well-known Professor of Political Science[11] at the Johns Hopkins University, Westel W. Willoughby, who had acted as a legal advisor to China in 1916–17 and who is recognized as a special authority on China, published a book in 1927 on foreign rights and interests in China[. In this book] he dedicated a chapter to the question of whether Japan really is entitled to declare a Monroe Doctrine with reference to China.[12] He was of course unable to dispute [the fact that] Japan, by geographical and political situation, had a 'special position' [English in original] with respect to China. The question for him was merely the rights that Japan could claim based upon recognized basic principles of international law and of 'Comity'. With reference to the 'right to economic existence and national security' the American scholar opines that even an economic or other emergency does not grant a right to the violation of treaty obligations with other states. These sorts of claims he labels 'claims of the same sort as German claims to a place in the sun.' Instead he gives Japan the sound advice to conquer the Chinese market in free competition. The gist of the argument is clear: a right to raw materials is only permitted [on the condition of] simultaneous subordination under the liberal capitalist world system. The response of the Allied powers to the German protest against the Versailles peace conditions from the year 1919, which tended in the same direction, is expressly cited. An industrialized country should purchase its raw materials on the world market. To this American Professor of Political Science, all additional entitlements were legally unfounded. Argumentation from the status quo alone, coupled with reference to existing treaties and the familiar *pacta sunt servanda*, dominated this part of Willoughby's discussion.

Alongside this appeal to the legality of the status quo of treaties, however, the principles of the liberal democratic *Weltanschauung* can be recognized just as clearly and just as decisively in the logic of the argument and the presentation of the evidence. The deep-seated character of the contradiction in world-views [*Wie tief der weltanschualiche Gegensatz liegt*] can be seen in the discussion of the question of whether the Monroe Doctrine could perhaps provide a 'precedent' [English in original] for Japan. The question is of course answered in the negative. The justification of [this] rejection is highly characteristic. The Monroe Doctrine, says Willoughby, never provided the United States with arguments for annexations, and if [it is true that] the United States exercises financial and administrative supervision in Central America and the West Indies, it is only ever and exclusively in the interests of its own citizens engaged in trade there, and likewise for the benefit of the population of these regions. In other words, only economic-capitalistic imperialism American-style should have the right to appeal to the Monroe Doctrine. Another author, Professor G.H. Blakeslee,[13] put forward a similar argument, saying that one may not compare Manchuria and Central America, for the United States, Blakeslee emphasizes, did not occupy Mexico militarily, did not take over its administration, organized no independence movements, and installed no new government. In view of the activities [*Vorgänge*] that led to the emergence of the republics of Cuba and Panama, this is not an effective [*gutes*] argument.

Another American, C. Walter Young, dedicated a searching study, which appeared in 1931, to the 'special position of Japan in Manchuria'.[14] The basic principle of the *Lebensrecht*, the 'Right to Live Doctrine', he says (pp. 298ff.), is not a doctrine of cooperation and reconciliation, but rather the one-sided claim of the unilateral right to take action against a state possessing raw materials. An Asian Monroe Doctrine following the American prototype has never formally been claimed by Japan for Asia or even just East Asia, but Japan wants to play the leading role with reference to China. Young stresses, nevertheless, that the so-called Caribbean Doctrine and the West-Indian, Panama Canal and Mexico policies of the United States should not be confused with the Monroe Doctrine, as Charles Evans Hughes [is] also [purported to have] rightly emphasized. The Monroe Doctrine is thus expressly distanced from the 'Caribbean' Doctrine. Also the right to protect one's own citizens [abroad] is something completely different from the Monroe Doctrine (pp. 344/345). This is undoubtedly correct. But where, then, lies the true and actual reason, according to Young, that the Japanese should have no right to appeal to an Asian Monroe Doctrine? In [the fact] that the dominance of Japan is not a 'natural' [dominance], that is, for the Americans, is not an economic or financial dominance, but is rather military in character (p. 343). This argument also plays a major role in the aforementioned book by Secretary of State Stimson about the crisis in the Far East. Here a great, world-historical friend–enemy grouping is even sketched out [*wird . . . an die Wand gemalt*] in terms of the contradiction between right and wrong, [between] Anglo-Saxon sense of justice [*Rechtsgefühl*] and Japanese militarism. Here one sees with what self-evidence the liberal-capitalistic interpretation of economic imperialism depicts its specific methods of expansion and domination as essentially 'peaceful' and 'natural', not only in order to deprive the political opponent of [appeal to] the Monroe Doctrine and to reserve [this doctrine] exclusively [*beschlagnahmen*] for itself, but also as intellectual armament for just war.

From the literature on the Asian Monroe Doctrine, finally, the treatise of a Chinese [scholar], Johnson Long, deserves mention[. It] appeared in 1933 in French and was provided with an introductory Foreword by de La Pradelle. In his Introduction, the French international jurist reproduces the typical treaty-positivist argument from the legality of the status quo. The true 'Doctrine' at issue is founded, according to [de La Pradelle] upon international treaties, especially the Nine-Power Pact of 6 December 1922, and upon two principles: equality of economic and industrial opportunity for all nations, without preferential treatment for Japan, and respect for the sovereignty and territorial integrity of China. Johnson Long himself speaks of an Asian Monroe Doctrine as merely a 'pseudo-doctrine' (p. 176). He summarizes his view of the great divergence of Japanese as against American principles in three points: 1. the American Monroe Doctrine guarantees the independence of American states and protects them from colonization whereas Japan, by contrast, wishes to make a Japanese colony out of China; 2. the American Monroe Doctrine contains the principle of non-intervention on the basis of democratic regimes and democratic freedom but, in contrast, the *Reich* of the Mikado is a feudalistic military state and already for this reason an inappropriate champion of the Monroe Doctrine; 3. the American Monroe Doctrine is a principle of isolation and as such obsolete in the age of transportation, and the Asia of the year 1933 is different from the America of the year 1823.

The three points contradict each other. Point 3 actually declares the entire Monroe Doctrine to be obsolete and appears to assume that modern transportation technology has already transformed the Earth into a single space open to all Anglo-Saxon interventions. Nevertheless such contradictory representations, too, have symptomatic significance. Namely, they make it possible to recognize how resilient and widely accepted is the connection that American policy has made between the Monroe Doctrine and the ideology of a liberal democratic imperialism.

The arguments of the *Führer*'s address of 28 April 1939 have with one blow put an end to this entire confusion. They have cleared the way for the restoration of the true and original Monroe Doctrine. 'Mr. Roosevelt will in this case (namely a question posed to him from our side [regarding] which goals he is pursuing in his foreign policy with respect to the Middle and South American states) surely appeal to the Monroe Doctrine and reject such a challenge [*Forderung*] as interference in the internal affairs of the Americas. We Germans advocate exactly the same doctrine for Europe, but in any case [certainly] for the region and the affairs of the Great German *Reich*.' With this the idea of a neat and peaceful [*schiedlich-friedlichen*] distinction between *Großräume* is expressed in plain sobriety and the confusion removed with which an economic imperialism had enveloped the Monroe Doctrine in fog, in that it bent [the latter's] reasonable logic of spatial separation [*Raumabgrenzunggedanken*] into an ideological claim to world interference. It would be terminological hair-splitting if one now wanted to ask whether this amounted to the declaration of a 'German Monroe Doctrine', or if – as has already happened once – a further discussion were inaugurated about whether and to what extent it is permissible to speak at all of a German, a Japanese or any other sort of Monroe Doctrine.

A view of the struggle over the international legal significance of the Monroe Doctrine, [a struggle] that has now been carried on for more than two decades, shows that it is not merely empty and arbitrarily interchangeable slogans that are at issue but rather the most elementary question of an international legal coexistence of peoples and states[. This question concerns] the opposition between a clear spatial order based on the non-intervention of extra-regional powers and a universalistic ideology that transforms the entire Earth into the battlefield for its interventions and [which] stands in the way of the natural growth of living peoples. We are thus not simply imitating an American model if we make reference to the Monroe Doctrine; we are merely excavating the healthy core of an international legal *Großraum*-principle, and developing it appropriately for our European *Großraum*.

Notes

1 ['Großraum gegen Universalismus: der völkerrechtliche Kampf um die Monroedoktrin', *Zeitschrift der Akademie fur Deutsches Recht* (15 May 1939) 333–7. Translation from the reprinted version appearing in C. Schmitt (1940), *Positionen und Begriffe: im Kampf mit Weimar–Genf–Versailles, 1923–1939*, Hamburg-Wandsbek: Hanseatische Verlagsanstalt, 295–302. New printing (1988): Berlin: Duncker und Humblot.

Throughout the text, Schmitt's own footnotes are interspersed with translator's notes, which appear in square brackets. Shorter translator insertions appear in square brackets in the text.

The term *Großraum* has been translated in a range of ways, all of which have in common, first, the idea of a territorial expanse exceeding the geographical boundaries of a single state, and second, the idea that a single hegemonic power actually or at least potentially dominates this region politically despite the nominal independence of states within its sphere. Thus 'territorial sphere of control', 'sphere of influence', 'global region' are all possible translations. Since the distinctiveness of the concept is central to Schmitt's argument, and since the German word *Großraum* (literally 'great space' or 'large region') is comparatively easily understood even for non-readers of German, it will be left in the German form. (Trans.)]

2 Among the numerous historical works on the Monroe Doctrine, the most recent, three-volume work of Dexter Perkins, entitled *The Monroe Doctrine* (the third volume of which ([covering] 1867–1937) appeared in Baltimore in 1937), deserves mention.
3 An exemplary, and in relation to our text very instructive, account of the absurdity of the sort of 'international' methods of conflict resolution evident in this opinion is to be found in the essay by Carl Bilfinger, 'Die deutsch-österreichische Zollunion vor dem Ständigen Internationalen Gerichtshof im Haag' ['The German-Austrian Customs Union before the Permanent International Court in the Hague'], *Deutsche Juristen-Zeitung* 1931, pp. 1205ff.
4 Cf. Carl Schmitt, *Die Kernfrage des Völkerbundes* [The Core Questions of the League of Nations], Berlin 1926, pp. 19ff.
5 Hans Römer, 'Strukturwandel der Nordamerikanischen Ibero-Amerika-Politik 1928–1934' ['Structural change in North American Ibero-American politics'], in *Ibero-Amerikanisches Archiv*, v. 8, pp. 231 ff; Gaston Nerval (pseudonym for Raúl Diez de Media), *Autopsy of the Monroe Doctrine: the strange story of Inter-American relations*, New York 1934. Also the efforts of Alejandro Alvarez to develop an [Inter-]American international law on the basis of the Monroe Doctrine recur, in sharp distinction [to more recent imperialistic extensions], to the original Monroe Doctrine. Compare as well the commentary of Jessup on the Mexican memorandum of October 1933, 'The generalisation of the Monroe Doctrine', in *American Journal of International Law*, v. 29 (1935), pp. 105ff.
6 Carl Schmitt, *Völkerrechtliche Großraumordnung mit Interventionsverbot für raumfremde Mächte* [Regional Order in International Law with a Ban on Intervention for Extra-Regional Powers], Berlin – Vienna 1939, pp. 37, 54.
7 [Legal positivism is the idea that the principles of law are to be sought in the accumulated body of legal decisions rather than in principles external to juridical practice. Study of the body of decisions, according to legal positivists, can thus reveal norms capable of guiding future decisions and interpretations. (Trans.)]
8 The note from the American Secretary of State Stimson from 7 January 1932 to the governments of China and Japan includes the declaration that the government of the United States will neither admit the legality of any *de facto* situation nor recognize treaties concluded between Japan and China that violate the treaty rights of the United States or of its citizens in China[. This] include[s] such treaties as relate to the sovereignty, the independence or the territorial or administrative inviolability of the Chinese Republic or that international policy relating to China known as the 'open door policy'. A decision of the Geneva League of Nations Assembly from 11 March 1932 accordingly establishes the basic principle of non-recognition of all situations or treaties that were concluded in contradiction to the Geneva League of Nations Pact or the Kellogg[-Briand] Pact.
9 *The Far Eastern Crisis*, New York and London 1936.
10 Such an individual argument lacking in fundamental character is exemplified by the observation of Parker Thomas Moon, *Imperialism and World Politics*, New York, 1927, p. 363, that the United States encompasses almost half of the population of the Western Hemisphere, while Japan has only 6 to 7 per cent of the Asian population.
11 ['Political Science' is rendered by Schmitt here and again a few lines down in English. Peter Stirk (personal communication) points out that this was a dig by Schmitt at the fact that Willoughby was not a jurist. (Trans.)]
12 *Foreign rights and interests in China*, Baltimore (The Johns Hopkins Press) 1927, pp. 402ff: 'Has Japan an [*sic*] Valid Right to Assent [*sic*] a Monroe Doctrine with Reference to China?'

13 The, in any case, superficial treatment of Georges Klévanski, *Le 'Monroisme' Japonais*, Paris 1935, is dependent in its essential train of thought upon Blakeslee, whose book *Conflicts of Politics in the Far East* [was published] in Boston in 1934. Blakeslee was an expert of the American government in the Lytton Commission.
14 *Japan's special position in Manchuria, its assertion, legal interpretation and present meaning*, Baltimore – London – Oxford 1931.

Part II
Historical geographies of the nomos

4 Appropriating, distributing, and producing space after 9/11

The newest nomos of the Earth?

Timothy W. Luke

This chapter examines how contemporary discourses among nation-states, transnational firms, and NGOs, which increasingly track threatening developments such as "failed states," "fragile states," or "rogue states," trigger opportunities to reconsider Carl Schmitt's call to envision a new "nomos of the Earth." Schmitt's appeal is a foundational one, because he demands all evaluate "the earth, the planet on which we live, as a whole, as a globe, and seek to understand its global division and order" (Schmitt 2006: 351). As he maintains, such fundamental rethinking is essential inasmuch as "nomos means *Nahme* [appropriation]; second, it also means division and distribution of what is taken; and third, utilization, management and usage of what has been obtained as the result of the division, i.e. production and consumption" (2006: 351).

Regarding this process as a historically driven, but naturally based, spatial challenge with both territorial and maritime dimensions, Schmitt gave tremendous weight to the richness of "the *nomos*." In these three articulations of its meaning, Schmitt asserts that the idea simultaneously implied a taking, a dividing, and a making power that all rest within the embedded performative appropriation, distribution, and production of legal-political order (2006: 324–330). There always has been "an order to the Earth" for Schmitt, but the original one for the West was shattered with the discovery of the New World and rise of Europe's new maritime empires that led, in turn, to a new modernizing Eurocentric nomos of the Earth, which was tied to an alternately stable and unstable territorial and maritime rezoning of world order that lasted until 1914 (2006: 352–353). A generation of war from 1914 through 1945 again remade the world. Yet, for Schmitt, the East–West blocs of 1947–1991 were germinating the *Großräume* of cohesive, grand groupings of major states— loyal to either the United States or the Soviet Union—capable of constituting a new nomos of the Earth, but this system of geopolitical ordering fell apart rapidly after the events of 1989–1991.

What would follow the Second World War was, for Schmitt, unclear, but it was obvious that "the new nomos of the Earth [was] growing irresistibly" (2006: 355) in the efforts of all those old and new forces seeking to establish more fixed relations of land and sea, order and disorder, stability and chaos. "Appropriation, distribution, and production," he noted (2006: 351), "are the primal processes of human history, three acts of primal drama." The anxieties that many have today about world order one can speculate that Schmitt would see as predictable concerns caused by a feeling of "boundlessness or a nothingness," rising out of the 1990s' New World Order where failed, failing, or failure-prone states are becoming the rule rather than the exception. The more elaborate arguments about space and order in *Empire* (Hardt and Negri 2000) would undoubtedly not persuade him.

When thinking about *Großräume*, the works of Samuel Huntington (1993; 1996; and 2004) written during this tumultuous era become interesting, particularly in light of his controversial visibility as a public intellectual (Jacoby 1987), who openly mused about the clash of civilizations, cultural conflict, and civil-military relations. These political topics are critically important, especially to the degree that Huntington imagines individuals in many countries experiencing their civilizations as forces clashing with others. Since differences, frictions, and conflicts between civilizations are what define the stakes of life for Huntington, finding the order needed to stage and survive this clash is critical. In a separate register, then, Huntington was thinking about the "nomos of the Earth." Yet, he also is probing the philosophical, political, and practical discourses of modernity (Habermas 1987), and he is tracking how the power/knowledge dynamic (Foucault 1980) seems to work in a very different fashion for *Realpolitikers* in Washington, DC. Most of his thinking about the clash of civilizations was widely criticized (Kaplan 2001), but he also squarely aimed his words at an American and world public in the spirit of an open debate of ideas.

Given Huntington's analyses and the Great Recession of 2008–2010, it is useful to speculate about the sovereign as an agent who decides upon invoking "the state of exception" to recreate, retain, or regain order. Admitting from the outset that it is a "borderline concept," Schmitt (1985 and 1996) centers this notion within his writings on dictatorship and political theology. Remembering this point, but then turning to another theme, the USA as a nation has been regarded by many in both liberal and conservative traditions of thought as "an exceptionalist state," because of its allegedly unique constitutional republican order, its remaking of Western civilization in supposedly an Edenic continent of its special expression of Judeo-Christian values in a modern capitalist economy. To bring these parallel lines of thought together in a treatment of "geographies of the nomos," this analysis will re-examine efforts by the USA since the mid-1990s to define and then manage some of the negative geopolitical backwash or blowback from failed states, rogue states, or fragile states. During a time when the *Großräume* are quite unclear, and the nomos perhaps is yet to solidify, one finds useful political moments for exploring these specific discourses about states and times of exception.

Finally, it is useful to bear in mind the "exceptional times" in which the entire contemporary world economy—one might even talk about a "core breach" to conflate the meanings of a term drawn both from nuclear power engineering and world-systems sociology—now finds itself. After nearly two years of concentrated financial meltdown in which over $11 trillion dollars have been incinerated in a 53 percent drop in the USA's stock market alone, a massive global stock exchange implosion abroad has burnt up over $12 trillion more, a worldwide crash of private housing and commercial property values, the rising worries about massive sovereign debt defaults and excesses all around the world and the first truly synchronized economic contraction in global GDP since World War II, one can imagine even Schmitt would admit that these seem to be exceptional times wracked by boundless nothingness.

Exceptional analysis

As one considers geographies of the nomos, it is fair to ask: has the USA in effect declared itself to be in a "state of exception" to both manage real and/or perceived terrorist threats to the USA and maneuver through the worsening financial collapse of the world economy, while maintaining the impression of adhering to a formal rule of law and the ordinary practices of liberal capitalism? When looking at American interventions in failed and fragile states, analysis soon presses up against the borderline nature of a state of exception. As Schmitt foresaw, power may in these circumstances bring new measures of operationally informal lawlessness to its lawful formal operationality.

This shift can be witnessed in American military actions in Sudan, Afghanistan, Somalia, Pakistan, Yemen, and Iraq, even though official American policy presents these efforts—at home and abroad—as well-intentioned efforts to contain aggressive threats from failed and fragile states by lessening American vulnerability. Likewise, the shift continues in the American government's exceptional interventions in the nation's credit markets, the banking sector, housing markets, and the industrial economy under the extraordinary cover of the Trouble Assets Relief Program (TARP) to track down, contain, and remediate toxic assets threatening the whole world economy. Facing such fragilities, flaws, and failures, the USA in 2008 passed its Emergency Economic Stabilization Act, and opened a new Office of Financial Stability, crystallizing a sense of America's role as the world's "stability officer" in this "emergency economy."

Schmitt (1996) saw "the political" resting in strategic existential distinctions that discriminate between who is a "friend" or an "enemy." The amicable ties of liberal economy and society pre-positions all of the resources—information, energy, matter, and people—terrorists need to wreak tremendous destruction upon the conduct of people's everyday life, rendering any faith in the surety behind pledges of security down to nearly dead letters. Merely choosing to brook the demilitarized, depoliticized, and desocialized assumptions of individual freedom in liberal exchange with the evocation of an *ad hoc*, or even some standing, declaration of war, allows terrorists to unleash embedded assets of destructive power hidden by the collaborative amorality of commercial exchange. If nomos is an objectification of the polis, and its power constellations pivot on the structuration of land and sea relations in the ordering of space, then the terrestriality of territoriality and maritime life clearly are now fully in question.

By 1950, Schmitt believed the normative order of the earth was undergoing radical revisions. In this regard, he observed, "it is not inconsequential whether the industrialized and mechanized world that men have created with the help of technology has a terrestrial or maritime foundation," and it also is quite "conceivable that the air will envelop the sea and perhaps the earth, and that men will transform their planet into a combination of produce warehouse and aircraft carrier" (2006: 49). As this occurs, he believed new lines of amity and enmity would form. The greater roles that air power, space power, and electronic warfare in cyberspace play after 1991 in ordering the earth must be recognized as major factors of spatial disruption in today's unsettled nomos.

State power in Schmitt's formulae defines itself at the interface of the juridical and political action in the consensual and coercive, amicable and inimical relations around sovereign authority. Indeed, "the exception reveals most clearly the essence of the state's authority," because whatever agency exerts authority here "proves that to produce law it need not be based on law" (Schmitt 1985: 13). Sovereignty is expected to operate normally in a juridical manner; but, the sovereign authority has the discretion to define "normality," and then decides, "whether this normal situation actually exists" (Schmitt 1985: 13). If not, the state determines when and where the exceptional condition exists within the normal, juridical, and functional order, and it can suspend the law in a state of exception.

For an exceptionalist state, such as the USA, the state of exception is not dictatorship, but rather it is increasingly a zone of tremendous ambiguity in which checks and balances, divided authority, and separation of powers coagulate in a flexible suspension of limits on the legitimate authority's decision-making and action-taking. Private/public, inside/outside, regular/irregular all are in place, but can be ignored, put aside or neglected as the state of exception works as a zone of suspension that defaces, and then, effaces the roots of juridical order in this or that campaign of determined mobilized concentration usually conducted on tightly constricted "need to know" bases.

To turn to the context of implementation, one must recall the odd qualities of what is now regarded in the USA as an already quite mythic time of tranquility, opportunity, and prosperity during the years between the tearing down of the Berlin Wall and the final attacks on Manhattan's twin World Trade Center towers. During that time, many well-meaning agents of global peace in the employ of that exceptionalist liberal state tied to, but also working around, governmental and non-governmental agencies in Washington, DC talked about a few "failed states" and their miserable conditions scattered around the periphery of the planet (Kaplan, 1994: 44–76). Of course, those years had their serious violent strife in Europe, Asia, and Africa. Today, the failed states of Afghanistan or Congo in the 1980s can be regarded as harbingers of bigger disasters to follow in Yugoslavia, Colombia, Belarus, Sudan, Iraq, Latvia, Iceland, Haiti, Georgia, Bolivia, Mexico, Ukraine, and many others. Such sites now appear to be not the discrete developments of localized governmental and/or economic collapse, but rather just the initial incidents of more endemic failures in the modern state form itself.

New World Order?

As Schmitt observes, there always has been some kind of nomos of the Earth. In all the ages of mankind, the Earth has been appropriated, divided, and cultivated (2006: 351). Recognizing how an old world order prevailed before capitalism, globalism, and informationalism eclipsed it with a New World Order of multiple dimensions and diverse motivations, Schmitt looked beneath, behind, and beside the geopolitical ordering for other spatial formations. On the other hand, he recognized a complex spatiality of transnational exchange was unfolding. That is, "over, under, and beside the state-political borders of what appeared to be a purely political international law between states spread a free, i.e., non-state sphere of economy permeating everything: a *global economy*" (Schmitt 2006: 235). And, on the other hand, Schmitt was grappling with how this global economy resulted, in theory and practice, "from the circumnavigation of the earth and the great discoveries of the 15th and 16th century" that clearly required a new spatial order (2006: 86). A planetary consciousness of space activated "the practical-philosophical need not only for a geometric surface division, but for a substantive spatial order of the Earth" (Schmitt 2006: 86).

The conceptual resources for such "an order applicable to the whole earth" (Schmitt 2006: 86) were scarce. Within the old nomos of the Earth, civilization was synonymous with European civilization. In this sense, Europe was still the center of the Earth. With the appearance of the "New World," Europe became the Old World... In 1492, when a "new world" actually emerged, the structure of all traditional concepts of the *center* and *age* of the Earth had the change (Schmitt 2006: 86–87). For Schmitt, these new unknown, non-European spaces arose not as spaces of a new enemy, "but as free space, as an area open to European occupation and expansion" (Schmitt 2006: 87).

Paradoxically, the latter condition, as Europe expanded and occupied this apparently open space, soon created sites for seeing new enemies as well as revitalizing conflict with old ones. For over 300 years, Europe was both affirmed and undercut, because the struggle to expand into and occupy these spaces led to an internal political struggle within Europe as well as external political frictions beyond Europe as "civilization" itself came into contestation. The New World of Anglo-Saxon and Latin America was assumed by some to be part of the European family of nations, but then it came to be seen in the frame of America's post-Monroe Doctrine isolationism and Cold War struggles with Communism as only qualifiedly so. The two Schmitt essays translated by Matthew Hannah, which open this volume, address these issues in "Discussing Forms of Modern Imperialism" (Schmitt 2011 [1932]) and "*Großraum* versus Universalism" (Schmitt 2011 [1939]).

Consequently, it became possible to find new lines of geopolitical amity and enmity with their own agonal meaning and character as the American state and civil society posed the problem of "civilization" being either synonymous with European civilization or equivalent to other substantively ordered spatialities of non-European civilization. Schmitt's elaborate exegesis of the Congo Conference of 1885, the Spanish *Conquista* in the New World, the post-1787 new American republic's self-legitimized isolation from the Old World, and the slow collapse of *Jus Publicum Europaeum* after initiating Japan into the once exclusive club of Great Powers all moved Schmitt to assert "the transition to a new, no longer Eurocentric world order began from Asia with the inclusion of an East Asian Great Power" (Schmitt 2006: 191).

After the horrendous era of the World Wars and Cold War, is it possible that the pluralization of civilizations plus the integration of their spatiality in global economies provides a new means of appropriating, distributing, and producing space? As Schmitt observes, "when an old world sees a new world arise beside it, it is challenged dialectically and is no longer old in the same sense" (2006: 87), does he set the stage for thinkers, like Samuel P. Huntington (1993 and 1996), to discover "the West" and "the Rest"? And, does some amalgam of ideological fragments left behind after internal European struggles for the new world come to regard those Old/New Worlds in the new fracture lines between of "The West" and "The Rest"?

Conflicts and civilizations?

Huntington's "clash of civilizations" (1993) thesis is a paradigm-shifting intervention, which surfaced in *Foreign Affairs* only two years after the 1991 collapse of the USSR. Asserting that the ideological blocs of the capitalist West and communist East were a brief historical interlude, he envisioned the new battle lines of struggle cycling back to something like those of 1452 or 1491 with a united European Christian West confronting a patchwork Arab/Turkish/Persian Islamic East as well as other threats. During the twenty-first century, then, "the fault lines between civilizations will be the battle lines of the future" (Huntington 1993: 22).

Arguing that a civilization is the widest and densest identification that peoples might share, he maps out seven major civilizations that appear to be groupings capable of being regarded as *Großräume*: Western, Confucian, Japanese, Islamic, Hindu, Slavic-Orthodox, Latin American (as well as perhaps Africa being the proto-foundation of a yet to be determined eighth civilization complex), Huntington's article (1993: 22–49) was a landmark publication in American intellectual life. As the editors of *Foreign Affairs* openly declared, no article in its history since the famous George Kennan piece about the Soviet Union, or the "X" (1947) article, sparked as much discussion.

Using generic categories, such as those Schmitt uses for *Großräume*, Huntington suggests, "civilizations are differentiated from each other by history, language, culture, tradition, and, most importantly, religion" (1993: 25).

Each of these identifiers is important, but they can be linked by prior events, shared linguistic codes, a shared set of beliefs, a common long-running experience, and some enduring institutional religious force. In light of these sticky, persistent, and heavy concentrations of human practices from years gone by, there are three central theses about how global affairs will unfold in this century:

1. For a variety of reasons, civilization-consciousness is rising; conflict between civilizations will supplant ideological and other forms of conflict as the dominant global forms of conflict.
2. Successful political, security, and economic institutions at the international level are more likely to develop within civilizations than across civilizations; conflicts between groups in different civilizations are likely to be more violent than conflicts between groups in the same civilization. And as a corollary, violent conflicts between groups in different civilizations are most likely to lead to global wars.
3. The dominant axis of future world politics will be the struggle between the West and the rest; elites in non-Western countries who are trying to make their countries part of the West thus will face major obstacles; and the locus of immediate conflict will be between the West and the several Islamic-Confucian states.

(Huntington 1993: 48)

During the last fifteen years, Huntington's grand generalizations about civilizational practices have gained considerable traction in policy-making and academic circles. Friction arose in Islamic societies against "Westoxification" and "Occidentalosis," but these resistances have not always taken statalized forms. Instead of ideological contradictions in which the political issue in question is "which side are you?," the flashpoint has been more centered upon psychosocial issues of values, identities, or communities, namely, "What are you?" (Huntington 1993: 26).

The relative destatalization of political conflict coupled with this retraditionalization of cultural friction exceeds the neat divisions of rigid territorial order. Because "the West" and "the Rest" are multitudes dispersed widely around the world, there has been a revitalization of cultural myths, traditional practices, or religious affiliations that "stretch back deep into history" (Huntington 1993: 26). As a result, polyglot, intermingling, co-residential, and multicultural populations "see an 'us' versus 'them' relation existing between themselves and people of different ethnicity or religion" (Huntington 1993: 29). While not quite Schmitt's strict "friend" vs. "foe" calculations, the coded constructions of the 9/11 attacks in the USA, the 3/11 violent incident in Madrid, the 7/7 bombings in London, and the 11/26–29 assault in Mumbai cast them as "foes" striking "friends" in attacks that frequently are chalked up to grand civilizational causes by many observers. Whether or not these trends have held in the 2008–2010 Great Recession remains to be seen. The economic hardships now being experienced around the world do not appear to be exclusively confined to only one or two civilizational formations. Rather the crisis is far more general, and cross-civilizational. Such common crises could reactivate familiar class-based populist, nationalist, or elitist politics, putting Huntington's thesis to the test as Chinese, Mexican, Japanese, Polish, Indian, and American workers all lose their jobs and/or wealth in today's worldwide economic collapse (Luttwak 1999; Rodrik 1997; and Soros 1998).

Ironically, President Woodrow Wilson took the USA into WWI as the "war to end all wars" and "make the world safe for democracy." Eighty-five years later, President George W. Bush plotted to make that more democratic world an allegedly safer place for freedom by preparing for, and then invading, Iraq. While some, such as Francis Fukuyama (2004), saw that moment in history as the seed bed for a Kantian perpetual peace and Friedmanite era of end-less accumulation on Earth, "the peace" of the 1990s and 2000s appears to be the antithesis of Wilsonian statecraft. That is, what seems to be now fully institutionalized is a permanent state of war against all in a "global war on liberty" (Paye 2007). While this war is a relatively low intensity one, it also creates an insincere peace that empties all prosperity and peace of any providential power.

While trying to live in freedom, Americans in "the post 9/11 threat environment" have not yet been enabled to live in complete safety and security. In part, tangible threats do exist to their collective security; but, in part, the continuing need to generate constant threat awareness via color-coded threat alerts, 24/7 policing, and continuous surveillance now guarantee, not the freedom from danger implied by security, but rather a subjection to, and fascination with, the existential dangers expressed by permanent insecurity. Americans may live freely, but also not from the fear, anxiety, care, doubt, and uncertainty caused by a peace that ends all peace. Whether it is the sub-prime mortgage crisis, Hurricane Katrina, the collapsing automobile industry, complete corporate corruption, transnational narco-capitalist wars, or the global banking meltdown, few people today in the USA share any sense of being free from care, being safe, feeling secure. At best, the civilization defense project of "the West" after 9/11 is distinguished by the mobilization of rationally planning for, heightened awareness of response to, and complete recovery from acts of (in) securitizing terror (Paye 2007) in positioning America as "the homeland" and by declaring war on liberty itself.

On May 1, 2003, when the President declared an "end to major hostilities" against Baghdad on the *USS Abraham Lincoln*, the entire Western "coalition of the willing" had incurred only 171 dead and wounded troops in the Iraqi war, while the US had only lost 110 in Operation Enduring Freedom. Yet, enduring freedom's operations in Iraq after the end of that battle, during what are supposedly months and then years of "peace," have clearly proven to be far more fatal to thousands of coalition soldiers than the initial "war" itself—here again is an odd quality of the peace that ends all peace. Meanwhile, the exceptionalist American state—now led by President Obama—continues to juggle new threats in Pakistan, Syria, Mexico, Iran, and North Korea.

Although the American war dead only number a few hundred for the days since his inauguration in January 2009, he has intensified the hunt for terrorists in Afghanistan, Iraq, Yemen, and Somalia as well as for Osama bin Laden in the tribal regions of Pakistan. Indeed, Obama's taste for robotic strikes with Predator UAVs in failed or fragile states has become a new "drone war" on terror fought at a distance by remote control.

Meanwhile, the USA has lost about 600,000 jobs a month since the 2008 presidential elections, and the stock market fell another 20 percent plus before coming back in March 2009. As 2010 arrived, in the USA, one in nine American mortgage holders needed some sort of financial assistance to avoid foreclosure, one out of thirty-one American adults is in prison, jail or penal detention, and one out of every fifty American children is homeless. Plainly, security is far from certain, and the peace that ends all peace is a troubled one. Perhaps this is a "change America needs," or maybe it is only another different path to experience the peace that ends all peace. Regardless, this posture remains part of that state of exception, as the statal apparatus does all of this just inside, or barely outside, of the law, eroding away the earlier promises of unending peace at "the end of history" in 1989.

The end of the Cold War actually brought with it neither "the end of history" nor "an end to war." Instead, there is this new variety of "peace" built atop drone wars and enduring freedom operations, but it is not peace-like, peaceful, or peaceable. It is free, but not with freedom from anxiety, care, doubt, or fear. Allegedly, there are no absolute enemies, no obvious warring alliances, and no menacing warriors, but many hidden enmities, underground antagonists, and angry multitudes are all lumped together by the American state as civilizational threats to be crushed by the West's ongoing "war on terror." The conditions of today's "peace," in turn, erase many peaceable and peaceful qualities in everyday life. And, this state of emergency rests on a vast state formation that sees danger emerging everywhere, all the time, and from anyone. If this is solidifying into a new nomos of the Earth, then it has few enthusiastic backers. One wonders if a new *anomos* of Earth shall follow?

Moving from disorderly states of nature to more structured states of society, as the nomos takes hold, is not a discrete, one-time, or dichotomous change; it is instead for Schmitt always a consolidated, constant, and continuous transformation, occurring all the time everyday. Finding some agency to fulfill the promises of surety behind security, or finagle some evasive nonsureties in episodes of security, is a new quality that consistently weaves in and out of everyday government with each its urgencies for the commission of both discretionary and necessary acts. Foucault's inversion of Clausewitz's dictum on war and politics, therefore, makes perfect sense. Politics—whether one looks in the public or private sphere—is the "continuation of war by other means" (Foucault 2003: 16).

The peaceful hopes of fiscal surpluses, sustained economic growth, and geopolitical supremacy, once widely assumed to be the future of the United States back at the century's end in 2000, now are long gone. Much of the world made by industrial modernization over the past 250 years is fraying or fragmented. Since 1979, a new dialectic of state privatization, territorial denationalization, and cultural hollowing-out is emerging with the largely unchecked capitalism of contemporary globalization (Soros 1998). Amid this marketplace, official streams of hi-tech, fast capitalist informational production increasingly coexist with, if not actually create, much more common, slow flows of material commerce in illegal, immoral, and illicit goods and services (Agger 1989). The binary ethic in capitalism of private vice and public virtue often nests its operations spatially in both successful and failed states where individuals and societies, which cannot always master waves of change, struggle to exist amid many different modes of production and consumption. From Russia to Iceland, Sierra Leone to Colombia, Thailand to Afghanistan, Congo to Greece, the twin threats of fragile states and fraying markets rapidly are making many states more fragile, if not failures, as their markets also sputter along.

As Schmitt observes, the root dispositions of liberal society and its commercialism with its insistent patterns of demilitarization and depoliticization are what have evaded politics, the state, and government in order to ensure individual freedom, private property, and commercial opportunity. The political, when necessary, must be ready and able to require individuals to sacrifice their lives often with comrades and friends in collective struggle against their enemies to preserve order. Security, even surety, requires always violence to continue. Schmitt, however, correctly concludes,

> Such a demand is in no way justifiable by the individual of liberal thought. No consistent individualism can entrust to someone other than to the individual himself the right to dispose of the physical life of the individual. An individualism in which anyone other than the free individual himself were to decide upon the substance and dimension of his freedom would be only an empty phrase. For the individual as such there is no enemy with whom he must enter into a life-and-death struggle if he personally does not want to do so. To compel him to fight against his will is, from the vision point of the private individual, lack of freedom and repression.
> (1996: 71)

Political conflicts, then, are pushed down, out, and away by liberals into other "heterogeneous spheres, namely, ethics and economics, intellect and trade, education and property" (Schmitt 1996: 70).

As the USSR collapsed, however, what little "stability" existed in many places around the world evaporated along with the other artifacts of Cold War alliances, leaving in their wake only pretend nation-states "without leadership, without order, without governance itself" (Atwood 1994: 21). From the currency crises of 1997–1998 through the Great Recession of 2008–2010, it is clear that no solid structures are arising as a basis for order. Little has improved since 1991, as Haiti, Hungary, Honduras, and Hong Kong, or Somalia, Sudan,

Serbia, and Syria or Pakistan, Philippines, Poland, and Palestine all continue to demonstrate at various levels of ineffectiveness and on different scales of illegality. Chaos becomes a strange entrepôt of capitalist opportunities marked by insufficient, ineffective, or insecure levels of governmentality. Even when regimes are "agovernmental" (Foucault 1991), or incapable of efficiently adjusting people to things within their designated space of sovereignty (Luke 1993) darker modes of commerce proliferate and prosper.

Global systems of production or consumption are denied easy access to their labor and resources, as with Somalia or Sudan, while these people and places miss out on the benefits of transnational commerce save through piracy or pillage. This condition of economic collapse frequently leads to massive flows of contraband products, as with Armenia or Afghanistan, into and out of the country along with cross-border incidents of destabilizing violence. Whether in Mexico, Russia, Nigeria, or Thailand, corrupt capitalists disrupt the civic stability of neighboring states, and civil society of distant wealthy cities, and the stable operations of legal transnational enterprise (Luke 1991).

Consequently, particular times and places of liberal development can deprive the state and its politics of any specific concrete meaning, leaving the specific technicities of national and international commodity chains to set the tone and tenor of collective life (Walker 1993; Luke 1993). One finds that:

> The state turns into society: on the ethical-intellectual side into an ideological humanitarian conception of humanity, and the other into an economic-technical system of production and traffic. The self-understood will to repel the enemy in a given battle situation turns into a rationally constructed social ideal or program, a tendency or an economic calculation. A politically united people becomes, on the other hand, a culturally interested public, and, on the other hand, partially an industrial concern, and its employers, partially a mass of consumers. At the intellectual pole, government and power turns into propaganda and mass manipulation, and at the economic pole, control.
>
> (Schmitt 1996: 72)

The material culture of too many contemporary liberal capitalist societies is riddled by these depoliticized and demilitarized, but still nonetheless highly political, qualities.

Civilizations as *Großräume*

Huntington questioned what he saw as the delusions of those holding Western universalist values and expecting that "people throughout the world should embrace Western values, institutions and culture because they embody the highest, most enlightened, most liberal, most rational, most modern, and most civilized thinking of mankind" (1996: 310). Realizing the world scene of the 1990s and 2000s would be one of "ethnic conflict and civilizational clash,"

Huntington recognized that "Western belief in the universality of Western culture suffers three problems: it is false; it is immoral; and it is dangerous" (1996: 310). The West's rational, liberal, modern civilization for Huntington is unique, but its cultural uniqueness is an embedded spatial particularity. In its civilizational life, many things capture its essential value, but valued essence "is valuable not because it is universal but because it is unique" (Huntington 1996: 311).

For many, this claim can be shocking, but Huntington believed it was essential for "the West" to leave "the Rest," both at rest and to the rest, rather than pursuing the aggressive moralistic universalism of the Carter-Reagan-Bush-Clinton-era evangelizing for legality, individualism, pluralism, commercialism, and neo-liberalism. If the USA did not forsake its Cold War imperial ventures, then the West might not be able "to learn to navigate the shallows, endure the miseries, moderate its venture, and safeguard its culture as it now rode on the shifting tides in the affairs of men" (Huntington 1996: 311). Huntington saw all civilization as enduring systems in perpetual clash inasmuch as civilizations are truly unique, exclusive, and particular rather than being inevitably general, inclusive, and universal. Such thoughts are not popular, but they do reflect accurately many different tensions building in the current conjuncture.

The Cold War brought to life two threats, as Huntington regards them, for America and the world at large—cosmopolitanism and imperialism. Caught in the hegemonic rhetorical spin of attempting to eliminate cultural, economic, political, or social differences at home and abroad, the USA constantly is tugged between an inner imperialistic imperative by which it must remake the world and a complex cosmopolitan consensus through which the world must remake America (Kennedy 1992). It is ironic that what Huntington calls "the Davos Culture" (1996: 57) captures both of these threats. When "Davos Man" wishes to hold forth about truth, progress, and justice, cosmopolitanism prevails; but, when those addressed recoil and/or resist, imperialism can work just as well. Huntington then alienates American conservative and liberals alike in repudiating their respective imperial and cosmopolitan missions in favor of preserving what he regards as the USA's deeply embedded Anglo-Protestant culture, engrained religiosity, and republican credo. Still, one wonders if there are the foundations for a new nomos of the Earth being poured in such theoretical frameworks.

On the whole, Huntington's cultural cartographies carry spatial content and categories that plainly are very questionable. Like the strange country maps drawn for the geopolitical board game, *Risk*, they bear enough relation to reality to be examined curiously as Huntington's civilizations (1996: 26–27). Yet, they do not have the real substance to be really taken seriously. On Huntington's maps, the West does not include Orthodox Christian zones or Latin America: both of them were, are, or will be sites of threat. So Huntington disconnects them from the classical and medieval Western civilization of the West. Likewise, Islamic civilization becomes *sui generis*, losing all of its ties to Judaism, Christianity, and the medieval moment in Europe. Sinic civilization appears to be a place-holder for Confucianism (or about anywhere a Chinese dynasty once might have ruled). Hindu civilization exists, but mostly in the subcontinent, and it is in some disarray. Jewish and Buddhist civilizational zones are considered, and yet they are not given their due because they occupy no set geopolitical autonomous space. Africa is just a quasi/proto/para-civilization except where it is Islamic. South of a line running more or less from Liberia to Uganda, Africa is left to becoming only a near civilization. North of that line except for the Horn, coastal Kenya and Tanzania, Africa is Islamic. For Huntington, however, the Republic of South Africa is not the West; it now is the African rest. Latin America is mapped off as a whole civilization running from Tijuana to Tierra del Fuego, except for the Falklands and the old French, Dutch, and British Guianas, which are a patchy quilted culture of Africa, Hindu, and the West. The Philippines are a similar mish-mash of Sinic, Islamic, and Western civilization. Japan is a civilization unto its own, but strangely Greenland is the West. Buddhist civilization is mapped almost Zen-like over Mongolia, Tibet, Myanmar, Cambodia, and Laos, but it is not a major player. Strangely enough, Antarctica is zoned "Buddhist" on the map as well. Israel is Jewish, but not the West nor Islam. And, nearby Cyprus is terra incognita.

The putative universals of Huntington's maps are fascinating. Like Carl Schmitt's (2006) *The Nomos of the Earth in the International Law of the Jus Publicum Europaeum*, a "new world order" concealps in the ideography/theography/ethnography/nomography of a cranky cartography. Like Schmitt, Huntington is disputing universalism, and entrenching his own New World Order out amid his civilizational myths. Accuracy and certainty stem not from the lines on maps, but the cultural forces Huntington sees pulling and pushing their powers across the map. Ultimately, Huntington shows how what was once "the West," or the old European imperia defined through rule by the West, and the autonomous independent "Rest" in 1920 (1996) morphs into the Cold War's zone regimes (1991), and now the nomos of the Earth is civilizational (1996).

His strange vision of civilization pervades a new cultural cartography, but it is most blatant in the case of the USA in another decade. For 2020, with his anxious fears about white, Protestant, "Western Civilization" America, he maps out darkening zones of Black, Asian, Native American, or Hispanic population enveloping "white spaces" of fewer than 10 percent non-white counties. Thus, spaces such as Washington, DC; metro Detroit; Clark County, NV; Coconino County, AZ; and Mora County, NM will apparently then be "the Rest," while "the West" remains Maine, Vermont, New Hampshire, West Virginia, and Iowa (Huntington 1996: 205). The cartography of this contradictory country is extraordinary, but Huntington's point is simple: ". . . Muslims pose the immediate problem to Europe, Mexicans pose the problem in the United States" (Huntington 1996: 204). The civilization of clash comes out plainly here, and it belies his truly big question for the next century, "Who Are We?" The audacity and continuity of his answers is admirable (Huntington 1981; 1991; and, 2004). Still, the complexity of his motivations, as well as perhaps an odd disregard about how his views, as a world-famous Harvard professor of government, can be misinterpreted by allies and enemies alike, is distressing.

Paradoxically, however, some of Huntington's conceptualizations of these world civilizations as zones of clash have been borne out by many events. In 1993, he saw civilizational imperatives shaping the direction of American domestic and foreign policies, and he spelled them out more clearly in 1996. That is, it was essential for the USA,

- to achieve greater political, economic, and military integration and to coordinate their policies so as to preclude states from other civilizations exploiting differences among them;
- to incorporate into the European Union and NATO the Western states of Central Europe that is, the Visegrad countries, the Baltic republics, Slovenia, and Croatia;
- to encourage the "Westernization" of Latin America and, as far as possible, the close alignment of Latin American countries with the West;
- to restrain the development of the conventional and unconventional military power of Islamic and Sinic countries;
- to slow the drift of Japan away from the West and toward accommodation with China;
- to accept Russia as the core state of Orthodoxy and a major regional power with legitimate interests in the security of its southern borders;
- to maintain Western technological and military superiority over other civilizations;
- and, most important, to recognize that Western intervention in the affairs of other civilizations is probably the single most dangerous source of instability and potential global conflict in a multicivilizational world.

(Huntington 1996: 312)

Despite the unusual inspirations behind his thinking, many in the USA and Europe would concur with this vision of geopolitical maneuvering; it appears to be a main current in the drift of twenty-first century events.

Responses to (in)security

The responses to an *anomos* of the Earth also point to the ready submission to a new level of surveillance, policing, and control unknown since the mass mobilization for WWII during 1941–1945. The examples set by the Ashcroft/ Gonzales Department of Justice and the George W. Bush Administration's PATRIOT Act unfortunately have pointed the USA down a road leading to an odd new dirigisme (Gill 1995). Attorney-General Holder and President

Obama are just now slowly backing away from this path, but not entirely, and only in certain situations. By wrapping the cloak of national, municipal, and personal security around the predicates of liberal society, the fetish for individual freedom sees liberty in recasting state repression as risk-management, constant surveillance as insurance, and aggressive policing as collective security. Amicality here is nationalized, class-focused, ethnified, and ultimately racialized, creating identifiable foreign, poor, ethnic, and racial others—from whom enmity is always suspected and amity is never expected. Trust evaporates in a fog of peace-seeking suspicion rather than the flashes of militant war.

Such responses turn the mythographical clash of Huntington's civilizations (1996) into a self-fulfilling strategic prophecy, but these "Other-based" myths also do not guarantee security (Ó Tuathail and Dalby 1998). Before the Oklahoma City bombing and the Washington sniper attacks, most citizens in America's liberal capitalist society believed that no one or, at least not one of us—that is, an ordinary American white man or black man such as Timothy McVeigh or John Allen Muhammed—could have "done what they did." Nonetheless, they did. And, even PATRIOT Act-driven anti-terrorist profiling, which can turn any airline ticket holder, suburban gun owner, average motorist, or former serviceman through sophisticated data mining into a ticking Islamic terrorist time bomb, cannot prevent new violent events from coming from other like-minded agents in the peace that ends all peace. Likewise, principles of liberalism militate against state repression and the commercial impulse behind daily standards of living require continuing liberalism's industrial practices, so ways of life maintaining inequalities at home and abroad are a peace that ends all peace.

Huntington's last book *Who Are We?* (2004) developed naturally out of his *Clash of Civilizations* book and earlier article in response to the upheavals of the 1990s. His spin on that moment in history is simple: it was "the eruption of a global identity crisis." Almost everywhere one looks, people have been asking, "Who are we?" "Where do we belong?" and "Who is not us?" (1996: 126). Whether Yugoslavia or India, South Africa or the USA, Huntington believed questions of national identity were being, and would continue to be, hotly debated. His 2004 book, however, was another contribution to that debate done again in broad strokes and with stark assertions. Huntington's last work directly asks "Who are we?" and once he raises this question against the backdrop of his clash of civilizations conundrum, the place of cultural ties in the everyday life of the world's publics cannot be ignored.

Since at least the 1960s, the USA's geographical borders as well as its diverse multicultural communities have become civilizational flash points where "we-ness" and "they-ness" have sparked some of Huntington's questioning. From daily interactions in civil society, the economy, and urban life, Huntington sees Americans being challenged to answer who we are, how we are as we are, and whom the who in question gathers to answer such questions. Most importantly, his discomforting answers to such queries ironically go beyond the easy acceptance of his earlier "clash of civilizations" thesis. Instead he recognizes the civilizing influence of constant cultural clash itself is an embedded means for posing, and then pushing, answers for such foundational questions. Without saying so, and with little consciousness of where his claims lead, Huntington touches upon how intellectuals—popular as well as expert—work in any society to shape individual and collective subjectivity to accept some decisive form of nomos.

While imperfect, Huntington's mappings for world civilizations stand in accord with Schmitt's views on a new nomos of the Earth. Because there is no single world sovereign, and the hegemonic power balance of the Eastern vs. the Western bloc has corroded away, the final option that Schmitt foresaw might be coming to pass. That is, "the third possibility, in equilibrium of several independent *Großräume* is rational, if the *Großräume* are differentiated meaningfully and are homogeneous internally" (Schmitt 2006: 355). Still, as Schmitt also notes, "the joint domination of sea and air, which only the United States is capable of doing," might well continue, since "America is, so to speak, the greater island" that still could "administer and guarantee the balance of the rest of the world" (2006: 351). Of course, the Departments of Defense and Homeland Security are hard at work on all these tasks, but it is not clear that they are prevailing, as many states continue to unbundle their sovereignty and security (Luke 2007).

From a world being "made safe for democracy" in 1918 by President Wilson to a world marked by a long war on "global terror" in 2008 by President George W. Bush, one must ask how and why the "democracy safe" world can now accomplish its contradictory mission. In fact, through ruthlessly enforcing or enacting a peace that ends all peace, does the *anomos* of anarchic life—as it can be experienced in the scrambled spatialities of contemporary aerospace, informatic, maritime, and terrestrial relations for appropriation, distribution, and production—now morph into the newest nomos of the Earth?

References

Agamben, G. (2005) *State of Exception*. Chicago: University of Chicago Press.
Agger, B. (1989) *Fast Capitalism*. Urbana: University of Illinois Press.
Atwood, B. (1994) "From the Cold War to Chaos and Cholera (Development or Recolonization)," *New Perspectives Quarterly*, 11, 4: 21–23.
Foucault, M. (1980) *Power/Knowledge: Selected Interviews & Other Writings*. New York: Pantheon.
Foucault, M. (1991) *The Foucault Effect: Studies in Governmentality* (Eds. G. Burchell, C. Gordon, P. Miller). Chicago: University of Chicago Press.
Foucault, M. (2003) *"Society Must Be Defended," Lectures at the Collége De France, 1975–1976*. New York: Picador.
Fukuyama, F. (2004) *State-Building: Governance and World Order in the 21st Century*. Ithaca, NY: Cornell University Press.
Gill, S. (1995) "The Global Panopticon? The NeoLiberal State, Economic Life, and Democratic Surveillance," *Alternatives*, 20, 1 (January/February): 1–49.

Habermas, J. (1987) *The Philosophical Discourse of Modernity*. Cambridge, MA: MIT Press.
Hardt, M. and Negri, A. (2000) *Empire*. Cambridge, MA: Harvard University Press.
Huntington, S.P. (1981) *American Politics: The Promise of Disharmony*. Cambridge, MA: Belknap Press.
Huntington, S.P. (1991) *The Third Wave: Democratization in the Late Twentieth Century*. Norman: University of Oklahoma Press.
Huntington, S.P. (1993) "The Clash of Civilizations?," *Foreign Affairs*, 72, 3: 22–49.
Huntington, S.P. (1996) *The Clash of Civilizations and the Remaking of World Order*. New York: Simon & Schuster.
Huntington, S.P. (2004) *Who Are We? The Challenges to America's National Identity*. New York: Simon & Schuster.
Jacoby, R. (1987) *The Last Intellectuals: American Culture in the Age of Academe*. New York: Basic Books.
Kaplan, R.D. (1994) "The Coming Anarchy," *The Atlantic Monthly*, 273, 2: 44–76.
Kaplan, R.D. (2001) "Looking the World in the Eye," *The Atlantic* (December) 12pp. Online. Available at www.theatlantic.com/doc/200112/kaplan.
Kennedy, P. (1992) *Preparing for the Twenty-First Century*. New York: Random House.
Luke, T.W. (1991) "Security, Sovereignty and Strategy: Reinterpreting the Lessons of Operation Desert Storm," *Crossroads: An International Socio-Political Journal*, 33 (December), 3–14.
Luke, T.W. (1993) "Discourses of Disintegration, Texts of Transformation: Re-Reading Realism," *Alternatives*, 18, 3 (September/October): 229–258.
Luke, T.W. (2007) "Unbundling the State: Iraq and the 'Recontainerization' of Rule, Production, and Identity," *Environment and Planning A*, 39: 1564–1581.
Luttwak, E. (1999) *Turbocapitalism: Winners and Losers in the Global Economy*. New York: Harper Collins.
Ó Tuathail, G. and Dalby, S. (1998) *Rethinking Geopolitics*. London: Routledge.
Paye, J.-C. (2007) *Global War on Liberty*. New York: Telos Press Publishing.
Rodrik, D. (1997) *Has Globalization Gone Too Far?* Washington, DC: Institute for International Economics.
Schmitt, C. (1985) *Political Theology: Four Chapters on the Concept of Sovereignty*. Cambridge, MA: MIT Press.
Schmitt, C. (1996) *The Concept of the Political*. Chicago: University of Chicago Press.
Schmitt, C. (2006 [1950]) *The Nomos of the Earth in the International Law of Jus Publicum Europaeum*. New York: Telos Press.
Schmitt, C. (2011 [1932]) "Forms of Modern Imperialism in International Law." (Trans. M. Hannah; Chapter 2 in this volume.)
Schmitt, C. (2011 [1939]) *Großraum* versus Universalism: The International Legal Struggle over the Monroe Doctrine. (Trans. M. Hannah, Chapter 3 in this volume.)
Soros, G. (1998) *The Crisis of Global Capitalism: Open Society Endangered*. New York: Public Affairs.
Walker, R.B.J. (1993) *Inside/Outside: International Relations as Political Theory*. Cambridge: Cambridge University Press.
X [Kennan, G. F.] (1947) "The Sources of Soviet Conduct," *Foreign Affairs*, XV (July): 575–576.

5 Echoes of Carl Schmitt among the ideologists of the new American Empire

Gerry Kearns

Mark Twain wrote that "History never repeats itself, but the kaleidoscopic combinations of the pictured present often seem to be constructed out of the broken fragments of antique legends" (Twain and Warner, 1874 [1873], 76). More pithily, he is widely quoted as having said some variant of the following: "History never repeats itself, but it sometimes rhymes." I hear Schmitt rhymed when Robert Kaplan (2002, 4) writes of danger in the twenty-first century as likely to come from "populist movements, taking advantage of democratization," and as requiring the establishment of order abroad, through self-interested leadership on the part of the United States. This "pagan" self-interested leadership must be prepared to set aside morality in the service of effectiveness, and thus, while "[t]he [US-] Mexican War [1846–1848] was probably unjust—motivated as it was by sheer territorial aggression," yet, "it was a war worth fighting: the United States acquired Texas and the entire Southwest, including California" (Kaplan, 2002, 130). George W. Bush rhymed Schmitt when, in defending Donald Rumsfeld in April 2006, he described his own style of government: "I hear the voices, and I read the front page, and I know the speculation. But I'm the decider, and I decide what is best" (Henry and Starr, 2006). The reading list for the Bush administration that took office in January 2001 included Terry Eastland's (1992) *Energy in the Executive: The Case for a Strong Presidency* and in Eastland's advocacy, and in Bush's practice, of a President with almost unlimited powers, a unitary executive, I hear more Schmitt rhymes (J. W. Dean, 2008 [2007], 100). I heard them too, when, in April 2004, George W. Bush set aside UN resolutions and, while advocating the creation of a Palestinian state, yet reassured Israeli Prime Minister, Ariel Sharon, that, "[i]n light of new realities on the ground, including already existing major Israeli populations centers, it is unrealistic to expect that the outcome of final status negotiations will be a full and complete return to the armistice lines of 1949" (Anon., 2004). I heard Bernard Lewis (1990) rhyme Schmitt when he spoke of a "civilizational jealousy" that meant the world of Islam hated the West for surpassing the Arab world in technology, wealth, and power and described a "clash of civilizations" between two global blocs defined essentially by religion, with Islam as the auld enemy of Christendom. And, having borrowed Lewis's incendiary phrase for his own study of international relations as *The Clash of Civilizations*, Samuel Huntington (1977) turned to the internal divisions within the United States and I heard rhymes of Schmitt in his bemoaning the dilution of WASP dominance through the immigration of Mexican Catholics (Huntington, 2004).

A week after the international crimes of 9/11, Congress passed an authorization for the use of force:

> the President is authorized to use all necessary and appropriate force against those nations, organizations, or persons he determines planned, authorized, committed, or aided the terrorist attacks that occurred on September 11, 2001, or harbored such organizations or persons, in order to prevent any future acts of international terrorism against the United States by such nations, organizations or persons.
>
> (Anon., 2001)

The Bush administration touched its house jurist, John Yoo, for a legal opinion that would give it unfettered war powers under this indefinite and unspecific mandate. Yoo obliged in terms that certainly rhyme easily with Schmitt. Some of these opinions have recently peeped out into the press and we now know that Yoo's sketch

> included assertions that the president could use the nation's military within the United States to combat people deemed as terrorists and to conduct raids without obtaining a search warrant. [... And] that the president could unilaterally abrogate foreign treaties, deal with detainees suspected of terrorism while rejecting input from Congress and conduct a warrantless eavesdropping program.
>
> (N. A. Lewis, 2009)

The Schmittian rhymes were there, too, a bare ten days after 9/11, when George Bush declared war on terror and enjoined his fellow Americans to recognize that "we have found our mission and our moment" (Bush, 2001a). A mere five days after the attacks, he had spoken also of "[t]his crusade, this war on terrorism" (Bush, 2001b). Asked a few years later if he had consulted his father, the former President, George H. W. Bush, about how to respond to 9/11, the son could not remember anything in detail but then added: "[y]ou know, he is the wrong father to appeal to in terms of strength. There is a higher father that I appeal to" (Woodward, 2004, 421). I hear Schmitt too in this theological politics.

Carl Schmitt's work seems to speak to our times. In our daily news, we find echoes of his accounts of states, of sovereignty, and of international relations. We might conclude that his work encapsulated some inescapable dimensions of politics; hard lessons that we must learn once again. Instead, I want to suggest that there are a variety of ways that states, sovereignty, and international relations have been and can be configured and that Schmitt argued in favor of certain ones of them: his approach was normative. Furthermore, he engaged with his own times and found much to criticize and occasionally things to praise in the way peoples, states, and foreign affairs were managed by his contemporaries. We find, today, people who share Schmitt's values and promote policies similar to those he promoted. Politicians, strategists, and intellectuals seem to echo Schmitt in part because desiring similar ends they see things in much the same way as did Schmitt. Schmitt would have strongly disagreed with this reading of his work. As a friendly critic, Leo Strauss noted of Schmitt's analysis of the political, "it is immaterial in Schmitt's express opinion, whether one regards the political as desirable or detestable: the intent of the position 'is neither bellicose or militarist, nor militarist nor pacifist.' Schmitt desires only to know *what is*" (Strauss, 2007 [1932], 108, quoting Schmitt, 2007 [1932], 33). I want to show some of the ways that this is a misleading characterization of Schmitt's geopolitical arguments. After a brief account of the context of Schmitt's geopolitical writings, I take up five aspects of these works. I consider first Schmitt's account of the different forms taken by the nomos of the Earth. I turn then to nation-states and outline Schmitt's critique of liberalism, before moving to a consideration of force (the reality that Schmitt insisted liberals avoid), and then to the notions of identity that he both described, and indeed advocated. I end by relating these themes to the theological tenor of Schmitt's politics.

Geopolitical justifications

Gopal Balakrishnan (2000) has tracked the ways that Schmitt's writings about his central concerns responded to contemporary political events. After defeat in World War I, Germany was rent by monarchic reaction and socialist revolution. Schmitt was one of those conservatives who made an anathema of socialism, thinking authoritarian reaction rather than mass democracy a safer bet for property, stability, and morality (Woods, 1997). In Germany during the 1920s the main political forces were: first, an authoritarian conservatism that wanted to organize the state through the army and the civil service as directed by an elite recruited from the landed and professional classes and responsive very largely to the needs of industrial corporations; second, a liberal middle class; third, a revolutionary proletariat that sought to expropriate private property and install Soviet socialism; and, finally, a radical nationalism stoking populist and racist anger to salve the continuing shame of the settlement imposed after military defeat. Schmitt identified with the first, was contemptuous of the fuzzy thinking of the second, detested the third, and joined the fourth when it became the dominant power in the land. Thus, after a prompt from Martin Heidegger, Schmitt joined the Nazi party on May 1, 1933, about five weeks after Hitler had effectively suspended civil liberties with the so-called Enabling Act to which Schmitt had given early and eager support (Bendersky, 1983, 203–204).

Schmitt reaped academic and public rewards for his loyalty but the party ideologists mistrusted him and others who had not been foot soldiers during the long rise to power and by 1936 Schmitt was forced out of his party positions despite his very public endorsing of anti-Semitic purges in intellectual and professional life (Schwab, 1989 [1970]). Schmitt blamed, in large part, some of his Jewish ex-students who, from exile outside Germany, expressed their disappointment with their former mentor by claiming that Schmitt's conversion to Nazism was not only late but insincere (Bendersky, 1983, 225). At the end of the war, Schmitt was held for some fourteen months by American forces while they investigated his responsibility for the waging of aggressive war before finally deciding to bring no charges. Schmitt refused to submit to de-Nazification and unlike many other Nazi academics he did not return to high professional office, living out his last two score of life in what he announced as internal exile by naming his house *San Casciano*, recalling both where Machiavelli spent his own internal exile under the Medicis and the third-century martyr who was executed at the hands of his own students (Hoelzl and Ward, 2008, 2).

One way of responding to Balakrishnan's analysis is to examine the place of geopolitical reasoning in the justifications for various policy options that Schmitt developed in his writings, almost all of which had distinct and immediate political purchase. Much of Schmitt's early work concerns what he saw as the problems of liberalism and it reflected his disdain for mass democracy and it justified government by elites. Two sets of ideas from these early writings recur in the later work on international politics. In the first place, Schmitt argues that individualism is an improper postulate for understanding society, religion, or law for the human being "is not alone in the world," but, rather, is always "in the company of other" people (Schmitt, 1996 [1917], 51). Schmitt's communitarian perspective is developed further as a justification for authoritarian government through the second strong theme in these early writings and that is his claim that democracy can only function when there is substantial equality among the members of the polity for, according to Schmitt (1985 [1926a], 9), "democracy requires homogeneity and [thus]—if the need arises—[the] elimination or eradication of heterogeneity." At the very least this required the articulation and inculcation of an integrative myth, which he believed must be "a national myth," with a "common spiritual enemy" (Schmitt, 1985 [1926b], 75). In the 1920s, this enemy was usually identified by Schmitt as communism and in the second half of the 1930s, the enemy was more frequently represented as Jewish people. Schmitt (2007 [1932], 32) was anxious that internal enemies be subdued so that civil war be avoided and thus also the "self-laceration" that "endangers the survival" of the state and "has the effect of weakening the common identity vis-à-vis another state." This anti-individualism and aggressive nationalism were later important themes in his geopolitical writings.

Schmitt's German patriotism inflamed his anger at the shaming of Germany at the hands of the allied powers after WWI. When he collected some of his writings from the 1920s and 1930s, Schmitt (1940) gave the collection the title *Positionen und Begriffe: im Kampf mit Weimar–Genf–Versailles, 1923–1939*

(Positions and Concepts in the Struggle against Weimar–Geneva–Versailles). Weimar, of course, was the republic constructed out of the compromised sovereignty allowed to Germany by the peace settlement of Versailles, and policed by the League of Nations, based in Geneva. Schmitt saw them as related aspects of Germany's humiliation. His early geopolitical writings were evident justification and provocation for a German policy of defying these arrangements. A central argument in these writings was that the League of Nations was based upon a hypocritical caesura between form and content. In form, the League announced itself as based upon the equality of states, the elimination of war, and the principle of non-interference by others in the internal affairs of sovereign states. Instead, observed Schmitt (2008 [1938a], 47), the League had an explicit civilizational scale in distinguishing between peoples who were capable of self-government and those "unable to forge an organizational apparatus character of a modern state" who were to be consigned to protectorates if on the way to self-government, or to colonies where their case was for the moment hopeless.

But, beyond his irritation with the hypocrisy of the League of Nations, Schmitt (2004 [1938b], 15) was yet more disturbed by the threat of a global federal government based upon the twin poles of "individualism and universalism." Schmitt saw the rights of states being dismembered between the two. Individuals, through the "so-called rights of minorities" (Schmitt, 2004 [1938b], 15) would have the protection of the League against their governments while states would lose the right to wage war with impunity since the League reserved to itself the right to adjudicate upon the causes of war and thus unite the free world against the unjust. In this way, Schmitt suggested, by means of a discriminating concept of war, dividing states into innocent victims and unjust aggressors, "the whole order of international law allows itself to be unhinged, yet [the League] creates no new order" (Schmitt, 2004 [1938b], 44–45). Schmitt was seeking to justify Germany's defiance of complaints about its treatment of Jewish people, with the revocation of naturalization in July 1933, and he was also reserving to Germany the right to wage war in exercise of "the will of self-assertion of free peoples" (Schmitt, 2004 [1938b], 5).

In defending the national autonomy and right to self-assertion of Germany, Schmitt claimed he was asking for no more than the United States had already arrogated to itself. In the two very interesting essays, one of 1933 on the "Forms of Modern Imperialism" and the other of 1939 on "*Großraum* versus Universalism," reprinted earlier in this book, Schmitt developed an analysis of the Monroe Doctrine (1823) that was central to his justification for German imperialism. He argued that the Monroe Doctrine was nothing more than a fig leaf for the assertion of the imperialistic policies of the United States both economically and militarily. The United States itself decided when and how to invoke the principle of non-interference by outside powers in the affairs of the Western hemisphere. Furthermore, he pointed out that the United States had forced the League of Nations to incorporate into its Covenant the basic rights claimed by the United States under the doctrine, even though the United

States chose ultimately to remain outside the League. Schmitt saw the Monroe Doctrine as another nail in the coffin of the League's claims to universalism and indeed he proposed that Germany was claiming no more in its European domain than the United States claimed in its American one. In March 1939 Germany invaded Czechoslovakia and a few weeks later Schmitt lectured in Kiel defending just this sort of action as a legitimate exercise of German power within its *Großraum* and he said that it was no more than the application in Europe of the principles of the Monroe Doctrine (Bendersky, 1983, 252). A few weeks later, on April 28, Hitler justified the aggression in the same precise terms, producing Schmitt's fawning observation of May 15 that his *Führer* had now "cleared the way to the restoration of the true and original Monroe doctrine" (Schmitt, 1939 [see Chapter 3 in this volume for Matthew Hannah's translation]).

The final justificatory theme to which I wish briefly to advert concerns Schmitt's rebuttal of the charge that Germany had been a reprehensible aggressor in either world war. Schmitt's discussion of the bracketing of war in eighteenth- and nineteenth-century Europe rested in part upon the claim that such wars were limited in nature because the belligerents did not claim for them the righteousness of total war, that the "so-called 'cabinet war' was essentially and deliberately a partial war" (Schmitt, 1999 [1937], 29). But the discussion also served as a justification for such wars, this "great accomplishment" (Schmitt, 1974 [2003], 140) of European civilization. WWI, he proposed, had begun as a limited conflict but absolute enmity had been "generated by the conflict itself" (Schmitt, 1999 [1937], 35). It had been generated out of the clash between two logics of war. Facing the German army with its continental tradition of limited war had been Great Britain, a country that early had "detached herself from the Continent, [had . . .] not passed through the [straits] of Continental statehood" (Schmitt, 2006 [1956], 55), and had never accepted the concept of limited war because

> naval wars were based on the idea of the necessity of treating the enemy's trade and economy as one. Hence the enemy was no longer the opponent in arms alone, but every inhabitant of the enemy nation, and ultimately, every neutral country that had economic links with the enemy.
> (Schmitt, 1997 [1954], 47)

Total war, self-righteous war, these were the fault of the maritime power not the land power. At the end of the war, the same totalistic struggle was waged by the Bolsheviks who began a "global civil war of revolutionary class enmity" (Schmitt, 2007 [1975], 95).

Schmitt made the same claim for Germany in the build-up to and during World War II. It was, he urged, the universalistic principles of the League of Nations that by claiming to make war illegal invited the international community to gang up on states that might be prosecuting the traditional form of limited war within their domain and in doing so threatened to convert every war "into an international civil war and therewith [the war] achieves a kind of totality that is as horrid and destructive [as] a facile propaganda has accused the national totality [of being]" (Schmitt, 1938c, 44–45).

It is evident, I hope, why I cannot agree with Bendersky (1983, 242) that in the face of criticisms of his lack of Nazi ideological commitment, after 1936, "[t]o avoid further complications, [Schmitt] never again dealt with domestic or party politics, but turned his attention to the study of international relations, and soon passed into obscurity." Rather than being a disengagement from ideology and politics, Schmitt's geopolitical writings grew out of his nationalism, his hostility to mass democracy, and his contempt for liberalism. The themes of rootedness and hierarchy, which were part of his organic and communitarian view of the state, likewise run through his geopolitical writings. Mitchell Dean (2007) has elaborated in detail how Schmitt developed a mythology around the concept of the nomos in order to justify Jewish exclusion and German expansion. Having sketched the political context of Schmitt's geopolitical writings and having asserted that they demonstrate a clear engagement with political debate and serve as explicit justifications for certain conservative, nationalistic, and fascist policies, I want now to show how Schmitt made his central geopolitical concepts carry the normative weight of his political position. I take up in turn the opposition of land and sea, the nature of liberal states, the glorification of force, and finally the theological meaning of global conflict.

Land and sea

Carl Schmitt (1974) described as the nomos of the Earth, the territorial processes of the incorporation of land into polities. In Roman times, this was organized by empires with the crucial relations being between empires, between empires and their subjects, and between empires and the nomadic tribes that existed at the margins of the territory claimed by the empire. With medieval Christendom, the world was divided between Christian Europe, the Islamic enemy around Europe's southern and eastern borders, and after 1492 new territory open for mission and commerce in the Americas. The Pope was the point of reference for the nomos and he licensed the unbridled violence practiced abroad as crusade, just war, and mission. Within Europe, he limited the scale of conflict between Catholic princes. With the Reformation, the Pope lost this spiritual monopoly and conflict within Europe took the form of unlimited just war as each side in religious wars fought to the finish. With the Peace of Westphalia (1648), a phase began where each monarch chose the religion for their subjects and did not go to war to change the religion of other European states. Beyond Europe were polities in Asia with whom Europeans established trading relations, African societies that were raided or rendered protectorates, and the new lands of America where the Europeans allowed each other to take colonies. The combination of limited war in Europe and common imperialism in the Americas was held together by British domination of the seas that left them open for commerce. This period of international European law, of the *Jus Publicum Europaeum*, was codified with the Treaty of Utrecht in 1713 and while it lasted until WWI, it was already called into question when, in 1823, the Americas were closed to further European colonialism with the Monroe Doctrine and the US declaration of a colonial exclusion zone for the Western hemisphere. The United States had thereby declared and created a large sphere of influence, or *Großraum*. The United States, however, remained semi-detached from Europe, claiming isolation while interfering in international treaties or making arrangements of its own from its recognition of the Belgian company controlling the Congo in 1884 to its attempts to practice an imperialism of its own in China with its call for an open door policy there in the early twentieth century. This indeterminacy lasted effectively until the Cold War when the *Großräume* of the United States and the Soviet Union were extended towards each other.

The normative dimensions of Schmitt's account are threefold. First, the limitation of war within Europe is celebrated as a "great accomplishment" resting upon the free seas ensured by British naval power, the balance of power in Europe created by the detached perspective of British sea power, and the draw of so-called "free lands" in the Americas (Schmitt, 2003 [1974], 140). The attempt to cut off access to free lands, then, either in the Americas after 1823 or in Africa after 1885, is understood to pose serious problems for the balance of power in Europe. For a late colonizer such as Germany, this insistence that it was only the possibility of colonialism and imperialism abroad that kept wars constrained in Europe, that protected the "great accomplishment," meant that its own colonial ambitions were not only justified but necessary for European peace, indeed part of the arrangement by which the concert of Great Powers had pacified Europe. In the second place, the singular imperialist projects of the United States, from declaring a European exclusion zone in 1823, to demanding an open door China, to extending its security zone far out to sea and skipping island by island across the Pacific, inaugurated a new global nomos of *Großräume*. From 1939, Schmitt argued that modern conditions of commerce, war, and politics, made states anachronistic and that only by copying the US example could a people survive. Thus Germans had to develop their own *Großraum* in central and eastern Europe if they were not to disappear (Kennedy, 2004, 26).

Finally, Schmitt makes significant use of the distinction between land and sea power. At one level, Schmitt follows Hegel in contrasting favorably sea with land power, for Hegel had suggested in *The Philosophy of Right* that "[b]y the substitution for the tenacious grasp of the soil, and for the limited round of appetites and enjoyments embraced within the civic life, of the fluid element of danger and destruction, the passion for gain is transformed" (Hegel, 2001 [1820], 190 [para. 247]). Schmitt goes further because for him the bourgeois love of safety is contemptible and thus the danger of the seas is akin to the riskiness of life and death, peace and war, which grounds the very notion of the political for Schmitt (Kennedy, 2004, 103). Schmitt set these arguments out in his 1942 work, *Land und Meer. Eine weltgeschichtliche Betrachtung* (Land and Sea: A Reflection upon Universal History). In *Land und Meer*, Schmitt argued that the British era of sea power, the Age of Leviathan, was nearing its end and Raphael Gross reports that in large part, Schmitt attributed this to Jewish people feasting upon the Leviathan, undermining the British (Gross, 2007 [2001], 161–162). Schmitt suggested that the Age of Leviathan would be superseded by the Reich, a land-based German *Großraum* (Gross, 2007 [2001], 161–162).

Schmitt argued, further, that it was precisely the sea power of the British that had introduced the notion of total war. Although in many places he traces the practice of total war to the religiously sanctioned violence of a just war, in *Nomos of the Earth*, he contrasted the limitations placed upon land war between Europeans, with its protection of civilians, its forbidding of plunder, and what Schmitt saw as the symmetry of soldiers on each side who equally risked death, with the lawlessness of the seas where booty and prize were unrestrained and where there was no limit to the acceptable forms of blockade or bombardment of the inhabitants of ports. It is sea power that provides the nearest model for the industrialized asymmetry of aerial bombardment and the projectile violence of total war (Schmitt, 2003 [1974], 312–320). Thus Schmitt argues that total war was pioneered by Britain, the sea power, and that they were long the only power able to prosecute total war (Kennedy, 2004, 115). The end of the Age of Leviathan can only be secured with war for "[o]nly in battle can the new *nomos* arise. [. . .] Some believe that they are experiencing the end of the world. In reality we are experiencing only the end of the previous relationship of land and sea" (Meier, 1995 [1988], 71; quoting Schmitt, 1997 [1954], 59). So Schmitt contrasted land and sea power and saw Germany as the rising land power but, furthermore, while prizing the adventure of sea power, he blamed it for letting out the genie of total war in Europe, and thus undoing the great accomplishment of the *Jus Publicum Europaeum*. The blame for the unbridled violence of the European world wars lay with those sea powers that prevented Germany from acquiring colonies: the United States for setting the example of *Großraum* development; and good share might be given to Britain for pioneering total war. The spatial dynamics of the nomos, then, led Germany to engage in a war essential to its survival and in which it but followed the lead of others. Land and sea power are something like floating signifiers for although there are certain fairly obvious and uncontroversial things to be said about each of them, in fact, they are usually opposed in ways that make the use of force in one mode less ethical than in the other. They are also regularly placed in series that present one or other as the wave of the future, or the march of progress.

Liberalism and states

Schmitt's arguments about the elimination of peoples through international competition placed great stress upon states organizing themselves to face their international challengers. In *Political Theology*, Schmitt (2005 [1934], 53) set out one of his many attacks upon romantics who, he claimed, "possess an odd habit: everlasting conversation." Although in his early writings Schmitt was very much concerned with literary and artistic topics, Ellen Kennedy (2004, 47) remarks that Schmitt came to criticize the aesthete as someone who refuses the decisions that are part of the true ethical life. Against what he terms political romanticism, Schmitt insists that in politics decisions are made with absolute finality (Strong, 2007, xiii). These decisions are not constrained by rules and law, instead Schmitt insists that the essence of sovereignty consists in choosing when to suspend law, when to make an exception and how to decide upon the exception. For Schmitt, liberalism was an obstacle to political decision-making. By institutionalizing social or religious divisions as parties, it fomented disagreement about policy. Indeed, if democracy was a system for expressing the will of the people, Schmitt was sure that liberalism was antithetical to democracy. Again, Schmitt related this failing of the state to the influence of Jewish people and Jewish thought (Kennedy, 2004, 179–180). Drawing upon a classic anti-Semitic figure, Schmitt said Jewish people were migratory and rootless, having a natural affinity for universal rather than nationalist ideas. Indeed, he saw Jewish people as the bearers of the idea of freedom of thought and thus as people who undermined public authority, which had to rest upon truth and authority, not pluralism and opinion.

Understanding mere opinion as inimical to authority, Schmitt approached liberalism as a form of value relativism that led people to forget the theological and mythological basis for the absolute values that alone could command obedience and deliver final decisions (Bielefeldt, 1998, 25). Dominique Leydet (1998, 109) writes that Schmitt viewed the liberal state as little more than the "aggregate of compromises between heterogeneous groups." He argued that under modern conditions of mass media and public interest in the affairs of parliament, representatives were held to account as delegates of interest groups rather than as disinterested rational disputants: "[t]he situation of parliamentarism is critical today because the development of modern mass democracy has made argumentative public discussion an empty formality" (Schmitt, 1985 [1926a], 6). Schmitt praised Marxists and anarchists for appreciating the distance between the balance of parties in a bourgeois parliament and the true interests of the people, a distance that might make a minority the agent of the general good. Setting aside the forms of parliamentarism, the truly political actor might embrace dictatorship and force instead of representation and chatter: "[a]s Trotsky justly reminded the democrat Kautsky, the awareness of relative truths never gives one the courage to use force and to spill blood" (Schmitt, 1985 [1926b], 64). While Schmitt was opposed to socialism and anarchism as political movements because he saw the identity of the people rooted in a spiritual *Volk* consciousness rather than in sectional economic interests, he shared their criticisms of modern representative systems and he came to prefer a plebiscitary leader who would have the legitimacy of popular endorsement but would be free from the legality of formal law, and thus could lead the people to a clearer understanding of their true interests. Only the decisive leader could unite the realms of norms in the state, of action in the political movement, and of identity in the people (Kennedy, 2004, 21–22).

Schmitt's distrust of representation is not really conservative since it does not rest upon a respect for historical precedent. It is rather a form of authoritarianism that seeks to justify government as a permanent state of exception, a continual state of war with the centralization of power typically claimed by the executive in dangerous times. Schmitt did not accept that there was anything positive in value pluralism, or in neutrality, that non-discrimination might even demand no less (Bielefeldt, 1998, 29). Jürgen Habermas (1998 [1996]) gives the best response to Schmitt when he contrasts Schmitt's substantive to his own procedural account of democracy. For Schmitt, democracy must express a national will that he assumes already exists, whereas Habermas suggests that it is through the democratic process that people discover their common interests. Dominique Leydet (1998, 124) makes the important point that norms can be effective even if not applied with absolute rigor because, where legislation must be argued for as being in the general interest, then, this places some limits upon the most egregious sectarianism. As Reinhard Mehring (1998, 148) suggests, majorities that, cognizant of the public virtue of tolerance, wish to avoid appearing despotic will choose to attend to the rights of minorities even though, as Schmitt observes, they do not have to. Moreover, in acting in this way they renew the liberal virtues that Schmitt insists must corrode and fade as soon as they are embodied in imperfect institutions. Heiner Bielefeldt (1998, 32) argues, further, that the exception need not be lawless in the manner anticipated by Schmitt. The exceptional circumstances will not be completely without precedent and the executive may use analogous cases to justify the measures taken. More effectively, perhaps we may insist that exceptional measures not carry blanket immunity and that conduct during emergencies should be examined more soberly after the event and the conduct of the executive subject to retrospective and tolerant review. Schmitt preferred an authoritarian regime but he reduces liberalism to absurd caricature in order to make it seem an unavoidable choice.

Force, death, and identity

For Schmitt (2007 [1932], 52), politics is the struggle for national survival and "[i]f a people is afraid of the trials and risks implied by existing in the sphere of politics, then another people will appear which will assume these trials by protecting it against foreign enemies and thereby taking over political rule." Schmitt's advocacy of force goes beyond the merely tactical. Whereas Habermas proposes that democratic engagement can forge identities, Schmitt insists that it is force alone that can manifest a people's intrinsic identity. He asserts that "[a] life which has only death as its antithesis is no longer life but powerlessness and helplessness," amounting to "a renunciation of the struggle" (Schmitt, 1996 [1929], 95). In other words, to be really living a person must be struggling against others while to survive a people must struggle against other peoples. This trial is what gives life its purpose, and identity its meaning, for, as Strong (2007, xv) puts it, "Schmitt [. . .] thought [. . .] that people will only be responsible for what they are if the reality of death and conflict remain present." According to Schmitt, the only rights people deserve are those they have fought for, and the only principles that matter are those that they will die for, or, rather, those that they will kill for. The effective leader is the one who can show a people their distinct nature by identifying their enemy, the one that poses an existential threat, the one that endangers "one's own way of life" (Schmitt, 2007 [1932], 49). Between June 30 and July 2, 1934, Hitler ordered the assassination of Ernest Röhm and between 250 and 1,000 others that he identified as political opponents. As Chancellor, he went to the Reichstag and in announcing and defending seventy-four of the murders, he declared: "If anyone reproaches me and asks why I did not resort to the regular courts of justice, then all I can say is this: In this hour I was responsible for the fate of the German people, and thereby I became the supreme judge of the German people" (Shirer, 1990 [1960], 226). Alone among leading German jurists, Carl Schmitt justified Hitler's actions (Kennedy, 2004, 24). Dyzenhaus remarks that, in his 1934 piece entitled "The *Führer* guards the law," Schmitt had praised Hitler for having

> done everything that Schmitt positively required of a leader. Hitler had made the distinction between friend and enemy, as proved in the murders, had established himself decisively as the supreme source and judge of all right and law, and had done away with the liberal and parliamentary "fictions" of Weimar. Most important of all, he had, through his personal representation of the German people as a substantive homogeneous unit, brought about the democratic identity that Schmitt prized above all else.
>
> (Dyzenhaus, 1998, 3)

Hitler had brought Germany from the false transcendence of liberal or universal ideals, to the real immanence of *Volk* consciousness (Strong, 2007, xxx).

For Schmitt, legitimacy was more important than legality, and legitimacy was based on articulating the national will by identifying the national enemies. You will know your enemies because they contradict the guiding principles of your own ideology. Schmitt shared the regime's anti-Semitism. He drew a contrast between the Nazi "Just State" and a liberal, or "Jewish constitutional state" (Gross, 2007 [2001], 34). The Just State was grounded in the legitimacy of a national consciousness, whereas the cosmopolitan alternative was based on the legality of a false universalism. Schmitt supported measures taken to make Jewish people visible as an alien presence within Germany who would thereby recall German people to their own distinctive national identity, one that Jewish people could not share. This national consciousness justified, for Schmitt writing in 1933, purging public life of "non-Aryan elements of a foreign kind" (Gross, 2007 [2001], 32). Schmitt believed that the new times required a total state and by this he meant a society where the friend–enemy distinction colonized all spheres of life. Thus whereas the separate spheres were based on distinct forms of antithesis (religion on belief/heresy; economics on profitable/unprofitable; aesthetics on beautiful/ugly etc.), "[e]very religious, moral, economic, ethical, or other antithesis transforms into a political one if it is sufficiently strong to group human beings effectively according to friend and enemy" (Schmitt, 2007 [1932], 37). Identifying a German and a non-German form of religion, of art, etc., would enable the state to colonize all spheres of life and thereby create social unity through a total state. Schmitt welcomed this development under Hitler.

Schmitt's version of German national values was a combination of religion and authoritarianism. Because he believed that humankind was essentially fallen, evil, or dangerous, he was an authoritarian rejecting the optimism of anarchist utopias where the people are instead to be trusted. He believed that Catholicism provided a good example and set of practices that instituted obedience and authority. In contrast, Protestant appeals to individual conscience and liberal appeals to fundamental rights, undermined authority and homogeneity. Hitler promised both authority and homogeneity, and Schmitt recognized a leader whose practice might restore German *Volk* consciousness and act upon it without the diversions of modernist individualism. Calling Germans to an orgy of national renewal and foreign aggression, Hitler was the politician needed for politics as defined by Schmitt. Schmitt's posthumously published *Glossarium* ended with this hope: "With each newly born child a new world is born. God will, each newly born child will be an aggressor!" (Strong, 2007, xxxi).

This was a vision of the national polity as resting upon an assumed internal homogeneity and an asserted external forcefulness. It presented aggression as redemptive, dismissing cooperation as a hostage to fortune, and legality as a false universalism. It was offered as a realistic description of the ways things actually were but its normative dimensions are evident. It is mere assertion to say that the only things that give meaning to life are those for which you would take another's life. Not only is this grim, it is manifestly untrue. Schmitt elided the taking of life and the self-sacrifice of risking one's life. People dedicate their lives to all sorts of causes and in all sorts of ways. Taking a decision to live your life in a certain way because of your fidelity to some set of values in many cases does not involve risking your life or accepting the responsibility of taking another person's life. Taking life is not in itself a guarantee of purity of purpose; it is all too easy for gangsters who have little nobility, merely greed.

Political theology

Religion was very important to Schmitt. Paul Gottfried (1990, 7–9), who writes of Schmitt's devotion to the Latin culture of the Catholic regions of south

Germany, notes that several of Schmitt's uncles were priests, and that about one half of his earliest publications were in Catholic journals. Schmitt appealed to both scriptural and papal authority in his political writings. Thus, in his arguments about friend and enemy, he felt impelled to navigate around the Sermon on the Mount where Jesus is reported as saying: "Ye have heard that it hath been said, Thou shalt love thy neighbour, and hate thine enemy. But I say unto you, Love your enemies, bless them that curse you, do good to them that hate you, and pray for them which despitefully use you, and persecute you" (Matthew 5:43–44; King James version). Schmitt's (2007 [1932], 29) response was that this referred only to private enemies but that public enemies were quite another matter (as shown by the papal blessing of crusades) for Christians had always defended Europe against their public enemy, the Saracens, Muslims in general. Schmitt noted that the concept of the just war developed from the identification of those who resist Christianity as permanent enemies. Thus, a missionary war was sanctioned both by papal practice and, on Schmitt's reading, from Christ's injunction to evangelize: "Go ye therefore, and teach all nations, baptizing them in the name of the Father, and of the Son, and of the Holy Ghost" (Matthew 28:19; King James version). But Schmitt's favorite biblical injunction was from Genesis where he found a life of struggle promised for the original sin of disobedience. When humanity fell through Adam's sin under Satan's temptation, Schmitt was sure it fell into a world of endless strife for the Bible had God promise: "And I will put enmity between you and the woman, and between your offspring and hers; he will crush your head, and you will strike his heel" (Genesis 3:15; King James version). Yet this is addressed to the serpent and unless Schmitt wanted to see foreign powers as spawn of the Devil, it is difficult to see its application to international relations. However, he had ample precedent and one that he quoted with relish was Oliver Cromwell who addressed his fellow English Puritans as follows: "The Spaniard is your enemy," his "enmity is put into him by God." He is "the natural enemy, the providential enemy," and he who considers him to be an "accidental enemy" is "not well acquainted with Scripture and the things of God," who says: "I will put enmity between your seed and her seed" (Schmitt, 2007 [1932], 68).

Religion was important to Schmitt in part because he saw most political concepts as secularized versions of religious concepts but also because this secularizing trend was one that he wanted to resist. Schmitt argued that while Jewish people had a transcendent view of God so that the law could be the unmediated realm of God's word, for Catholics God also was immanent and thus had a representative on Earth, so that in this way papal direction gave law and society a hierarchical basis that reached back to divine authority (Gross, 2007 [2001], 97). He wanted as far as possible to re-enchant society with the truth of Revelation. In this way, a principled Christian nation might help delay the End of Days, might act as a constraint, or *Katechon*, against the Antichrist. Whereas Schmitt praised the limited war of the period of European international law, it is quite clear that the common European ground was

Christendom and the respect Christian princes could cultivate towards each other based on their common faith. Beyond Europe, there was ever only just war with Christian heel being laid upon heretic head. Only the conversion of all nations would end missionary wars. With God on his side, Schmitt set out a geopolitics that justified a political practice based on a sense of one's own exceptionalism, an appeal to national homogeneity, an authoritarian form of government, the use of violence as redemptive, a rejection of international law as a fraud, and a religiously sanctioned crusade against the permanent enemies of the righteous. These goals are widely shared and thus we find time and again people using state power in precisely the way Schmitt advocated. This repeats his beliefs rather than vindicating his analysis.

References

Anon. (2001) The Authorization for the Use of Military Force Against Terrorists (Pub.L. 107–40, 115 Stat., enacted September 18, 2001. Accessed on March 22, 2009 at http://frwebgate.access.gpo.gov/cgi-bin/getdoc/cgi?dbname=107 cong public laws& docid=f:publ040.107.

—— (2004) Bush Letter to Sharon Recognizes "Facts on the Ground" *Foundation for Middle East Peace. Settlement Report 14:3* May-June. Accessed on March 22, 2009 at www.fmep.org/reports/archive/vol.-14/no.-3/bush-letter-to-sharon-recognizes-facts-on-the-ground.

Balakrishnan, G. (2000) *The Enemy: An Intellectual Portrait of Carl Schmitt*. Verso: London.

Bendersky, J. W. (1983) *Carl Schmitt: Theorist for the Reich*. Princeton University Press: Princeton, NJ.

Bielefeldt, H. (1998) Carl Schmitt's Critique of Liberalism: Systematic Reconstruction and Countercriticism. In *Law as Politics: Carl Schmitt's Critique of Liberalism* (Ed. D. Dyzenhaus). Duke University Press: Durham, NC, pp. 23–36.

Bush, G. W. (2001a) Address to a Joint Session of Congress and the American People, 20 September 2001. Accessed on March 21, 2009 at www.dhs.gov/xnews/speeches/speech 0016.shtm.

—— (2001b) Remarks by the President; White House Lawn, September 16, 2001. Accessed on March 21, 2009 at http://avalon.law.yale.edu/sept11/president 015.asp.

Dean, J. W. (2008 [2007]) *Broken Government: How Republican Rule Destroyed the Legislative, Executive, and Judicial Branches*. Penguin: New York.

Dean, M. (2007) *Nomos*: Word and Myth. In *The International Thought of Carl Schmitt* (Eds. L. Odysseos and F. Petito). Routledge: New York, pp. 242–258.

Dyzenhaus, D. (1998) Introduction: Why Carl Schmitt? In *Law as Politics: Carl Schmitt's Critique of Liberalism* (Ed. D. Dyzenhaus). Duke University Press: Durham, NC, pp. 1–20.

Eastland, T. (1992) *Energy in the Executive: The Case for the Strong Presidency*. Free Press: New York.

Gottfried, P. (1990) *Thinkers of Our Time: Carl Schmitt*. Claridge Press: London.

Gross, R. (2007 [2001]) *Carl Schmitt and the Jews: The "Jewish Question," the Holocaust, and German Legal Theory*. University of Wisconsin Press: Madison, WI.

Habermas, J. (1998 [1996]) On the Relation between the Nation, the Rule of Law, and Democracy (trans. C. Cronin). In J. Habermas, *The Inclusion of the Other*. MIT Press: Cambridge MA, pp. 129–153.

Hegel, G. W. F. (2001 [1820]) *Philosophy of Right* (trans. S. W. Dyde). Batloche Books: Kitchener, Ontario.

Henry, E. and Starr, B. (2006) Bush: "I'm the Decider" on Rumsfeld. Defense Secretary: Changes in Military Meet Resistance, *CNN News* April 18. Accessed on March 22, 2009 at www.cnn.com/2006/POLITICS/04/18/rumsfeld/index.html.

Hoelzl, M. and Ward, G. (2008) Editors' Introduction. In C. Schmitt, *Political Theology II: The Myth of the Closure of Any Political Theology*. Polity: Cambridge, pp. 1–29.

Huntington, S. (1997) *The Clash of Civilizations and the Remaking of World Order*. Simon & Schuster: New York.

—— (2004) *Who are We? The Challenges to America's National Identity*. Simon & Schuster: New York.

Kaplan, R. D. (2002) *Warrior Politics: Why Leadership Demands a Pagan Ethos*. Random House: New York.

Kennedy, E. (2004) *Constitutional Failure: Carl Schmitt in Weimar*. Duke University Press: Durham, NC.

Lewis, B. (1990) The Roots of Muslim Rage *Atlantic Monthly* 266:3, 47–60.

Lewis, N. A. (2009) Bush Administration Memos Claimed Vast Powers, *International Herald Tribune* 3 March. Accessed on March 22, 2009 at http://iht.com/articles/2009/03/03/america/terror.php.

Leydet, D. (1998) Pluralism and the Crisis of Parliamentary Democracy. In *Law as Politics: Carl Schmitt's Critique of Liberalism* (Ed. D. Dyzenhaus). Duke University Press: Durham, NC, pp. 109–130.

Mehring, R. (1998) Liberalism as a "Metaphysical System": The Methodological Structure of Carl Schmitt's Critique of Political Rationalism. In *Law as Politics: Carl Schmitt's Critique of Liberalism* (Ed. D. Dyzenhaus). Duke University Press: Durham, NC, pp. 131–158.

Meier, H. (1995 [1988]) *Carl Schmitt and Leo Strauss: The Hidden Dialogue* (trans. J. H. Lomax). University of Chicago Press: Chicago.

Schmitt, C. (1940) *Positionen und Begriffe: im Kampf mit Weimar–Genf–Versailles*. Hanseatiscner Verlaganstal: Hamburg.

—— (1985 [1926a]) Preface to the Second Edition (1926): On the Contradiction between Parliamentarism and Democracy (trans. E. Kennedy). In C. Schmitt, *The Crisis of Parliamentary Democracy*. MIT Press: Cambridge, MA, pp. 1–17.

—— (1985 [1926b]) *The Crisis of Parliamentary Democracy* second edition (trans. E. Kennedy; first edition, 1923). MIT Press: Cambridge, MA.

—— (1996 [1917]) The Visibility of the Church: A Scholastic Consideration (trans. G. L. Ulmen). In C. Schmitt, *Roman Catholicism and Political Form*. Greenwood Press: Westport, CT.

—— (1996 [1929]) The Age of Neutralizations and Depoliticizations (trans. M. Konzett and J. P. McCormick). In C. Schmitt, *The Concept of the Political*. University of Chicago Press: Chicago, pp. 80–96.

—— (1997 [1954]) *Land and Sea* (trans. S. Draghici; first edition 1942). Plutarch Press: Washington, DC.

—— (1999 [1937]) Total Enemy, Total War and Total State. In C. Schmitt, *Four Articles 1931–1938* (trans. S. Draghici). Plutarch Press: Washington, DC, pp. 28–36.

—— (1999 [1938c]) Neutrality According to International Law and National Totality. In C. Schmitt, *Four Articles 1931–1938* (trans. S. Draghici). Plutarch Press: Washington, DC, pp. 37–45.

—— (2003 [1974]) *The* Nomos *of the Earth in International Law of the Jus Publicum Europaeum*, second edition (trans. G. L. Ulmen; first edition, 1950). Telos Press: New York.

—— (2004 [1938b]) *War/Non-War* (trans. S. Draghici). Plutarch Press: Corvallis, OR.

—— (2005 [1934]) *Political Theology: Four Chapters on the Concept of Sovereignty* second edition (trans. G. Schwab; first edition, 1922). University of Chicago Press: Chicago.

—— (2006 [1956]) *Hamlet or Hecuba: The Irruption of Time into Play* (trans. S. Draghici). Plutarch Press: Corvallis, OR.

—— (2007 [1932]) *The Concept of the Political* second edition (trans. G. Schwab; first edition, 1928). University of Chicago Press: Chicago.

—— (2007 [1975]) *Theory of the Partisan: Intermediate Commentary on the Concept of the Political*, second edition (trans. G. L. Ulmen; first edition, 1963). Telos: New York.

—— (2008 [1938a]) *The Leviathan in the State Theory of Thomas Hobbes: Meaning and Failure of a Political Symbol* (trans. G. Schwab and E. Hilfstein). University of Chicago Press: Chicago.

—— (2011 [1939]) *Großraum* versus Universalism: The International Legal Struggle over the Monroe Doctrine (trans. M. Hannah), Chapter 3 in this volume.

Schwab, G. (1989 [1970]) *The Challenge of the Exception: An Introduction to the Political Ideas of Carl Schmitt between 1921 and 1936*. Greenwood Press: Westport, CT.

Shirer, W. L. (1990 [1960]) *The Rise and Fall of the Third Reich: A History of Nazi Germany*. Simon & Schuster: New York.

Strauss, L. (2007 [1932]) Notes on Carl Schmitt, *The Concept of the Political* (trans. J. H. Lomax). In C. Schmitt, *The Concept of the Political*. University of Chicago Press: Chicago, pp. 97–122.

Strong, T. B. (2007) Foreword: Dimensions of the New Debate around Carl Schmitt. In C. Schmitt, *The Concept of the Political*. University of Chicago Press: Chicago, pp. ix-xxxi.

Twain, M. and Warner, C. D. (1874 [1873]) *The Gilded Age: A Tale of Today, Volume III*. George Routledge & Sons: London.

Woods, R. (1997) *The Conservative Revolution in the Weimar Republic*. Palgrave Macmillan: London.

Woodward, B. (2004) *Plan of Attack*. Simon & Schuster: New York.

6 Reading Schmitt geopolitically
Nomos, territory and *Großraum*[1]

Stuart Elden

With the 2003 translation of *The Nomos of the Earth*, a rather different set of Carl Schmitt's ideas became accessible to an Anglophone audience. While previously his work had shaped debates on politics, the political, the friend–enemy distinction, the question of democracy and the sovereign decision (see Dyzenhaus 1998; Mouffe 1999), his ideas on international politics became available. A 2004 conference session led to a symposium in the *Leiden Journal of International Law* and an edited book on his 'international political thought' (Odysseos and Petito 2006; 2007), in which *The Nomos of the Earth* is hailed as a 'missing classic' of international relations (2007: 2). In a recent book William Hooker describes him as 'one of the most profound and most prolific theorists of international order in the twentieth century', with *The Nomos of the Earth* likely to be guaranteed a place 'in the canon of essential IR reading' (2009: 3). In another volume we are told that Schmitt's work 'involves a complex theory of political territory' (Shapiro 2008: 68). Hooker also suggests that Schmitt's 'bold vision of the importance of spatial concepts in shaping the possibility of political order' qualifies him as a geographer (2009: 196). The interest in Schmitt, to an extent, parallels both the appropriations of Giorgio Agamben, whose own ideas draw greatly on Schmitt, particularly in terms of the 'space of exception', and the impact of Hardt and Negri's *Empire* on the thinking of global order. Schmitt apparently can help us understand terrorism, the 'war on terror', responses in terms of security, the post-Cold War world, the European Union and globalisation (see also Rasch 2005; Slomp 2009).

But if Schmitt is to be read geopolitically, then the same cautions that were made about reading him politically should be heeded. Schmitt's complicity with National Socialism should never be forgotten; nor should it be thought that this was merely opportunistic, or unconnected to his work on international politics. As Mark Neocleous argued fifteen years ago, Schmitt was a 'conservative revolutionary, fascist and an *enemy* of the Left', and to turn him 'into a debating adversary . . . is a dangerous political manoeuvre' (1996: 21; see Müller 2003; Neocleous 2009). As I have argued with Heidegger, what insights he has can only be used having passed through detailed textual, contextual and political analysis (Elden 2006). Here I want to make three moves in contesting the turn to Schmitt as a geopolitical theorist. First, I suggest that we cannot simply read *The* Nomos *of the Earth* alone, but must situate it both in its time and in relation to earlier parts of Schmitt's work. Second, I interrogate what Schmitt says about the concept of territory, surely one of the notions central to any adequate theory of international politics or geopolitics, and following the first point, relate it to the notion of *Großraum*. Third, and more briefly, I look at Schmitt's understandings of global order and the shifts he saw in his own time. The argument is that Schmitt's work on territory, the world and global order is both politically compromised and intellectually limited, and that this is important in terms of his worth to IR or political geography. Yet rather than dismiss Schmitt out of hand, I want to show why it is compromised and how it is limited (see Kalyvas and Scheuerman 2004).

The Nomos *of the Earth*: resituating Schmitt

Until relatively recently the two works by Schmitt that have had most impact – at least in Anglophone debates – have been *Political Theology* (2009 [1922]; 1985) and *The Concept of the Political* (2002 [1932]; 1996). While both predate his joining of the Nazi party they are works of that period in his intellectual development; deeply critical of the existing Weimar Republic. Many years later Schmitt published books that were direct reflections on these works: *Theory of the Partisan: Intermediate Commentary on the Concept of the Political* (2006 [1963]; 2007) and *Political Theology II: The Myth of the Closure of any Political Theology* (1970; 2008). While both these later works shed a great deal of light on his earlier ideas, nobody would turn to them alone for his views on political theology or the concept of the political. Yet there is a danger we do exactly that when we read *The* Nomos *of the Earth* (1997 [1950]; 2003 [1950]). *The* Nomos *of the Earth* was published in 1950, after the war and during Germany's period of de-Nazification. Yet this was not the first time Schmitt had written on such topics. This book, like *Theory of the Partisan* and *Political Theology II*, must be read as his post-war reflections on earlier themes, and to an extent as exculpations. Schmitt himself liked to think that *The* Nomos *of the Earth* was a crucial moment and the beginning of his post-war work: Müller tells the story that Schmitt asked that a collection of his political writings begin with this book (2003 [1950]: 87). We should resist accepting that decision.

Although a long-term critic of the Treaty of Versailles, Schmitt turned to international issues in earnest around 1938. The year is not insignificant. It was connected both to his own position in the party, where debates on international politics were somewhat less policed, and events on the world stage (Bendersky 1983: 250–1; Balakrishnan 2000: 226). While Hitler had broken the terms of Versailles when he marched troops into the demilitarised Rhineland in 1936, and through rearmament, 1938 was when his expansionist aspirations became most evident. March of that year saw the *Anschluß* with Austria – also forbidden under Versailles – and in September the Munich conference signed over the Sudetenland from Czechoslovakia. Schmitt's key work is *Völkerrechtliche Großraumordnung mit Interventionsverbot für raumfremde Mächte: Ein Beitrag zum Reichsbegriff im Völkerrecht*, published in 1939 (1991a [1941]). This book had its beginnings in a lecture Schmitt delivered in Kiel on 1 April 1939, two weeks after the invasion of the remains of Czechoslovakia (1988 [1940]: 317). Translating this title into English is no easy task. *International Law of* Großraum-*Ordering with a Prohibition on Intervention for Extra-Regional Powers: A Contribution to the Concept of* Reich *in International Law* is probably as close as can be achieved, although this leaves two terms untranslated. *Reich*, empire, is well known, and in 1939 this could only have had one connotation. *Großraum* is much more of an issue. Literally it means 'great space', but has a sense of a 'sphere' of influence, and 'geopolitical space' may be closer to the meaning. By the term Schmitt intends to grasp an area or region that goes beyond a single state (that is, a specific territory), to comprehend much larger-scale spatial orderings, complexes or arrangements (1991a [1941]: 11–12).[2] As Ulmen notes, the term emerged in economic thought first, to comprehend how the provision of key utilities such as gas and electricity could be integrated and provided as part of a *Großraumwirtschaft*, a large-scale spatial economy rather than a *Kleinraum*, small space or small-scale organisation (Ulmen 2003a: 23; see Schmitt 1991a [1941]: 12). Before further discussion of *Großraum*, however, it is worth noting one other word in the title: *raumfremde*. A word combining the German words for 'space' and 'stranger' sounds rather sinister, but it really just means external or extra-regional. Schmitt's particular focus is on countries outside the specific sphere of influence, the *Großraum*. These should have no right of intervention within it.

Schmitt's classic example of a *Großraum* in the wider international political-economic sense is the Monroe Doctrine, where the United States declared that the whole of the Americas was off-limits to European powers, both in terms of colonization and influence. Something similar happened in Eastern Europe after the end of the Second World War. This was not universalism, but competing spheres: what would be called a multipolar rather than unified or unipolar world (1988 [1940]: 295–302). In the 1930s though, his analysis of space and spatial politics was not simply for analytical reasons; but their legal context as part of his service of the regime. This had been the case in the 1920s in his analysis of the Rhine region (1988 [1940]: 26–33, 97–108). In the 1930s, Schmitt did not simply analyse the existence of these regions, but actively campaigned for one. This was for a kind of German-dominated *Mitteleuropa* (Schmitt 1991a [1941]: 12; see Naumann 1915; Meyer 1955: 194–217; Stirk 1994). *Mitteleuropa* meant 'middle' or 'central' Europe; an extent of the continent exceeding Germany's own boundaries where they would hold strategic domination. While this would, in practice, include German-speaking peoples, and was therefore tied to the presence of a *Volk*, it was not explicitly dependent on the *Blut und Boden* (blood and soil) elements of racialist discourse. Rather the basis for the argument was a legalistic account of land law, partly derived from John Locke's argument about cultivation: adding value to the land gave a right of propriety ownership. As such, it came close to arguments made about 'land without people', that should be filled with people without – or without sufficient – land (Grimm 1926). While Schmitt only occasionally uses the vocabulary of *Lebensraum*, his ideas at this time were hardly critical of, and sometimes explicitly endorsed, National Socialism's expansionist politics into the East (1991a [1941]: 23, 42–8).

The line drawn through Poland by the Molotov–Ribbentrop pact was one such division into regions (Schmitt 1991a [1941]: 47); the key point being that central and eastern Europe was Germany's sphere of influence, and that other world-powers should not be involved in the region. Schmitt later declares that this world war is a *Raumordnungskrieg*, a war for spatial ordering (1995: 433). In Schmitt's analysis, the *Großraum* cannot be reduced to the *Reich*, but it is the *Reich* that will dominate it (1991a [1941]: 49, 67). If this means his position has some distance from a policy of explicit annexation, this is little comfort. While some parts of the lands seized by Hitler were annexed to a greater *Reich*, and some were occupied, other countries were simply subjugated while retaining nominal independence. The establishment of the *Reichskommissariat* Ukraine and Ostland was part of a multifaceted policy of occupation. Similarly, for Schmitt, a *Reich* was more than a mere state, territorially confined, but exercising authority beyond any nominal boundaries (Balakrishnan 2000: 237). As Bendersky notes, press coverage of the time indicates that Schmitt was seen, at least by his enemies, as articulating the claims of the National Socialist movement (1983: 258). Indeed, later in April 1939 Hitler began to articulate ideas of a German-dominated Monroe Doctrine for Europe, as a response to President Roosevelt's demands on him to cease his territorial ambitions. Hitler declared that this was a European matter; off-limits for America. Schmitt was apparently warned from trying to assert his own prior articulation of such claims (Bendersky 1983: 258–9; see Gruchmann 1962). Schmitt complied and clearly followed the tide of opinion in his attitude to Nazi foreign policy: he says some of his most explicitly supportive comments in 1941 in a piece added to the last edition of *Völkerrechtliche Großraumordnung* (1991a [1941]: 64–73).

It has been suggested that Schmitt began *The* Nomos *of the Earth* between 1942 and 1945 (Ulmen 2003b: 35). This was after Operation Barbarossa, which Schmitt considered a disaster,[3] and the entry of the Americans into the war. These events meant that it was increasingly clear that the tide had turned and that the German loss of the war only a matter of time. Although in 1942 Schmitt claimed that the entry of the US into the war was not decisive, he acknowledged its seemingly unstoppable power in 1943 (1995: 431, 447). That in 1942 and after Schmitt was able to take positions that do not openly seem National Socialist tells us little. Indeed, there is an effective denial of the context of the writing and publication of *The* Nomos *of the Earth* since, as Zarmanian notes, 'there is no mention of the Nazi occupation of much of Europe, let alone the horrors of the Holocaust, in the entire book' (2006: 55).[4] The key point to be stressed is that what Schmitt writes about international politics in the post-war book bears the boot-print of what he said about such issues in the context of National Socialist Germany.

Indeed, *The* Nomos *of the Earth* makes a number of similar moves to *Völkerrechtliche Großraumordnung* in analytic terms, though apparently shorn of their political resonances. Schmitt suggests that for Locke, 'the essence of political power, first and foremost, is jurisdiction over the land'. He reinforces this by quoting Locke to the effect that 'government has a direct jurisdiction only over the land' (Schmitt 1997 [1950]: 18; 2003 [1950]: 47; see Locke 1988 [1690]: 349). His other key source is Immanuel Kant's (1887 [1796]) argument about the distinction between *Obereigentum* and *Landesherrschaft*, supreme proprietorship and land rulership, which Kant links to the Latin terms *dominium* and *imperium*. The first set of terms invoke private property; the second public property (Schmitt 1997 [1950]: 17; 2003 [1950]: 46).[5] Individuals can own land; states control territory. Schmitt reminds us that the Greek word *nemein*, from which nomos is derived, means both 'to divide' and 'to pasture' (1997 [1950]: 40; 2003 [1950]: 70). Hannah Arendt has similarly noted the relation between 'law and hedge in the word *nomos*', stressing the relation between law and boundary line or zone, and pointing out that 'the Greek word for law, *nomos*, derives from *nemein*, which means to distribute, to possess (what has been distributed) and to dwell' (1958: 63 n. 62). The legal is thus tied directly to the land. As Schmitt continues:

> *Nomos* is the *measure* by which the ground and soil of the earth [*Grund und Boden der Erde*] in a particular order is divided and situated; it is also the form of political, social, and religious order determined by this process. Here, measure, order, and form constitute a spatially concrete unity.
> (1997 [1950]: 40; 2003 [1950]: 70)[6]

Schmitt on territory

In his pre-1938 writings, Schmitt says relatively little about territory. He seemingly saw the relation of territory to the state to be essential, but equally unproblematic. As he says in *The Concept of the Political*:

> The concept of the state presupposes the concept of the political. According to modern linguistic usage, the state is the political status of an organised people in an enclosed territorial area [*territorialer Geschlossenheit*]. This is nothing more than a general description [*Umschreibung*], not a conceptual determination [*Begriffsbestimmung*] of the state.
> (2002 [1932]: 20; 1996: 19; translation modified)

While often reduced to simply the first line, this is an important formulation of which two things need to be underscored. First, that the territorial determination is inherent to Schmitt's understanding of the state. But, second, that this is insufficient. It is merely a paraphrase or circumlocution, an analytic judgement, an explication of terms, rather than the synthetic work that goes beyond this and which Schmitt believes is necessary. In *Political Theology* he makes another oft-quoted claim, but one which is similarly frequently reduced to a single sentence:

> All central concepts of the modern theory of the state are secularized theological concepts. This is not only because of their historical development – in which they were transferred from theology to the theory of the state, whereby, for example, the omnipotent God became the omnipotent lawgiver – but also because of their systematic structure, the recognition of which is necessary for a sociological consideration of those concepts.
> (2009 [1922]: 43; 1985: 36; translation modified)

There are two aspects to the claim being made here. While the first part – 'not only' – is certainly important and worthy of investigation, the second part – 'but also' – is much more challenging. Political theory puts the sovereign in a privileged position, just as theology did God: that much is straightforward. But what is it about the systematic structure of state theoretical concepts that owes a debt to theology, even if this is masked through a process of secularisation? The point is not to wish to restore the theological, but rather to note what has been transformed in the process of secularisation. To what extent is this the case with the notion of territory?

Schmitt's analysis in *The* Nomos *of the Earth* covers a long historical period. His suggestion is that modern territorial politics emerges, in part, as a consequence of the conquest of the new world and the different sense of the world this gave. Before this time, there were empires [*Reiche*] that could be understood as *Großräume*, but they lacked any kind of order, because the idea of the Earth as a whole, as a common space [*gemeinsamen Raume*] and its overall spatial order was lacking (1997 [1950]: 25; 2003 [1950]: 55). As he says in the opening lines of part II:

> No sooner had the form [*Gestalt*] of the earth emerged as a real *globe* [*Globus*] – not just sensed as myth, but apprehensible as fact and measurable as space – than there arose a wholly new and hitherto unimaginable problem: the spatial ordering of the entire earth [*Erdenballes*] in terms of international law. The new global image [*globale Raumbild*] required a new global spatial order. This was the situation resulting from the circumnavigation of the earth and the great discoveries of the 15th and 16th centuries.
> (1997 [1950]: 54; 2003 [1950]: 86)

There are a number of issues at stake here. Schmitt is suggesting that it was only with the explorations of the late fifteenth century that Earth as a globe actually became tangible. Of course, even the Ancient Greeks knew Earth was a sphere, but it was not demonstrably shown through circumnavigation until Magellan's voyage of the early sixteenth century. At the same time, a number of scientific techniques were developed to map and survey the lands and seas encountered. This is the basis for the notion of measurability he suggests here (see 1955: 97; 2003 [1950]: 341). These had been anticipated by decisions such as the Treaty of Tordesillas in 1494 that had proposed a line being drawn from pole to pole through the Atlantic to divide Portuguese and Spanish claims to the new world (1997 [1950]: 56–7; 2003 [1950]: 88–9). The 'global image' he talks of is, literally, a 'global space-picture'; and one of the words he uses for 'earth' is the 'earth-as-ball'. In these he is reminiscent of language Martin Heidegger uses in the pre-war lectures *An Introduction to Metaphysics*, although these were not published until 1953 (1983: 28–9; see Elden 2006: 103–4). Throughout *The Nomos of the Earth*, Schmitt outlines the ways in which political theory and nascent international law provided a basis for such an understanding to arise.

Schmitt sees a primitive relation between *Ortung* and *Ordnung*, placing and ordering (see 1991a [1941]: 81). Thus political order is always a *geopolitical* order. This appears to be valuable to IR, whose neglect of the spatial aspects of its questions is well known; but is superficial at best. Schmitt tends to work as if all ages have operated with a sense of territory and spatial ordering, just in different ways, rather than tracing the emergence of the categories themselves. Schmitt, as with most accounts, sees the conquest of the new world and the religious wars in Europe following the Reformation as the basis for the emergence of a distinctively modern political-legal understanding of the relation between space and politics. But there is a frustrating lack of detail and textual specificity to his arguments. Indeed, given his suggestion of the secularisation of the theological, it is striking how little attention he pays to the theological arguments about the division between secular and temporal power, and how theorists of temporal power began to articulate the spatially limited and circumscribed extent of political rule as opposed to universalist aspirations. This spatial extent became both the object and possibility of what was later understood as the idea of sovereignty. Nor, surprisingly for a legal theorist, does Schmitt pay attention to the impact of the rediscovery and reinterpretation of Roman law on political theory, especially for the relation between territory and jurisdiction, in the fourteenth century. He takes up the story with the more familiar sixteenth- and seventeenth-century figures of de Vitoria, Grotius and Pufendorf, rather than returning to Bartolus and Baldus.[7] While understandable in terms of his focus on *international* law, and the relation between the two spatial orders of firm land and free sea, this obscures the emergence of the modern relation between a state and its territory. Schmitt contends that if the focus is

> isolated, sovereign, territorial states [*souveränen Flächenstaates*], then the facts of the matter are clear: the territory of the state [*Staatsgebiet*] is the theatre of rule [*Schauplatz des Imperiums*]; with a territorial change

[*Gebietswechsel*], the agent of rule relinquishes the theatre and another sovereign agent appears on the stage.

(1997 [1950]: 166; 2003 [1950]: 194)

For Schmitt, the complexities are in the international dimensions. The simplicity of his formulation obscures a lot; the English translation even more. His understanding of territory is far too static, and seemingly ahistorical. Territory, for Schmitt, remains a bounded space under the control of a group; a quasi-Weberian definition that may provide the terms to be analysed, but is hardly a theory in itself.[8] From Schmitt's time or before, the work of Otto Gierke, the Carlyle brothers and even his fellow National Socialist Otto Brunner is more informative for more properly historical conceptual inquiries (Gierke 1868–1913; Carlyle and Carlyle 1903–36; Brunner 1942 [1939]).

Perhaps most intriguingly, Schmitt uses a range of German words for his concept of 'territory'. He talks, for instance, of 'the new territorial order [*Flächenordnung*] of the state' (1997 [1950]: 96; 2003 [1950]: 126), one that he later glosses as 'spatially self-contained, impermeable, unburdened with the problem of estate, ecclesiastical, and creedal civil wars' (1997 [1950]: 99; 2003 [1950]: 129). *Territoriale* is usually used as an adjective; like Weber he uses the term *Gebiet*, often in the phrase *Staatsgebiet*, or state-territory; here we see the use of *Flächenordnung*; and he sometimes uses the earlier term *Landeshoheit*, which was the German translation of *jus territorialis* in the treaties of Westphalia.[9] This shows that, for him, at least four terms have a sense close to the English 'territory'. Historically and politically much more needs to be said about these concepts and vocabulary, and how they relate to earlier terms that demarcate the relation between place and power. But Schmitt is frustratingly imprecise: reason enough to be cautious about appropriating what he does say, especially when mediated through translation. Hooker suggests that 'territory is as close as we come to a foundation in Schmitt's thought, and the idea of trying to situate real politics without it seems absurd and fanciful' (2009: 101). But it is not at all clear that Schmitt means the cohesion that the collapsing of these terms in English translation implies. He makes the valid claim that 'space, soil, land, field, area, terrain, territory and district [*Raum, Boden, Land, Feld, Fläche, Gelände, Gebiet, Bezirk*]' are not simply terminological nuances and interchangeable terms (1991a [1941]: 76), but never spells out the differences or accounts for their conceptual histories. He also sometimes runs the different concepts together to strong rhetorical effect. At one point in 1939, for instance, he suggests that legal doctrine's idea of a *Raumtheorie* actually implied the very opposite of a 'concrete representation of space and grasped land, soil, territory, state-territory [*Land, Boden, Territorium, Staatsgebiet*] indifferently as a 'space' in the sense of an empty flat area with added depth and linear borders [*einer leeren Flächen- und Tiefendimension mit Lineargrenzen*]' (1991a [1941]: 16). Schmitt wants to rescue the idea of territory – and more explicitly *Großraum* – from a 'mathematically-neutral, empty concept of space' (1991a [1941]: 14, 75, 76, 79). Such an argument concerning space and territory has been made elsewhere. Yet while for Schmitt this is because it is neglectful of a spiritual, Völkish sense of place (1991a [1941]: 77), other accounts see this more powerfully as being complicit with the calculative strategies of the state and capitalism.

A new world order?

If the transitions Schmitt alludes to gave birth to the 'modern' spatial order, he is clear that in the twentieth century there was yet another transition. This is the key claim of *The Nomos of the Earth*, that a new spatial-political order is taking shape; and there is a need to understand it. It is here that the concepts of *Großraum* and territory are disassociated. Within a *Großraum*, Schmitt now claims, dominant powers exercise influence, but do not seek to incorporate the land as with previous colonisation. The first step, Schmitt suggests, is that the dominant power is not seeking the territorial annexation [*territoriale Annexation*] of the controlled state; but rather to absorb it into its spatial sphere of influence, its *spatiale Bereich*, spatial field or area, which Schmitt calls its *Raumhoheit*, its spatial supremacy (1997 [1950]: 225–6; 2003 [1950]: 252–3).

> The external, emptied space [*äußere, entleerte Raum*] of the controlled state's territorial sovereignty [*territorialen Souveränität*] remains inviolate, but the functional [*sachliche*] content of this sovereignty is changed by the guarantees of the controlling power's economic *Großraum*. This is how the modern type of intervention treaties came about. Political control and domination were based on intervention, while the territorial *status quo* remained guaranteed. The controlling state had the right to protect independence or private property, the maintenance of order and security, and the preservation of the legitimacy or legality of a government. Simultaneously, on other grounds, it was free, at its own discretion, to interfere in the affairs of the controlled state. Its right of intervention was secured by footholds, naval bases, refuelling stations, military and administrative outposts, and other forms of cooperation, both internal and external. The controlling state's right of intervention was recognized in treaties and agreements, so that, in a strictly legal sense, it was possible to claim that this was no longer intervention.
> (1997 [1950]: 225; 2003 [1950]: 252)

Schmitt, then, is suggesting that there is a fragmentation of how state control of space is understood. On the one hand, there is the preservation of existing territorial divisions, fixing of boundaries and the reinforcement of settlements. In 1950, with the UN Charter only five years old, this would seem to make sense. It was the culmination of previous attempts to fix boundaries in Europe, such as the Locarno treaty of twenty years before. But Schmitt is simultaneously saying that this space, while fixed in terms of its external limits, is emptied out, hollowed out. Internally, the idea that a state is sovereign within its boundaries – the late medieval notion of *Rex est imperator in regno suo*, that the king is the emperor within his own kingdom – is dissolved. A situation that was wrestled from the Pope only with struggle both in practice and ideas is no more. Economically, at least, sovereignty is worth little; even if it appears that the 'territorial *status quo*' is preserved. Schmitt proposes that in the early modern period the struggle was over the enactment of the principle *cuius regio, eius religio* (1970: 107; 1997 [1950]: 99; 2003 [1950]: 128; 2008: 114) – to whom the region, the religion; a principle of religious freedom put forward at the 1555 Diet of Augsburg – and that the secular equivalent of this was *cuius regio, eius economica* – to whom the region, the economy. A fundamental aspect of a sovereign state is not simply to decide on 'such concepts as independence, public order, legality, and legitimacy', but also on 'its constitution of property and economy' (1997 [1950]: 226; 2003 [1950]: 252–3). Today this has been reversed to *cuius economica, eius regio* (1991b: 179; 1997 [1950]: 285; 2003 [1950]: 308), economic power gives regional control. Economic power in that fundamental sense is no longer an option for most states. Religious struggles give birth to modern politics; economics is the central decision of a political regime; now politics becomes reduced as economics is predetermined.[10] As Schmitt suggests:

> Territorial sovereignty [*territoriale Souveränität*] was transformed into an empty space for socio-economic processes. The external territorial form [*territorial Gebietsbestand*] with its linear boundaries was guaranteed, but not the substance of territorial integrity [*territorialen Integrität*], its social and economic content. The space of economic power determined the sphere [*Bereich*] of international law.
> (1997 [1950]: 226; 2003 [1950]: 252)

If it is true that individuals own land but states control territory, then it is the *Reich* that will dominate the *Großraum*. In the immediate post-war period, this may make a lot of sense of the relative spheres of the USA and USSR. Indeed, in one of the many seemingly concluding statements of the book, Schmitt mentions the London Charter of 8 August 1945 as a moment when 'East and West finally came together and agreed. Criminalization now took its course' (1997 [1950]: 255; 2003 [1950]: 280).[11] What was this charter and why was this date significant? The charter was that setting up the Nuremberg International Military Tribunal for war crimes; on the same day the Soviet Union declared war on Japan, invading Manchuria.

But the idea of competing *Großräumen* with their own rules and enforcements needs to be much more thoroughly interrogated if it is to help understand the post-Cold War period, where such understandings have become more truly global. As I have argued at length elsewhere, the term used in the UN Charter, 'territorial integrity', has much more generally been split apart: territorial preservation seen as non-negotiable; territorial sovereignty as entirely contingent (Elden 2009). The US-led interventions in 2001 and 2003 took the sovereignty of Iraq and Afghanistan as subject to intervention because of their failure to meet particular codes of behaviour, yet subsequently the polities themselves were to be preserved at all costs. In particular, questioning their spatial constitution was entirely off the table, even as their sovereignty remains profoundly compromised through occupation. Similar situations can be found in Kosovo and Sierra Leone with the notion of 'humanitarian intervention'. Indeed, it was long a rhetorical trope of Tony Blair to insist on the territorial integrity of places he was about to bomb. Yet for the Schmitt of *The* Nomos *of the Earth* there is no clear sense of why any of this might be happening, what it produces and to what extent we should find it worthy of embrace or critique. Schmitt sees the 'plurality of *großer Räume* or the global spatial order of a unitary dominated world [*einer einheitlich beherrschten Welt*]' as 'the great antithesis of world politics', as if these were the only possibilities (1997 [1950]: 220; 2003 [1950]: 247). Schmittian accounts today founder on similar rocks. Are different spheres of US, European, Chinese and Russian *Großräumen* really to be preferred to a unipolar world (Mouffe 2005)?

Conclusion

Schmitt is more geopolitical than most international relations' theorists. He undoubtedly says more about territory – historically, conceptually and politically – than most accounts of the international order. But these are hardly major challenges. He explicitly acknowledges the influence of geographers on his work, singling out the imperialist figure of Halford Mackinder, who proposed the heartland theory of global control (1997 [1950]: 5; 2003 [1950]: 37).[12] His debt to Friedrich Ratzel, the writer of the 1901 essay 'Lebensraum', is also important.[13] It would be a regressive step indeed if Schmitt's use of Mackinder or Ratzel somehow became an influence on modern political geography, or if his work proved to be the basis of the injection of a political-spatial sensibility that international relations so sorely needs.[14] If such themes deserve attention, as they surely do, then a dialogue between these disciplines might be a better start. If the search is outside, then other theorists such as Lefebvre and Foucault have much more to offer. Foucault, especially in recently published lectures, offers much more by way of a historical and conceptual purchase on territory; Lefebvre enables a much more progressive understanding of the political and economic aspects of such questions (see Elden 2007; Brenner and Elden 2009). But the history of the concept of territory remains to be written. The one area where Schmitt's work here may be worth a little more interrogation is his use of a broader vocabulary than simply the German *Territorium*, but the range of complicated terms including *Gebiet*, *Land* and words derived from *Fläche*.

To what extent the concept exceeds the practice is debatable. In this regard we should also remember that the notion of territory is frequently subsumed in his work into a wider *Großraum*, for which we lack a simple English equivalent. If somewhat obscured in the post-war *The* Nomos *of the Earth*, the lineage of this term is essential to bear in mind. Even in his later work this remains the dominant concept for world ordering. Yet here again, the gains from Schmitt seem minimal. In fact, one of the reasons that Schmitt seems so amenable to IR is that he repeats, anticipates and lends a spurious credibility to so many of the tired clichés of that discipline, concerning, for example, the Westphalian system and the challenges to it today. Most fundamentally, it must be remembered that Schmitt is not only offering something approaching a theory of geopolitical space, but was once a passionate advocate of a German *Großraum*. As much as he tries to obscure the explicit political context in which its ideas were forged, *The* Nomos *of the Earth* is a deeply reactionary text. He must always be read politically, and, if he is to be appropriated for insights into international relations or political geography, *geopolitically*. This is a deliberately chosen term. Over the past couple of decades, attempts have been made to reappropriate the notion of 'geopolitics', with its imperial connotations, as a 'critical geopolitics'. But just as Mackinder, Ratzel, Rudolf Kjellén, Karl Haushofer and others need careful, historical, contextual and political readings in such a project, in order to recognise the limits of their work and the reactionary politics that accompanies them, so too does Schmitt. Hooker makes the point that Schmitt is often characterised as 'an arcane and reductive Nazi who has little to offer current debates', and that 'the invocation of Schmitt is dangerous, seductive and destructive'. He claims that both cannot be true (2009: 2). Yet it is entirely possible that they are. While Schmitt's work does have little to offer, it is precisely because he appears to be useful that he is so dangerous. The seductiveness is that he seems to transcend his circumstances and political views, when remaining deeply rooted in them. The anointing of Schmitt as a geopolitical theorist with contemporary relevance is thus a serious error, intellectually and politically.

Notes

1 This chapter previously appeared as 'Reading Schmitt Geopolitically: *Nomos*, Territory and *Großraum*', *Radical Philosophy*, 161, May/June 2010, pp. 18–28.
2 The literature on this in English is not extensive. See Bendersky 1983: 250–62; Kervégan 1999; Luoma-aho 2007; Hooker 2009: 126–55; and – by far the best – Stirk 1999. In German see Michiels 2004 and Voigt 2008.
3 Balakrishnan (2000: 240) suggests that this is the subtext of Schmitt's book *Land und Meer* (1942).
4 For minor exceptions, see 1997 [1950]: 214–6, 221 n. 1; 2003 [1950]: 242–3, 248 n. 10 on Abyssinia and the Munich Agreement.
5 See also 1997 [1950]: 171; 2003 [1950]: 199 where this is related to state and colonial territory. See Kant 1887: 182. The public/private division made here by Schmitt parallels his well-known distinction in *The Concept of the Political* between the public enemy, *polemios*, and the private one, *ekhthros*.
6 Ulmen's translation masks the extent of the spatialised language, rendering *Grund und Boden der Erde* simply as 'land'.
7 Baldus de Ubaldis is never mentioned; the one substantive reference to Bartolus of Sassoferrato (1997 [1950]: 33–4; 2003 [1950]: 64) is misleading.

8 In his early analysis of dictatorship (1921: 190), Schmitt describes the 'state of emergency' in terms reminiscent of Weber, as establishing 'an unconstitutional situation for a determined territory [*ein bestimmtes Gebiet*]'.
9 The term *Landeshoheit*, of fundamental importance to politics within the Holy Roman Empire, is helpfully analysed in Gagliardo 1980.
10 On the notion of *oikonomia* as a religious issue, see Agamben 2008.
11 Schmitt also blames the interwar politics of the allies at Yalta for Czechoslovakia's ending up in the 'eastern *Großraum*' (1997 [1950]: 221 n. 1; 2003 [1950]: 248 n. 10).
12 For an excellent recent study, see Kearns 2009.
13 The explicit references (1997 [1950]: 56, 258; 2003 [1950]: 88, 283) are rather muted. See, though, 1991a [1941]: 76, 78.
14 See, for example, Hooker 2009: 69–101.

References

Agamben, G. (2008) *Le règne et la gloire: Pour une généalogie théologique de l'économie et du gouvernement*, trans. by J. Gayraud and M. Rueff, Paris: Seuil.
Arendt, H. (1958) *The Human Condition*, Chicago: University of Chicago Press.
Balakrishnan, G. (2000) *The Enemy: An Intellectual Portrait of Carl Schmitt*, London: Verso.
Bendersky, J.W. (1983) *Carl Schmitt: Theorist for the Reich*, Princeton, NJ: Princeton University Press.
Brenner, N. and Elden, S. (2009) 'Henri Lefebvre on State, Space, Territory', *International Political Sociology*, 3: 353–77.
Brunner, O. (1942 [1939]) *Land und Herrschaft: Grundfragen der territorialen Verfassungsgeschichte Südostdeutschlands im Mittelalter*, Wien: Zweite Auflage.
Carlyle, R.W. and Carlyle, A.J. (1903–36) *A History of Mediæval Political Theory in the West*, Edinburgh: William Blackwell & Sons, six volumes.
Dyzenhaus, D. (ed.) (1998) *Law as Politics: Carl Schmitt's Critique of Liberalism*, Durham, NC: Duke University Press.
Elden, S. (2006) *Speaking Against Number: Heidegger, Language and the Politics of Calculation*, Edinburgh: Edinburgh University Press.
Elden, S. (2007) 'Governmentality, Calculation, Territory', *Environment and Planning D: Society and Space*, 25: 562–80.
Elden, S. (2009) *Terror and Territory: The Spatial Extent of Sovereignty*, Minneapolis: University of Minnesota Press.
Gagliardo, J.G. (1980) *Reich and Nation: The Holy Roman Empire as Idea and Reality*, Bloomington: Indiana University Press.
Gierke, O. (1868–1913) *Das Deutsche Genossenschaftsrecht*, Berlin: Weidmannsche Buchhandlung, four volumes.
Grimm, H. (1926) *Volk ohne Raum*, Munich: Albert Langen.
Gruchmann, L. (1962) *Nationalsozialistische Grossraumordnung: Die Konstruktion einer deutscher Monroe-Doctrin*, Stuttgart: Deutsche Verlags-Anstalt.
Heidegger, M. (1983) *Einführung in die Metaphysik: Gesamtausgabe Band 40*, Frankfurt am Main: Vittorio Klostermann.
Hoelzl, M. and Ward, G. (2008) 'Editors' Introduction', in Schmitt, *Political Theology II*, pp. 1–29.
Hooker, W. (2009) *Carl Schmitt's International Thought: Order and Orientation*, Cambridge: Cambridge University Press.

Kalyvas, A. and Scheuerman, W.E. (2004) 'Schmitt's Nomos of the Earth', *Constellations: An International Journal of Critical and Democratic Theory*, 11: 492–550.
Kant, I. (1887 [1796]) *The Philosophy of Law: An Explosition of the Fundamental Principles of Jurisprudence as the Science of Right*, trans. W. Hastie, Edinburgh: T&T Clark.
Kearns, G. (2009) *Geopolitics and Empire: The Legacy of Halford Mackinder*, Oxford: Oxford University Press.
Kervégan, J.-F. (1999) 'Carl Schmitt and "World Unity"', in C. Mouffe (ed.), *The Challenge of Carl Schmitt*, pp. 54–74.
Locke, J. (1988) *Two Treatises of Government*, edited by P. Laslett, Cambridge: Cambridge University Press, third edition.
Luoma-aho, M. (2007) 'Geopolitics and Grosspolitics: From Carl Schmitt to E.H. Carr and James Burnham', in L. Odysseos and F. Petito (eds), *The International Political Thought of Carl Schmitt: Terror, Liberal War and the Crisis of Global Order*, London: Routledge, pp. 36–55.
Meyer, H.C. (1955) *Mitteleuropa in German Thought and Action 1815–1945*, The Hague: Martinus Nijhoff.
Michiels, H. (2004) *Die Großraumtheorie von Carl Schmitt*, Munich: Grin.
Mouffe, C. (ed.) (1999) *The Challenge of Carl Schmitt*, London: Verso.
Mouffe, C. (2005) 'Schmitt's Vision of a Multipolar World', *South Atlantic Quarterly*, 104: 245–51.
Müller, J.-W. (2003) *A Dangerous Mind: Carl Schmitt in Post-War European Thought*, New Haven, CT: Yale University Press.
Naumann, F. (1915) *Mitteleuropa*, Berlin: Georg Reimer.
Neocleous, M. (1996) 'Friend or Enemy? Reading Schmitt Politically', *Radical Philosophy*, 79: 13–23.
Neocleous, M. (2009) 'The Fascist Moment: Security, Exclusion, Extermination', *Studies in Social Justice*, 3: 23–37.
Odysseos, L. and Petito, F. (eds) (2006) 'The International Theory of Carl Schmitt', *Leiden Journal of International Law*, 19: 1–103.
Odysseos, L. and Petito, F. (2007) 'Introduction: The International Political Thought of Carl Schmitt', in L. Odysseos and F. Petito (eds), *The International Political Thought of Carl Schmitt: Terror, Liberal War and the Crisis of Global Order*, London: Routledge, pp. 1–17.
Rasch, W. (ed.) (2005) 'World Orders: Confronting Carl Schmitt's The Nomos of the Earth', *South Atlantic Quarterly*, 104: 177–392.
Schmitt, C. (1921) *Die Diktatur von den Anfängen des modernen Souveränitätsgedankens, bis zum proletarischen Klassenkampf*, Munich: Duncker & Humblot.
Schmitt, C. (1942) *Land und Meer: Eine weltgeschichtliche Betrachtung*, Leipzig: Philipp Reclam.
Schmitt, C. (1955) 'Nomos–Nahme–Name', in S. Behn (ed.), *Der beständige Aufbruch: Festschrift für Erich Przywara*, Nürnberg: Glock und Lutz, pp. 92–105.
Schmitt, C. (1970) *Politische Theologie II: Die Legende von der Erledigung jeder Politischen Theologie*, Berlin: Duncker & Humblot.
Schmitt, C. (1985) *Political Theology: Four Chapters on the Concept of Sovereignty*, trans. George Schwab, Cambridge: MIT Press.
Schmitt, C. (1988 [1940]) *Positionen und Begriffe: im Kampf mit Weimar–Genf–Versailles, 1923–1939*, Berlin: Duncker & Humblot.

Schmitt, C. (1991a [1941]) *Völkerrechtliche Großraumordnung mit Interventionsverbot für raumfremde Mächte: Ein Beitrag zum Reichsbegriff im Völkerrecht*, Berlin: Duncker & Humblot.
Schmitt, C. (1991b) *Glossarium: Aufzeichnungen der Jahre 1947–1951*, edited by Eberhard Freiherr von Medem, Berlin: Duncker & Humblot.
Schmitt, C. (1995) *Staat, Großraum, Nomos: Arbeiten aus den Jahren 1916–1969*, edited by G. Maschke, Berlin: Duncker & Humblot.
Schmitt, C. (1996) *The Concept of the Political*, trans. George Schwab, Chicago: University of Chicago Press.
Schmitt, C. (1997 [1950]) *Der Nomos der Erde im Völkerrecht des Jus Publicum Europaeum*, Berlin: Duncker & Humblot, Vierte Auflage.
Schmitt, C. (2002 [1932]) *Der Begriff des Politischen: Text von 1932 mit einem Vorwort und drei Corollarien*, Berlin: Duncker & Humblot, Siebente Auflage.
Schmitt, C. (2003 [1950]) *The* Nomos *of the Earth in the International Law of the* Jus Publicum Europaeum, trans. G.L. Ulmen, New York: Telos Press.
Schmitt, C. (2006 [1963]) *Theorie des Partisanen: Zwischenbemerkung zum Begriff des Politischen*, Berlin: Duncker & Humblot, Sechste Auflage.
Schmitt, C. (2007) *Theory of the Partisan: Intermediate Commentary on the Concept of the Political*, trans. G.L. Ulmen, New York: Telos Press.
Schmitt, C. (2008) *Political Theology II: The Myth of the Closure of any Political Theology*, trans. M. Hoelzl and G. Ward, Cambridge: Polity.
Schmitt, C. (2009 [1922]) *Politische Theologie: Vier Kapitel zur Lehre von der Souveränität*, Berlin: Duncker & Humblot, Neunte Auflage.
Shapiro, K. (2008) *Carl Schmitt and the Intensification of Politics*, Lanham: Rowman & Littlefield.
Slomp, G. (2009) *Carl Schmitt and the Politics of Hostility, Violence and Terror*, London: Palgrave.
Stirk, P. (ed.) (1994) *Mitteleuropa: History and Prospects*, Edinburgh: Edinburgh University Press.
Stirk, P. (1999) 'Carl Schmitt's Völkerrechtliche Grossraumordnung', *History of Political Thought*, 20: 357–74.
Ulmen, G.L. (2003a) 'Translator's Introduction', in Schmitt, C. *The* Nomos *of the Earth in the International Law of the* Jus Publicum Europaeum, trans. G.L. Ulmen, New York: Telos Press.
Ulmen, G.L. (2003b) 'Translator's Note and Acknowledgements', in Schmitt, C. *The* Nomos *of the Earth in the International Law of the* Jus Publicum Europaeum, trans. G.L. Ulmen, New York: Telos Press.
Voigt, R. (ed.) (2008) *Großraum-Denken: Carl Schmitt's Kategorie der Großraumordnung*, Stuttgart: Franz Steiner.
Zarmanian, T. (2006) 'Carl Schmitt and the Problem of Legal Order: From Domestic to International', *Leiden Journal of International Law*, 19: 41–67.

7 Interwar spatial chaos?
Imperialism, internationalism and the League of Nations

Stephen Legg

Reading Carl Schmitt demands an appreciation of context: that in which he wrote; the contexts through which his work has travelled and been translated; and the contexts in which we now read and apply his work. Various authors have contextualised Schmitt in different ways, through his intellectual biography (Balakrishnan, 2000), his ongoing theoretical engagements (Slomp, 2009) and the international relations of Germany (Stirk, 2005). This chapter will seek an alternative route into engaging and problematising Schmitt's writings on the nomos. Rather than taking as its focus a person, concept or interpretation related to Schmitt, it will seek insights into his thought through examining his treatment of an institution. The League of Nations recurred as a focus of ire throughout Schmitt's writings, culminating in the *Nomos* where it signified the decline of European world order, the rise of US economic imperialism and global interventionism, and a reign of 'spatial chaos' (Schmitt, 2003 [1950], 257). As such, the League of Nations has a synecdochical position in Schmitt's writings. It represents for him the granting to small nations parity with the great powers, the stifling of international politics (which had previously allowed friend–enemy relationships to be resolved by bracketed wars), the occlusion of American hegemony beneath the mask of ethical-humanitarian intervention, and the ossification of European imperialist privilege through the defence of the 1919 status quo.

As a scholar of colonialism, this is the most fascinating aspect of the *Nomos* for me. Schmitt provided a jurisprudential and political account of the rise of Europe as a world-ordering force. This unambiguously began with Spanish and Portuguese colonial acquisitions in the late fifteenth century, spread through the French and British empires, faltered while resolving the 'scramble for Africa' at the Berlin Conference of 1884–5, and finally capitulated during the Versailles Peace Conference of 1919. Schmitt provides an alternative to Marxist political-economic, Foucauldian biopolitical, or post-colonial culturalist interpretations of the imperial past and present (see Buck-Morss, 2008, 149). However, his focus on elite law-making, and his own political persuasions, blind him to a more nuanced understanding of capitalism, industrialisation, democratisation (Hallward, 2005) and, despite his decisionistic commitment to studying concrete situations, the working of international law on the ground.

Schmitt's oversights can, in large part, be explained by his nostalgia. Unlike other commentators of the right, Schmitt's nostalgia is not for a heterogeneous, rural past/milieu (Legg, 2005). Rather, it is a form of 'postcolonial melancholy' (Gilroy, 2006) for the age of European exploration and discovery, in which the rise of anti-colonial nationalism is associated with the demise of Man himself (Levinson, 2005, 206). This elegiac tone runs through Schmitt's earlier work in the 1920–30s on decisionism, exception, sovereignty and politics, through to his 1940–50s work on the spatial dimensions of politics, the nomos and the land–sea relation (Galli, 2008), all of which condemn the League of Nations. This chapter will proceed in three parts: the first will examine colonialism and the nomos, considering Schmitt's work in relation to Orientalism and imperial history; the second will examine internationalism and the nomos, in terms of both the League of Nations and America's global Monroe Doctrine; while the final section will examine the League's actual functioning to suggest that a more Foucauldian approach to its governmentalities provides a pivot from which we can tilt our appreciation of Schmitt's world-view.

Colonialism and the nomos

One way of thinking through the connections between Schmitt's earlier work and *The Nomos of the Earth* is to consider how his understanding of sovereignty and politics were altered by his shifting concern from the domestic to the international realm. Did Europe become the global sovereign, deciding which nation or peoples would be considered friend or enemy? Did these decisions map out the East from the West? As such, can Schmitt's friend–enemy distinction be thought of productively alongside the occident/orient-self/other distinction that Edward Said (1978) discursively cartographised in *Orientalism*? There is some evidence to think so. In the *Nomos* Schmitt pays extensive attention to the amity (friendliness) lines that Europe used to inscribe the Earth with zones in which '. . . treaties, peace and friendship applied only to Europe, to the Old World, to the area on this side of the line' (Schmitt, 2003 [1950], 92). The rest of the world was not necessarily that of enemies, but of unrestrained, free space for acquisition. Schmitt did, however, quote Hobbes's reclamation of the axiom *homo homini lupus* (man is a wolf to man) to suggest that the land beyond the amity line, and the people who inhabited it, was in a state of nature.

The connections between friend–self and enemy–other can, however, be rejected on various levels. Reflecting on similar questions regarding Levinas and Schmitt, Botwinick (2005) considered whether the other must be decided to be friend or enemy, or whether the other must be subdivided into friends and enemies. The friend–enemy self–other dichotomies were, however, ultimately rejected as theoretically antagonistic. The same can be said for the binaries as used by Said and Schmitt due, first, to Schmitt's subordination of all other binaries to those of the political and, second, to his complex spatialities of the nomos that eschew the geopolitical dualism of West–East, as explained below.

In *The Concept of the Political* Schmitt (1996 [1927], 26) argued that the political could always be reduced to the ability to make the distinction between friend and enemies, and that this distinction was independent of those in morality (good/evil), aesthetics (beautiful/ugly) and economics (profitable/unprofitable). While these distinctions could be related and drew upon each other, politics could not be traced to, or based on, any other distinction:

> The political enemy need not be morally evil or aesthetically ugly; he need not appear as an economic competitor, and it may even be advantageous to engage with him in business transactions. But he is, nevertheless, the other, the stranger; and it is sufficient for his nature that he is, in a specially intense way, existentially something different and alien, so that in the extreme case conflicts with him are possible.
> (Schmitt, 1996 [1927], 27)

Schmitt's commitment to analysing concrete decisions made in specific situations meant that his political conception of friend–enemy could not be judged by a previous norm (in time) or a neutral third party (in space). As against this, Said's self–other distinction was one borne in discourse, defined by capillary mechanisms whose origins were distant in time and space, and was as much based on culture as politics. Broadly cultural assumptions and decisions do circulate through Schmitt's concept of the political, however. He insisted that: 'Every religious, moral, economic, ethical, or other antithesis transforms into a political one if it is sufficiently strong to group human beings effectively according to friend and enemy' (Schmitt, 1996 [1927], 37). Similarly, the appraisal of the threat posed by a group must necessarily inform the decision made as to their status: 'Therefore, a cultural and partially aesthetic representational aspect precedes the foundational moment of politics' (Pan and Berman, 2008, 4). Slomp (2009, 6) has stressed that (contrary to those who would claim him unambiguously as a realist battling against interwar utopian liberals) Schmitt did *not* describe the world as it was but as he thought it, and its politics, should be. However, while we can see the political distinction blurring with that of the cultural, any comparison between Said's and Schmitt's dichotomies break down completely when Schmitt explicates his own geographical imagination of colonialism and imperialism in the *Nomos*.

> The new global image, resulting from the circumnavigation of the earth and the great discoveries of the 15th and 16th centuries, required a new spatial order. Thus began the epoch of modern international law that lasted until the 20th century.
> (Schmitt, 2003 [1950], 86)

The beginning of Europe's colonial enterprise is central to Schmitt's project, although the New World is stressed from the beginning to be a free space, not a space of enemies. Schmitt described the English approach to land beyond the constitutional restraints of their own soil as a clear example of the construction of a state of exception, of martial law, which was analogous to a zone of free and empty space (Schmitt, 2003 [1950], 98). Schmitt's solely metropolitan viewpoint conflated most colonial lands into one empty mass, or, at best, subdivided them among the categories of 'firm land' (1: state territory; 2: colonies; 3: protectorates; 4: exotic countries with European extraterritoriality and 5: free occupiable land – see Schmitt, 2003 [1950], 184). Much more attention was paid, however, to the relationship between *Land and Sea* (Schmitt, 1997 [1954]). Like the *Nomos* this book was mostly written in the 1940s and was published in the 1950s. It dealt with the history of colonialism in greater detail, examining the contests between land and sea powers, the capacity of one empire to act as a *katechon* (restrainer) of another, the role of technological innovation in driving exploration and, centrally, England's forceful domination of the world's seas so as to make them 'free'. From the early actions of pirates, privateers and 'corsair capitalists', to royal chartered explorers and eventual naval supremacy, the English achieved a spatial revolution in placing the sea at the centre of the collective existence of its islanded people. For Schmitt, the English then British Empire was barely territorial at all; but an empire of bases and lines of communication. The industrial revolution of the eighteenth century had turned the metaphorical British 'fish into a machine' (Schmitt, 1997 [1954], 53) but one that had been strong enough to maintain its supremacy throughout the nineteenth century.

This, then, was how imperialism operated beyond the amity line of European consensus and cordiality. While empires were based on appropriation of land that was viewed to be abandoned or free (what Stepputat, 2008, 338, refers to as juridical primitive accumulation), liberal imperialism operated through the policed freedom of seas and subjects. Trade was not just of merchandise or capital, but of enmity and violence; European conflict outside of Europe imported peace and stability while exporting competition and conflict (Galli, 2008). This was, however, the situation under the imperialism of only the second type of global line. Even in Schmitt's (2011 [1932]) earlier work he had identified three modern forms of imperialism. The first functioned around the Christian/non-Christian distinction and resulted in mutual exemptions from foreign jurisprudence and the extraterritoriality of Europeans in 'exotic lands' (as still referenced in Schmitt, 2003 [1950], 184). This imperialism was secularised in the nineteenth and twentieth centuries into that between civilised, half-civilised and uncivilised peoples, resulting in colonies (of empires) and protectorates (of the League of Nations). But the imperialism of the United States augmented its colonies and talk of civilisations with the distinction of creditors/debtors and a whole new world of concepts, institutions and methods, which Schmitt described as moving alongside the development of the American state like a shadow; the Monroe Doctrine.

Internationalism and the nomos

In an early interpretative piece on the nomos and American imperialism Ulmen (1987, 49) showed that for Schmitt (2003 [1950], 286) the Monroe Doctrine succeeded the *rayas* and amity lines by etching a new global partition. The address of President Monroe in December 1823 sketched a hemispherical line that made the New World into a separate order and established a *Großraum* orchestrated around US soil that would continue in that form until 1917. For Schmitt (1939) the Monroe Doctrine operated through three simple principles: the independence of states in the Americas; non-colonisation of this space; and the non-interference of extra-American powers in this space, or of the USA in extra-American spaces. This for Schmitt represented an ideally limited and confined spatial *appropriation* of space, a *distribution* of capacities within it, and thus the *production* of a regulated space; the three key functions of a nomos (Schmitt, 2003 [1950], 324).

This purity had, for Schmitt, been polluted by the irresistible draw of 'dollar diplomacy' in the nineteenth century, and was further compromised after America got drawn into the 1914–18 war (Schmitt, 2011 [1939]). The Monroe Doctrine had been bent to the will of liberal-capitalism and economic imperialism, although for Schmitt the isolationism of the doctrine stood in express contradiction to the space-disregarding transformation of the Earth into an abstract world and capital market (also see Smith, 2005, 49). Schmitt would later acknowledge the diplomatic consequences of this global Monroe Doctrine, highlighting the USA's growing influence in both hemispheres. Cuba had been granted its freedom from Spain on the condition that it constitutionally acknowledged the right of the USA to intervene to enforce this freedom should it be threatened, by forces from without or within. While the territorial status of states within the American *Großraum* remained unchanged they were within the 'spatial sovereignty' of the controlling state: 'The external, emptied space of the controlled state's territorial sovereignty remains inviolate, but the material context of this sovereignty is changed by the guarantees of the controlling power's economic *Großraum*' (Schmitt, 2003 [1950], 252). But America's interests reached beyond the western hemisphere. It had recognised the International Congo Society in 1884 which, through the lens of the *Jus Publicum Europaeum*, was not a state, and the USA used its absent imperial presence to encourage the neutralisation of the Congo Basin without participating in the resultant Berlin Conference of 1884–5 (Schmitt, 2003 [1950], 217).

The USA alone would, by the 1930s, decide when its non-interventionist stance with regards to the rest of the world applied or did not, although no one else was permitted to demand action from it (Schmitt, 2011 [1932]). This achievement marked for Schmitt a phenomenon of world historical significance. As global hegemon the USA did not so much divide the world into friends and enemies, as to cast an imperial control over the power of definition (*Caesar dominus et supra grammaticam* [the emperor is ruler over grammar as well]): What is peace? When is war? What is intervention?

While American imperialism would be free to make this decision everywhere while territorially needing to be nowhere other than the USA, Europe was increasingly bogged down in the muddled spaces of colonialism. The liberal states of the nineteenth century had failed to definitively appropriate colonial space in the age of 'geography militant' (Driver, 1999), leading to a confusion of scientific discoveries and explorations, cartographic surveys, symbolic occupations, treaties and inter-state conferences. The Berlin Conference of 1884–5 attempted to impose order on the 'scramble for Africa' but, for Schmitt:

> Essentially, the whole enterprise already was a helpless confusion of lines dividing spheres of interest and influence, as well as of failed amity lines simultaneously overarched and undermined by a Eurocentrically conceived, free, global economy ignoring all territorial boundaries. In this confusion, the old *nomos* of the earth determined by Europe dissolved.
> (Schmitt, 2003 [1950], 226)

The third explanatory factor Schmitt put forward regarding the collapse of the *Jus Publicum Europaeum*, besides geographical confusion over European appropriations and the rise of American interventionist isolationism, was the spread of universalist international law. Rather than appropriating and ordering the world for, or by, one body or collection of bodies, the new international law was 'spaceless' (Schmitt, 2003 [1950], 233). It had recognised states whose forms of sovereignty bore little in common with their European predecessors, treaties were signed that further hemmed in the possibility of bracketed wars, and regional *Großraum* had emerged and been tolerated not just in the Americas but also in East Asia (Aravamudan, 2005). But this did not suggest that liberal internationalist law was weak; far from it. For Schmitt, it could be more oppressive than colonial domination (Scheurman, 1999, 143). The danger arose from: liberal international law's alignment with the spacelessness of a global economy that most benefitted the Anglo-Saxon powers of the USA and Great Britain; the ushering in of a language of ethical-humanitarianism that masked Anglo-American economic imperialism and territorial colonialism; and, most keenly for Schmitt, the provision of a model and justification for the punishment of Germany in the interwar years, under the orchestration of the League of Nations.

Despite its obvious significance to Schmitt's writings, the Treaty of Versailles and the resultant League of Nations have not been the subject of sustained investigation in the existing literature (even Carty's, 2001, 29, comprehensive review of Schmitt's work on the liberal international legal order admits that it is not concerned with the Versailles Treaty and Schmitt's opposition to it). Galli (2008, also see Scheurman, 1999, 143, and Axtmann, 2007), however, gives 'Genevan universalism' its rightful place as Schmitt's first polemical target, as identified in 1925. For Schmitt, it represented the worst of individualism, liberalism, normativism, and the attempt to eradicate the 'political' from internal and external politics:

Universalism, then, is the representation of the international scene as a smooth and homogenous space which is morally and legally malleable; but for Schmitt, this space is actually functional for those in power (the Anglo-Saxons and their economic potential) who act politically by way of the moral disqualification of their enemies.

(Galli, 2008)

For Schmitt, President Woodrow Wilson personified the union of dollar diplomacy with liberal internationalism. He saw Wilson using the 1914–18 war as one of human liberty, which could then be used to press for global self determination, human rights and a reconfiguration of Europe and its colonies (Axtmann, 2007, 534; also see Smith, 2003). The cloaking of America's geopolitical and economic objectives beneath the veil of humanitarianism infuriated Schmitt, and it was the League's seeming obliviousness to this that fuelled his twenty-year campaign to denounce this institutional manifestation of liberal internationalism.

Schmitt's loathing for the League of Nations

The *Nomos* book explicitly situates the League of Nations between chapters describing the collapse of the European nomos and the transformed and more dangerous meaning of war, American influence and modern means of destruction. This positioning was by no means incidental and worked to situate the League at the crossfire of two damning narratives; the decline of European influence and its world stability, and the emergence of new and unbracketed forms of war. This was, however, a conclusion Schmitt had been simultaneously affirmed of and working towards throughout his publishing career. In his discussion of the sovereign's ability to decide the exception in *Political Theology*, Schmitt (2005 [1922], 11) detailed the way in which article 48 of the German constitution of 1919 effectively denied the German state full sovereignty. The Versailles influenced constitution stipulated that an exception could be declared by the President of the Reich but only under the control of Parliament, which could demand its suspension. This liberal constitutional state, for Schmitt, divided control of competences in a way that denied Germany the status of state. As Schmitt (2011 [1932]) would later comment: 'A people is only conquered when it subordinates itself to the foreign vocabulary, the foreign construction [*Vortellung*] of what law, especially international law, is. Then in addition to the surrender of weapons [one has] surrender[ed] one's own law.'

Six years after the Treaty of Versailles the lack of improvement in Germany's state of affairs led Schmitt (1925) to question the League's support for the status quo that had emerged in 1919. The term was taken both from contemporary usage in reference to political proposals and ideas such as security, inviolable treaties and the sanctity of borders. However, for people such as Schmitt who felt that the peace treaty had been woefully unfair, the

Interwar spatial chaos? 113

status quo meant a perpetuation of gross indignity and oppression. Using the example of the occupation of Rhineland territory through the 1919 Treaty, the status quo was one of a militarised presence, confiscated houses, expelled Germans and German demilitarisation. This last act especially divided the national territory of Germany, but through international law. This was, in effect, an international *occupation*, orchestrated by the League. The latter also reserved the right of investigation into German constitutional affairs more broadly and organised the 'territorial rupture' of the eastern German border, the separation of German 'tribes' from the Reich, the payment of reparations, and the foreign control of German banks, railroads and aircraft construction. The Rhineland was thus just an especially burdened part of an abused state. This status quo suited the English, who could pursue commerce and the maintenance of their empire in such conditions, and France, which Schmitt suggested strove towards military and political dominance over Europe. Hinting at themes that he would develop in the 1930s, Schmitt contrasted this emphasis on the status quo with an external world of rapid change, technical progress and intellectual thinking that emphasised eternal becoming, flow and substanceless functioning. Hinting at a deeper concern with what he would later call the collapsing European nomos, Schmitt argued that the desire for calm, peace and justice combined with the inability to find a sufficient legal principle could stabilise the present, but would surely lead to new conflicts. Just as the nineteenth century had seen the Holy Alliance and the Napoleonic Empire described as the arbiters of 'peace', now the status quo and the League of Nations jointly claimed this mantle. The latter was denounced as a legalised but unbearable intermediate state between war and peace in which the politically powerful deprived the politically weak not only of their life, but also of their right and their honour.

In his 1932 piece on 'Forms of modern imperialism in international law' Schmitt outlined the three historical phases of imperial relationship (orchestrated around the Christian, the civilised and the creditor imperialist). But threaded through this discussion was a denouncement of the indeterminate position of the League. While not a barefaced imperialist organisation, it retained a relic of the un/civilised distinction in its division of mandates ('. . . where the victors [in the 1914–18 War] take as spoils previously Turkish regions and the German colonies', Schmitt, 2011 [1932]) into those more or less able to govern themselves ('. . . a consciously pathetic form . . .', Schmitt, 2011 [1932]). Schmitt denounced this as the most compromised example of the division of humanity on the lines of civilisation, but also the classic representation of nineteenth-century European imperialism. Yet while the League had inherited some of the vestiges of the passing imperial age, it seemed oblivious to the new methods of securing influence that America had been experimenting with. It was the USA that pushed for a League of Nations that it did not then join, although eighteen 'American states' (from its *Großraum* in the western hemisphere) could now vote on European affairs through the League. Most gallingly for Schmitt, article 21 of the League Covenant had recognised the Monroe Doctrine, thus foregoing any possibility of intervention into 'American affairs'. This effectively made the League 'lame in the American leg, though the Americans enjoy full participation in European affairs' (Schmitt, 2011 [1932]). Through its interventionist isolation and its absent presence, the USA had, for Schmitt, *understood* international law, while the League had not. The Monroe Doctrine was, as such, not something that Schmitt despised; rather, he admired its ingenuity and wished for something similar for Germany in central Europe: 'as a German I can only feel in these discussions of American imperialism like a beggar in rags [might feel] speaking of the riches and treasures of others'(Schmitt, 2011 [1932]).

With the Nazi ascent to power imminent, in 1932 Schmitt published a revised version of his 1927 text *The Concept of the Political*. Here his previously described isolation of the political friend–enemy distinction was used to articulate a series of implicit and explicit arguments against the League of Nations. Just as Schmitt's insistence that the political cannot be judged by a previous norm or neutral third party distanced him from Said's world-view, so it condemned the League and its universalistic international law. Only 'actual participants' were qualified to judge a concrete situation and settle conflict (Schmitt, 1996 [1932], 27). The political was thus not an intellectual, abstract or pedagogic concept; a broadside against interwar utopians or idealists (see Carr, 1993 [1939]). Were idealist notions of neutrality to prevail in the world, then wars might decrease in number, but would increase in ferocity. In contrast to the mournful but restrained tone of Schmitt's post-1945 writings on the nomos, these earlier works crackle with anti-democratic sentiment (as in *Political Theology*'s suggestion that constitutional democracy annuls the sovereignty of a state). A pacified globe would mean, for Schmitt (1996 [1932], 35) a world without war that would lack friend–enemy distinctions and thus politics, depriving the world of meaningful antitheses, and anything to kill for. The only form of pacifist political energy would be a pacifist war against non-pacifists; a war against war. The League was, of course, unwilling and unable to do this, so it did something Schmitt found altogether more unnerving. Instead, it justified wars in the name of humanity. This, for Schmitt, would make war unusually intense and inhuman because a moral category was becoming blurred with that of the political. This made the opponent not a political enemy, but an immoral monster that should be destroyed, not just defeated and forced back into its territorial borders; that is, humanity can have no enemy that is a human being.

Schmitt's specific complaint was that humanitarianism was not even being used for peace, but for profit and domination: 'The concept of humanity is an especially useful ideological instrument of imperialist expansion, and in its ethical-humanitarian form it is a specific vehicle of economic imperialism' (Schmitt, 1996 [1932], 54). So as to leave no grounds for misinterpretation of the object of his criticism, Schmitt immediately went on to discuss the irrelevance of a League of Nations without a League of Monarchs to oppose, and to decry the utopian ideal of depoliticisation, which would necessarily lead, for Schmitt (1996 [1932], 55), to the nonexistence of states. The League was thus an 'incongruous' organisation that was *not* international, as it did not transcend the borders of states, but was merely inter-state. It neither abolished wars nor states: 'It introduces new possibilities for wars, permits wars to take place, sanctions coalition wars, and by legitimizing and sanctioning certain wars it sweeps away many obstacles to war' (Schmitt, 1996 [1932], 36). Changing tack, Schmitt then went on to outline his critique of liberal individualism, which in his eyes undermined the ability of the community and state to make friend–enemy distinctions and persistently returned its attentions to two heterogenous spheres; ethics (including intellect and education) and economics (trade and property). The attempt to annihilate politics through liberalism could thus be traced across the following spheres in which, for instance, the political concept of battle was transformed into the intellectual pursuit of discussion and the economic act of competition (Schmitt, 1996 [1932], 70–2) (see Table 8.1).

Vitally, Schmitt immediately followed this typology of ways in which liberalism subjugated the state and politics to law, morality and economy by insisting that the ideological structure of the Peace of Versailles corresponded exactly to this polarity of ethical pathos and economic calculation. Ethically, Germany had been forced to accept *responsibility* for all war damages and losses. This laid the foundation for a juridical and moral value judgement but one that avoided annexation. Thus: Alsace and Lorraine were 'ceded' to France as recognition of an injustice; the cession of Polish and Danish served the ideological claims of nationalism; while German colonies were seized on the grounds of humanity. Economically, *reparations* constituted an unlimited economic exploitation of the politically vanquished. This polarity of ethics and economics was unable to depoliticise the world, as an economic power position of superiority *was* warlike and would enforce the conditions on the world to ensure its hegemony through economic and thus, technically, non-political means (Schmitt, 1996 [1932], 78). The League of Nations, at the opposite pole to what we must presume was Anglo-American economic dominance, also had at its disposal sanctions, protection and the possibility of international policing, amounting to what Schmitt (1996 [1932], 79) termed the 'modern means of annihilation'.

Table 8.1 Schmitt's analysis of the effects of liberalism

Liberalism =	*Ethics*	*Economics*
Politics →	Moral pathos	Materialist reality
Battle →	Discussion	Competition
State →	Humanity	Production – traffic
People →	Public	Consumers – employers
Government →	Propaganda	Control

Carty (2001, 34) has argued that while Schmitt continued to criticise the League of Nations, he also started to articulate his vision of an alternative international order. This was outlined in his *Völkerrechtliche Grossraumordnung* (1939, 4th edition in 1941; see Elden this volume) in which he detailed his vision of international law for 'greater space' regions, which included a prohibition of intervention for powers external to that space (see Stirk, 2005, 71). This would create a world divided into *Großraum* blocs, although the role of a *Reich* or regional hegemon was an ambiguous one (for the critical reception of Schmitt's theory see Stirk, 2008, 434). In his 1939 text on '*Großraum* versus universalism' it became clear that this international vision was one in which Germany would be allowed her own Monroe Doctrine. But the text also adapted this new world-view such that Schmitt could continue his attack on the League, an institution he now referred to in the past tense. The League was said to have: 'perished on the disparity between its universalistic construction and the objective necessity of an internal self-ordering of the European *Großraum*' (Schmitt, 2011 [1939]). Combining his comments in *The Concept of the Political* on the violent potential of universalism with his new interest in *Großraum*, Schmitt posed the future of international coexistence as a choice between two options. One was the League view, and the other one which clearly vindicated German domination of Europe as a measure to avoid international conflict. Schmitt's options and conclusion were:

1 A clear spatial order based on the non-intervention of extra-regional powers
2 A universalistic ideology which transforms the entire Earth into the battlefield for its interventions and which stands in the way of any natural growth of vital peoples.

We are thus not simply imitating an American model if we make reference to the Monroe Doctrine; we are merely excavating the healthy core of an international legal *Großraum*-principle, and developing it appropriately [. . .] for our European *Großraum*.

(Schmitt, 2011 [1939], 8)

Largely written during the 1940s, contemplated during his incarceration in Nuremberg and published in the 1950s, Schmitt's Nomos *of the Earth* unsurprisingly contained fewer references to a European *Großraum*. After exploring the term nomos, the imperial expansion of Europe and the *Jus Publicum Europaeum* that resulted, Schmitt turned to the question of the new nomos of the Earth arising from America's newfound status and the emergence of international law. This prefaced his chapter: 'The League of Nations and the Problem of the Spatial Order of the Earth' (Schmitt, 2003 [1950], 240–58). Earlier in the book Schmitt (2003 [1950], 186) had made it clear that the role of international law was not to protect the 'status quo' but to protect the nomos, the spatial structure of unity and orientation. If wars between Great Powers were not allowed a free space they could become total and force a new spatial order. In contrast the League was worse than anarchy because it made no distinction between meaningful and destructive wars. Worse still, it had no concrete spatial structure, unlike the previous nomos that had been firmly grounded in Europe (Schmitt, 2003 [1950], 190).

Instead, the Versailles conference was denounced for having accepted the US Monroe Doctrine and Japan's interests in East Asia, while failing to address the absence of the USSR, Europe's imperial possessions or the freedom of the sea (Schmitt, 2003 [1950], 240). While previous European conferences had determined the order of the Earth, Versailles perversely inverted this relationship and let the rest of the world determine Europe. The League had failed to prevent Italy's invasion of Ethiopia, suggesting for Schmitt the residual imperialism within the internationalist order:

> An extraordinary league! Perhaps, in the case of Ethiopia, subconsciously the distinction of traditional European international law was at work, i.e., in the fact that war on non-European soil fell outside its order and that Africa was considered to be colonial territory.
> (Schmitt, 2003 [1950], 243)

This desire to be both a European and an international order crippled any attempt at a League nomos: 'Given this lack of decision with respect to the basic question of spatial order, the League was unable to develop an internally consistent and unifying principle of the territorial *status quo*' (Schmitt, 2003 [1950], 244–5). As described earlier, the inappropriate universalisation of the American Monroe Doctrine was also blamed, but the League was particularly lambasted for subjugating itself from the outset. The League, which effectively ceased to operate with the outbreak of the Second World War in 1939, did not feature substantially in Schmitt's future writings. As in the broader literature, it was consigned to the scrapheap of history alongside much of the 'utopian' liberal thinking on international relations that it had produced and relied upon.

League governmentalities?

The object of this chapter is not to defend the League of Nations against Schmitt's critical onslaughts, nor to defend its achievements. One of the League's core aims was to prevent war and on this objective it undeniably ended in catastrophic failure. However, Schmitt's reading can be challenged on two grounds: first, and least unsettling, one can challenge Schmitt's reading of the League; second, and more productively, one can question the perspective from which Schmitt's comments were made. Through taking him at his word and looking at the concrete situations into which the League intervened, it is possible to gain critical insights not just into the logic of Schmitt's philosophy, but into the oversights of his world-view that necessarily impact back upon his politics and the utility of his theories to readers today.

First, Schmitt's portrayal of the League as instituting an era of spatial chaos can be questioned. This questioning, indeed, was hinted at in his 1932 paper where he suggested that the League had assumed imperial hierarchies and in the *Nomos* where he questioned the League's treatment of Ethiopia. Yet neither of these comments led to a consideration of the way the League itself made decisions about the capacities or freedoms of its member states. Schmitt's 1932 criticism was aimed at the mandates, the League's treatment of which is attracting increasing comment (Callahan, 1999; Pedersen, 2006). Anghie (2004) and Grovogui (1996) have both criticised the League's division of mandates into three categories of development (and also of race): A, Ottoman Arabs; B, African and Pacific Islanders; and C, South-West Africa and the German Pacific. But beyond this there were further partitions of the world into spatial categories. The League created a new global cartography of members, non-members, mandates and dependencies of members of the League. The latter were colonies that had no direct say in their membership, but were instead signed up for the League on their behalf by their colonial overlords. As such, the League could be argued to have had a spatial order that was inherited from the imperial age and recouched in the language of international law. Indeed, the liberal international relations scholar Alfred Zimmern believed the League to be the saviour (*deus ex machina*) of the *Third British Empire* (Zimmern, 1927, 75). However, the League still lacked the capacity to decide on friends and enemies on the basis of threat posed to the international community, or on any clear and consistent racial or constitutional lines. For instance, India had secured a place as a member of the League due to its signing of the Treaty of Versailles, on account of the number of men it sacrificed during the war. This was despite not being a self-governing nation itself, in which case it should have been present as a dependency (Schmidt, 1994).

A more challenging approach to Schmitt's reading is to question those activities of the League that he chose to focus on. Schmitt examined the League as a body that orchestrated the 'occupation' of Germany, which failed to prevent armament and war and, to a lesser extent, which allowed Anglo-Saxon economic imperialism to further spread worldwide. But the League also had other concerns, including those termed 'technical work', in which it is increasingly acknowledged to have found some success (see Weindling, 1995). The League Health Organisation successfully promoted public health values, circulated epidemiological intelligence and statistics, encouraged personnel interchange and offered technical assistance to governments. The League cooperated with and assisted the International Labour Office in securing fairer working conditions, while the Social Questions Section of the League campaigned against the drugs trade, obscene publications and trafficking in women and children. Though not without conflict, the League managed through these measures to challenge practices in which member states were often reluctant to invest. It did this through practices that Schmitt would have dismissed as 'empty normativism'; through recommending, advising and conducting rather than through censoring, outlawing or dividing. Mapping such relations would need to go beyond the state-by-state cartography of membership, or the *raya*, amity or Monroe lines of global partition. Rather, it would have to map the circulation of information (see Manderson, 1995) or of travelling commissions (Legg, 2009) that share the spatial logic of America's global intervention through absent presence as much as the colonial hierarchies of Europe's empires.

Such practices would contribute to the ongoing reassessment of League achievements outside of the theatre of war (Pedersen, 2008). But they can also contribute to questioning not just Schmitt's condemnation of the League, but the comprehensiveness of his broader world-view. This can be illustrated through the work of Alfred Zimmern, whose approach to the League is diametrically opposed to that of Schmitt. His *The League of Nations and the Rule of Law, 1918–1935* (Zimmern, 1945 [1936]) was actually similar in structure to Schmitt's *Nomos* book; it began with an analysis of the emergence of pre-war international law with its sole focus on war ('little more than a decorous name for a convenience of the Chancelleries', Zimmern, 1945 [1936], 99), which introduced a critical but favourable discussion of the League. There are other points on which Zimmern and Schmitt actually converge: on the idea of the League being an 'improved and enlarged Monroe Doctrine' for President Wilson (216); on the weakening of the League by the parity of positions held by Great and Small Powers (294); that international law supplied a spiritual (or political theological) need (100); and that the League *could* provide a dangerous new arena for the play of power politics (291). However, Zimmern actually had great faith in the League, believing that it was politically important and that its main capacity was as an instrument of cooperation within the realm of responsibility politics and harmonious interests (289). Most importantly for this argument, Zimmern drew attention to the 'technical work' of the League. This was, for him, impossible to summarise because it demanded attention not on the centre but on the influence exerted, and results achieved, in the various countries to which this work extended (325). But these achievements *did* relate to a 'theory of the League', which was that use could be made of 'experts' in international affairs. These people could draw on reservoirs of knowledge and public spirit, uniting 'non-political', technical men together: 'Thus the League was becoming, in a sense and to a degree of which this could be said of no national centre of government, a *point of convergence between Knowledge and Power*' (Zimmern, 1945 [1936], 319, original emphasis). This development went beyond technical work to effect the dominance of old style diplomacy in the League, although the influence of tradition and state politics could not be immediately overturned (see Dunbabin, 1993). Rather, the new and old styles had settled into appropriate spheres of interpenetration: 'The methods of the Old Diplomacy have found their way to Geneva, while Geneva in its turn has cast its shadow over the Chancelleries' (Zimmern, 1945 [1936], 494).

In one sense, Zimmern's hope for the League and for peace introduced a politically naive belief in the subsumption of power politics beneath responsibility politics in the international realm, for which he has been thoroughly castigated. Most famously, E. H. Carr (1993 [1939]; see Wilson, 1995) placed Zimmern highly among the interwar liberal utopianists he damned for having set their course to high-minded ideals, not the realities of political developments on the ground (or the 'free' seas). Although Carr (1993 [1939], 186–7) was more critical than Schmitt of the influence of power politics on international relations, the parallels between their works are startling (Luoma-aho, 2007, concludes that it is likely Carr knew of Schmitt's work). On the nature of the political, Carr (1993 [1939], 180) insisted that the political arena was one of near constant *conflict*, and that every system of law was based on a political *decision* as to the authority who could make or unmake law. Like Schmitt, Carr argued against *a priori* solutions to the problem of security (106) because law was not an abstraction, but depended on political interests (179). The League itself had been exposed as saturated with power relations through its treatment of Italy over the Ethiopian invasion (104), its dismemberment and disarmament of Germany (105), and its maintenance of the status quo under the *pacta sunt servanda* (181) commitment to keeping all agreements (a term used in Schmitt, 2011 [1939]). Carr's (231) reaction to this was to call for international relations dominated by something very similar to *Großraum* politics, in which units of former states would form under the effective authority of one centre.

However, in his attention paid to the technical work of the League, but also to the 'theory of the League' to which this work gave rise, Zimmern was anything but a utopian moraliser. This was not just because Zimmern was a 'cautious idealist' (Rich, 1995) but because he had been actively involved with the League since its inception, in the Foreign Office in London, then as a Deputy Director at the League and a summer school teacher in Geneva (Markwell, 1986). His involvement with the working of the League highlighted to him the awkward triangulation of old sovereign powers and new international diplomacies; it stressed upon him the need to examine the workings out of new power-knowledge formations by experts in the field; and it opened up to him the realm of cooperation and responsibility as realms for international governance. In Foucault's terms these equate to: the intersection of bio- and sovereign-powers in international governmentalities; their capillary and circulatory logic through travelling 'experts' (also see Mitchell, 2002); and their functioning through the conduct of conduct as much as through surveillance, force or spectacle.

Using this terminology brings a different League to light because Schmitt and Foucault's views of sovereignty are so different. As Barder and Debrix (Forthcoming, 9) have argued, Schmitt's view of sovereignty was centralised and tied to the individual persona of an authoritarian decision maker, while Foucault focused on the fragmented, pluralised sovereignty distributed through governmental techniques throughout society (as Zimmern, 1933, 25, commented of post-Revolutionary European and American democracies: 'the sovereign monarch gave place to the sovereign people. His power, his glory, and his so-called 'rights' were taken from him and divided into thousands and millions of fractions distributed among the uncrowned sovereigns of the mass'). While Foucault extracted considerations of sovereignty solely from the juridico-institutional realm to consider it 'from below', Schmitt remained focused solely on the law, the state and sovereignty 'from above' (Barder and Debrix, Forthcoming, 9). Indeed, 'governmentalities' were exactly what Schmitt was critical of, in theory and in practice (McCormick, 1997, 6), while his placing of land appropriation as the founding moment of a nomos suggests an un-Foucauldian attachment to a singular origin of sovereignty (Bosteels, 2005, 300). However, in other ways Schmitt and Foucault complement shortcomings in each other's work. While Schmitt described the collapse of the *Respublica Christiania*, Foucault detailed the early modern crisis of pastoral power and the collapse of the papal-imperial compact that created the need for a 'balance of Europe' (Foucault, 2007, 297). Schmitt's nomos work sketches out the international orders and conquests that framed the governmentalities Foucault described in Europe, while both are interested in the 'where' as well as the 'how' of power (Dean, 2004). Deuber-Mankowsky (2008) has examined the parallels between Foucault's critical genealogies of liberal governmentality and Schmitt's denouncement of the quantitatively but not qualitatively total state of liberal constitutional democracies (also see Crombez, 2008): while one detailed the introduction of economy into politics, the other spoke of the depoliticisation through which politics became economic; for one the political was a field of state intervention, for the other, one of decision. If concepts of state presume the political (Schmitt, 1996 [1927], 19), then surely they also presume the rationalisation of governmental practice and the economisation of politics that Foucault detailed (Deuber-Mankowsky, 2008, 149)? For all his insistence to the contrary, Schmitt did not study concrete situations, but their legal representation, eschewing life, place and resistance. As such, Schmitt's persistent interchanging of 'League of Nations' for 'Geneva' or 'Versailles' in his writings is indicative. For him, the League was essentially the decisions made in France or Switzerland. But League governmentalities occurred in every town hall, bazaar, factory, poppy field or speakeasy in which conduct was incrementally altered by publicity, rumour, propaganda or state obligation emanating from Geneva.

As such, there is much to remain critically aware of in Schmitt's writings. Just as his definition of politics was political itself (Axtmann, 2007, 537), so his denunciation of the League of Nations was as political as it was personal. Schmitt's view of the nomos was constructed from the European core and from the position of law, and thus took little account of the operation of the nomos on the ground, those it oppressed, and also those who resisted it (Aravamudan, 2005). These shortcomings suggest that Schmitt's approach to the nomos would benefit from an examination of its imbrication with government, resistance and place. Such an engagement with governmentalities would also encourage a consideration of the latter in their global and international functions (Larner and Walters, 2004), and would place international law alongside other forms of sovereign power being reintegrated into a Foucauldian analysis (Golder and Fitzpatrick, 2008). Such a joint approach would not, for me, be put together so as to recuperate the League. Schmitt's criticisms are startlingly incisive and *do* highlight the vacillation and inaction, the pandering to imperial will, and the problematic appropriation of humanitarian language, of the League. But attention to League governmentalities would open up the different geographies through which advice, censoring, innovations and sanctions emanating from Geneva transgressed scalar sovereignties and global linear lines through mobile and capillary forms which, from Schmitt's juridical perspective, were simply part of Europe's, and the world's, *fin de siècle* spatial chaos.

References

Anghie, A. (2004) *Imperialism, Sovereignty and the Making of International Law*. Cambridge University Press: Cambridge.
Aravamudan, S. (2005) Carl Schmitt's The Nomos of the Earth: Four Corollaries *South Atlantic Quarterly* 104, 227–36.
Axtmann, R. (2007) Humanity or Enmity? Carl Schmitt on International Politics *International Politics* 44, 531–51.
Balakrishnan, G. (2000) *The Enemy: An Intellectual Portrait of Carl Schmitt*. Verso: London; New York.
Barder, A. B. and Debrix, F. (Forthcoming) Agonal Sovereignty: Rethinking War and Politics with Schmitt, Arendt, and Foucault *Philosophy and Social Criticism*.
Bosteels, B. (2005) The Obscure Subject: Sovereignty and Geopolitics in Carl Schmitt's The Nomos of the Earth *South Atlantic Quarterly* 104, 295–305.
Botwinick, A. (2005) Same/Other Versus Friend/Enemy: Levinas Contra Schmitt *Telos* 2005, 46–63.
Buck-Morss, S. (2008) Sovereign Right and the Global Left *Cultural Critique* 69, 145–71.
Callahan, M. D. (1999) *Mandates and Empire: The League of Nations and Africa, 1914–1931*. Sussex Academic Press: Brighton; Portland.
Carr, E. H. (1993 [1939]) *The Twenty Years' Crisis 1919–1939: An Introduction to the Study of International Relations*. Macmillan Press & Papermac: London.
Carty, A. (2001) Carl Schmitt's Critique of Liberal International Legal Order between 1933 and 1945 *Leiden Journal of International Law* 14, 25–76.
Crombez, T. (2008) 'The Sovereign Disappears in the Voting Booth': Carl Schmitt and Martin Heidegger on Sovereignty and (Perhaps) Governmentality. In *Anti-Democratic Thought* (ed. E. Kofnel). Imprint-Academic: Exeter, pp. 101–21.
Dean, M. (2004) *Nomos* and the Politics of World Order. In *Global Governmentality: Governing International Spaces* (eds W. Larner and W. Walters). Routledge: New York; London, pp. 40–58.
Deuber-Mankowsky, A. (2008) Nothing Is Political, Everything Can Be Politicized: On the Concept of the Political in Michel Foucault and Carl Schmitt *Telos* 2008, 135–61.
Driver, F. (1999) *Geography Militant: Cultures of Exploration in the Age of Empire*. Blackwell: Oxford.

Dunbabin, J. (1993) The League of Nations' Place in the International System *History* 78, 421–42.
Foucault, M. (2007) *Security, Territory, Population: Lectures at the Collège De France 1977–78*. Palgrave Macmillan: Basingstoke; New York.
Galli, C. (2008) Carl Schmitt and the Global Age. Presented at Buffalo Conference on Political Philosophy 'New Paths in Political Philosophy'.
Gilroy, P. (2006) *Postcolonial Melancholia*. Columbia University Press: New York.
Golder, B. and Fitzpatrick, P. (2008) *Foucault's Law*. Routledge: London.
Grovogui, S. N. Z. (1996) *Sovereigns, Quasi-Sovereigns and Africans*. University of Minnesota Press: Minneapolis; London.
Hallward, P. (2005) Beyond Salvage *South Atlantic Quarterly* 104, 237–44.
Larner, W. and Walters, W. (2004) *Global Governmentality: Governing International Spaces*. Routledge: London; New York.
Legg, S. (2005) Contesting and Surviving Memory: Space, Nation and Nostalgia in *Les Lieux De Mémoire*. *Environment and Planning D: Society and Space* 23, 481–504.
—— (2009) Of Scales, Networks and Assemblages: The League of Nations Apparatus and the Scalar Sovereignty of the Government of India *Transactions of the Institute of British Geographers NS* 34, 234–53.
Levinson, B. (2005) The Coming Nomos; or, the Decline of Other Orders in Schmitt *South Atlantic Quarterly* 104, 205–15.
Luoma-aho, M. (2007) Geopolitics and Grosspolitics: From Carl Schmitt to E. H. Carr and James Burnham. In *The International Political Thought of Carl Schmitt: Terror, Liberal War and the Crisis of Global Order* (eds L. Odysseos and F. Petito). Routledge, London, pp. 36–55.
Manderson, L. (1995) Wireless Wars in the Eastern Area: Epidemiological Surveillance, Disease Prevention and the Work of the Eastern Bureau of the League of Nations Headquarters. In *International Health Organisations and Movements, 1918–39* (ed. P. Weindling). Cambridge University Press: Cambridge, pp. 109–33.
Markwell, D. J. (1986) Sir Alfred Zimmern Revisited: Fifty Years On *Review of International Studies* 12, 279–92.
McCormick, J. P. (1997) *Carl Schmitt's Critique of Liberalism: Against Politics as Technology*. Cambridge University Press: Cambridge.
Mitchell, T. (2002) *Rule of Experts: Egypt, Techno-Politics, Modernity*. University of California Press: Berkeley; London.
Pan, D. and Berman, R. A. (2008) Introduction: Culture and Politics in Carl Schmitt *Telos* 2008, 3–6.
Pedersen, S. (2006) The Meaning of the Mandates System: An Argument *Geschichte und Gesellschaft* 32, 560–82.
—— (2008) Back to the League of Nations *The American Historical Review* 112, 1091–1117.
Rich, P. (1995) Alfred Zimmern's Cautious Idealism: The League of Nations, International Education, and the Commonwealth. In *Thinkers of the Twenty Years' Crisis* (eds D. Long and P. Wilson). Clarendon Press: Oxford, pp. 79–99.
Said, E. (1978) *Orientalism: Western Conceptions of the Orient*. Routledge & Kegan Paul: London.
Scheurman, W. E. (1999) *Carl Schmitt: The End of Law*. Rowman & Littlefield: Lanham, MD.

Schmidt, K. J. (1994) *India's Role in the League of Nations, 1919–1939*. Florida State University: Unpublished doctoral thesis.
Schmitt, C. (1925) The Status Quo and the Peace. In *Weimar: A Jurisprudence of Crisis* (eds A. J. Jacobson and B. Schlink). University of California Press: Berkeley, pp. 290–93.
—— (1996 [1927]) *The Concept of the Political*. University of Chicago Press: Chicago.
—— (1996 [1932]) *The Concept of the Political*. University of Chicago Press: Chicago.
—— (1997 [1954]) *Land and Sea*. Plutarch Press: Washington, DC.
—— (2003 [1950]) *The* Nomos *of the Earth in the International Law of the Jus Publicum Europaeum*. Telos Press: New York.
—— (2005 [1922]) *Political Theology: Four Chapters on the Concept of Sovereignty*. University of Chicago Press: Chicago.
—— (2011 [1932]) Forms of Modern Imperialism in International Law (Trans. M. G. Hannah, Chapter 2 in this volume).
—— (2011 [1939]) *Großraum* versus Universalism: The International Legal Struggle over the Monroe Doctrine (Trans. M. G. Hannah, Chapter 3 in this volume).
Slomp, G. (2009) *Carl Schmitt and the Politics of Hostility, Violence and Terror*. Palgrave Macmillan: Basingstoke.
Smith, N. (2003) *American Empire: Roosevelt's Geographer and the Prelude to Globalization*. University of California Press: Berkeley; Los Angeles; London.
—— (2005) *The Endgame of Globalization*. Routledge: London.
Stepputat, F. (2008) Forced Migration, Land and Sovereignty *Government and Opposition* 43, 337–57.
Stirk, P. M. R. (2005) *Carl Schmitt, Crown Jurist of the Third Reich: On Pre-Emptive War, Military Occupation, and World Empire*. Edwin Mellen Press: Lampeter.
—— (2008) John H. Herz and the International Law of the Third Reich *International Relations* 22, 427–40.
Ulmen, G. (1987) American Imperialism and International Law: Carl Schmitt on the US in World Affairs *Telos* 72, 43–73.
Weindling, P. (ed.) (1995) *International Health Organisations and Movements, 1918–39*. Cambridge University Press: Cambridge.
Wilson, P. (1995) Introduction: The Twenty Years' Crisis and the Category of 'Idealism' in International Relations. In *Thinkers of the Twenty Years' Crisis* (eds D. Long and P. Wilson). Clarendon Press: Oxford, pp. 1–24.
Zimmern, A. (1927) *The Third British Empire: Being a Course of Lectures Delivered at Columbia University*. New York Oxford University Press: London.
—— (1933) India and the World Situation. In *India Analysed Volume I: International* (eds F. M. Houlston and B. P. L. Bedi). Victor Gollancz: London, pp. 13–29.
—— (1945 [1936]) *The League of Nations and the Rule of Law, 1918–1935*. Macmillan: London.

Part III
Analytical geographies of the nomos

8 Colonial war
Carl Schmitt's deterritorialization of enmity

Mathew Coleman

> [W]orld history remains open and fluid ... Every new age and every new epoch in the co-existence of peoples, empires, and countries, of rulers and power formations of every sort, is founded on new spatial divisions, new enclosures, and new spatial orders of the earth.
>
> (Schmitt 2003 [1950], 78–79)

Carl Schmitt is often understood as an intellectual forerunner of the hard-nosed, power politics modeling of inter-state relations developed in the social and behavioral sciences, post-1945. Schmitt's realist credentials in part reflect his Weimar-era relationship with Hans J. Morgenthau, so-called "founding father" of the discipline of international relations at the University of Chicago. But there is also the fact that Schmitt's writings on sovereignty, war, and the immutability of conflict, particularly in the guise of his well-cited friend–enemy relation, read intuitively as a sort of proto-realism. So, for example, Williams (2005, 93) summarizes Schmitt's friend–enemy relation and defense of sovereign decisionism as an illiberal *realpolitik* focused on a "mythologized unity of nation and state within a defining context of enmity." Chandler (2008, 37), contra various poststructuralist appropriations of Schmitt, likewise describes him as properly "the founding theorist of a geopolitical framework of international relations." Burchard (2006) too argues that if Schmitt's rendering of politics as a mass-scale public phenomenon (*hostis*, not *inimicus*) is not specific to states, it nonetheless lends itself to a "Westphalian" interpretation of the political as a heterogeneous pluriverse of states constituted through strife. Others see Schmitt as an "institutional realist" because of his emphasis on rules that have tempered inter-state politics since 1648 (Zarmanian 2006). Critical international relations scholars too, while warning of the dangers of a "hyper-realist" take on Schmitt (Odysseos and Petito 2008), have traced realism's "dangerous ontology" of inter-state warfare in part to Schmitt's friend–enemy distinction (Huysmans 1998; Odysseos 2002).

But is enmity in Schmitt necessarily state-territorial? Is the state a "fundamental, irrefragable, existential verity" in Schmitt's work, as charges prominent critic Richard Wolin (1992, 432)? My argument here is that there is a much richer vein of thought in Schmitt's work that is displaced by linking the friend–enemy problematic to a proto-realism of state power and inter-state conflict. What we get in the recent English translation of Schmitt's Nomos *of the Earth* (2003 [1950]), for example, is an extended discussion of an important theme found throughout Schmitt's work: that enmity hews to no particular spatiality. Indeed, what I hope to accomplish in this chapter is to use *Nomos*, among other of Schmitt's texts, to problematize a reading of Schmitt as committed to a geopolitical ontology of states, or better, as a thinker who maps geopolitical enmity onto competitive blocs of state-territorial space as an inescapable aspect of a specifically inter-national politics. As I argue, Schmitt breaks with the "modern geopolitical imagination" (Agnew 2003) insofar as he scrambles what typically counts as geopolitics and where we might find it. Specifically, Schmitt nowhere articulates the "inside = politics, outside = force" logic (Agnew and Corbridge 1995, 86) that underwrites realist international relations (and political geography) scholarship. Indeed, for Schmitt, a billiard ball modeling of the political, i.e. of states projecting power beyond their peaceable boundaries into an abstracted inter-state space, misses out on the ways in which all sorts of practices at the domestic scale are in fact warring.

What is geopolitics, then, for Schmitt? What Schmitt offers as definitional of geopolitics is not state action in the realm of foreign policy practice, but an imploded domestic/foreign polarity in which there is no necessary distinction between a "peaceful community of presence" within the state and a "primordial absence of community" without (Ashley 1987). For Schmitt, the geopolitical percolates through all places and social relationships, even those typically understood as exceptional by virtue of their "domestication." Indeed, Schmitt's insistence that the political not be understood narrowly as an inter-state foreign policy problematic recalls Campbell's (1992) exploration of geopolitics in terms of merged public and foreign policy practices that cease to make sense as specifically spatialized tactics of governance, i.e. relevant to either the "domestic" or the "international." This is the geographical challenge that Schmitt poses.

The state, however, is not anathema to Schmitt. This is so in several ways. First, Schmitt's take on geopolitics emphasizes the way in which states themselves undo the very inside/outside territoriality that their authority and legitimacy depends on and yet how states continue to matter as institutionalized centers of violence (although under the cover of legal and bureaucratic neutrality). In other words, Schmitt's discussion of geopolitics offers us a paradoxical and contradicted rendering of the state as a site of subversion and reappropriation to new ends. This marks a distinct break from other ways of imagining the political beyond the problem of state territoriality. Because Schmitt understands transformations in the state and statecraft from roughly the late nineteenth century forward as central to what we might call the deterritorialization of geopolitics, he avoids a "globalist" reframing of politics in which the state is hitched to state territoriality in a strict sense and rendered an historical artefact (Walker 2002).

Second, it is important to note that a fully unproblematized account of the state as it once was haunts Schmitt's work. Indeed, perhaps the central guiding thread in Schmitt's research is a conservative lament for a "classical" period of conflict in which warfare was waged between states and territorial sovereigns possessing *jus belli* (the right to war). In *Theory of the Partisan* (2007 [1975]), for example, Schmitt's Cold War-era critique of the "spaceless universalism" of twentieth-century guerrilla warfare (Odysseos 2007) takes place against the backdrop of a once territorially ordered realm of inter-state conflict in which state armies fought state armies and in which peace was possible through territorial compromises between sovereigns. In this sense, we can say that for Schmitt the modern geopolitical imagination was once a valid description of international politics but now no longer holds.

Lastly, we should add that, particularly in his Weimar-era scholarship, Schmitt unambiguously celebrates the virtues of strong and centralized state authority. Schmitt's insights about the "quantitative total state" are instructive. The latter, for example in Schmitt's *Legality and Legitimacy* (2004 [1932]), describes a situation in which the state has been fragmented between competing societal interests and turned into an interventionist, inwards-looking, and ham-fisted disunity of governmental tactics. As I review below, Schmitt understands the quantitative total state as a distinctly liberal problematic. The important thing to note for the moment, however, as Scheuerman (1999, 85–112) argues persuasively, is that Schmitt uses the disorder and divisive qualities of the quantitative total state to defend a reactionary, state-based authoritarianism. Indeed, it is via his critique of the quantitative total state that Schmitt, in *Political Theology* (2005 [1934]), both endorses Bodin's notion of sovereignty as the unfettered power to make laws and exact obedience to them as well as advances his infamous definition of state legitimacy in terms of the sovereign's ability to decide on the nature and scope of extra-legal powers. It goes without saying that this side of Schmitt's work is entirely worrisome given his accommodation to the Nazi regime in the 1930s (Kennedy 2004, 11–37)—although it is Schmitt's focus on the spatial implosion of state geopolitical practice and his claims about the dangers posed by "internal enemies" that is arguably much more alarming in light of his role as the "crown jurist" of the Third Reich (Bendersky 1983). Either way, Schmitt's reinterpretation of geopolitical practice beyond the state-territorial fiction should not be confused as a progressive critique of the state.

In the first section below I examine Schmitt's civilizational cartography of law and violence, as outlined in *Nomos*. I argue that Schmitt's appeal to civilization is problematic because it fixes what Agamben calls the force of ~~law~~ (the force of law without law) to an extra-European world. Second, I review Schmitt's claims about colonial war in *Nomos*. I read colonial war as Schmitt's ambivalence about the "where" of enmity and geopolitical practice, and suggest that the problem of colonial war means moving beyond Schmitt's well-recorded lament for the state–sovereignty–law trifecta of centuries past without mistaking this for what Schmitt describes as the stuff of geopolitics today.

130 *Mathew Coleman*

In a third section I review Schmitt's work on the quantitative total state and liberal geopolitics in order to draw linkages between the "internationalist" arguments in *Nomos* and his earlier "domestic" work on law. At the close of the chapter I investigate briefly the literature linking Schmitt to Morgenthau, as noted above. I conclude that if there is a substantive thread linking the two then Morgenthau's rendering of geopolitics is notwithstanding far less provocative than Schmitt's.

Schmitt's metacartography

I want to start off by querying Schmitt's "global diagram" of the *Jus Publicum Europaeum*, described in *Nomos* as a "distinction between the surface areas of firm land, the soil of European states, i.e. state areas in a specific sense, and the soil of overseas possessions, i.e. colonial lands" (2003 [1950], 184). This distinction grounds Schmitt's claim that between the sixteenth and nineteenth centuries there was a limiting of European wars, and that this achievement was made against a geopolitical free-for-all in Europe's colonial hinterlands—an explanation reminiscent of the ways in which Mackinder spoke, at the beginning of the twentieth century, of geostrategic elbow room for European powers before the post-Columbian "world as closed system" (Kearns 2009, 127–161). How can we explain this simple cartography at the heart of *Nomos*? One might see it as an uncomfortable geopolitical truth. As Rasch (2005, 259) asks in his review of *Nomos*:

> If . . . we are rightly horrified by the distinction between civilized and uncivilized when it is used to describe the relationship of Old Europe and its colonial subjects . . . then why do we persist today in using those very distinctions when combating our latest enemies?

While Rasch's insistence that we not shy away from naming (and problematizing) enmity as a structuring principle in war is laudable, I prefer to see Schmitt's geography of soils as a metacartographical elision of what Agamben calls, in his *The State of Exception* (2005, 36), "the force of ~~law~~" (the force of law without law). By this Agamben means "a field of juridical tensions in which a minimum of being-in-force [of a norm] coincides with a maximum of real application, and vice-versa" (2005, 36).

Agamben argues (2005, 33) that Schmitt's work opens up for discussion "an outside of the law within the law" by virtue of his examination of the state of exception, which we can consider a suspension of the law during an emergency. For Agamben, the state of exception, as more or less a question of fact, is too often considered a short-lived political decision that stands removed from a still-signifying realm of law. Agamben sees the state of exception differently: as a constitutive moment of sovereign power which, because it stands at the threshold between things political and things juridical, means doing away with a standard differentiation between democratic (i.e.

constitutional, juridical) and absolutist (i.e. unconstitutional, extra-juridical) forms of government. But if Schmitt opens the door to such questions he at once closes it, Agamben charges. This is because Schmitt confuses the state of exception with dictatorship, with the result that the exception is shorthand for a fullness of sovereign power in literally the body of the sovereign. For example, Schmitt's concept of constitutional or commissarial dictatorship describes a suspension of the constitution in order to uphold the constitution; here sovereign violence with a minimum of legal backing is a defensive maneuver for a temporarily shelved state of law. Schmitt pursues a similar recuperation in his discussion of unconstitutional or sovereign dictatorship. For Schmitt, sovereign dictatorship describes a sovereign's application of force which if contradicting an existing constitution nonetheless stands at the sharp end of a newly emerging, proto-legal order. In both cases, the gulf between the norm of the law and its concrete application—Agamben's force of law without law—is closed down. In other words, violence is always in law's orbit in Schmitt's work. Schmitt's 1958 afterword to *Legality and Legitimacy* is a good example of this. Defending his then two decades old critique of the bureaucratic-constitutional state as a mode of mass "blind obedience" to a free-floating, discrete, and impersonal legal system, Schmitt writes that his call to presidential decisionism therein "was a despairing attempt to safeguard the last hope of the Weimar constitution, the presidential system, from a form of jurisprudence that refused to pose the question of the friend and enemy of the constitution" (2004 [1932], 95).

As Agamben remarks, the effect of Schmitt's identity of exception and dictatorship is to step back from the abyss of violence with no relation to the law—or, to tether the specter of an ungrounded violence to a juridical anchor. In other words, Schmitt makes violence intelligible in terms of the law, and vice versa. It is this intelligibility of the exception that ultimately describes the break between Agamben and Schmitt. The difference is that for Schmitt the state of exception is largely *topographical*: it is a matter of boundaries between the law and violence (the exception), and the temporary shifting of authority from the legal realm to the realm of violence while the former continues to signify. Accordingly, the law and violence are relative concepts for Schmitt: they are held apart as distinct identities; yet they are made each other's frame of reference by virtue of the sovereign's ability to straddle both and ultimately to change the mix of law and violence in any given situation. In contrast, for Agamben, the state of exception is *topological*. Contra Schmitt's relative account, Agamben suggests that law and violence are relational concepts, i.e. impossible to disentangle at the level of their constitution. This means that the identities law and violence cease to be meaningful as distinct anchor points for each other, and as such that there is no stable sphere of pure law in relation to which a sovereign violence can be justified. For Agamben, then, that the state of exception is topological means a non-signifying void at the heart of sovereign authority that is always and everywhere the force of law without law, or violence with but a nominal relation to law. As Agamben argues, against

Schmitt, the state of exception "is not a dictatorship . . . but a space devoid of law, a zone of anomie in which all legal determinations—and above all the distinction between public and private—are deactivated" (2005, 50–51).

Making violence intelligible in terms of the law is precisely what Schmitt does in *Nomos* via his distinction between European and colonial soils. The New World is "a sphere outside the law and open to the use of force" (2003 [1950], 98); it is indeed there that Schmitt notes that *homo homini lupus* (man is a wolf to man). In contrast, in the Old World, despite its many ferocious wars, we have order and orientation derived from the structured space of civilized European practice: man here is no wolf to man. Indeed, for Schmitt, Europe's violences are what he calls "bracketed," i.e. they are rational, humane, and non-discriminatory; they are familial feuds rather than wars proper; they heed to a shared civilizational imperative, and ultimately stop short of being total war, as in the annihilation of one's enemy and the complete destruction of inter-state order, conceived both politically and legally. In contrast, one cannot count on such assurances or intelligibilities beyond Europe's amity lines, which mark out a "free space" of "zones for agonal tests of strength" as well as a "desolate chaos of mutual destruction" (2003 [1950], 99).

This orientalist trope effectively allows Schmitt to minimize the "ends that do not meet" between law and violence within the body of the *Jus Publicum Europaeum*. Indeed, Schmitt provides a spatial fix of sorts to the problem of law and violence insofar as he exports the possibility of violence without reference to law to an anomic non-European world without. The result is a deeply problematic inside/outside, continental as well as civilizational inscription of European order and non-European violence. In contrast, imagine the impossibility of this mapping given Agamben's provocation to treat law and violence as topological. The result would be to expose the fiction of a Eurocentric, civilizational experience in which violence is bracketed due to an overriding set of norms—or, to map a placeless catastrophe in which law and violence are in nonrelation everywhere, i.e. where violence is violence despite pronouncements about its lawfulness or relation to law.

Colonial war

Schmitt's reading of European order is deeply problematic, but if we do our own bracketing and work with the story that Schmitt gives us regarding the erstwhile *Jus Publicum Europaeum* and the dissolution of its *guerre en forme*, Schmitt's account of a "new" nomos of the Earth is insightful insofar as it signals something out of the ordinary about what war is and where it happens. Schmitt's cartographic elision allows him to articulate, first, the growing importance of civil war—or territorially "disordered" or "entropic" war—to warfare more generally, and second, the centrality of law specifically to civil war. This focus on civil war and law means ultimately that Agamben's critique of Schmitt is specific to a certain strand of argument found within the latter's work. On the one hand, and as noted above, Schmitt keeps law and violence apart insofar as he justifies decisionism and the emergency situation as a constitutional safeguard of sorts. Here there is little possibility of violence without some relation to law, however attenuated. On the other hand, Schmitt is not always and everywhere a topographic thinker of the relation between law and violence. If Schmitt's apology for dictatorship and/or decisionism generally does work by making the violence of the state of exception intelligible in terms of a defensive constitutional maneuver, i.e. a still functioning sphere of law, his discussion of liberal geopolitics from the late nineteenth century forward pursues, I argue, an explicitly topological understanding of law and violence. Indeed, Schmitt posits the indefensibility and inhumanity of conflict in *Nomos*—and also during his Weimar-era writings—precisely on account of a "zone of indifference, where inside and outside [the law] do not exclude each other but rather blur with each other," to use Agamben's phrasing (2005, 23). In terms of the former argument, Schmitt blocks an understanding of violent state practices with only a token relation to the law and offers up a Eurocentric exceptionalism; in terms of the latter argument, and what interests me in particular, Schmitt prompts us to consider a geopolitics of law in which the law is folded into violence, and vice versa, such that violence is simply violence rather than justified by some adjacent or referential sphere of law. In other words, Schmitt's focus on civil war and the centrality of law to civil war suggests the relevance of a geopolitics structured around the force of law without law, i.e. violence in the name of a law that is not a law in the "pure" sense advocated by legal positivists. What I am suggesting then is that Agamben's critique of Schmitt works in terms of Schmitt's defense of authoritarianism but does not quite get at Schmitt's critique of liberal geopolitics. This also suggests that Schmitt is inconsistent when it comes to theorizing the relationship between law and violence in the sense that he moves between competing topographic and topological accounts of their interconnection depending on whether he is defending authoritarianism or critiquing liberal constitutionalism.

The warring qualities of law are front and center in *Nomos*, inasmuch as Schmitt defines nomos as "radical title"—as active appropriation/distribution/production—rather than as a free-floating statute or legislation. This reflects Schmitt's career-long critique of legal positivism and its fixation on law as constituted institutions, as if law is an extra-sociological fact without a basis in conflict or constitutive acts. As Schmitt explains in *Political Theology* (2005 [1934], 33), law is "situational" and as such properly "sociological" before being "juridical"; "*autoritas, no veritas facit legem* [power, not truth, makes law]." In many ways this constitutive formulation of law echoes Michel Foucault's emphasis, in *Society Must be Defended* (2003, 50–51) that "law is born of real battles, victories, massacres and conquests," that "law was born in burning towns and ravaged fields." For both thinkers, law can be considered neither above the sociological fray nor a moment of political domestication. However, there are differences between Schmitt and Foucault on the political constitution of the law. Foucault's object of criticism—the apparently legitimate rights of the sovereign in much of the "Roman history" on princely power, as well as the legal obligation to obey—is exactly the content of Schmitt's lament for the *Jus Publicum Europaeum*. Moreover, unlike Foucault Schmitt strictly periodizes the law-as-politics argument: for Foucault the prompt is philosophical, whereas for Schmitt it is in the conduct of statecraft at the end of the nineteenth century that we arrive specifically at a true intimacy of war to law, and as such at law as a sort of violent decree with no relation to law per se. As sketched out in *Nomos*, and also in *Theory of the Partisan*, the dissolution of the *Jus Publicum Europaeum* enables a first-time war–law hybrid and ushers in the transformation of war from *justus hostis*—where war between states cannot be rationalized as either legitimate or illegitimate—to a form of quasi "just war" where questions of legitimacy and culpability reign supreme. Schmitt sums up this transformation as the mutation of European war into so-called "colonial war."

Schmitt's discussion of the mechanics of colonial war is interesting because it provides good grounds for rethinking what I described at the outset as a dominant state-territorial reading of Schmitt. By colonial war Schmitt means legal war, or making war a legal problem—as well as a closely related shift from what he calls "real" to "absolute" enmity. First, the making of war into a legal object or problem. For Schmitt, the 1884–1885 Congo Conference, which divided up the African continent for European powers and which marked the birth of the "classical" imperial period, brought about the de-differentiation of European and colonial territories as, similarly, legal objects of abstract soil parity. The result was that European states were no longer understood as united by a common spatial, civilizational order but instead as members of an international legal community of states, and as such subject to overarching constraints on inter-state conflict. Second, the shift from real to absolute enmity, which Schmitt understands as part and parcel of the legalization of war. For Schmitt the juridicalization of war, in the wake of the Berlin Conference, marks the birth of a modern discriminatory concept of "just war" in which "the distinction between the justice and injustice of war makes the enemy a felon, who is no longer treated as a *justus hostis*, but as a criminal ... Thus, the action against him is no more war than a police action against a gangster," "social pest control," or "a measure taken against a parasite or trouble-maker" (2003 [1950], 124). For Schmitt this means that unlike with the *Jus Publicum Europaeum*, war will no longer be resolved through territorial gains/losses between equally sovereign "person states." Rather, war will take on a "total" character in which the endgame is the pursuit of the enemy's absolute elimination. And, as Schmitt argues in *Nomos* as well as *Theory of the Partisan*, "total war" ultimately means the replacement of inter-state war with a form of civil war in which the distinctions between war and peace, combatants and non-combatants, military and police powers, domestic and foreign policy, and inter- and intra-state affairs are obliterated. These wars are—in the language used above—territorially disorganized and disorderly, or entropic.

Schmitt's Weimar-era scholarship on liberal geopolitics

Those familiar with Schmitt's earlier scholarship might recognize in the discussion of colonial war in *Nomos* a repetition of his mostly interwar critique of liberalism—which in political geography and international relations has received short shrift in comparison to Schmitt's related musings on the friend–enemy distinction. In that earlier work Schmitt reads liberalism as a double-pronged "internal" and "external" maneuver aimed at dethroning strong state authority. A very brief discussion of Schmitt's assessment of liberalism will clarify his argument as well as help draw linkages to Schmitt's later case against the "new" nomos.

Schmitt's many-fronted salvo against liberalism during the Weimar era takes the form of both philosophical criticism as well as more grounded observations about changes in statecraft. As found in *The Concept of the Political* (in the form of Schmitt's analysis of the League of Nations as a depoliticization of the state and politicization of civil society), *Crisis of Parliamentary Democracy* (in the form of Schmitt's critique of parliamentarism as a politics of conversation rather than decisionism), *Political Theology* (in the form of Schmitt's critique of legal normativism and proceduralism), *The Leviathan in the State Theory of Thomas Hobbes* (in the form of Schmitt's critique of the split in Hobbes between public confession and private faith, leading to a hollowing out of state authority via Spinoza), as well as in Schmitt's *Legality and Legitimacy* (in the form of Schmitt's critique of bureaucracy and the law as value-neutral), among other texts, Schmitt's attack on liberalism centers on two general points. First, Schmitt claims that liberalism misidentifies political legitimacy as a question of legality, or as given by the limitation of sovereign power over the pursuit of private aims through constitutional checks and balances. For Schmitt, whereas legality refers to a neutralizing power of obedience to law, legitimacy is about a more meaningful constituting power that flows from a moment of existential identification. Second, Schmitt argues that liberals misunderstand the problem of political order. As with his critique of political legitimacy, Schmitt finds political order to depend properly not on procedure and law but on existential identification with a sovereign standing quasi-objectively above the people in a defensive as well as offensive posture.

This critique of liberalism is rooted in the tumultuous and violent everyday of the Weimar Republic. In *Political Theology* and *Legality and Legitimacy*, for example, Schmitt argues explicitly that liberal reliance on law and legislative deliberation necessarily founders when faced with civil unrest or emergent civil war. This is so for two reasons. On the one hand, liberalism prohibits the sovereign from acting unilaterally at the edges of the law. On the other hand, its divisibility of power "shifts all political activity onto the plane of conversation" (2005 [1934], 59) and in so doing essentially perpetuates disorder. The outcome, according to Schmitt, is that liberalism—government by jurisprudence and dialogue—impairs the concrete authoritarian power of the sovereign to act decisively in the name of public security. However, Schmitt's critique is not about liberalism's apparent inability to deal with conflict. Schmitt understands an intimate, productive relation between liberalism and public disorder: liberalism's making of the citizen into an autonomous and disconnected subject lends itself to the dissolution of public law and order. But, again, Schmitt does not mean to inventory the unintended consequences of liberal government. His claim, to be clear, is that liberalism intentionally throws the public sphere into crisis: the liberal revolution—its constitutional checks and balances, its double-pronged privatization and pluralization of once publicly held commitments, its free marketization—is a technology "that saps the world of meaning, and establishes the possibility for novel and harsher modes of domination . . . an overly quantitative and abstract force that eradicates the concrete and qualitative particularities of human existence" (McCormick 1997, 18). The result is what Schmitt calls an 'identity of state and society' (1976 [1932], 22), meaning that the state is fractured into various disarticulated arms in response to all number of petty conflicts and disagreements, and as such loses its coherence and transcendence. Schmitt derides this as the development of the quantitative total state—in which "everything is at least potentially political, and in referring to the state it is no longer possible to assert for it a specifically political characteristic" (1976 [1932], 22).

For Schmitt, the internal turmoil and fragmentation bred by liberalism and perpetuated by the resulting quantitative total state had extremely important geostrategic implications. For example, in *The Concept of the Political* Schmitt in no uncertain terms argues that interwar liberal reform efforts transformed the "total peace within the state and its territory" (1976 [1932], 46), which Schmitt imagined as "territorially enclosed," "impenetrable to aliens" as well as "internally peaceful" (1976 [1932], 47), into an unbordered and undefended territorial unit, fractured by cultural and economic warfare, which by definition put at risk the public's collective ability to decide "in a concrete situation upon the enemy and . . . to fight" (1976 [1932], 45). In other words, despite its pronouncements about peace, liberalism left economically reformed and constitutionalized states literally open to annihilation by others less pacifically inclined, or better, in thrall to those who engineered the liberalization project. Schmitt was particularly concerned about the League of Nations project that sought to hitch state decision-making abilities to international law. As Ulmen (1987) has argued, for Schmitt, the geostrategic legal reforms introduced at the domestic/national scale were part and parcel of a much broader "legal world revolution" characterized by the surrender of individual state authority to centralized global legislatures, as well as to attendant planetary trade networks under specifically American tutelage (see also Schmitt 1987).

This is an abbreviated account of Schmitt's account of liberalism as a geopolitical technology. But we can nonetheless see in it how and why Schmittian commentators have called liberalism a secreted "politics of getting rid of politics" (Dyzenhaus 1998) or an "invisibilised" politics (Rasch 2004). Indeed, Schmitt's point is that liberalism masquerades as legal reform when it is actually a form of unmediated warfare or violence propelled by the friend–enemy distinction, or what was called above the force of law without law; liberalism is for Schmitt about the covert advancement of enemies against the (now dismantled) state under the thin guise of law. We might further note that this is an explicitly geographical critique that Schmitt offers us. On the one hand, liberalism deterritorializes statist modes of identification and affiliation; in their place Schmitt finds private conflict, i.e. conflict related to the economy, culture, religion, etc. On the other hand, as a counterpart to this ultimately centrifugal development, liberalism is centripetal in the sense that it makes newly hollowed-out states into culpable/responsible spaces through overarching and interventionist international organizations and global legal covenants. This development is summed up very concisely in Schmitt's later *Nomos*: "Territorial sovereignty was transformed into an empty space for socio-economic processes. The external territorial form with its linear boundaries was [legally] guaranteed, but not its substance, i.e. not the social and economic content of territorial integrity" (2003 [1950], 252).

For Schmitt, then, liberalism is a global and essentially deterritorializing set of geopolitical technologies that operate precisely by folding domestic and international spaces into one interlinked field of geopolitical practice. Liberal reform works from the inside out as well as from the outside in, via newly repurposed arms of the state. The upshot is that public policy and foreign policy arenas and programs are rendered interchangeable. Or we could say it more strongly, based on Schmitt's characterization of the new nomos of the Earth as the "spacelessness of a general universalism" (2003 [1950], 230): that the domestic and the foreign, and public policy and foreign policy, become indistinguishable components of a single field of geopolitical contest written by the all-pervasive friend–enemy antagonism (in the guise of liberal law).

Common to both Schmitt's Weimar-era writing as well as his explanation of colonial war in *Nomos* is, then, an effort to think enmity beyond state-territorial forms. Indeed, what we find in Schmitt via liberal geopolitics as well as later via the problem of colonial war is certainly not the sequestering of geopolitical practice and enmity to an anarchic realm of inter-state power politics. Rather we have in both accounts something like a deterritorializing geography of enmity defined by a tension—between states as juridical objects of intervention and correction by global bodies, and states as no longer existentially signifying cultural and economic spaces. This may strike political geographers as commonsensical but such a reading, as I noted at the outset, cuts across the grain of much Schmittian scholarship that reads enmity as a strictly state-territorial phenomenon—or, alternately, reads Schmitt's ontology of enmity as an ontology of states. This has the unfortunate effect of blunting Schmitt's provocative understanding of enmity through the lens of nomos, i.e. as constituting power, as spatialized struggles of appropriation, distribution, and production. In other words, while the political, i.e. the friend–enemy antagonism, is certainly an unavoidable part of Schmitt's work, this antagonism can take place anywhere; it is the animating moment behind *so many* appropriations, distributions, and productions.

Carl Schmitt and Hans Morgenthau

By way of conclusion, and in order to draw a contrast with Schmitt's deterritorializing interpretation of twentieth-century geopolitics, I want to look briefly at Schmitt's influence in international relations, and specifically at Schmitt's intellectual influence on Hans J. Morgenthau, commonly understood as the originator of international relations in the US post-World War Two (Honig 1996; Koskenniemi 2000; Frei 2001). Based on Morgenthau's own recollections (1978) of his first and only encounter with Schmitt before his republication of *The Concept of the Political* in 1932 (the original was published in 1921), in which apparently significant changes to the original text were taken unacknowledged from Morgenthau's work, this research emphasizes in general the "hidden dialogue" between Schmitt and Morgenthau as well as their shared approach to international politics (Scheuerman 1999, 225–251). And indeed there are some striking similarities between the two thinkers, despite Morgenthau's Cold War assessment of Schmitt as "the most evil man alive" (1978, 68). Scheuerman (2010), for instance, argues that Schmitt and Morgenthau shared a critique of liberalism, nostalgia for the *Jus Publicum Europaeum*, as well as an appreciation of politics through the lens of conflict—even if Schmitt was a "realist of war" and Morgenthau a "realist of peace" (cf. Brown 2010). But far more important are the differences. Indeed, it is with Morgenthau that we might isolate something of an ontology of state enmity in ways that narrow what counts as geopolitics and where we might find it to the world of foreign policy practice and representation.

Morgenthau's *realpolitik* description of inter-state politics—even if celebrated as an American Cold War outlook founded and nurtured at the University of Chicago (where Morgenthau was based between 1943 and 1971)—owed much to Schmitt's earlier, Weimar-era problematization of liberalism as well as his development of the friend–enemy concept. Morgenthau's Schmittian debts are generally obscured in his post-World War Two work, but are front and center in his first major post-doctoral publication which, in print in France just one year after Schmitt's reworked edition of *The Concept of the Political*, is titled *La Notion du 'Politique'* (1933). If frequently misplaced as part of his official bibliography, this short text is nonetheless an important part of Morgenthau's progression as a scholar.

In *La Notion du 'Politique'*, Morgenthau deals at length with the application of law to international conflicts as well as explicitly with Schmitt's analysis of politics in terms of the friend–enemy distinction. The basis of Morgenthau's argument is that the international is not exclusively a sphere of legal dispute and resolution (*différends juridiques*) as much as it is an uneven landscape of varying degrees of political, or interest-based, conflicts (*les différends politiques*) that in the end can at best be but partially and temporarily mediated by law. As such, Morgenthau blunts Schmitt's harsh critique of liberalism in that he leaves the door open to the possibility of workable judicial dispute mechanisms between states. But Morgenthau nonetheless shares Schmitt's critique of legal positivism as "pure law". Indeed, for Morgenthau, by approaching the international as an abstract realm of judicial possibility, i.e. as governable through legal institutions and agreements, liberal positivists generally underestimate international politics (*la politique interétatique*) in sociological terms. To address this oversight, Morgenthau puts forth what would come to be known as a realist conception of politics that he refers to in this early work as simply a material theory of political life (*la notion matérielle du politique*).

Morgenthau's realist conception of the political in *La Notion du "Politique"* centers on four central propositions. First, as a dry run for his later theorizing of the inter-national, post-World War Two, Morgenthau claims that sociological reality is defined by the will to power (*la volonté de puissance*) or a threefold maintenance of power (*maintenir la puissance*), augmentation of power (*augmenter la puissance*), and affirmation of power (*manifester la puissance*). Second, based on a detailed discussion of Schmitt's friend–enemy distinction, Morgenthau (1933: 44–61) claims that sociological reality is at root about the formation of antagonistic social groups: political friends (*amis politiques*) and political enemies (*ennemis politiques*). This is not a straightforward appropriation of Schmitt, however. Morgenthau criticizes Schmitt's definition of the friend–enemy distinction as metaphysical guesswork. Moreover, he is critical of Schmitt's rendering of politics as somehow apart from religion, morality, aesthetics, the economy, culture, etc. on account of the supposed primacy and autonomy of the friend–enemy distinction. Indeed, Morgenthau's qualification of "friend" and "enemy" through use of the adjective "political," i.e. *amis politiques* and *ennemis politiques*, is meant to, first, ground the political in material interests and goals and, second, emphasize politics as inter-group competition that develops into particularly acute forms of sociological and psychological enmity, and that finds its roots in any number of economic, religious, moral, etc. spheres of life. In other words, Morgenthau criticizes Schmitt's existential definition of the political at the same time as affirming Schmitt's focus on politics as enmity. Third, Morgenthau claims that sociological reality is about the life of states, inter-state relations, and the exercise of foreign policy. Indeed, Morgenthau observes that although the formation of *amis politiques* and *ennemis politiques* may be relevant at both domestic and international scales, the domestic (*l'étatique*) and the international (*l'interétatique, l'étrangère*) are nonetheless two different domains of the political, with the latter of much greater significance than the former. Lastly, Morgenthau argues for an inherent disconnect between the status quo posture of law and the dynamic quality of international sociological reality. He argues that there will always be non-adjudicable oppositional claims between states—particularly intense expressions of the friend–enemy distinction—that will challenge static legal orders to the point that they become unworkable.

La Notion du 'Politique' is remarkable in contrast to the ways in which Schmitt is absent in name when some of the themes therein are reworked in Morgenthau's major post-war publications—such as his definitive *Politics Among Nations*

(1948), which is still in print and a staple in realist international relations classrooms. In the latter text, for example, Morgenthau criticizes exclusively legalistic approaches to world politics on account of their inability to comprehend power politics, and advances a notion of politics as inimical "power drives" between competing constituencies. However, if a roughly Schmitt-inspired characterization of politics as particularly intense forms of "friend" and "enemy" conflict that escape legal mitigation remains a fundamental feature of his post-war writing, Morgenthau diverges significantly from Schmitt in terms of the spatiality of the political.

The crucial difference between Morgenthau and Schmitt is what Morgenthau discusses as the "essence of national power" (1948, 73–121). In order to explain how it is that foreign policy is relatively coherent, Morgenthau starts off by noting that power qua "the power of man [sic] over the minds and actions of other men [sic]," is a problem "to be found whenever human beings live in social contact with each other," i.e. at all scales of social organization. However, Morgenthau notes that due to "rules of conduct and institutional devices for controlling individual power drives" the latter are curtailed at the domestic scale, where only very few individuals exercise power without limitation. Morgenthau specifically names "law, ethics, and mores, innumerable social institutions and arrangements, such as competitive examinations, election contests, sports, social clubs, and fraternal organizations" as responsible for this pacification of the political such that, as he puts it, "most people are unable to satisfy their desire for power within the national community" (1948, 73–75). This leads, Morgenthau suggests, to an aggregation of frustrated power drives and their direction outwards to the world of inter-state relations. This "compensatory identification" with power as foreign policy-based projections of force is a mainly middle- and working-class phenomenon:

> Not being able to find full satisfaction of their desire for power within the national boundaries, the people project those unsatisfied aspirations onto the international scene. There they find vicarious satisfaction in identification with the power drives of the nation ... It is as though we all, not as individuals but collectively, as members of the same nation, owned and controlled so magnificent a power. The power which our representatives wield on the international scene becomes our own, and the frustrations which we experience within the national community are compensated for by the vicarious enjoyment of the power of the nation.
>
> (Morgenthau 1948: 74)

This marks a significant geographical departure from Schmitt. Whereas the Weimar conservative suggests geopolitics as a deterritorializing phenomenon encompassing both the domestic and the international, for Morgenthau the domestic sphere can be meaningfully held apart from the international. Morgenthau does concede that the struggle for power occurs at both scales, but he also argues for a depreciation of the political within state borders on account of social cohesion, hierarchical political and legal organization, technological development, cultural uniformity as well as the threat of external invasion (in the US case Morgenthau notes explicitly the problem of geographical interconnectedness as well as the threats posed by communism and atomic warfare as modes of global insecurity that work to channel domestic conflict outwards). What we have, then, in Morgenthau, is the sequestering of a realm of geopolitics on the outside from a realm of politics on the inside such that "the domestic political order is . . . more stable and to a lesser degree subject to violent change than is the international order" (1948, 21).

The point then is that if Morgenthau's often unacknowledged intellectual debtor is Schmitt, it does not follow that Morgenthau's specifically state-territorial rendering of world politics follows from Schmitt. Nor does it follow that Schmitt is easily the forerunner of political realism qua state-territorial enmities. Indeed, Schmitt and Morgenthau pursued very different geographical imaginations of twentieth-century geopolitics. The crucial difference is that for Morgenthau law and violence can be fixed to state and inter-state spaces, respectively; in Schmitt we have something altogether much more geographically convoluted.

References

Agamben, G. (2005) *The State of Exception*, Chicago: University of Chicago Press.
Agnew, J. A. (2003) *Geopolitics: Revisioning World Politics*, London: Routledge.
Agnew, J. A. and S. Corbridge (1995) *Mastering Space*, London: Routledge.
Ashley, R. K. (1987) "The Geopolitics of Geopolitical Space: Toward a Critical Social Theory of International Politics," *Alternatives* 12: 403–434.
Bendersky, J. W. (1983) *Carl Schmitt: Theorist for the Reich*, Princeton, NJ: Princeton University Press.
Brown, C. (2010) "The Twilight of International Morality? Hans J Morgenthau and Carl Schmitt on the End of the *Jus Publicum Europaeum*" in *Realism Reconsidered*, M. C. Williams (Ed.), Oxford: Oxford University Press, 62–92.
Burchard, C. (2006) "Interlinking the Domestic with the International: Carl Schmitt on Democracy and International Relations," *Leiden Journal of International Law* 19: 9–40.
Campbell, D. (1992) *Writing Security: United States Foreign Policy and the Politics of Identity*, Minneapolis: University of Minnesota Press.
Chandler, D. (2008) "The Revival of Carl Schmitt in International Relations: The Last Refuge of Critical Theorists," *Millennium* 37: 27–48.
Dyzenhaus, D. (1998) *Law as Politics*, Durham, NC: Duke University Press.
Foucault, M. (2003) *Society Must be Defended*, New York: Picador.
Frei, C. (2001) *Hans J. Morgenthau – An Intellectual Biography*, Baton Rouge: Louisiana State University Press.
Honig, J. W. (1996) "Totalitarianism and Realism: Hans Morgenthau's German Years" in *The Roots of Realism*, B. Frankel (Ed.), London: Frank Cass, 283–313.
Huysmans, J. (1998) "Security! What Do You Mean? From Concept to Thick Signifier," *European Journal of International Relations* 4: 226–255.

Kearns, G. (2009) *Geopolitics and Empire*, Oxford: Oxford University Press.
Kennedy, E. (2004) *Constitutional Failure: Carl Schmitt in Weimar*, Durham, NC: Duke University Press.
Koskenniemi, M. (2000) "Carl Schmitt, Hans Morgenthau, and the Image of Law in International Relations" in *The Role of Law in International Politics*, M. Byers (Ed.), Oxford: Oxford University Press, 17–34.
McCormick, J. P. (1997) *Carl Schmitt's Critique of Liberalism*, Cambridge: Cambridge University Press.
Morgenthau, H. J. (1933) *La Notion du "Politique" et la Théorie des Différends Internationaux*, Paris: Recueil Sirey.
Morgenthau, H. J. (1948) *Politics Among Nations*, New York: Alfred A. Knopf.
Morgenthau, H. J. (1978) "An Intellectual Autobiography," *Society* 15: 63–68.
Odysseos, L. (2002) "Dangerous Ontologies: The Ethos of Survival and Ethical Theorizing in International Relations," *Review of International Studies* 28: 403–418.
Odysseos, L. (2007) "Crossing the Line? Carl Schmitt and the 'Spaceless Universalism' of Cosmopolitanism in the War on Terror" in *International Political Thought of Carl Schmitt*, L. Odysseos and F. Petito (Eds.), London: Routledge, 124–143.
Odysseos, L. and F. Petito (2008) "Vagaries of Interpretation: A Rejoinder to David Chandler's Reductionist Reading of Carl Schmitt," *Millennium – Journal of International Studies* 37: 463–475.
Rasch, W. (2004) *Sovereignty and its Discontents*, Portland, OR: Birbeck Law Press.
Rasch, W. (2005) "Lines in the Sand: Enmity as a Structuring Principle," *The South Atlantic Quarterly* 104: 253–262.
Scheuerman, W. E. (1999) *Carl Schmitt: The End of Law*, Lanham, MD: Rowman & Littlefield.
Scheuerman, W. E. (2010) "Carl Schmitt and Hans Morgenthau: Realism and Beyond" in *Realism Reconsidered*, M. C. Williams (Ed.) Oxford: Oxford University Press, 62–92.
Schmitt, C. (1976 [1932]) *The Concept of the Political*, New Brunswick, NJ: Rutgers University Press.
Schmitt, C. (1985 [1923]) *The Crisis of Parliamentary Democracy*, Cambridge: MIT Press.
Schmitt, C. (1987) The Legal World Revolution, *Telos* 72: 73–89.
Schmitt, C. (2003 [1950]) *The Nomos of the Earth*, New York: Telos Press.
Schmitt, C. (2004 [1932]) *Legality and Legitimacy*, Durham, NC: Duke University Press.
Schmitt, C. (2005 [1934]) *Political Theology*, Chicago: Chicago University Press.
Schmitt, C. (2007 [1975]) *Theory of the Partisan*, New York: Telos Press.
Schmitt, C. (2008 [1938]) *The Leviathan in the State Theory of Thomas Hobbes*, Westport, CT: Greenwood Press.
Ulmen, G. L. (1987) "American Imperialism and International Law: Carl Schmitt on the US in World Affairs," *Telos* 72: 43–71.
Walker, R. B. J. (2002) "After the Future: Enclosures, Connections, Politics" in *Reframing the International*, R. Falk, L. E. J. Ruiz, and R. B. J. Walker (Eds.), London: Routledge, 3–25.
Williams, M. (2005) *The Realist Tradition and the Limits of International Relations*, Cambridge: Cambridge University Press.
Wolin, R. (1992) "Carl Schmitt, the Conservative Revolutionary Habitus and the Aesthetics of Horror," *Political Theory* 20: 424–447.
Zarmanian, T. (2006) "Carl Schmitt and the Problem of Legal Order: From Domestic to International," *Leiden Journal of International Law* 19: 41–67.

9 A new nomos of post-nomos?

Multipolarity, space, and constituent power

Rory Rowan

Introduction

Jan-Werner Müller has noted that for Schmitt 'clarity is an appropriate distribution of light and shadow' (Müller 2003: 9).[1] This seems an appropriate description of Schmitt's own work that appears to offer startlingly sharp conceptual insights but leaves them cloaked in ambiguity, concealing as much as they reveal. As Müller argues, Schmitt's writing 'freely mixes supposedly crystal-clear definitions and distinctions with images, metaphors and myths' (Müller 2003: 9). If this rich aesthetic and analytic brew is partly what makes Schmitt's work so engaging it is also arguably the source of its dangerously seductive power. *The* Nomos *of the Earth* is not an exception to this rule but rather amplifies it, taking Schmitt's thought into extremely suggestive if uncertain territories in a tangled thicket of philosophical analysis, political polemic and mythological allusion that seems at once mired in apologist inconsistency and pregnant with world-historical insight. Despite entering murkier waters the book follows an odyssey familiar from his earlier work, where order, cast adrift on an unsteady ontological sea, seeks to return to the firm land of authentic legitimacy. If such a 'ground' for order was sought in a 'groundless' sovereign decisionism in *Political Theology* or antagonistic relations with the enemy in *The Concept of the Political*, in *The* Nomos *of the Earth* it is identified all too literally with the geopolitical ordering of space. A geopolitical vision that firmly fixes order to space may be appealing at a time when the 'markers of certainty' are dissolving but we should steadfastly steer clear of this reactionary siren call. But it is precisely Schmitt's vision of a multipolar global order fixed to a number of 'Big Spaces' that a number of critical leftist thinkers have adopted from his book. Chantal Mouffe, Fabio Petito and Danilo Zolo are among those that have directly appropriated Schmitt's geopolitical thought in appealing for a new multipolar order of the Earth. I argue that these calls for a new multipolar world order replicate the worst of Schmitt's understanding of the relationship between space and political order and adopt his regressive understanding of political pluralism contained within a set of large-scale spatial units. These multipolar arguments are, however, to my mind, based upon a limited reading of *The* Nomos *of the Earth* that ignores the radical conception of constituent power Schmitt locates at the heart of his book. I argue that by returning to a fundamental tension between constituent and constituted powers at the conceptual core of Schmitt's philosophical project it is possible to develop an alternative reading that locates constituent power in relation to the production of space. Such a reading allows the relationship between space and politics to be rearticulated in radically democratic terms that resist the rocky lure of 'Big Space' geopolitics.

Multipolarity

The Nomos *of the Earth* contains a critique of liberal ideology, 'humanitarian wars' and U.S. imperialism that is undeniably powerful. Schmitt's analysis of how the 'pseudo-universalism' of liberal international law and the doctrine of 'humanitarian war' have been cynically employed by powerful states to pursue their particular interests in the name of all seems particularly prescient today in the wake of the 'war on terror'. It is no surprise then that Schmitt's book has attracted the attention of many leftist and post-structuralist critics opposed to U.S. power and keen to highlight liberalism's blindspots. I do not wish to dwell on these arguments here as they have been extensively covered elsewhere; rather I want to focus on a group of theorists who have drawn on a different, and arguably more controversial, aspect of *The* Nomos *of the Earth*, namely Schmitt's appeal for a new multipolar world order to counteract liberal hegemony and U.S. domination. Chantal Mouffe, Fabio Petito, Danilo Zolo and others have moved far beyond other readers of Schmitt's work in using his theory of nomos to make normative suggestions for a multipolar world order based around a number of *Großraum*, or 'Great Spaces'.[2] In my view this appropriation of Schmitt's thought is fraught with danger as it serves to replicate the reactionary geopolitical imaginaries embedded in *The* Nomos *of the Earth*. On the other hand these multipolar readings miss what is, for me, the most important aspect of the book, and that which gives it relevance for a radical democratic politics: the relationship Schmitt sketches between constituent power and the production of space.

Closely following Schmitt's analysis in *The* Nomos *of the Earth*, Mouffe, Petito and Zolo argue that the hegemony of liberal ideology, market economics and the power of the United States have produced an unjust, unstable and violent unipolar world (dis)order. While this assemblage of forces is certainly hegemonic it is very much open to question whether or not it can be understood to constitute anything as coherent as a unipolar world order. Although the United States undoubtedly remains the sole global superpower, with a disproportionate share of the Earth's wealth, fire-power and technological expertise, this position of strength is constrained by the perilous indebtedness of the economy, the limitations of a conventional force in fighting so-called 'Twenty First Century wars' (state building and asymmetric guerrilla conflict in multiple theatres) and the relative power of other states, notably of course rising powers and creditor nations such as China.[3] However, bracketing these concerns and acknowledging that resistance to the hegemony of liberal ideology, market economics and U.S. power are noble goals, my apprehension lies with the proposed alternatives to a unipolar world. The fundamental problems arise in Mouffe's, Petito's and Zolo's arguments when they conflate the question of an alternative to unipolarity with Schmitt's search for a new nomos of the Earth. The alternative to unipolarity is obviously to be found in some form of pluralism but by remaining within Schmitt's framework the numerous possibilities for understanding pluralism are reduced to the necessity of a multipolar world order conceived in the framework of traditional 'Big Space' geopolitics. As Chantal Mouffe states

> I will argue, using Schmitt's insights, that it is the fact that we are now living in a unipolar world, with the unchallenged hegemony of the United States, which is at the origin of our current predicament, and that the *only way out* lies in the establishment of a multipolar world order.
> (Mouffe 2007: 147, emphasis added)

Zolo insists, equally emphatically, that there are 'no alternatives' to Schmitt's 'macro-spatial perspective' if the unipolar nihilism of U.S. domination is to be avoided (Zolo 2007: 162). In my view, such 'macro-spatial' multipolarity posits an understanding of the relationship between space and politics that puts severe limits on how pluralism can be conceived and thus on the political possibilities considered open. These thinkers impose a false choice between unipolarity and multipolarity that overlooks the political potential in the complex realities of the contemporary world and condemns it to the logic of the lesser evil. Although Mouffe, Petito and Zolo aim to produce a less violent and unjust global order, by taking up Schmitt's call for a new multipolar nomos of the Earth they replicate his reactionary geopolitical imaginary and propose an extremely regressive understanding of the politics of space.

It is important to unpack the nature of the relationship between space and politics implicit in these multipolar visions in order to understand the limits it puts on pluralism, what motivates this approach and how an alternative understanding, open to radically democratic articulation, may be developed. It must be noted first however that differences exist in how Mouffe, Petito and Zolo conceive of the pluralism their proposed multipolar nomos would allow. Petito and Zolo both appeal to distinct 'cultural and religious' identities and argue that multipolarity would lay the grounds for a 'dialogue of civilizations', although Petito notably puts this phrase inside inverted commas, apparently aware that 'civilization' is a questionably essentializing category (Petito 2007: 180; Zolo 2007: 162). It appears that both authors understand these 'cultural' or 'civilizational' identities they appeal to as more-or-less located in particular regional spaces. Zolo is certainly the cruder thinker of the two and makes direct reference to Latin America, China and a united Europe as viable future 'poles' to offset the United States, presumably another pole (Zolo 2007: 162). Indeed, Zolo's call for a Europe that would rediscover its 'cultural identity – its Mediterranean roots' and open a dialogue with 'Arab-Islamic cultures in general' seems to rely on a particularly regressive understanding of politics rooted in culture and culture rooted in regional geography (Zolo 2007: 162). Chantal Mouffe makes a more sophisticated argument built upon a relational conception of subjectivity and an understanding of hegemonic dynamics. The blind spot of Mouffe's argument is that while the 'institution of society' is exactly that over which hegemonic struggle allegedly takes place the fundamental institutional framework (and presumably the geopolitical framework) must not be questioned. 'A democratic society' she argues 'can not treat those who put its basic institutions into question as legitimate adversaries' (Mouffe 2005: 120). She attempts to shore up her position against this obvious contradiction with reference to the necessity of a more fundamental 'shared symbolic space' that would set limits upon legitimate hegemonic struggles (Mouffe 2005: 121). In this logic however a 'shared symbolic space' is constituted precisely to the extent that basic institutions are not questioned. Thus, although Mouffe's conception of political subjectivity is considerably more nuanced than that advanced by Petito and Zolo there are certain institutions, principles and presumably political subject positions that must remain fixed. Further, she approvingly quotes Massimo Cacciari to the effect that a multipolar world order means 'working towards the establishment of an international system of law based on the idea of regional poles and cultural identities federated among themselves in the recognition of full autonomy', which threatens to see her position lapse into the same neo-regional essentialism as Zolo's (Mouffe 2005: 117). Thus, while the internal ordering of the poles may rely on the hegemonic (and supposedly democratic) dynamics between a plurality of smaller powers or rest directly upon stable, unified 'cultural; and religious' identities in all three cases a 'macro-spatial' world order is proposed that maps separate political subjectivities to distinct regional and 'cultural' poles.

This regressive conception of the relationship between space, politics and subjectivity underlying the plea Mouffe, Petito and Zolo make for a multipolar world order directly adopts the concept of *Großraum* from *The* Nomos *of the Earth*. Schmitt conceived of the *Großraum*, literally 'Big Space', as a new large-scale unit of territorial sovereignty that could replace the state, which in his view had been eclipsed in the twentieth century by a pseudo-universalist law of nations and the imperial power of the United States. For Schmitt, the Monroe Doctrine, where the United States unilaterally awarded itself ultimate sovereignty over the entire 'Western Hemisphere' including of course its neighbours, offered an effective model for *Großraum* power. Schmitt proposed that in the wake of Cold War bipolarity, whose quick collapse he predicted, a new nomos of the Earth characterized by the balance of powers between a number of *Großraum* would provide the most stable form of global order. By appealing for 'a neo-regionalist revival of the idea of *Großraum*', as Zolo refers to it, Schmitt's multipolar readers place themselves squarely within the reactionary geopolitical tradition Schmitt himself was clearly a part of (Zolo 2007: 160). Such 'Big Space' geopolitics, or '*gross*politics' as Mika Luoma-aho refers to it, has a long and controversial history running from Halford Mackinder (whom Schmitt cites as an influence in the introduction to his book) and Friedrich Ratzel through Haushofer and the English School of International Relations up to contemporary figures such as Samuel Huntington and Alexander Dugin (Luoma-aho 2007: 36).[4] The multipolar visions that Schmitt's recent readers have advanced display the classic symptoms of such 'Big Space' thought: the adoption of a pseudo-objective 'God's eye view' and a conception of political identities as fixed within spatial containers.[5] What would motivate critical left thinkers to align themselves with such a regressive geopolitical imaginary? The answer lies in their understanding of Schmitt's concept of the political and its consequences for the relationship between difference, order and space.

For Schmitt's multipolar readers the concept of the political, or the ineradicable nature of the friend–enemy distinction, means that disorder and war are inescapable facts that arise directly from ontological difference. Or rather, they develop a realism that filters this ontology of difference through Schmitt's 'political anthropology' that understands man to be a 'dangerous and dynamic being' (Schmitt 1996: 61).[6] These authors take it as an axiom that because there is difference war is inescapable. As William Rasch bluntly states, 'there is a war' (Rasch 2005: 253). As war, in this view, arises out of the very ontological conditions of human existence and cannot be overcome the best that can be hoped for is to manage it. As Fabio Petito argues, the aim of a pluralistic world order 'is not to create a paradise on earth but rather and in the first instance to prevent the earth from becoming a hell' (Petito 2007: 180). Following Schmitt, his multipolar readers argue that war cannot be limited in a unipolar world order because it fails to provide the grounds for making distinctions between war and peace and between combatants and non-combatants. When the world is dominated by a single superpower, so the argument goes, war and peace dissolve into a global regime of militarized policing that the dominant power leads in its own interests. It is argued that multipolarity on the other hand provides the basis for distinguishing a number of powers and a number of discreet spaces, thus making the distinction between combatants and non-combatants and between zones of war and peace possible. The presence of a number of relatively equal powers would allow the collective to recognize the existence of clearly distinct conditions of war and peace, thus to contain the former. Further, a balance of powers would put a check on the war-making capacity of any one power and allow rules to be agreed for waging war and establishing peace. The central argument in this multipolar logic is that while ontological difference makes war inevitable, giving expression to this difference in a pluralistic order is the only way in which it can be contained. Or in other words, because difference is an ontological condition the political is ineradicable, but recognizing this antagonistic difference allows the effects of the political to be limited, or diffused.

In my view this subtle shift from recognizing the political to diffusing it, is central to the appeal Mouffe, Petito and Zolo make for a multipolar nomos of the Earth. While these authors argue that a pluralist geopolitics allows a 'return of the political', to use Chantal Mouffe's phrase, their implicit aim is to domesticate the political in a depoliticized order (Mouffe 1993). Indeed, limiting the effects of the political and containing war are presented as the principal achievement and goal of the proposed neo-regional *Großraum* order. Mouffe, Petito and Zolo are arguably therefore not so much theorists of the political as they are theorists of depoliticization. The point I want to emphasize here, however, is that this depoliticization is understood to be grounded directly in the multipolar geopolitics these thinkers draw from Schmitt's work. It is in fact the multipolar geopolitical arrangements themselves that are understood to facilitate the construction of a depoliticized order. Multipolarity, for these neo-Schmittians, is fundamentally a means with which to limit the scope of the political by grounding a necessarily limited pluralism. While the explicit argument made on behalf of a multipolar nomos of the Earth is that it would allow the expression of difference and political antagonisms, the implicit argument is that these differences would be fixed to a certain set of spaces. Hence, by fixing certain subjects to certain spaces the play of difference is brought to a close and the expression of the political restrained. Depoliticization and the limitation of pluralism are embedded in the geopolitical imaginary of multipolarity because it assumes only a limited set of macro-political units can exist. In my view the principal aim of a *Großraum* order then is not the recognition of pluralism but rather its limitation. The pluralism of the proposed multipolar nomos is evidently based upon a fixed set of differences rather than openness to difference as such, upon difference qua difference, despite the analogy Mouffe draws between the Schmittian political and Heideggerian ontology (Mouffe 2005: 8–9).

Thus, the multipolar nomos of the Earth, that Mouffe, Petito and Zolo call for, appeals to space to establish a depoliticized order by affixing a set of 'proper' political subjects to a set number of 'proper places'. Although it can be objected that none of these authors are so crass as to actually suggest a set number of poles, and that the question of 'how many' is therefore left open, this would miss the point. The problem is not simply one of number, or how much pluralism is the right amount, but arises from the very logic of affixing a 'proper' subject to its 'proper' place, regardless of number. This logic of 'the proper' relies, in my view, on a certain understanding of space that must be interrogated as it has serious consequences, first, for how the relationship between space and politics is understood, and second, for the political possibilities deemed available as a result. The division of the globe into a series of *Großraum* provides a *Katechon*, to use Schmitt's term: a framework that serves to *restrain* the destructive power of the political.[7] As such the division of space is understood to *ground* order. As a *ground* for order space is conceived to be stable, objective and hence extra-political. Indeed, it is precisely the extra-political status attributed to space that allows it to act as a depoliticizing tool of order: it provides an objectively given platform on which distinctions can be drawn and to which differences can be fixed without the risk that the ground itself will change. Affixing subjects to a divided space, that is itself understood to be extra-political, closes new possibilities for rearticulating the division of space, and hence the 'proper' number and nature of legitimate political subjects. Thus, by grounding order in an extra-political space the very grounds of order are depoliticized and put beyond question. In my view, these fantasies of multipolar order resonate strongly with the politics of the proper variously described as the 'state of the situation' by Alain Badiou, the 'diagram of order' by Giles Deleuze and the 'distribution of the sensible' by Jacques Ranciere. In all cases it is the very impropriety of the political, the fact that the emergence of the political disrupts the established arrangement of proper subjects and places, that leads dominant forces to try to contain it.[8]

This conception of the relationship between space and politics implicit in the multipolar geopolitics proposed by Mouffe, Petito and Zolo has grave consequences for how politics can be imagined. A multipolar '*gross*politics' necessarily understands political power to be held in the hands of the few. Not only does this *Großraum* model fix legitimate political subjectivity to a set number of 'Big Spaces' but their internal political relations are left open to question, which intensifies the inherent problems of such a regime of the 'proper'. It seems necessary that the relations internal to *Großraum* would be arranged hierarchically if such wide areas were to coalesce into unified political subjects. Such unity could be secured in a number of ways, including through representative institutional processes, hegemonic ideologies (read also 'cultural' identifications), repressive force or some combination of these. Chantal Mouffe goes furthest to address this issue, arguing that each regional pole would be organized internally through hegemonic processes. However, despite the theoretical position that Mouffe has long staked between hegemony and democracy there is nothing necessarily democratic about the nature of hegemony, even if we concede that politics as such, and hence democracy, must operate within hegemonic dynamics. The appeal these thinkers make to cultural, religious and 'civilizational' categories make a democratic pluralism aware of its contingent hegemonic grounds, such as Mouffe imagines, highly unlikely. Thus, any stability such multipolarity may bring would come at the price of alienating many people from power and at worst rely on massive repressive violence.

Such fantasies of multipolar order put both the nature of political subjects and the fundamental organization of political space beyond question. Needless to say such an arrangement severally limits the way in which a pluralist politics can be conceived and makes the radicalization of democracy unlikely in the extreme. The power of people to constitute themselves as 'the people' and to have control over the spatial organization of their lives and communities would be vastly diminished within a system where subjectivities are locked into a set of 'macro-spatial' units. There is however nothing necessary about limiting pluralism within a multipolar geopolitics despite the insistence of Mouffe and Zolo that it is the 'only' alternative available to stave off unipolar annihilation. It is possible to conceive an alternate understanding of the relationship between space and politics, one where the constitution of political subjectivities and the organization of political space lies in the hands of self-constituting communities. Indeed, I believe that there are resources for building such a radically democratic politics of space to be found in *The* Nomos *of the Earth*. To my mind, Mouffe, Petito and Zolo all propose an extremely limited and 'one-sided' reading of *The* Nomos *of the Earth* that emphasizes space as a ground for constituted order. Doubtless this geopolitical imaginary plays a powerful role in Schmitt's *Großraum* theory, which is clearly aimed at establishing a new foundation for authority in the wake of the state, but this is only one element of a more complex relationship Schmitt traces between space and politics that is open to different readings.[9] In my understanding, the relationship between constituent power and space is central to *The* Nomos *of the Earth*. Not only does Schmitt claim that all normative institutional order is grounded in a fundamental spatial order but, further, argues that this spatial order is founded upon exceptional acts of constituent power he refers to as 'land appropriations'. This central element of Schmitt's argument is largely ignored by his multipolar readers who emphasize instead the institutional value of multipolarity and the role of space in grounding order. By excluding the relationship between constituent power and space these theorists miss what I understand to be the potential for extracting a radically democratic theory of spatial politics from Schmitt's work. I believe that by returning to the '*geo*philosophical' core of *The* Nomos *of the Earth* it is possible to mine an alternative understanding of the relationship between space and politics within Schmitt's thought (Kervégan 1999: 64). However, in order to fully appreciate this '*geo*philosophical' core it is necessary to return to the essential conceptual structure of Schmitt's work as a whole and locate the tension between constituent and constituted powers running through it.

Founding rupture

In my reading *The* Nomos *of the Earth* plays out a fundamental tension that structures Schmitt's thought as a whole. Throughout his work Schmitt repeatedly presents indeterminacy as an ontological condition on the one hand and, on the other, ceaselessly attempts to bring this indeterminacy to a close by grounding order in some form of authentic legitimacy. Schmitt's entire body of work can be characterized, in my view, by this tension between events that open a field of ontological indeterminacy, revealing the absence of firm grounds for order, and the contingent attempts to establish such grounds. However, this oscillation should not be understood to indicate a contradiction or weakness in Schmitt's thought. It, on the contrary, constitutes the productive nucleus of his work and animates all his core concepts; the groundless sovereign decision that establishes order, the existential threat of the enemy that unifies the body politic, the baseless 'existential total decision' of the people on the constitution, the acts of land appropriation that establish a new nomos of the Earth. As Thalin Zarmanian has argued:

A new nomos of post-nomos? 151

> Schmitt's theoretical move was [...] to assume plurality, conflict and chaos as ontologically given and take charge of what Carlo Galli calls the 'tragedy of modernity' – the fact that on the one hand after the collapse of a Medieval Christian unity an ultimate and uncontested foundation for legitimacy is no longer possible and that, on the other hand, such legitimacy is unavoidable for any order.
>
> (Zarmanian 2006: 48)

In Galli's view, the absence of firm theological grounds for order meant, for Schmitt, that 'modern politics is marked by an original, tragical, nondialectical contradiction between the necessity of constructing order, and the impossibility of founding it firmly' (Galli 2000: 1606). For Schmitt, 'no individual subject, no political institution, no rational thinking, can ever overcome this fact: In the beginning there was disorder, and disorder is insuperable' (Galli 2000: 1606). Thus, due to the ontological primacy accorded to indeterminacy the core of Schmitt's thought is not simply an authoritarian insistence on order, as is often claimed, but rather a necessary tension between order and disorder. To take one well-known example, in *Political Theology* Schmitt argues sovereignty is a 'borderline concept', inhabiting a liminal position, both inside and outside the law (Schmitt 2005: 5). As Giorgio Agamben has famously argued, for Schmitt, 'the paradox of sovereignty consists of the fact that the sovereign is, at the same time, outside and inside, the juridical order' (Agamben 1998: 15). Therefore, the core category of sovereignty occupies neither a sphere of order nor a sphere of disorder in Schmitt's work but rather marks the tension between them.

It is crucial to recognize that this tension does not simply structure the relation between two sets of opposed ideas in Schmitt's work but rather constitutes the internal structure of each of his core concepts. Thus, in the example of sovereignty, the norms of an institutional order and the exceptional act of decision that found that order are contained within a single concept. While sovereignty is introduced as an additional term in the set it does not play the role of a 'higher third' that dialectically resolves the tension. Rather, the concept indicates that norms and exceptions, institutional order and foundational acts, order and disorder, exist in a permanent tension that resists all dialectical resolution. Thus, as Mika Ojakangas argues, Schmitt's core concepts maintain at once an 'insurmountable gap' and an 'insurmountable togetherness' between two binary terms (Ojakangas 2006: 209–10). Ojakangas locates this conceptual structure, which he refers to as the 'founding rupture', at the very heart of Schmitt's thought.[10] He employs this paradoxical formulation to argue that for Schmitt the norms of a constituted order and the exceptional acts of constituent power that found that order are always coterminous.[11] In this analysis, order is founded in an event that simultaneously introduces a rupture into the existing state of affairs or, recalling Galli, the act that produces order arises from disorder. Indeed, in Ojakangas' reading, it is because indeterminacy, or disorder, is an ontological condition that the freedom to act, the very possibility of change, exists. The primacy of disorder ensures that all order is contingent. Moreover, any order remains open to contestation as all new attempts to found order arise in the process whereby existing foundations are undone. 'For Schmitt', Ojakangas notes, 'it is the moment of the opening up of order which constitutes order' (Ojakangas 2006: 203). Or as Sergei Prozorov has argued, the 'founding rupture' at the centre of Schmitt's thought indicates that, 'all foundation is transgressive, but transgression is still foundational' (Prozorov 2007: 89).

If Schmitt's core concepts operate by maintaining a tension between order and disorder, between exceptional events and normative order, located in the structure of the 'founding rupture' they also always indicate a mediating act. In all instances a foundational act takes place within a field of ontological indeterminacy that contingently institutes order. For example: the sovereign decision on the legal order, the people's 'total existential decision' on the constitution, the recognition of the enemy threat, acts of land appropriation that found a nomic order. Further, for each of these acts to take place a subject is presupposed with the capacity to act. This active subject is of course most often associated with the figure of the sovereign in Schmitt's work. This can largely be attributed to the fact that *Political Theology* and *The Concept of the Political*, where most emphasis falls on sovereignty, have been the principal texts through which Schmitt has become known to English-speaking readers, no doubt reaffirmed by the influence of Agamben's reading on the recent reception of Schmitt's thought. A powerful and undeniable 'metaphysics of the subject' certainly accompanies Schmitt's conception of the sovereign, which is identified as the indivisible source of authority with the exclusive power over decision. However, this does not exhaust the subjective forms that Schmitt associated with founding acts of rupture, or the subjective mediation between order and disorder. In his recently translated *Constitutional Theory* Schmitt casts the tension that animates his work, between order and disorder, norm and exception, in the classical terms of constituent and constituted powers that he draws from Sieyes (Kalyvas 1999: 96).[12] It is useful to view Schmitt's thought more broadly through the lens of this distinction as it makes clear the central role that acts of constituent power have in the formation of order in all his core concepts. For example, as Andreas Kalyvas has argued, the sovereign can be understood precisely 'as the one that carries the constituent power of a society' although sovereignty is not the only form this constituent power can take (Kalyvas 1999: 110). Further, the distinction between constituent power and constituted power allows forms of political subjectivity to be conceived that are untainted by the authoritarian conception of sovereignty in Schmitt's work and more obviously open to radically democratic articulation. While any formulation of constituent power may suppose a subject defined by a minimum of unity in order for action to be conceivable it need not therefore be burdened with the metaphysical demands of indivisibility associated with Schmitt's sovereign subject. It is not inconceivable that those elements of Schmitt's work that emphasize constituent

A new nomos of post-nomos? 153

power can be located in the modern tradition of republican thought running from Sieyes and Rousseau up to thinkers such as Fanon and Negri.

In my view, recent multipolar readings of *The* Nomos *of the Earth* have emphasized the institutional moment in the concept of nomos, the moment of constituted power, but paid scant attention to the acts of constituent power Schmitt argued found spatial order. This partial reading has unsurprisingly led Mouffe, Petito and Zolo to stress the role of space in grounding multipolar order and ignore the possibilities of a more democratic articulation of the relationship between space and politics. It is therefore important to re-examine the concept of nomos in light of the 'founding rupture' that maintains a tension between constituent power and constituted power in Schmitt's work. By contextualizing the concept of nomos within the fundamental structures operating in Schmitt's thought, I believe, it is possible to develop an alternative reading of *The* Nomos *of the Earth* in strict opposition to the Schmittian model of multipolar geopolitics.

Nomos

Just as is the case with Schmitt's other core concepts, nomos has the structure of a 'founding rupture' and contains a tension between ontological indeterminacy and contingent attempts to establish order, a moment of constituent power and a moment of constituted power. Therefore, in my understanding, Schmitt proposes two sides to the concept of nomos, only one of which his multipolar readers have drawn upon. First, Schmitt conceives of nomos as the institutional relation between order and space. It refers to both, the necessary relation between political order and space as such, or between 'order and orientation' as Schmitt writes, and to the institution of spatial order that all subsequent forms of order are based upon (Schmitt 2003 [1950]: 42). Nomos, Schmitt states, 'constitutes the original spatial order, the source of all further concrete order and all further law' (Schmitt 2003 [1950]: 48). Thus, for Schmitt every order is fundamentally grounded in a certain arrangement of space. Second, however, nomos indicates the foundational acts of land appropriation that establish such a relationship between order and space and make order possible. For order to be grounded in space it first has to be made available through appropriation and division. As Schmitt writes, 'not only logically, but also historically, land-appropriation precedes the order that follows from it' (Schmitt 2003 [1950]: 48). Nomos is therefore a concept that has clearly distinguishable elements: foundational acts and institutional structures, moments of constituent and constituted power. It is a concept that indicates both a form of *institutional order* grounded in space and *foundational acts* that produce new forms of spatial order. It is this latter understanding of nomos, as a foundational act of constituent power, which recent multipolar readings of Schmitt have failed to address.

For Schmitt, therefore, any nomos of the Earth owes its foundations and its norms to the exceptional act of land appropriation. In *The* Nomos *of the Earth* acts of land appropriation simultaneously introduce a rupture into the existing state of affairs and lay the foundation for a new spatial order. This has important consequences for how the relationships between space and order and space and constituent power are conceived. First, it must be remembered that although the 'founding rupture' indicates the simultaneity of rupture and foundation and maintains the tension between order and disorder, disorder retains ontological precedence even after order is established. As Carlo Galli notes: 'In Schmitt's thought, disorder, the lack of substance, is the inescapable origin of modern political order, which goes on marking it even once the order is established' (Galli 2000: 39). Thus, *nomic* order, rather than having escaped disorder in the very act of its foundation, remains structurally dependent on *anomie*. The foundational status of *anomie* is structural rather than simply originary and thus, rather than being overcome by *nomic* order, it persists in the role of 'constitutive outside'. This constitutive disorder is clear in Schmitt's description of the *Jus Publicum Europaeum*, which he considered to be the first global nomos of the Earth that structured European international law from the sixteenth to nineteenth centuries. Continental Europe, in Schmitt's analysis, could be established as a space of order only insofar as it remained structurally dependent on spaces of *anomie* in the 'New World' and the high seas. One obvious outcome of this relationship between order and disorder is that all *nomic* order remains contingent and vulnerable to collapse due to its foundations in *anomie*.[13] Thus, in failing to address the fact that nomos has a necessary relation not only to order but also to disorder Schmitt's multipolar readers build their argument on shaky foundations and leave their proposed order exposed to the very instability it seeks to contain. The fundamental point I want to stress, however, is that, in Schmitt's thought, the foundations of spatial order are politically produced through subjective acts of constitutive power, land appropriations. This transforms not only the way in which the relationship between space and order is understood, but the concept of space itself.

If in Schmitt's analysis all *nomic* orders rely upon exceptional acts of land appropriation then it can be said that the relationship between space and order is articulated through political action. There is thus nothing inherent to space that allows it to act as a ground for order, rather, space and order are simultaneously produced through subjective political acts, through acts of ground*ing* that fuse space and order in a new relation. Thus, I believe that it is possible to draw the conclusion from *The* Nomos *of the Earth* that space is fundamentally politically produced. Space is not a stable, objectively given and extra-political foundation to which order can be fixed but a malleable tool political subjects use in dynamic processes of ordering. Further, precisely because it is politically produced, space is a plural, contingent and contested category that can be understood in a plurality of different ways by different subjects. Thus, there is no necessary relation between a proper subject and a proper place but rather various contested relations between space and order that are contingently produced through the actions of a variety of political subjects. The understanding of space as a stable, objective and extra-political ground for order implicit within the multipolar geopolitics of Schmitt's recent

A new nomos of post-nomos? 155

readers is thus challenged by the much more complex relationship Schmitt charts between space and constituent power in the foundational acts of land appropriation.

Drawing on the understanding of space as politically produced through acts of constitutive power I believe it is possible to dredge out the beginnings of a radically democratic theory of spatial politics from *The* Nomos *of the Earth*. This was evidently not Schmitt's intention and I am in no way suggesting that such a programme is present within the book. But by approaching the question of pluralism and space in relation to Schmitt's radical conception of constituent power it may be possible to build an alternative understanding of spatial politics that would resist the reactionary *Großraum* fantasies he and his multipolar readers conjure. It is certainly plausible to develop an understanding of a democratic political subject using its constitutive power to order its own political space and resist the imposition of a 'macro-spatial' order from above that would affix proper political subjects to proper spaces. Of course, this would involve developing a democratic concept of constituent power unfixed from the 'metaphysics of the subject' associated with Schmitt's sovereign and an understanding of foundational *nomic* acts of spatial production that does not remain trapped within the territorial logic of land appropriation. Even if Schmitt's work cannot furnish us with the means to develop it, and in fact must largely be rejected, it is worth salvaging the importance of this relation from his thought. Indeed, thinking constituent power in relation to the production of space can help theorize the vital connections between radical democracy and space being forged in many instances across the globe today.

Glasgow

One of the failings of the 'macro-spatial' perspective adopted by Mouffe, Petito and Zolo is that it overlooks many of the innovations already at work in specific situated struggles where the relationship between space and politics is being reformulated against dominant geopolitical imaginaries. There are many instances where people are producing forms of radically democratic space through acts of constituent power in resistance to the dominant models of political power and spatial ordering. To take just one example of how a radically democratic politics of space is being enacted in a specific politically contested site it is possible to look to the council estates of Glasgow. As was reported in the *Guardian* newspaper in June 2008 the residents of the Kingsway estate in Glasgow mounted a successful campaign of resistance against the deportation of asylum seekers in the community (*The Guardian*, 'Land of No Return', Friday, 13 June 2008).[14] Hundreds of asylum seekers from places such as Iraq, Afghanistan, Algeria and Uganda had been housed in the six fifteen-storey tower blocks of the Kingsway estate pending decisions on their applications for asylum in the United Kingdom. Despite their pariah status in the right-wing media, local residents claimed that the asylum seekers were warmly accepted and the new families quickly became part of the community.

It was therefore a shock to residents when immigration authorities began to make regular dawn raids to seize asylum seekers for deportation. In response residents began dawn patrols to monitor for and frustrate the deportation raids. When the immigration authorities appeared a phone system would go into operation warning asylum seekers and enabling them to escape. In the *Guardian* report residents recounted how their knowledge of the estate's architecture allowed them to evade the authorities and turn their homes into collective escape routes.[15] Large crowds would appear to frustrate the authorities' attempts to arrest the asylum seekers, allowing them to melt into the crowd leaving the deportation vans empty. This campaign ran for two years until forced removals were stopped altogether at Kingsway.

Although this case may seem rather insignificant when contrasted to the '*gross*politics' of *The Nomos of the Earth* I believe we can see in this community's actions a radically democratic politics of space in practice. The residents of the Kingsway estate in Glasgow introduced a rupture into the established spatial order through an act of constitutive power that transformed these blocks of flats into a space of asylum, of equality and hospitality. Their actions contested the state's understanding of the relationship between space and political order whereby the asylum seekers have no 'proper place' in the community. Through a subjective commitment to equality the residents transformed their flats into a space that contested an order that affixes proper subjects to proper spaces and instituted an order in line with their own conception of themselves and the space of their community. The space of the estate may not have physically changed but its relationship to political order was transformed through the residents' subjective commitment and collective action. The flats became a space for the community to reclaim its constituent power and in so doing to reconstitute understandings of who makes up that community and the spatial politics of their daily lives.[16]

I do not think it is an exaggeration to say that this is a case, like so many, which sees a democratic rearticulation of the relationship between 'the people' and space. Crucially, although the subjective claim to be 'the people' is made from within, and in relation to, a specific space it is made on the basis of equality. Further, equality is not understood in terms either of homogeneity or the allotting of 'proper places' but in an open relation to difference and hospitality. Thus, here we see a universalist politics staged within the context, and on the basis of a particular site. While cases such as this too often remain isolated instances that fail to build strategic links with similar groups in other sites and at other scales this is by no means a rule and indeed the anti-deportation activities of the Kingsway community are part of a broader national movement involving a variety of groups across the UK.[17] The point to draw from this example, however, is that forms of radically democratic spatial politics are already at work in a number of contexts that fuse democratic acts of constituent power and the production of space. It is possible, in my view, to, perhaps surprisingly, extract from Schmitt's work some core conceptual building blocks with which to understand the nature and significance of such cases.

Conclusion

In conclusion, I argue that the 'Big Space' geopolitics that Schmitt's multipolar readers adopt from *The* Nomos *of the Earth* is based upon a deeply reactionary understanding of space as a 'ground' for order. In my view, while these thinkers claim to support a pluralist politics based upon a 'return of the political' they in fact seek to establish a depoliticizing order that limits pluralism by affixing a set number of 'proper' subjectivities to a set number of 'proper' spaces. However, I argue that their arguments are based upon a selective reading of *The* Nomos *of the Earth* that ignores the fundamental tensions that run through Schmitt's thought. In my view Schmitt's core concepts are structured around a 'founding rupture' that maintains a tension between constituent and constituted powers. Schmitt's multipolar readers emphasize the relationship between space and institutional order but neglect the equally important relationship between space and constituent power that Schmitt places at the heart of *The* Nomos *of the Earth* in the figure of land appropriation. I argue that it is possible to develop from this relationship between constituent power and space a radically democratic theory of spatial politics in opposition to the regressive geopolitical imaginaries embedded in calls for a new nomos of the Earth, including Schmitt's. Further, this theory of a democratic politics of space can be used as an analytic tool with which to understand a range of existing political movements, such as the campaign to resist the deportation of asylum seekers in Glasgow's Kingsway estate, and develop their logic into wider movements.

There are of course several thorny challenges in attempting to utilize Schmitt's thought in this way. Mitchell Dean has rightly warned of the dangers of adopting the 'mythopoetics' at work in Schmitt's thought and a reading that emphasizes acts of constituent power may be just as vulnerable to the dangers inherent in Schmitt's work as one that draws on the normative institutional elements of his thought (Dean 2007: 242). Further, it is possible that in celebrating the return of a forceful active political subject this reading falls prey to what Simon Critchley has referred to, in relation to Alain Badiou's work, as the 'heroism of the decision', a tragic and potentially violent rush to decision (Critchley 2008: 48). More specifically, attempting to construct an understanding of the democratic production of space in terms of land appropriation is evidently extremely problematic and risks falling into a territorial logic of conquest. It would certainly be necessary to distinguish the democratic production of space from land appropriation as Schmitt understood it, i.e. in relation to a violent imperial history of which he remained scandalously proud. There is also the difficulty of how a democratic understanding of subjectivity with an ethico-political commitment to equality can be developed on the basis of a Schmittian concept of the political fundamentally structured around antagonistic difference. There are however resources for imaging such a universalist politics that remains tied to a logic of antagonism in the work of Badiou, Ernesto Laclau, Ranciere and others, and indeed opening paths to examining these conceptions of the political in relation to the politics of space is arguably one of the valuable contributions Schmitt's thought can make to radically democratic thought. Lastly there is of course the problem of scale and how a viable democratic politics can be developed across a variety of sites and scales to face very real challenges that do require a functional global politics. There is not space available to address these pressing concerns here but I believe it would be foolhardy to reject outright the idea that *The* Nomos *of the Earth* can provide valuable conceptual tools for a radically democratic politics of space. Doubtless, Schmitt's late masterwork must be approached with extreme caution and kept at a critical distance but it is not to my mind totally 'beyond salvage' (Hallward 2005). The question is not whether *The* Nomos *of the Earth* should be accepted or rejected as a whole but rather which concepts can be utilized and how. I believe it is possible to employ Schmitt's insights into the disorderly foundations of spatial order in constituent power to build a radically democratic politics of space starting from this, thankfully, groundless ground. Yet, while some of Schmitt's recent multipolar readers urge us 'to go "beyond Schmitt" in search for a new nomos of the earth' I think we must not only go 'beyond Schmitt' but also beyond the search for a new nomos (Odysseos and Petito 2007: 15). When the fantasy of a final order grounded in space is rendered obsolete that which Schmitt feared becomes an opportunity: 'That is the new *nomos* of the earth; no more *nomos*' (Schmitt, quoted in Berman and Marder 2009: 3).

Notes

1 Schmitt is, as Müller notes, quoting Goethe, who in turn was quoting Hamann.
2 See also, the typically more tentative, William Rasch (2004, 2005) and many of the articles collected in Odysseos and Petito (2007a).
3 Giovanni Arrighi (2005), Peter Gowan (1999), David Harvey (2005) and Immanuel Wallenstein (2003), among others, have convincingly argued that the long-term stability of US hegemony lies on shaky economic, ideological and military grounds despite their apparent global supremacy.
4 For more on the influence of Schmitt on Dugin see Ingram (2001) and Dugin's Eurasian Party website: http://evrazia.info. The website also contains accounts of the Moscow lectures of Alain de Benoist, a key thinker of the French *Nouvelle droit*, which promotes a similarly Schmitt-inspired vision of multipolar world order. His work has also recently appeared alongside Mouffe, Petito, and Zolo (de Benoist 2007).
5 See for example Gearóid Ó Tuathail's seminal *Critical Geopolitics* (1996).
6 As Chantal Mouffe likewise argues, politics must be based upon 'an anthropology which acknowledges the ambivalent character of human sociability' (Mouffe 2005: 3).
7 The term *Katechon*, which Schmitt famously takes from Saint Paul's Second Letter to the Thessalonians, plays a crucial role in his eschatological philosophy of history and its relationship to his geopolitics deserves a rigorous analysis. Although the space is not available here see Hooker (2009) for a discussion of this term in relation to Schmitt's thought on international order. Agamben (2005), Koskenniemi (2001), Meier (1995), Ojakangas (2006), Prozorov (2009) and Taubes (2004) all offer insights into the role of the *Katechon* in Schmitt's philosophy more broadly but largely leave its relation to spatial concepts underdeveloped.

A new nomos of post-nomos?   159

8 See, for example, Badiou (2005), Deleuze (1988) and Ranciere (1999).
9 Another extremely reactionary aspect of Schmitt's geopolitical imaginary, which I unfortunately do not have space to address here, is the vulgar distinction between 'elemental' land and sea spaces that he repeatedly emphasized in *Land and Sea* (1942), *The Nomos of the Earth* (1950) and *The Theory of the Partisan* (1963). In his recent *The Enemy of All* (2009) Daniel Heller-Roazen carries out a fascinating deconstruction of this land–sea distinction that not only troubles the divide but shows how faltering Schmitt appeared to be in positing it.
10 Ojakangas makes a powerful case for identifying the 'metaphysical core' of Schmitt's thought in the resistance to conceptions of absolute immanence. The 'founding rupture' is crucial for Schmitt, in Ojakangas' view, because it marks the impossibility of an absolutely self-immanent order that could rid itself of an 'outside', and as such it ensures a necessary openness to contingency.
11 The structure of the 'founding rupture' will be familiar to many from Agamben's analysis of the 'paradox of sovereignty' in *Homo Sacer* noted above. The benefit of Ojakangas' formulation, however, is that it abstracts this conceptual structure from Agamben's focus on sovereignty avoiding his somewhat hyperbolic conflation of sovereignty with the violent production of bare life and allowing it a wider application. The very formalism of the 'founding rupture' structure allows the relations between constituted order and constituent power to be re-imagined in a variety of ways. To my mind it allows us to imagine forms of democratic subjectivity analogous to sovereignty seemingly foreclosed by Agamben's biopolitical binary between violent sovereignty and bare life.
12 In his recent book, *Democracy and the Politics of the Extraordinary* (2008), Kalyvas provides a powerful account of the use of Schmitt's *Constitutional Theory* for democratic thought. Its importance in the future reception of Schmitt's work will likely increase in the coming years as familiarity grows with Schmitt's core constitutional text.
13 The structural role of disorder in spatial order also begs the question of where such a space of disorder may be in the 'Big Space' carve-up Schmitt and his multipolar readers suggest. Unless some form of new amity line can be drawn between those inside and those outside order, which although seemingly plausible given the growing disparities of wealth and political power emerging between the world's powerful nations and its poorest citizens, seems unlikely to provide stability and is clearly not mappable against distinct 'Big Spaces'. In fact the complexity of the spatial make-up of overlapping sites, scales and mobile networks of power in today's globe makes such multipolar partitioning a mere fantasy. If no space of disorder is located 'outside' order, so to speak, then it will simply appear 'inside' order, thus threatening the structural stability of the proposed multipolar order from the inside, and dissolving the distinction between order and disorder. This would, of course, replicate the 'spaceless' conditions that Schmitt and his multipolar readers accuse unipolarity of creating. If all the borders between outside and inside are *internal* to a global *Großraum* order then the coherence of Schmitt's 'anti-immanentism' is threatened and his rejection of universalism becomes complicated. There is not sufficient space to develop this here but it points to the inconsistencies within and between Schmitt's critiques of immanence and universalism and his reduction of both categories to renditions of 'the same'. It is precisely through developing more nuanced understandings of these categories that it may be possible to set Schmitt's work in dialogue with a radically democratic politics that goes beyond his polemical reductionism.
14 For further information on the resistance to deportation raids in the Kingsway estate and the broader campaign in Glasgow see the articles available on the websites of organizations such as Positive Action in Housing (PAIH), Glasgow

Anti-Racism Organization, Unity Centre Glasgow and the National Coalition for Anti-Deportation Campaigns (NCADC) and on the website of the Glasgow published free magazine *Variant*. I would like to thank David Featherstone for pointing me to some of these sources.

15 As one resident interviewed by the *Guardian* said, 'There's more than one way of getting out of the flats – there's two staircases and two lifts, so you could play games if you knew how. If we were a thorn in their flesh, then good' ('Land of No Return', Friday, 13 June 2008). One of the most fascinating aspects of this campaign is the way in which the architecture of the estate itself was utilized as a counter-apparatus to state control. The residents' deep knowledge of their everyday spatial and architectural reality allowed them to evade capture even within the extremely limited space of a block of flats. This *becoming fortress* of the Kingsway estate, to use a slightly tongue-in-cheek Deleuzian formulation, points to the crucial dynamic whereby a group claims a specific site's autonomy from authority while simultaneously opening it to forms of political community beyond the identitarian regime of the 'proper' that the state's asylum policy relies upon.

16 Many statements of the residents and activists point to how the local communities involved in the anti-deportation struggle define themselves in relation to the asylum seekers and against the immigration authorities. As one of the activists at Kingsway said of the asylum seekers, 'they are the local communities' (see the PAIH website: http://paihnews.wordpress.com/category/against-dawn-raids/page/22/). This is a sentiment echoed by another activist involved in the wider protests against deportation raids in Glasgow: 'They *all* belong to Glasgow' (see the *Variant* website: www.variant.org.uk/25texts/brand25.html). This is not of course to say that the asylum seekers have been welcomed by all members of the community and that there are no racial tensions among the residents. The articles above report these divisions but the scale of the protests, sometimes involving hundreds of people, points to the widespread sense that the majority of residents define the asylum seekers as a key part of their community. The protestors reject the government's attempts to forcibly remove asylum seekers not simply only on the grounds that it is an inhumane procedure but because they understand the asylum seekers to belong there as part of the community.

17 For a luminous analysis of the spatial aspects of how activist groups such as these can develop strategically into forceful political movements see David Featherstone's *Resistance, Space and Political Identities* (2008).

References

Agamben, G. (1998) *Homo Sacer*, Stanford, CA: Stanford University Press.
Agamben, G. (2005) *The Time That Remains: A Commentary on the Letter to the Romans*, Stanford, CA: Stanford University Press.
Arrighi, G. (2005) 'Hegemony unravelling 2', *New Left Review*, 33: 83–116.
Badiou, A. (2005) *Being and Event*, London: Continuum.
Berman, R.A. and Marder, M. (eds) (2009) 'Introduction', *Telos*, 147: 3–13.
Critchley, S. (2008) *Infinitely Demanding: Ethics of Commitment, Politics of Resistance*, London: Verso.
Dean, M. (2007) '*Nomos*: word and myth', in Odysseos, L. and Petito, F. (eds) *The International Political Thought of Carl Schmitt: Terror, Liberal War and the Crisis of Global Order*, London: Routledge.
de Benoist, A. (2007) 'Global terrorism and the state of permanent exception: the significance of Carl Schmitt's thought today', Odysseos, L. and Petito, F. (eds)

The International Political Thought of Carl Schmitt: Terror, Liberal War and the Crisis of Global Order, London: Routledge.

Deleuze, G. (1988) *Foucault*, Minneapolis: University of Minnesota Press.

Featherstone, D. (2008) *Resistance, Space and Political Identities*, Chichester, West Sussex: Wiley-Blackwell.

Galli, C. (2000) 'The critic of liberalism: Carl Schmitt's antiliberalism; its theoretical and historical sources and its philosophical and political meaning', *Cardozo Law Review*, 21: 1597–617.

Gowan, P. (1999) *The Global Gamble: Washington's Faustian Bid for Global Dominance*, London: Verso.

Grant, H. and Stevenson, R. (2008) 'Land of no return' in *The Guardian* (Friday 13 June).

Hallward, P. (2005) 'Beyond salvage', *South Atlantic Quarterly*, 104, 2: 237–44.

Harvey, D. (2005) *The New Imperialism*, Oxford: Oxford University Press.

Heller-Roazen, D. (2009) *The Enemy of All: Piracy & The Law of Nations*, New York: Zone Books.

Hooker, W. (2009) *Carl Schmitt's International Thought: Order and Orientation*, Cambridge: Cambridge University Press.

Ingram, A. (2001) 'Alexander Dugin: geopolitics and neo-fascism in post-Soviet Russia', *Political Geography*, 20, 8: 1029–51.

Kalyvas, A. (1999) 'Who's afraid of Carl Schmitt?' *Philosophy Social Criticism*, 25: 87–111.

Kalyvas, A. (2008) *Democracy and the Politics of the Extraordinary: Max Weber, Carl Schmitt, and Hannah Arendt*, Cambridge: Cambridge University Press.

Kervégan, J.-F. (1999) 'Carl Schmitt and "world unity"' in Mouffe, C. (ed) *The Challenge of Carl Schmitt*, London: Verso.

Koskenniemi, M. (2001) *The Gentle Civilizer of Nations: The Rise and Fall of International Law, 1870–1960*, Cambridge: Cambridge University Press.

Luoma-aho, M. (2007) 'Geopolitics and *gross*politics: from Carl Schmitt to E.H. Carr and James Burnham', in Odysseos, L. and Petito, F. (eds) *The International Political Thought of Carl Schmitt: Terror, Liberal War and the Crisis of Global Order*, London: Routledge.

Meier, H. (1995) *The Lesson of Carl Schmitt: Four Chapters on the Distinction Between Political Theology and Political Philosophy*, Chicago: Chicago University Press.

Mouffe, C. (1993) *The Return of the Political*, London: Verso.

Mouffe, C. (ed) (1999) *The Challenge of Carl Schmitt*, London: Verso.

Mouffe, C. (2005) *On the Political*, London: Routledge.

Mouffe, C. (2007) 'Carl Schmitt's warning on the dangers of a unipolar world', in Odysseos, L. and Petito, F. (eds) *The International Political Thought of Carl Schmitt: Terror, Liberal War and the Crisis of Global Order*, London: Routledge.

Müller, J.W. (2003) *A Dangerous Mind: Carl Schmitt in Post-War European Thought*, New Haven, CT: Yale University Press.

Ó Tuathail, G. (1996) *Critical Geopolitics: The Politics of Writing Global Space*, London: Routledge.

Odysseos, L. and Petito, F. (2007) 'Introduction: the international political thought of Carl Schmitt', in Odysseos, L. and Petito, F. (eds) *The International Political Thought of Carl Schmitt: Terror, Liberal War and the Crisis of Global Order*, London: Routledge.

Ojakangas, M. (2006) *Concrete Life: Carl Schmitt and the Political Thought of Late Modernity*, Bern: Peter Lang.
Petito, P. (2007) 'Against world unity: Carl Schmitt and the western-centric and liberal global order', in Odysseos, L. and Petito, F. (eds) *The International Political Thought of Carl Schmitt: Terror, Liberal War and the Crisis of Global Order*, London: Routledge.
Prozorov, S. (2007) *Foucault, Freedom, Sovereignty*, Aldershot and Burlington, VT: Ashgate.
Prozorov, S. (2009) 'The appropriation of abandonment: Giorgio Agamben on the state of nature and the political', *Continental Philosophy Review*, 42, 3: 327–53.
Rasch, W. (2004) *Sovereignty & Its Discontents*, London: Birkbeck University Press.
Rasch, W. (2005) 'Lines in the sand: enmity as a structuring principle', *South Atlantic Quarterly*, 104, 2: 253–62.
Ranciere, J. (1999) *Disagreement: Politics & Philosophy*, Minneapolis: University of Minnesota Press.
Schmitt, C. (1996) *The Concept of the Political*, Chicago: University of Chicago Press.
Schmitt, C. (2001) *Land and Sea*, Corvallis, OR: Plutarch Press.
Schmitt, C. (2003 [1950]) *The Nomos of the Earth*, New York: Telos Press.
Schmitt, C. (2005) *Political Theology: Four Chapters on the Concept of Sovereignty*, Chicago: University of Chicago Press.
Schmitt, C. (2007) *The Theory of the Partisan*, New York: Telos Press.
Schmitt, C. (2008) *Constitutional Theory*, Durham, NC: Duke University Press.
Taubes, J. (2004) *The Political Theology of Paul*, Stanford, CA: Stanford University Press.
Wallenstein, I. (2003) *The Decline of American Power: The US in a Chaotic World*, New York: New Press.
Zarmanian, T. (2006) 'Carl Schmitt and the problem of legal order: from domestic to international', *Leiden Journal of International Law*, 19, 1: 41–67.
Zolo, D. (2007) 'The re-emerging notion of empire and the influence of Carl Schmitt's thought', in Odysseos, L. and Petito, F. (eds) *The International Political Thought of Carl Schmitt: Terror, Liberal War and the Crisis of Global Order*, London: Routledge.

10 Carl Schmitt and the question of spatial ontology

Claudio Minca

> Every ontological judgment derives from the land.
> (Schmitt 2003 [1950], 45)

Schmitt rediscovered

Andrea Cavalletti's recent book, *La città biopolitica*, opens with Schmitt's well-known dictum: 'there are no political ideas without a spatial referent, just as there are no spaces (or spatial principles) without corresponding political ideas' (2005: 1).[1] The choice is not by chance, for Cavalletti's work provides what is perhaps the most perceptive investigation of the relationship between Schmitt and the question of spatial ontology. The very notion of a 'spatial ontology' is highly controversial. While some authors accept the existence of a distinct Schmittian spatial ontology and subject it to critical analysis (see, for example, Rowan's contribution to this volume), others seem to deny its very possibility (see Elden 2010; also his chapter in this book). This chapter will not engage directly with that controversy, but will rather reflect on how 'ontological' the question of space was for Schmitt, and on how this understanding of space can be of relevance for geography.

What appears to be a foundational claim on 'the political' – that is, the co-implication between space and politics – is, for Cavalletti, a necessary starting point for any speculation on Schmitt's spatial thinking, as well as for any reflection on the nature of biopolitics. For the Italian philosopher, this claim not only discloses a sort of spatial reasoning in political philosophy, but also reveals the eminently political–philosophical tone of any theory that declaredly adopts a predetermined and neutral concept of space (Cavalletti 2005: 1). But this is nothing new to most geographers.

Nonetheless, this formula, which represents a crucial passage in Schmitt's theoretical edifice, does not simply mark its recognition of the importance of spatial categories that are linked to political qualifications. Since this connotation is presented by Schmitt in *absolute* terms, for Cavalletti, it implies that spaces de-coupled from politics are simply inconceivable, and that, before any qualification of the two terms – space and politics – is discussed, together with their relation, we must reflect on the inseparable dyad space–power – a deeper co-implication already discussed by Foucault in *Discipline and Punish* and many others after him (Cavalletti 2005: 2).

This fact alone could possibly justify the sudden interest for Schmitt in political theory and international relations (see, among others, Balakrishnan 2000; Hooker 2009; Kalyvas 2008; Müller 2003; Shapiro 2008) and, more recently, in Anglophone human geography (see Legg in this volume). Why and how has Schmitt become a new academic icon in the English-speaking world (can Schmitt be thought of as 'new' in any possible way?) is, intentionally, *not* the subject of this chapter. Having said that, his distinct personal trajectory, especially his involvement in Nazi politics, should always be kept in mind when engaging with his conceptual ruminations (see Legg and Vasudevan in this volume).

It is widely accepted by now that this renewed interest for Schmitt may be attributed to a series of concomitant events. In the first place, to the fact that Giorgio Agamben's seminal work on biopolitics relies heavily on (though it subsequently departs from) Schmitt's theory of sovereign exception and his concept of the nomos (Agamben 1998; 2007). The second factor is the growing interest in Schmitt's understanding of 'the political' on the part of many post-foundational political theorists, an interest that inherently also invests mainstream discussions in contemporary political philosophy (see Marchart 2007; Mouffe 1999; 2005a; Ojakangas 2006). Third, on a more popular (if not populist) level, Schmitt's terminology and apparently accessible formulae have appealed to the advocates of several, often contradictory, narratives on the nature of contemporary global (dis)order, attracted to the possibility of confronting the war on terror and its (presumably) de-territorialised geographies with a set of (presumably) robust grand claims of the Schmittian kind: from the neo-conservative geopolitical projections of Washington-based think tanks, to anti-liberal counter-narratives that find in Schmitt's deep critique of global liberalism a ready-made, over-simplified (and thus media-friendly) framework (see, for example, Neocleous 1996; also Legg and Vasudevan in this volume).

In a recent critique of the superficial and contradictory ways in which Schmitt's spatialities have been treated, Stuart Elden underlines how

> with the 2003 translation of *The* Nomos *of the Earth*, a rather different set of Carl Schmitt's ideas became accessible to an Anglophone audience. While previously his work had shaped debates on politics, the political, the friend/enemy distinction, the question of democracy and the sovereign decision, now his ideas on international politics became available.
>
> (Elden, this volume: 91)

In what remains to date one of the few interventions of this kind on the part of a geographer, Elden then denounces the equally superficial reception of the *Nomos* in the discipline of international relations, noting how Schmitt was

The question of spatial ontology   165

recently described as 'one of the most profound and most prolific theorists of international order in the twentieth century', with the *Nomos* likely to be guaranteed a place 'in the canon of essential IR reading' (Hooker 2009: 3). More importantly for the core argument of this chapter, however, Elden dismisses Hooker's suggestion that Schmitt's 'bold vision of the importance of spatial concepts in shaping the possibility of political order' qualifies him as a geographer (2009: 196).

Can Carl Schmitt (also) be considered a geographer in disguise, or a 'geomythographer', as suggested by Mitchell Dean (2007: 249)? Is this preoccupation with the disciplinary appropriation of Schmitt's spatial thinking relevant? Probably not, especially if it remains simply a question on the production and circulation of academic capital where attributions, and intended or unintended affiliations, are what is really at stake. But if we are to consider, instead, the 'question of spatial ontology', then the relationship between the geographical tradition and Schmitt's work is perhaps of some relevance.

Be this as it may, after this brief introductory detour, allow me to start again. The reasons for opening this chapter with a direct reference to Andrea Cavalletti's work are twofold. The first has to do with the fact that Carl Schmitt's work has been circulating in Italian for several decades now (although *The Nomos of the Earth* was first translated into Italian only in 1991, this was still 12 years before the English translation) and Schmitt has long been seen as a key figure not only by political and urban theorists, but also by some geographers (see, for example, Farinelli 2003; Galluccio 2002, 2006; Minca 2006). This consolidated literature 'on Schmitt' has, by now, thoroughly 'digested' some of his key ideas about space and the political, and have become part of a sort of 'mature' debate in the field of political theory (see, among others, Galli 2008; also Miglio 1972; Petito 2007; Ruschi 2007, 2008; Volpi 2002; Zolo 2007). What is more, in the post-war period, Schmitt continued to have direct academic and personal ties with Italy and Italian intellectuals, as is demonstrated, for example, by the introduction that he wrote specifically for the Italian re-edition of *The Concept of the Political* (1972a, 1972b). This should come as no surprise, since in the post-war period both conservative and progressive Italian intellectuals have fully engaged with the so-called German Conservative Revolution (see Herf 1986; Müller 2003), as demonstrated by the translation of Junger's and Spengler's work, this latter edited by a thinker like Julius Evola and commented by progressive Jewish historian Furio Jesi. I am saying this not to claim any privileged reading of Schmitt's work 'on space', but rather to explain why I find it useful to ground some of the reflections that will follow in a well-established debate to which Cavalletti's book, I believe, represents a very important contribution.

The second reason is only partially related to the first: Cavalletti's book treats Schmitt's work as a milestone in the understanding of the ontological foundations of modern biopolitics. At the same time, Cavalletti is also very explicit in linking Schmitt's spatial framework to the work of Friedrich Ratzel and, more generally, to modern geography and its understanding of the 'bio'

166   *Claudio Minca*

in the human. So, while Rory Rowan, in another chapter of this book, investigates the question of spatial ontology by looking at the tensions that 'structure Schmitt's thought as a whole by repeatedly presenting indeterminacy as an ontological condition on the one hand and, on the other, ceaselessly attempting to bring this indeterminacy to a close by grounding order in some form of authentic legitimacy' (Rowan, in this book), I will try here a different kind of operation. I will attempt, in fact, to de-link this discussion from the spatial fetishism of the contemporary debates on Schmitt vehemently denounced by Elden, and locate it, instead, within the long-standing discussion on the spatial nature of biopolitics that has been developed in particular by Andrea Cavalletti and, through a different route, by Giorgio Agamben, both inheritors and innovators of a certain branch of Italian political and philosophical thought.

I will therefore start by briefly noting how some of Schmitt's grand claims on space and spatial theory were his own, distinct, way of dealing with 'the spatial' and 'the political' at the same time. I will do so by highlighting how some of these claims were foundational in the most banal sense of the word; they were inherently ontological since based on his intuition and his arcane and millenarian vision of the world and of history. Without keeping this dimension in mind, I argue, it is very difficult to make sense of the relationship that he envisaged between 'Man' (*sic*) and the Earth, and also in part between space and politics, a relationship that is also linked to his very conservative and eminently Catholic understanding of culture and society, as well as the question of order.

The final part of the paper will reflect on how space is sometimes presented by Schmitt as an ontological issue, while in other instances it is treated as a way of thinking and managing the world, or a concrete framework for our 'realities'. Is this just an untenable contradiction in Schmitt's work, or is 'the ontological' a domain that intersects with his quite prescriptive (but also arcane) categories of the political? By investigating how these conceptions of 'the spatial' enter into a complex dialogue with ideas of *Land and Sea* (1997 [1954]; orig. *Land und Meer* 1942) when conceived as *the* fundamental elements of human life, I will conclude by asking whether the idea of a nomos – of the *Nomos* of the Earth – is inherently linked to a spatial ontology. Is the Schmittian nomos nothing other than an attempt to qualify a (his?) spatial ontology? And, finally, is the question of spatial ontology, as put by Schmitt, an eminently geographical question?

Space

If Schmitt's declared faith in the foundational act of 'land signification and appropriation' (dwelling?) was intended, as I believe it was, as an 'ontological gesture', then the universal nature of this gesture (as presented in *The* Nomos *of the Earth*) must be considered in its complex and somewhat contradictory relationship with Schmitt's idea of 'concrete' space (see also Ojakangas

2006). Space and place exist, in fact, in a tense relationship in Schmitt's imagined political geographies. Space for Schmitt is, at once, a fundamental measure of the world *and* something out there; the potential realm of the political, grounded by a specific, historically determined (spatial) ordering:

> the constitutive process of a land-appropriation is found at the beginning of the history of every settled people, every commonwealth, every empire. This is true as well for the beginning of every historical epoch. Not only logically, but also historically, land-appropriation precedes the order (*ordering/ordnung*) that follows from it. It constitutes the original spatial order(ing), the source of all further concrete order and all further law.
> (2003 [1950]: 48)

Land appropriation is presented here as the founding and foundational act of every human consortium, as the source of all forms of order and ordering, as the origin of all the categories adopted to describe the world. These categories, for Schmitt, are eminently of a spatial–political kind:

> all [. . .] subsequent regulations of a written or unwritten kind derive their power from the inner measure of an original, constitutive act of spatial ordering. This original act is the nomos [. . .] nomos is a matter of the fundamental process of apportioning space that is essential to every historical epoch – a matter of the structure-determining convergence of order and orientation in the cohabitation of peoples on this now scientifically surveyed (measured) planet. This is the sense in which the nomos of the Earth is spoken of here. Every new age and every new epoch in the coexistence of peoples, empires, and countries, of rulers and power formations of every sort, is founded on new spatial divisions, new enclosures (boundaries/delimitations), and a new spatial order of the Earth.
> (2003 [1950]: 78–9)

The nomos is conceived here as what Cavalletti would define as an *original spatialisation*, as the (founding and necessary) nexus between order(ing) (*Ordnung*) and orientation/localisation (*Ortung*); again, perhaps, as a sort of spatial ontology. According to Carlo Galli (2008), Schmitt, with this 'move', attempts to convert nature into politics via the spatialisation of a fundamentally ontological act. Within this perspective, the nomos is the fundamental *geographical act* that translates into land appropriation, but also into land partition, denomination, delimitation, measurement. Space is here intended, at the same time, as a sort of *original* measure, as a theory, as a way of theorising real or presumed terrestrial connections, as a set of ideas and practices, as a process of ordering – but *also* as a thing, out there, waiting to be ordered.

This supposed (spatial) ontology is thus immediately performative. Act and meaning, location and order, come together and become the same thing.

Without an 'original spatialisation', no order and no politics is possible. According to Schmitt, no norm is applicable to chaos. To obtain juridical-political order, a 'normal' situation must first be created. And yet any such order is senseless without territorial grounding, and without the (spatio-political) meaning conferred by such grounding. The occupation and denomination of land can thus be seen as a spatial ontological gesture from which 'all rights emanate', and within which space and right, order and its localisation, come together.[2] All rights, all laws are thus applicable only to specific 'territorial situations', and can only be suspended, with respect to such specific 'situations' by a sovereign exception. Schmitt's theory of exception is therefore premised upon the recognition of the necessity of a fundamental spatial 'measure' of the Earth – of a spatial theory – starting from which both order and the suspension of order gain meaning (Schmitt 2003 [1950]: 46; see also Minca 2006).

This is an eminently 'geographical' preoccupation, needless to say: the search for a spatial 'measure' of the Earth, a measure which, at a certain point in time, came to be termed 'geographical space' (see Farinelli 2003). So too is the attempt at the definition of some sort of territorial order. In this sense, Cavalletti is correct in saying that Schmitt's spatial thinking reflects in many ways the ontologies of the Ratzelian project and, to some extent, of all modern geography. A certain geographical tradition is, indeed, closely entangled with Schmitt's theorisation of the nomos, as these two citations highlight:

> No sooner had the form [*Gestalt*] of the Earth emerged as a real globe [*Globus*]—not just sensed as myth, but apprehensible as fact and measurable as space—then there arose a wholly new and hitherto unimaginable problem: the spatial ordering of the entire Earth [*Erdenballes*] in terms of international law. The new global image [*globale Raumbild*] required a new global spatial order. This was the situation resulting from the circumnavigation of the Earth and the great discoveries of the 15th and 16th centuries.
>
> ... when historical and scientific consciousness had assimilated [. . .] the planet down to the last cartographical and statistical details, the practical-political need not only for a geometric surface division, but for a substantial spatial order (for a spatial order loaded with meaning) of the Earth became evident.
>
> (2003 [1950]: 86)

Stuart Elden, however, is overtly critical of the relationship that Schmitt seems to establish between his ideas of space and his concept of territory, between spatial theory and the concrete (that is, place-based) nature of their production and implementation. According to Elden, in establishing 'a primitive relation between *Ortung* and *Ordnung*' Schmitt adopts an understanding of territory that is far too static, and seemingly ahistorical. For Schmitt, he argues, 'territory [. . .] remains a bounded space under the control of a group; a quasi-Weberian definition that may provide the terms to be

The question of spatial ontology 169

analysed, but is hardly a theory in itself' (2010: 23). Elden goes a long way in showing how Schmitt's use of territory is often confused and sometimes conflated with other terms and concepts, like that of land, soil and even space (2010: 22). And this is particularly true when the very concept of *Großraum* is evoked by the German theorist (Schmitt 1991, 1995; see also Elden 2010; Ruschi 2007).

I do not have the space here to expand on this. However, it is important to note that this preoccupation with the nature of Schmitt's supposed spatial ontology is also at the core of Rowan's own criticism of the way in which mainstream literature has received his conceptualisations of space. Rowan (in this book) argues that the Schmittian nomos has 'the structure of a "founding rupture" and contains a tension between ontological indeterminacy and contingent attempts to establish order, a moment of constituent power and a moment of constituted power'. In his view, Schmitt proposes two sides to the concept of nomos. In the first interpretation, it is 'the original spatial order, the source of all further concrete order and all further law' (Schmitt 2003 [1950]: 48); in the second, nomos indicates the foundational acts of land appropriation that establish such a relationship between order and space and make order possible (Rowan, in this book). Nomos is therefore a concept that has clearly distinguishable elements: foundational acts and institutional structures, as well as moments of constituent and constituted power. For Schmitt, therefore, 'any *nomos* of the Earth owes its foundations and its norms to the exceptional act of land appropriation. In *The* Nomos *of the Earth* acts of land appropriation simultaneously introduce a rupture into the existing state of affairs and lay the foundation for a new spatial order' (Rowan, in this book).

As Rowan rightly points out, there is nothing inherent to space that allows it to act as a ground for order: rather, space and order are simultaneously produced through subjective political acts, that is, through acts of ground*ing* that fuse space and order in a new relation. The understanding of space as a stable, objective and extra-political ground for order implicit within some recent geopolitical readings of Schmitt is therefore a poor rendition of the much more complex relationship that Schmitt traces between space and constituent power in the foundational act of land appropriation (Rowan, in this book). This is an important point. However, since the nomos of the land is not universal, Galli (2008) wonders how we can conceive the possibility of overlapping, differentiated, co-existing, spatial ontologies together with the question of global order(ing) so central to Schmitt's geo-political preoccupations (see also Mouffe 1999; 2005b; Petito 2007). Perhaps the question of spatial ontology should/could be approached from a different angle.

Mitchell Dean (2007: 248) has noted that in a recent extension of this notion of nomos, Giorgio Agamben has added nativity, with its etymological affinity with 'nation', as a third term in the modern nomos of the nation-state:

> For Agamben, it is along the axis of birth, citizenship and life that the nation-state is today being thrown into crisis. The consequence, according

to his thesis, is that the camp, as the site of the inclusive exclusion of naked life, is the new biopolitical nomos of the planet.

In so doing – argues Dean – Agamben ignores the overall fundamental framework in which the terrestrial character of nomos is located by producing an account that focuses on the spatial manifestations of the disqualification of citizenship rights as a condition of a failing territorial national sovereignty. Agamben thus links the exception – concludes Dean – with the territoriality of the taking of land, of land appropriation: 'While this is a striking critical gesture, its cost is to so enclose the nomos in the camp as to render the struggles over the rest of the planet and international law scarcely intelligible' (2007: 248).

I only partially agree with these considerations. However, what matters for the argument of this essay is that the link between Schmitt's and Agamben's conceptualisations of the sovereign exception can be conceived as a form of 'original spatialisation' – that is, also, a form of spatial ontology. In his analysis of the constitution of the sovereign exception, Agamben is indeed heavily (albeit critically) reliant on Schmitt and insists on the spatialisation of the exception as the fundamental condition of the sovereign subject. What is important above all, however, is that this 'original spatialisation' produces its own exception/transgression. It is a genuine 'space of exception' that the sovereign act of land appropriation and delimitation produces, via a strategy of inclusive exclusion (Agamben 1998). If this link is a valid path to the question of spatial ontology in Schmitt, then two issues deserve further investigation: first, the Schmittian call for an existentialist (and essentialist) recovering of the land and the sea as fundamental elements of human (and political) life; and, second, the question of the 'void' that the crisis of the nation-state reveals at the core of the political, stripped as it is of a supposed ontological link to the nomos of the Earth.

Land (and Sea)

In *Land and Sea*, Schmitt is explicit about the terrestrial foundation of any form of civilisation and even of human life:

> Man is a terrestrial being, a being that treads the land. Man stands and walks on solid land. It is the land that provides his location and determines his point of view, his impressions and his way of living in the world. From the land where he is born and across which he travels, he inherits his horizons, his appearance, and his way of moving.
> (1942/2002: 11)[3]

This explains, for Schmitt, the fact that, in many myths and legends, the land appears as a sort of Great Mother. But he goes even further when he asserts that 'human existence and human beings are, in their very essence, purely terrestrial and the land is their only essential referent' (1942/2002: 12) and, especially, when he asks: 'which is our true element? Are we sons of the land or of the sea?' (1942/2002: 14).

A key question for my own specific interrogation of Schmitt's thought is thus whether the relation between Man and land/Earth (and, by extension, the sea) is indeed conceived by him as an ontological question. A first problem here is that he does not always make a clear distinction between Earth and land, or even between Earth and world, as other philosophers of his day had done. Second, he presents a rather simplified understanding of the very concept of the land/Earth, without fully engaging with the genealogy of its relationship with human history, as famously done by Heidegger (1950, and in more popular form by Franz Rosenzweig in *Globus* 1984/2007), or by Franco Farinelli (2007) in his recent *L'invenzione della Terra* (The Invention of the Earth). For Schmitt, it seems that before the first fundamental spatial act on the part of Man there was only pure nature – *no physis ante nomos*. According to Agamben, however, world and Earth – though opposed in an essential conflict – are never separable, as argued by Heidegger:

> the Earth is the spontaneous emerging toward nothing of that which constantly closes itself and thus saves itself. World and Earth are essentially different from one another and yet are never separated. The world ground itself on the Earth, and Earth juts through world.
> (1950: 33–34; cited in Agamben 2004: 72)

This is not only a key philosophical question, but also the source of every original political conflict, the conflict that transverses and decides/defines the very confine between the humanity and the animality of Man:

> Heidegger was perhaps the last philosopher to believe in good faith that the 'place' of the polis [. . .] was still practicable, and that it was still possible for men, for a people [. . .] to find their own historical destiny. He was the last to believe – at least up to a certain point, and not without doubts and contradictions – that the anthropological machine, which each time decides upon and recomposes the conflict between man and animal [. . .] could still produce history and destiny for a people.
> (Agamben 2004: 74)

Schmitt, however, while showing a strong proclivity for grand and millenarian considerations, never really problematised the distinction between these two terms, using them in distinct but at the same time often confused ways. Perhaps this was due to the fact that his ruminations about the spatial history of humankind and the concept of the Earth drew inspiration from rather different sources (and were possibly targeting a different audience), and for this reason were intentionally deprived of any critical analysis of the genealogy of the terms implied (the re-invention of the 'nomos' in a sense represents a sort of philological shortcut). In fact, if *Land and Sea* is where Schmitt rediscovers, through the adoption of a rather popular (populist?) argument and jargon, the fundamental (Earthly) elements at the origin of human history, it is also where he implicitly reveals his own interest for their mythopoietic power (see Mendieta, in this book) (for instance, he draws mystical inspiration from the work of Triestine poet Theodor Daubler – see Schmitt 1991). According to Franco Volpi (2002: 121), in Schmitt, the elementary and the arcane coincide in a realm of obscure power and all his spatial thinking seems to be driven by this dual dimension. Arguably, there was a third monster, beyond Leviathan and Behemoth, that troubled Schmitt, and that he explicitly mentions in his private correspondence with Ernst Junger: the monster bird Ziz, the king of all winged beings. Ziz is the sovereign of the new global space that has started a new planetary revolution in the kingdom of the air . . . airplanes are the locusts of the apocalypse (see Junger and Schmitt 1999; Volpi 2002: 122; also, Hussain, in this book).

Furthermore, if 'history' was moving towards the formation of greater spaces exceeding the territory of the State, one key question for Schmitt was which political and juridical order would be able to secure peace in the new 'situation'. Troubled as he was by the collapse of the *ius publicum europeum*, Schmitt seemed to be terrified by the opening up of an 'empty' space in the midst of global politics, a kind of emptiness that he perceived as an ontological void. And it is at this point that he turned his attention to the power of the 'elements' (as expressed in *Land and Sea*), since in his millennial vision of history they represented an original and fundamental source of power and legitimacy; again, a spatial ontology of sorts. All his following speculations on the spatial concepts of *Großraum*, *Reich* and, finally, *Nomos* are, in a sense, tributaries of this ontological turn to the fundamental 'elements' of life (Volpi 2002: 131). The initial statement about the fundamental act of appropriation and apportion of the land in *The Nomos of the Earth* should also be read in this light. I will return to this mystical element in Schmitt's work in the closing remarks, after a brief reflection on how this 'geography of the origin', this original spatialisation, was translated into spatial theory – and biopolitics.

The original spatialisation

I would like to come back, once again, to Schmitt's opening sentence: 'there are no political ideas without a spatial referent, just as there are no spaces (or spatial principles) without corresponding political ideas'. In reflecting on this sentence, Cavalletti suggests that if every spatial concept is a political concept then the conception of an 'original temporality' should also be understood as a specific (concrete) 'situation' of power. But the question is whether what Schmitt was trying to address here is a specific concrete 'situation' or, rather, the very link/association between *any* 'situation' and power. If this latter is the case, what would be at stake, then, is not so much the specific character of that relation, but rather the relation itself: that which locates 'ontologically' each and every 'situation' (Cavalletti 2005: 8). Any political perspective capable of moving beyond this political-spatial relation, insists Cavalletti, will thus be accessible only via a history of space conceived, at the same time, as a history of power. But this was clearly not the task that Schmitt committed himself to, also because his spatial conceptualisations always contained an ontological stance/element and, more importantly, because he did not consider such a perspective either possible or desirable. On the contrary, Schmitt's main concern was that of being able to think of 'the political' in the light of the deep breach that the modern nation-state had opened at its very core, a core that he saw as dangerously empty and that he desperately attempted to imbue with a distinct Christian ontology.

According to Cavalletti, again, if every spatial concept is necessarily political and vice versa, the concept of population as it was developed from the eighteenth century onwards is also a spatio-political concept and can be conceived as a sort of positive 'intensity' capable of drawing a peculiar amity line (Cavalletti 2005: 51). This is an important consideration for my investigation of the question of spatial ontology. For Cavalletti, in this new concept of population, which will be entirely adopted by Schmitt, each and every relation between population and the environment became possible only with a 'primary' spatialisation of the human species (2005: 79). This primary spatialisation, in fact, produces an understanding of the human that is immediately political, since based on a calculative concept, that of population, which defines an endless series of caesurae in the body politic by identifying the right, just or necessary shape of the population (2005: 79). In other words, as soon as it appears as a scientific concept, the human species is already divided into a part that is necessary and a part that is not necessary in order to produce and reproduce the (spatialised) population of a State (2005: 80). Ratzel's biogeographies and, in particular, his idea of *Lebensraum*, were particularly important in translating this concept of population at the very beginning of the twentieth century into a robust geographical theory that would influence directly or indirectly the work of many political theorists (and spatial demographers) in the following decades (Ratzel 1897). Cavalletti is adamant about this influence:

> from this moment on any relation between population and territory loses its traditional geographical meaning, to become a sort of geo-biopolitics: space becomes vital and life becomes spatial, in an intensive way [...] The density of life is the concept that denominates life fighting with life [...] density intended as a form of primary (original?) spatialisation that permeates every spatial-political organism.
>
> (2005: 202, 206)

Space–population and space–density, according to Cavalletti, are key concepts in a vision of the world that will be largely appropriated/adopted by Schmitt a few decades later. In particular, Schmitt will take up these ideas through the writings of Italian fascist pseudo-demographer Luigi Valli whose book – *Il diritto dei popoli alla terra* (1926) – was read and cited by Schmitt in his National-Socialist interpretation of the Monroe Doctrine of greater spaces published in 1939 (Schmitt 1992, 1995; Cavalletti 2005: 210).

Schmitt's concern for 'the political' in a brave new world deprived of a political theology is thus addressed towards the conceptualisation of the friend–foe relationship as a form of primary spatialisation, with the consequence, according to Cavalletti, of translating demography into an essential spatialised politics, that is, into biopolitics (2005: 212). The unity of the German people, as envisaged by Schmitt, was then conceived as a spatial organism capable of expanding or shrinking while keeping the same demographic 'intensity'. A key objective of this project was the perfect coincidence between people and population in a unified, endlessly perfectable, biopolitical space (see Giaccaria and Minca, forthcoming). The 'other', the ontological enemy, who was not-of-that-space, resided (or had to be forced to reside) beyond and/or outside that space–population body politic[4] (Schmitt 1996 [1932]). The essential relationship between friend and foe is thus a spatio-ontological one, since it is based on a supposed primary spatialisation that defined, once and forever, the true body politic *in fieri* (and the very human essence, the definitive de-animalisation) of the German *Volk* (see Giaccaria and Minca, forthcoming). The political, as the result of the co-implication of life and space, is thus where the ontological nature of this spatialisation emerges in all its evidence. It is not by chance that Schmitt defined also the 'friend' (and not only the foe) in biopolitical terms, through a direct implication of life and death: 'in case of need, the political entity must demand the sacrifice of life' (Schmitt 1996 [1932]: 71; on this issue see also Axtmann 2007; Botwinick 2005; Rasch 2005; Slomp 2009).

For Schmitt, the primary spatialisation at the origin of the friend–foe relationship is thus a natural human condition; it is what precedes any form of civilised and political life; it is a fundamental act of the humanisation of the human (or of certain humans). This explains why Schmitt was convinced that any political theory was also a sort of anthropology. He identified, in fact, two fundamental anthropological-political visions, from which all other political theories should derive: one that believed that humans were naturally good, and the other that considered them essentially bad and prone to violence (Cavalletti 2005: 243). Affirming such a radical distinction was nothing but an attempt to establish a philosophical and political anthropology capable of qualifying the friend–foe relationship as an 'essential constitution of Man': a definitely Hobbesian understanding of human (political?) nature.

Agamben's reflection on the nature of anthropogenesis is of some use at this point: 'Anthropogenesis is what results from the caesura and articulation between human and animal. This caesura passes first of all within man' (2004: 79). In the 1920s, when Schmitt was busy writing *The Concept of the Political* (1996 [1932]), it was already clear that with the end of the First World War, European nation-states were no longer capable of fulfilling their 'historical mission', and that peoples and nations were bound to disappear. According to Agamben, at that point, the stakes became different and much higher, for it was a question of taking on as a task the very existence of the population, 'the assumption of the burden – and the total management – of biological life, that is, of the very animality of Man' (2004: 76, 77):

> Ontology, or first philosophy, is not an innocuous academic discipline, but in every sense the fundamental operation in which anthropogenesis, the becoming human of the living being, is realised. From the beginning, metaphysics is taken up in this strategy: it concerns that meta that competes and preserves the overcoming of animal physis in the direction of human history. This overcoming is not an event that has been completed once and for all, but an occurrence that is always under way, that every time and in each individual decides between the human and the animal, between nature and history, between life and death.
> (Agamben 2004: 79)

For Agamben, if the decisive political conflict (which determines every other conflict) is that between the animality and the humanity of Man, and if the anthropological machine is the engine of the historical becoming of Man, then the announced end of philosophy and the completion of any epochal destiny/destination of the Being after the Great War meant that the nation-state machine began spinning around an empty core, and it still does today (2004: 82).

Schmitt, aware as he was of the void at the core of this political machine, thus sought a new spatial political theology; a theology that he translated into a sort of ontological stance in which spatial theory and arcane and religious beliefs merged into an untenable cocktail of millenarian historical visions and an analysis of the newly formed spatial order(ing)s.

Horror vacui

According to Schmitt, Man has a specific awareness of his own space, since different forms of life correspond to equally different spaces. Ideas about space are even more differentiated, and this has been particularly true with the development of modern science: geometry, physics, psychology, biology, to name a few, have all produced various concepts of space (2002: 57). Yet a unified concept of space was missing, according to Schmitt's writing in the early 1940s. This lack allowed for the concurrent presence of a plethora of unrelated understandings (or misunderstandings) of space: something that Schmitt found deeply troubling. Even philosophy and gneosology were incapable of providing a synthetic and simple answer to the question of space (see also Mendieta, in this book). This was the very essence of the grand political, economic and cultural transformations that had accompanied the Enlightenment and the hegemony of modern culture (2002: 59). After Newton, in particular, a new idea of space had emerged in all of Europe and, for the first time ever, humankind was capable of imagining an empty space, something that before was inconceivable: 'Try to think of a really empty space [...] it corresponds to imagining the absolute nothing [...]' (2002: 68).

While liberal thinkers derided this *horror vacui*, in Schmitt's view, this horror was understandable, especially considering the fact that Man found himself facing, for the very first time, 'the void of death produced by nihilism'. Such a shocking revolution produced by the emergence of an infinite empty space, for Schmitt, could not be explained merely as the discovery of formerly unknown lands; if anything, these discoveries were only the consequence of a more substantial metamorphosis:

> it is not exaggerated to affirm that all spheres of life, all forms of existence, all species of Man's creative energy [...] are involved in the formation of this new concept of space [...] the grand mutations in the geographical image of the Earth are just a superficial manifestation of this metamorphosis that we normally describe as spatial revolution.
>
> (2002: 71)

From these few passages it is clear that Schmitt was very concerned about the overall implications of this new concept of space, a concept that, in his view, was the reflection of another void, that of the political institutions created by liberalism and by the dismissal of the *ius publicum europeum* without any 'grounding' in the cultural specificities of national cultures and in the 'concrete situation' in which they were supposed to operate (see Dyzenhaus 1998).

Agamben's most recent interpretation of the nomos is strongly implicated with this element of Schmitt's work. In *Means Without End* he asserts that while the decline of the nation-state maintained everywhere its empty shell, as a pure structure of dominion, the theorists of sovereign politics like Schmitt saw in this event the most evident sign of the end of politics (2000: 112). Schmitt was indeed obsessed with the question of political 'order', and his spatial theorisations should be read also as a reflection of this concern/obsession and of the deep belief in the existence of a sort of original, anthropogenic order that should be reflected in each society/state. However, in *Il Regno e la Gloria* (2007) Agamben argues that order is an equally empty concept, or, better, it is not a concept proper but rather what he terms a '*signatura*': something that, in a sign or a concept, tends to exceed it, evoking a particular interpretation or moving it into a different 'situation' altogether in order to create new meaning – all the while never leaving the semiotic sphere. The concepts that the *signatura* 'order' signifies are, he argues, genuinely ontological ones: the *signatura* 'order' thus produces 'a displacement of ontology from the category of substance to that of relation and praxis – perhaps the most important contribution of Mediaeval thought to ontology' (2007: 102; see also Agamben 2008).

This is also true for Schmitt's understanding of the concept of social and political order, intended by him as the desirable final objective of any 'primary' human spatialisation. It is within this framework that Schmitt's overall project can be seen as somehow driven by a spatial ontology, a half rational and half mystical ontology that acquires its full meaning only when confronted with his own grand historical vision. Agamben, again, reflects at length on this vision. In *Un Giurista davanti a se stesso* (2005: 14) he argues that this understanding was constructed around a set of Christian paradigms. The first has to do with the ways in which the twentieth century has been interpreted in Christian eschatology: in particular, the idea of the end of time/history, the idea of a time that is running out. Within Christian understandings of history, this sort of modern eschatological paralysis is set against the image of the *katechon*, as presented in Paul's Second Letter to the Thessalonians: that is, the idea of a power that delays and defers the end of time/history ('*la fine del tempo*'). In *The Nomos of the Earth*, for Agamben, this idea is at the core of Schmitt's understanding of a Christian empire:

> I do not believe that any historical concept other than *katechon* would have been possible for the original Christian faith. The belief that a restrainer holds back the end of the world provides the only bridge between the notion of an eschatological paralysis of all human events and a tremendous historical monolith like that of the Christian empire of the Germanic kings.
>
> (Schmitt 2003 [1950]: 60)

Such millenarian visions are directly related to Schmitt's 'rediscovery' of the fundamental elements of Nature. As stated numerous times in *Land and Sea*, Man is by nature a terrestrial animal and the land has always represented, through the millennia, his 'natural space', to occupy and to colonise. It is here, in this context, that Schmitt recalls for the first time the *katechon*, by applying it to the emergent global power of the United States, although in a rather minimalist sense, and not yet in its full politico-theological meaning as he will do after the war (Volpi 2002: 133). Schmitt argued, in fact, that the United States' entry into 'the realm of history' transformed once and for all the 'restrainers' of the world. In his view, the USA represented a sort of involuntary and unaware accelerator of history, much like a large rudderless ship, that tumbles into the maelstrom of history (Volpi 2002; see also Ulmen 1987).

What I am trying to suggest here is that the nomos and the question of spatial ontology must be read also, if not above all, in the light of Schmitt's previous writings, and especially in the light of his populist call for a return to the 'elementary elements'. According to Volpi, and I would agree with him, *Land and Sea* is 'an intriguing melting pot of historical interpretation and political theory; of mythography and theology, of philosophy and esoterism' (2002: 137). What Schmitt described as historical consciousness was instead an esoteric form of knowledge, to which he alone, and perhaps very few other 'initiates', had full access. Schmitt felt himself to be the custodian of the deep mysteries of history as an 'initiated' individual, and this explains his frequent adoption of the term *arcanum* (2002: 137). The presumed latent (and millennial) conflict between Judaism and Catholicism over the interpretation of history was another major obsession for Schmitt. For him, modernity was the field of this decisive clash. The combination of Jewish-led universalism and cosmopolitan capitalism and the British dominion of the seas made this clash even more dramatic – and, in his mind, entangled with apocalyptic scenarios (see Mendieta, in this book). Indeed, Schmitt's schizophrenic vision of the end of history was marked by the pressing need to unveil the Jews' secret art of dealing with the Leviathan – and to penetrate their true *Arcanum imperii* (Volpi 2002: 140).

Schmitt's spatial theory therefore needs to be read also in the light of this dark background in which millennial forces were fighting a decisive battle: a battle that Schmitt envisioned with a significant degree of paranoia about the end of the (Christian) world. The tension between a concept of space intended as a fundamental 'measure of the Earth/land' and a concept of space intended as something 'concrete' (a privileged term in Schmitt's writings), something historically determined that represented the 'actual' stage of human life and of the life of nations and peoples – this very tension could not (and cannot) be solved on epistemological grounds, since it is not just an argumentative problem as has often been assumed. Agamben rightly points out that the nexus between *Ortung* and *Ordnung* that constitutes the '*nomos* of the Earth' for Schmitt contains within it 'a fundamental ambiguity, an unlocalizable zone of indistinction or exception that acts against it as a principle of its infinite dislocation' (1998: 19–20).

Indeed, the question of space (and, with it, of order) is often presented by Schmitt as an ontological question for, to his mind, it is founded on a geographical *arcanum*, it is a gnosological project, driven by an esoteric Christian understanding of human history. Schmitt's 'spatial *arcanum*' must thus be read precisely as an (entirely political) attempt to match a rational spatial theory of the Earth – and a related geopolitical explanation of the present – with a millenarian, apocalyptic vision of history. It is in this vision that Schmitt found the very *raison d'être* of his grand project, its guiding force, but also a sort a 'spatial' credo that identified in the link with the 'fundamental' terrestrial elements the roots of the 'human'. In this sense, his was a truly populist, arch-conservative – and biopolitical project.

The by now famous Schmittian declamation of identifying in the appropriation of land the beginning of all things civilised (and human?) that opens his *The Nomos of the Earth*, thus cannot be simply reduced to Schmitt's inclination to think geographically – or to provide alternative epistemic grounds for a spatial theory. This gesture needs to be relocated within the spatial mystique in which Schmitt collocated his overall vision of history and his own project aimed at saving the world (or better yet, saving European, perhaps just German, civilisation) from the vortex produced by the ontological void of the modern (read: liberal and non-theological) project. Contemporary explorers of Schmitt's spatial and geopolitical thought should never forget how the German jurist's spatial/geographical *arcanum* was based on an untenable compromise between a simplified interpretation of the Ratzelian bio-geographical legacy and an esoteric belief in a specific (Christian) understanding of the nature of Man as an exquisitely 'spatial', de-animalised terrestrial being.

Notes

1 *La città biopolitica* is a seminal contribution to the discussion on the relationship between space and biopolitics. In particular, Cavalletti shows here in a very convincing way how Schmitt's spatialisation of the political is inherently 'biopolitical'. The genealogy and the trajectory of the notion of 'space–population' in Western political thought is central to his argument. Unfortunately, the book exists only in its original version in Italian.
2 Here Schmitt has in mind especially the 'rights' that emanate from 'concrete space', from the 'reality' of the (German) land.
3 Any direct reference to *Land und Meer* (1942) is here based on its Italian translation (*Terra e mare* 2002), since the English translation was not available. All citations have been translated into English by the author.
4 The two most immediate 'geographical' consequences of this conceptualisation of the enemy were an essentialised understanding of culture and/in space (as expressed by the organic nature of the nation-state) and the progressive ghettoisation (in whatever form this was conceived) of the putative enemy. This ontological stance on the enemy, when translated into the spaces of the political by the Nazi regime, became one key expression of the 'reactionary modernist' culture that provided a fundamental ideological and scientific support to the realisation of the Third Reich (see Herf 1986). According to Herf, Carl Schmitt was one influential academic 'mandarin' of what he describes as the reactionary modernist movement (together with Junger, Sombart and many other conservative thinkers of the day).

References

Agamben, G. (1998) *Homo Sacer: Sovereign Power and Bare Life*, Stanford, CA: Stanford University Press.
—— (2000) *Means Without End*, Minneapolis: University of Minnesota Press.
—— (2004) *The Open*, Stanford, CA: Stanford University Press.
—— (2005) *Schmitt. Un giurista davanti a se stesso*, Vicenza: Neri Pozza.
—— (2007) *Il Regno e la Gloria*, Vicenza: Neri Pozza.
—— (2008) *Signatura Rerum*, Torino: Bollati Boringhieri.
Axtmann, R. (2007) 'Humanity or Enmity? Carl Schmitt on International Politics', *International Politics*, 44: 531–51.
Balakrishnan, G. (2000) *The Enemy: An Intellectual Portrait of Carl Schmitt*, Verso: London.
Botwinick, A. (2005) 'Same/Other versus Friend/Enemy: Levinas contra Schmitt', *Telos*, 132(Fall): 46–63.
Cavalletti, A. (2005) *La città biopolitica*, Milan: Mondadori.
Dean, M. (2007) '*Nomos*: Word and Myth', in L. Odysseos and F. Petito (eds) *The International Political Thought of Carl Schmitt*, London: Routledge.
Dyzenhaus, D. (ed.) (1998) *Law as Politics: Carl Schmitt's Critique of Liberalism*, Durham: Duke University Press.

Elden, S. (2010) 'Reading Schmitt Geopolitically: Nomos, Territory and Großraum', *Radical Philosophy*, 161: 18–26.
Farinelli, F. (2003) *Geografia*, Torino: Einaudi.
—— (2007) *L'invenzione della terra*, Palermo: Sellerio.
Galli, C. (2008) *Lo Sguardo di Giano. Saggi su Carl Schmitt*, Bologna: il Mulino.
Galluccio, F. (2002) 'Della delimitazione e dello Stato: per una lettura geografica di Carl Schmitt', *Rivista Geografica Italiana*, 109: 255–80.
—— (2006) 'L'Impero e le sue scale', *Rivista Geografica Italiana*, 113: 27–45.
Giaccaria P. and C. Minca (forthcoming) 'Nazi Geopolitics and the Dark Geographies of the *Selva*'. *Journal of Genocide Research*.
Heidegger, M. (1950) *Holzwege*, Frankfurt: Klostermann.
Herf, J. (1986) *Reactionary Modernism*. Cambridge: Cambridge University Press.
Hooker, W. (2009) *Carl Schmitt's International Thought: Order and Orientation*, Cambridge: Cambridge University Press.
Junger, E. and C. Schmitt (1999) *Briefe 1930–1983*, H. Kiesel (ed.), Stuttgart: Klett-Cotta.
Kalyvas, A. (2008) *Democracy and the Politics of the Extraordinary: Max Weber, Carl Schmitt, and Hannah Arendt*, Cambridge: Cambridge University Press.
Marchart, O. (2007) *Post-foundational Political Thought: Political Difference in Nancy, Lefort, Badiou and Laclau*, Edinburgh: Edinburgh University Press.
Miglio, G. (1972) 'Presentazione', in C. Schmitt, *Le Categorie del 'politico'*, Bologna: il Mulino.
Minca, C. (2006) 'Giorgio Agamben and the New Biopolitical Nomos', *Geografiska Annaler B*, 88(4): 387–403.
Mouffe, C. (ed.) (1999) *The Challenge of Carl Schmitt*, London: Verso.
—— (2005a) *On the Political*, London: Routledge.
—— (2005b) 'Schmitt's Vision of a Multipolar World', *South Atlantic Quarterly*, 104(2): 245–51.
Müller, J.W. (2003) *A Dangerous Mind: Carl Schmitt in Post-War European Thought*, New Haven, CT: Yale University Press.
Neocleous, M. (1996) 'Friend or Enemy? Reading Schmitt Politically', *Radical Philosophy*, 79(Sept/Oct): 13–23.
Ojakangas, M. (2006) *Concrete Life: Carl Schmitt and the Political Thought of Late Modernity*, Bern: Peter Lang.
Petito, P. (2007) 'Against World Unity: Carl Schmitt and the Western-centric and Liberal Global Order', in L. Odysseos and F. Petito (eds) *The International Political Thought of Carl Schmitt*, London: Routledge.
Rasch, W. (2005) 'Lines in the Sand: Enmity as a Structuring Principle', *South Atlantic Quarterly*, 104(2): 253–62.
Ratzel, F. (1897) *Politische geographie oder die geographie der staaten, des verkehrs und des krieges*, Berlin: Oldenburg.
Rosenzweig, F. (2007) (orig. 1984) *Globus*, Milan: Marietti.
Ruschi, F. (2008) 'Space, Law and Power in Carl Schmitt', *Jura Gentium*. Online. Available at www.juragentium.unifi.it/en/surveys/thil/nomos.htm (accessed 5 July 2010).
—— (2007) 'Leviathan e Behemoth. Modelli egemonici e spazi coloniali in Carl Schmitt', *Jura Gentium*. Online. Available at www.juragentium.unifi.it/it/surveys/thil/ruschi.htm (accessed 3 July 2010).

Schmitt, C. (1932) 'Forms of modern imperialism in international law', in S. Legg (ed.) (2011) *Geographies of the Nomos*, London: Routledge.

—— (1939) '*Großraum* versus Universalism: the International Legal Struggle over the Monroe Doctrine', in S. Legg (ed.) (2011) *Geographies of the* Nomos, London: Routledge.

—— (1942) *Land und Meer: Eine weltgeschichtliche Betrachtung*, Leipzig: Philipp Reclam.

—— (1972a) *Le Categorie del 'politico'*, Bologna: il Mulino.

—— (1972b) 'Premessa all'edizione italiana', in C. Schmitt, *Le Categorie del 'politico'*, Bologna: il Mulino.

—— (1991) *Theodor Daublers 'Nordlicht'*, Berlin: Duncker & Humblot.

—— (1992) *Völkerrechtliche Großraumordnung mit Interventionsverbot für raumfremde Mächte: Ein Beitrag zum Reichsbegriff im Völkerrecht*, Berlin: Duncker & Humblot.

—— (1995) *Staat, Großraum, Nomos: Arbeiten aus den Jahren 1916–1969*, G. Maschke (ed.), Berlin: Duncker & Humblot.

—— (1996 [1932]) *The Concept of the Political*. Chicago: University of Chicago Press.

—— (1997 [1954]) *Land and Sea*, Washington, DC: Plutarch Press.

—— (2002) *Terra e Mare*, Milan: Adelphi.

—— (2003 [1950]) *The* Nomos *of the Earth in the International Law of the* Jus Publicum Europaeum. New York: Telos Press.

—— (2003) *The* Nomos *of the Earth*, New York: Telos Press.

—— (2005) *Political Theology: Four Chapters on the Concept of Sovereignty*, Chicago: University of Chicago Press.

Shapiro, K. (2008) *Carl Schmitt and the Intensification of Politics*, Lanham, MD: Rowman & Littlefield.

Slomp, G. (2009) *Carl Schmitt and the Politics of Hostility, Violence and Terror*, Basingstoke: Palgrave Macmillan.

Ulmen, G. (1987) 'American Imperialism and International Law: Carl Schmitt on the US in World Affairs', *Telos*, 72(Summer): 43–73.

Valli, L. (1926) *Il diritto dei popoli alla terra*, Milan: Alpes.

Volpi, F. (2002) 'Potere degli elementi', in C. Schmitt, *Terra e Mare*, Milan: Adelphi.

Zolo, D. (2007) 'The Re-emerging Notion of Empire and the Influence of Carl Schmitt's Thought', in L. Odysseos and F. Petito (eds) *The International Political Thought of Carl Schmitt*, London: Routledge.

11 Between nomos and everyday life

Securing the spatial order of Foucault and Schmitt

Peter Rogers

Introduction

This chapter grew from what was originally thought of as an 'alternative reading' of Foucault and Schmitt along the themes of order, territory and security. It is at no point the intention of this work to move point by point through all of the potential connections or disjunctions between the work of Schmitt and the work of Foucault.[1] Nor is it my intention to recount and describe the original theories of either in complete or comprehensive detail; that task is left to others in this and other volumes. Here my aim is to offer an alternative reading of security, order and territory as themes that emerge in both Schmitt and Foucault; by doing so I aim to create a point of departure for rethinking how we understand the spatial order of 'everyday life' – used here, in a broad sense, to articulate how we understand normative relations that order the conduct of day-to-day activities. The tension between Schmitt's anti-liberal critique of politics as indecisive, ordinary and fragile has a sharp, if notional, contrast with Foucault's critique of neo-liberal politics as technically expert in refining the order of subject populations in everyday time and space.

Both Schmitt and Foucault offer a unique insight into the formative processes by which the state emerges as a system for creating social order, how a system of spatial conflict or of spatial control is established, and how this acts as a regulatory influence on social order. Each offers a unique perspective on the problems inherent in a systemic ordering, both of spaces and of people in those spaces. Even more so both offer unique ways of de-essentialising the state and sovereign, but through critique each offers a distinctly different reappraisal of their importance. In the first instance this can be seen to centralise the sovereign determination of exceptions as formative of the power to order from the top down, and in the second a more nuanced interpretation of power as constituted through the mechanising techniques of governing. Of particular interest in this chapter are the 'conditions of possibility' for particular relations of normative ordering that emerge from concepts of spatial order when these are explained using security, territory and population as key analytical factors. I will argue that using

Schmitt's approach to security and territory, in the first case, and then adding to these a Foucauldian reading of population allows for a deeper reflection on which variables should be considered most influential in: (a) the creation of an 'everyday' normalising sense of order; (b) how this order becomes manifest in the government of everyday life; and (c) how important it is to understand the role of space in creating order, be that the territory of a nation-state or one's own body. In making thematic connections between my reading of Schmitt's concept of 'nomos' – as informing the concrete spatial order of a community – and the attempt to apply this to a broad understanding of 'everyday life' it is hoped that this reflection on the interplay between security, territory and population can help develop some grounded links between the theoretical discourse of spatial order and empirical research.

Schmitt: the foundations of nomos as spatial order

Schmitt's *The* Nomos *of the Earth* is a book concerned with the emergence of order over time, including the juridical ordering of relations between nation-states as a strong theme. This has a significant relationship with his concern over sovereignty, the forms of determination by which authority is understood to be legitimate, and the creation of legitimate exceptions to sovereign rule. One way of reading *The* Nomos *of the Earth*, developed in brief here, suggests that Schmitt argues for an approach to the legitimacy of sovereign rule as a variable of order that is initially made manifest in the authority of that ruling body over proprietorial relations linked to a given territory. A simple interpretation of 'territory', in its broadest sense, is the codification of ownership, initially of land (as productive soil) from which the principles and practices of law emanate as normative and regulatory relations, guiding the interaction between people as individuals and collectives. Such relations develop over time to become a 'concrete order' aligned with a totalising concept of 'political enmity'. This concept of 'political enmity' allows for different collectives of people to make distinctions between their 'right to own' (a territorially defined concept, distinct from liberal 'human rights') and that of others, seen by Schmitt as enemies who might challenge such 'rights'. The legal codification of relations thus creates the 'conditions of possibility' for normative interactions between individuals and groups to be created, codified and enforced by a governing body responsible for regulating a particular territorial 'space'.

The spatial order of a community is as such, first and foremost, a process of installing a right of ownership upon the productive soil, i.e. land as a territory belonging to someone who is able to draw resources from it. Securing a legitimate form of localised spatial ordering is thus central to *The* Nomos *of the Earth* and in fact forms the opening salvo for the exposition of nomos as a core concept, particularly in the second and third of the threefold roots of law and justice offered in the opening discussion of Schmitt's five introductory corollaries (Schmitt, 2003 [1950]: 42–84). The second of the threefold roots of law emphasises the demarcation of land use through the geomorphic imprint of agriculture and cultivation activities, and the third the distinct delineation of ownership implicit in 'fences, enclosures, boundaries, walls, houses, and other constructs' (Schmitt, 2003 [1950]: 42). Territory at this basic level is ordered through embedding ownership to individuals through proprietorial division. Land is ordered through the symbolic and practical breaking of space into owned segments, for specific purposes, i.e. the production of resources for fulfilling the basic conditions of human need (food, shelter, clothing, etc.). At its most fundamental level the appropriation of territory is bound to the ownership of the soil itself (i.e. the land as a productive resource). The imposition of order upon that soil as a bounded space (i.e. land) therefore relates to the *internal* ordering of ownership and property relations – where property includes the land inclusive of the resources cultivated from the productive soil.

Simply put this suggests that the internal order necessarily incorporates both individual ownership of a specific location and the *supreme ownership* of a territory by the collective group, i.e. who *does* the nomos maintains it. If we suggest that this is an attempt to solve the problem of an 'actualisation' of the *law* and of *rights*, in their broadest sense, then the legal rules of ownership must be seen as emanating from land appropriations. This therefore creates the conditions of possibility for an ordering of both internal and external relations. To expand on this, Schmitt argues that to avoid internal conflict and maintain internal order reference must also be made to an *external* order, through the awareness of an existentially different, opposing or alternate group. The friend–enemy distinction, developed in Schmitt's other works, is here very useful.[2] Internal spatial order as established by codified relations establishes the legitimacy of sovereign authority to direct the population to behave in certain ways; to maintain this order and regulate interactions between members of the community awareness is required of others who are not of the community. The internal spatial order of the group – in the case of a community or a 'state' – relies on a distinction between those inside the group among whom an order is tacitly agreed, and another group comprised of 'others' that may contest the legitimacy of this consensus through their own external order. It relies upon the conflict of interests that may thus arise between different groups that emphasises distinctions between the 'friend' like us and the 'enemy' like them, but also between legitimacy of communal ordering imbued in the rules that enforce the proprietary claims of each group. This 'final distinction' creates the conditions of possibility for 'rules' as a 'system of laws' to be established and legitimated as a sovereign authority, but it is concomitant with the collective (or community) acknowledgement of external challenges to ownership, and thus the power of sovereign authority to direct actions as emanating from law being required to regulate interactions between these groups. A legal order is that which is given shape as an empirical reality by the decisions of sovereigns (Zarmanian, 2006: 50), but a spatial order is more than strictly legal decision-making, it incorporates the *decision*, the *act of appropriation* and the *distinction between others*. This complex framework forges the concrete form of a spatial order. The spatial order is the means by which occupation of a given territory by a given community is rendered legitimate but also how it is regulated, therefore ordered. As such spatial order includes territory and the security of productive land, resources of the land, the exchange of resources, and so on; the regulatory practices for ensuring orderly conduct and orderly relations of exchange are at the heart of understanding why nomos is important. Spatial order, territory and security are bound to become central themes in the discussion of nomos.

The changing order and security of territory

The discussion thus far situates territory and security in *The* Nomos *of the Earth*, but the understanding of territory framed above at best lays a rough understanding of the state as a juridical framework for regulating productive land and resources, as secured for a specific population. How do we move from this broad theory to the interrogation of a concrete spatial order? To understand how a system of government authority for structured regulation of everyday activity is brought forth we need to look deeper into the concrete spatial order as the 'interplay' of distinct variables. These variables, as identified above in Schmitt's work, are first and foremost spatial order, but this order must be understood through the complementary lens of territory and security to bring the complexity of the interplay into focus. These are not static concrete things, or discrete objects, but fluent variables subject to change over time, each affecting and informing, and thus altering, the impact of the others in the everyday lives of a population. This requires that we understand: (a) how Schmitt develops a concrete spatial order as bound to an understanding of conflict and war between antagonistic groups competing for territory; (b) how the stability of a spatial order (that which makes it concrete) is tied to the forms of authority manifest within the community it reflects, for example *Respublica Christiana* and the presupposed authority of the church, *potestas spiritualis* (spiritual power) (Schmitt, 2003 [1950]: 120); and (c) that for Schmitt these forms are subject to change, and are epochal in nature.

The spectre of history emerges through the appreciation of this epochal change enshrined in the rules of war and conflict, as no order and no territory is static. The legitimacy of authority over a population has, in particular, been shown throughout history to be particularly susceptible to the vagaries of human intrigue, thus the *security* of a spatial order is rarely entirely stable. For Schmitt the emergence of the modern juridical order of the state is indicative of the dissolution of traditional understanding of the spatial order of statehood and the formation of a unipolar global territorial order (Mouffe, 2007). Building on Schmitt we can suggest that such changes to the nature, conduct and regulation of conflict and war have implications for the regulation of everyday life through the changes to the security of the territory and the means of ensuring order through the changing role of law. The concept of a legal war is thus: (a) a means to enforce acceptance among the 'collective of others' (i.e. nation-states) that a land appropriation was legitimate; (b) used to justify a violent act of war as legitimate often as a result of its outcome in changing the types of appropriations and subsequent proprietorial relations manifest in a given territory (i.e. bringing the approved order to disordered territory); and (c) as the means of limiting violence to military relations between nation-states thus protecting the established order (i.e. the external ordering of land appropriations assisted in maintaining the approved internal order of the state). The 'conditions of possibility' created by competition between nation-states over the resources and riches of new territory emerge as negotiations not only on the individual level between citizens and/or rulers, but between types of collective 'others'. In *The Nomos of the Earth* Schmitt details the epochal shift from a *Respublica Christiana* as a concrete spatial order to the *Jus Publicum Europaeum* through the centralisation of administrative authority in the heads of state, *magni hominus*, which allowed the nation-state as a personalised entity to lay claim to given territory, impose an order of internal appropriations that suited their needs and forged a new form of state-based authority divorced from spiritual right to the collective rights of the community, a form of authority made legitimate insofar as it is manifest in the will of a sovereign ruler. The shift from an old to a new nomos was thus tied[3] to a shift in the theological and administrative ordering of land appropriations, with significant impact on the forms of legitimate authority and thus the conduct of everyday life over this period.

The administrative authorities of territorial rulers were themselves realigned by international competition for land and resources. Subsequent land appropriations necessarily require a conception of territory far beyond that of a localised farm, homestead or ranch, or of a brotherhood of collectives with similar beliefs. It requires a collective sense of territory as an ensemble of interests and the creation of a collective sense of supremacy in opposition to a territorially external 'other'. For Schmitt the international order of land appropriations in the Middle Ages underpins all other appropriations and regulations (i.e. laws) because the authority upon which these appropriations are predicated emerges out of the sovereign–state. The right of rule when aligned with the rewards of land appropriations in the New World (particularly the Americas) required a rethinking of means and methods by which the enemy was defined as enemy.[4] This placed a higher premium on the rewards of proprietorial occupation of the New World above any spiritual or theological alignment between the *Respublica Christiana* as a European fraternity of rulers. The result of such shifts in the pressures of securing the new territory and imposing an order that would maximise economic rewards for that ownership increased inter-state competition and effectively concretised the shift away from recognition of a theological authority to that of the sovereign–state. In the interests of the sovereign nation-state the primary juridical authority was removed from the spiritual, mythological and theological realm into the administrative, realist and pragmatic realm of government, thus maximising the benefit of land appropriations occurring in the New World. This contributed to a range of shifts in the rights of nobility and aristocracy, realigning what it was to rule with authority over a new type of territory, and managing different reasons for conflict between 'us' and 'them':

> Practically speaking, it meant not only discarding the concepts on which the previous spatial order of the *respublica Christiana* had rested, but eliminating the justification of war they had entailed. This spelled the end of the medieval doctrine of tyrant, i.e. of the rights of challenge and resistance, and of the old 'peace of God'. These were supplanted by a peace guaranteed by the state.
> (Schmitt, 2003 [1950]: 128, original emphasis)

This shift away from *postestas spiritualis* (spiritual power) towards a more mundane earthly power of *civitates* (commonwealth) emerges in synch with a rise in rationalism and scientific thinking. A wider change in the interplay of values poses a significant ethical shift away from the theological, mythical and spiritual authority, to one subsumed by the ethical rationalism of modern and positivist forms of scientific thinking. These changes included the incorporation of the monarch and court methods of estate management, patrimonial administrations, Prussian models of absolutism, and the eventual rise of an administrative constitutionalism linked to increasingly secular nationalism (Poggi, 1990: 42–62). Distinctions of them and us became made not on a religious communitarian basis such as that which underpinned papal authority but on that of a secularised and hybrid nationalism, a different criterion emerged for legitimating regulating conflict as *just*, i.e. in pitting French against Spaniard against English against German, the implication is often made that 'God is with us' in the identification of a just cause for any conflict. It is here that the political is given coherency through the constitutive conflict of land appropriation and land occupation. The forms of normative authority within a territory over a collective population are not given meaning solely through the functional differentiation between internal and external needs, i.e. this is our land, and that which is of the land belongs to us NOT you – but also through the creation of defined boundaries of national territory, the centralisation of bureaucracy under the administrative and judiciary authority of the monarch or ruling body, and often the binding of conflict over land appropriations to religious *just causa belli* (just cause of war) aligned with a national identity, which Schmitt acknowledges in a primitive adage '*cujus regio, cujus religio*' [whose is the territory, his is the religion] centred on the ruler of the nation-state rather than an Emperor or Pope.

In Schmitt's reading of history the epochal change from *Respublica Christiana* to *Jus Publicum Europaeum* indicates only one shift in spatial ordering, another emerges throughout the late nineteenth century into the twentieth century. Problematising this change is the main goal of '*Nomos*'. Particularly emphasised are the rise in influence of American and Asiatic international interests against the explicitly European juridical framework for inter-state relations, which became formative of a shift towards a globalising sense of international law transcending EU continental interests. This is a central component of the shift to a new and more modern 'nomos of the Earth'. Schmitt argues that the spatial order of *Jus Publicum Europaeum* was destabilised by, among other variables: the confusion of minimal requirements of constitutional order in the recognition of statehood among developing countries; the disorientation of juridical thinking between public and private spheres (blurring domestic internal and inter-state external regulations); the juridical separation of the state-public sphere and private sphere of property, trade and economy (e.g. in the growth of free trade doctrines); and the lack of a concrete spatial order to the laws of economic exchanges that gained primacy over the laws of land appropriations. In the emerging global international law these factors effectively destabilised the 'bracketing of war' as legitimate actions of sovereign nation-states and signalled the epochal shift into a new unstable nomic form that lacked any concrete sense of spatial order. While Schmitt emphasises the juridical aspects of these changes the wider impacts on social, cultural, political exchanges are also widespread. The sense of epochal change is limited by an assumption of a holistic and cohesive interest in the preservation of the existing internal order by all members of a collective. It is possible that an anthropological archaeology could be used to interrogate these themes to display more in depth the 'conditions of possibility' for normative interactions between members of a collective, beyond the codes of legalised appropriation and conflict as 'state war'. What is being described are primarily juridical elements of changes to the wider conditions by which particular spatial orders are secured; laying a groundwork for a more critical inclusion of the juridical into our appreciation of economic, political and geographic discussions of statehood, but of limited suitability to uncovering lived experiences within a modern spatial order. These threads that have been reintroduced through the reappreciation of Schmitt are perhaps most useful in discussions of emergency, terrorism and the new security of everyday life elsewhere in this volume. To reach our goals of offering an alternative articulation of the orderly conduct of day-to-day activities we need to look at different approaches to the means by which states attempt to secure everyday life on behalf of their populations.

From Schmitt to Foucault: the order and security of populations

The themes that play out in Foucault have a different emphasis in subject and in focus to Schmitt, articulating the emergence of order over time but in different ways and for a different purpose. For example, where Schmitt was writing many of his early works on 'the political' during the tumultuous reconstitution of Europe after the First World War, expanding the critique of liberal democracy, inter-state relations and the reconstitution of law in the post-war era with *The* Nomos *of the Earth*, Foucault was writing during the political and intellectual struggles of post-war France in the context of the emergent European Union readjusting to the challenges of a globalising capitalism and the rise of alternative lifestyles and ideologies. A shift in focus towards ideological conflict, gender emancipation and increased sexual liberalism, the clash of communism and capitalist values, liberal and neo-liberal political growth, and the ascendance of capitalism over communism in the post-war era began to place the mind and body of the citizen, particularly in relation to the structures of political economy, much more at the heart of the ongoing debate. For thinkers like Foucault this supplanted the concerns of Schmitt and other juridical theorists over the territorial influence of the nation-state and international law with a focus on the population, the citizen and the role of legitimate state authority in their everyday lives. As such there is less concern in Foucault with the appropriation of land and 'productive soil', as the bulk of territory had been (ill)defined by the wars of the early twentieth century. The emphasis of struggle had shifted away from geo-juridical state formation and international relations thereof to the internal spatial discipline through which the order of everyday life is secured.

The discussion of order and security becomes, then, less often about the control of a territorial space in terms of Earth itself. It is now a discussion over securing order itself by embedding discipline in the *population* (Foucault, 2004 [1977]). Less central are the forms of land appropriations as constitutive of a community with a normative ordering of distinctions between 'us and them', between 'friends and enemies' and the juridical ordering emanating from these decisions. Spatial order is being defined here through the isolation and segmentation of spaces through disciplinary forms of power; the mechanisms of that power are able to fully function without constraint as they operate as a bio-politic form of regulation. The bio-political is a vital aspect of this approach as it forms the lens that at once encompasses the specific technologies but also the constitutive process of creating a collective susceptible to this form of rule (Deuber-Mankowsky, 2008: 135). We see a growing emphasis in Foucault's bio-politics on the interplay of variables, such as the regulation of knowledge, the rationalisation of law, and mechanisms of discipline and security paralleling on the nuanced land appropriations of Schmitt's discussion in a more elegant way to demonstrate the interplay of soil-grain through political economy and the disciplining spaces of planned urban environments as constitutive elements of ordering in everyday life. The discussion must emphasise the networked interplay by which disciplinary mechanisms and techniques reconstitute the processes of everyday life. This security-based emphasis differs from the juridical approach of Schmitt, a difference well pointed out in the 1978 lectures at the *Collège de France*:

> In other words, the law prohibits and discipline proscribes, and the essential function of security, without prohibiting or prescribing, but

possibly making use of some instruments of prescription and prohibition, is to respond to a reality in such a way that this response cancels out the reality to which it responds – nullifies it, or limits, checks or regulates it.
(Foucault, 2003 [1975]: 47)

This regulatory emphasis of the apparatus of security is one that seeks to stabilise and ensure the continuance of a given status quo in what could be called an 'orderly' fashion, supplementing and at times sublating the stricter functions of law through mechanisms of ordering largely ignored by Schmitt, such as policing. Particularly interesting variables for Foucault are thus: the government of individual people and collective populations; the ways in which discipline orders through mechanisms, apparatus and processes; the normative influences of sovereign authority on the bodies of individuals; and the emergence of disciplined bodies as functional outcome of the mechanisms and processes of government. These variables can be seen to act as constituent elements through which the broader *episteme* of a given epoch is developed, thus ordering the relations between people *within* and *with* the State rather than between collective populations *as* nation-states. Foucault appreciates the sovereign–state differently to Schmitt. Rather than dissolution of sovereign statehood as a global ordering mechanism Foucault emphasises the transformation of the sovereign state into the 'governmentalised' state. Rather than discussing the juridical implications of an administrative transformation in terms of inter-state relations or the constitution of authority (which Foucault considered to be reductive), the focus is on interrogating the interplay of sovereignty, discipline and governmental management as a triangulation of authority upon the population, using the apparatus of security as the primary mechanisms of ordering (Foucault, 2003 [1975]: 107–9). A simpler way of saying this might be to suggest that we do not here discuss the construction and form of the state, but rather on the state of government as an ensemble or dressage of interventions into the order of everyday life.

The changing order and security of everyday life

Developing this useful contrast between Foucault and Schmitt we can further these distinctions by addressing the different readings of change between epochs as indicative of a particular form or type of order. In particular, regarding the lectures given at the *Collège de France* between 1975 and 1979, reference is often made to the same shift between medieval, renaissance and enlightenment periods[5] discussed in *The Nomos of the Earth* (Schmitt, 2003 [1950]). Our attention is directed towards familiar elements of how a spatial order can be secured, for example: the relationship between war, power and law; a theory of sovereignty; juridical and economic conceptions of power; the shift in the focus of authority from a pastoral (religious) to administrative power of the authoritative sovereign. However, there are a number of key differences that we need to understand to frame the variant approaches to sovereignty and space in Foucault and Schmitt.

Our first issue of note in developing the discussion here is the striking similarity between the friend–enemy distinction made by Schmitt and Foucault's claim that 'we are all inevitably someone's adversary' (Foucault, 2003: 51). However, there are key differences of note. Schmitt's approach to authority in *Nomos* suggests that the distinction between friend and enemy is bound to the juridical frameworks of political power underpinning the transformation of legal justifications for war between states.[6] Foucault explicitly shifts the focus out of the juridical realm of right, law and sovereignty to a political realm seeking to analyse a perpetual war of agitation against powerful forces of domination and subjugation. In its essence this is a study of the strategic struggle between the freedom of action in everyday life and the disciplined government of an ordered everyday life. The distinction draws on what is seen here as the inevitably adversarial nature of the human subject. The goal is not to grasp at a unified philosophical truth, but to demonstrate the point of view used to legitimate the right of the collective (tribe, nation-state, etc.) to engage in violent conflict. Such conflict being primarily in this case undertaken for the appropriation of land or the eradication of a competitor for that land. The understanding of adversarial difference here suggests that these binary relationships of force are flawed, perspectival, dissymmetric and uneven. As such any claim to truth and legitimate right is a false claim, resulting in a perpetual war that is permanently anchored in the historical field of juridical thinking (and therefore difficult to displace) yet politically decentralised from the knowing subject going about their day-to-day routine. For Foucault we must move beyond these juridical representations of authority and power to a more nuanced genealogy of how order emerges, how a 'pact of security' is made between the government and the population.

Second, the presentation of this discussion as less of a historico-juridical discourse and more a historico-political discourse is striking, and gives a very different emphasis in interpretation of security, order and territory. One example of this difference is in the role of conflict in the guise of war. Both Foucault and Schmitt offer a discussion of war as a central concern for understanding the constitution of the modern social order, but where Schmitt arguably offers a '*where* of power' through the formation of the sovereign territorial state, Foucault attempts to ask about the '*how* of power'. By changing the focus of the question asked the emphasis moves away from a juridical emphasis on the codified formation of a unified sovereign authority further towards the study of mechanisms and processes by which this sovereign authority is enacted, from the unified authority of the ruler to the multiplicity of cyclical power relations used to rule:

> the theory of sovereignty shows, or attempts to show, how a power can be constituted, not exactly in accordance with the law, but in accordance with a certain basic legitimacy that is more basic than any law and that allows for laws to function as such. The theory of sovereignty is, in other words, the subject-to-subject cycle, the cycle of power and powers, and

the cycle of legitimacy and law . . . It therefore assumes the existence of three 'primitive' elements: a subject who has to be subjectified, the unity of power, and the legitimacy that has to be respected. Subject, unitary power, and law . . .

(Foucault, 2003: 44)

The emphasis here is on moving beyond the juridical to understand the subject at a micro-level, as an individual citizen, yes, but also as a member of a population, and it is the population that is the particular target of government intervention via the juridico-legal code, the mechanisms of discipline and the apparatus of security (*dispositifs*). This is a move away from a focus on the international relations *between* sovereign nation-states to the everyday relations of individuals to each other *within* states, away from the external ordering of exchanges to the internal ordering of experiences. The move is from a historic-juridical sense of external war between others as a precondition of an ordered society to a sense of a historic-political and internal war fought to preserve the social order against 'threats born of and within its own body' (Foucault, 2003: 216). States are therefore the arbiters of legitimate relations of violence, in the form of war, and when this can be undertaken on behalf of the personified nation-state (external regulations) but also the custodians of the law, and of punishment as examples of the many mechanisms mobilised to regulate everyday life (internal regulations). War is seen as principally a historico-political discourse (Foucault, 2003: 49) of everyday relations, this makes the *internal war* 'the motor behind institutions and order' (Foucault, 2003: 50) and is therefore central to understanding the methods by which a 'normal' everyday conduct among the population is made secure.

Third, when looking into the themes we have set up in this discussion as we compare and contrast the approaches of Schmitt and Foucault there is a subtle realignment of those themes. While we began here outlining the themes of order-territory-security in Schmitt, we have moved to a reconstitution of these concepts in Foucault's use of security-territory-population. However, Foucault himself makes note that this is not exactly what the focus of his argument emphasises, but on the one hand the series of security-population-government (Foucault, 2003: 88) and the other furthering the broader concept of 'govermentality' (Foucault, 2003: 108). What is meant by government is not in and of itself juridical, this must move past a limiting sense of man's right under the guidance of sovereign authority. It is far more an interrogation of the strategic mechanisms used to ensure ordered circulations in everyday life, i.e. a genealogy of order emerging through analysis of the disciplined conduct of the disciplined subject under the guiding influence of an 'art of government' (see for example Foucault, 2004 [1977]: 79, 100–5), a key rejection of the founding principles of Schmitt's argument. This is a shift in thinking away from the external ordering of territory in terms of inter-state relations towards ensuring that things move around in an efficient and orderly way, be they resources, people or the requirements of survival – such as air in a plague-ridden town. Probably among the better examples of this realignment of territory in the thinking of Foucault comes in his treatment of the police. Drawing on the work of Domas the suggestion is made that the rise of the police is synchronised with modern sensibility of the urban, not simply through the disciplining influence of militating forms in urban space, but also through the ways in which problems that were typically urban required regulation, many being born from the growth of urban commerce in the town and city marketplace, the dense cohabitation of so many people in towns and cities, and the rise of mercantile international relations between European states (Foucault, 2004: 333–40). Through Foucault I would argue that we can realign our use of order, security and territory to bring out a more nuanced reading of nomos. The nomic ordering of space is through such a reading embedded deeper than the strictly juridical sense, it is also linked to the organisation of everyday spaces, the organisation of institutions of order, the mechanisms and practices of ordering, embedding discipline in the everydayness of particular locations but further into the moral and ethical understanding of what is acceptable underpinning the collective sense of community.

Nomos and everyday life?

When rethinking the themes of *order* and *territory*, for example, it is clear that for Schmitt an understanding of order is necessarily tied to the law but that this had limited aspirations and specific goals that emphasised the reformation of jurisprudence, the dangers of a world without a concrete spatial, or *nomic*, order and a broader critique of the liberal project of market globalisation (Levinson, 2005: 206–7). In applying a sense of the law as broadly *nomic*, the law forms the codified juridical framework emanating from appropriations and distinctions of otherness that legitimates the concrete spatial order of a community. At the core of Schmitt's approach to 'the political' is the mediation of order between the insider and the other, effectively between 'us' and 'them'. The exercise of power over either of these groups is imposed through the nomic order, made manifest in law. The political and the nomic come together as a means of developing and ensuring *security* of 'us', defined in opposition to 'them'. As such we need a clearer understanding of security. This raises a number of questions for a discussion of our three keys themes, for example: is the community necessarily something territorial? How do different communities secure their coexistence if they are defined in opposition to one another? Put differently, how do different 'nomic orders' *interplay* across territories to create a secure international community? It is at this point that two things happen: (a) it becomes sensible to answer these questions by studying both order and security as being inherently *spatial*; (b) we cannot apply this sense of order to everyday life in direct or meaningful terms, another lens is needed to give focus to the impact of a *nomic* order on the everyday lives of the population.

In the first instance, Schmitt operationalises the law as an applicable set of relations and conditions with meaning only insofar as they are applied to a particular defined territory, thus making the discussion a discussion of giving *order* to a *space*. This ordering of the territory occurs for the purpose of increasing 'security' – be it for the security of the state, the body-politic, the citizen, the ruling decision-makers, the productive soil from which resources are drawn, etc. As such the purpose and role of governance and government in relation to the population of the territory (i.e. the people living there) is also a factor in determining the form of any sensical 'order' as it is they who decide what to secure, who to secure and what are the legitimate ways and means of creating, and enforcing, security.[7] This presents avenues into understanding everyday life but they are largely limited to the justification of codified rules of engagement between enemies, and most often as collective groups under the guise of nation-statehood.

Similar themes but different problems emerge from this reading of Foucault. For example, I have pointed out above that in the collected works of Schmitt there is a preoccupation with the importance of the law. Though this is inevitable given his occupation it is perhaps the shifting sense of security as the order of everyday life, bounded by space as a territorial framework for relations, that bind us to a given 'way of doing' everyday life that forms the central interest here. This is intended to create a more meaningful understanding of the struggle or 'internal war' over the appropriate and legitimate constitution of sovereign power as a means of decision-making – hence the appropriate use of power to secure order within national boundaries (territory). In the work of Foucault a key emphasis is placed not on the normative power of a legal order – and therefore the secure spatial order of the community but on the law as one of many 'technical operations' or 'mechanisms of security' used by decision-makers to direct the 'everyday experience' of populations *within* spaces. In particular, for Foucault, the themes of discipline and social order as tied to the spatial can be linked to a discussion of wider freedoms among the population of a nation-state, the appropriate use of authority to secure the people themselves as well as the territory they inhabit, and as a result emphasising the relationships between the transgression of norms and the responses to those transgressions by those tasked with creating the growth, development and maintenance of a given order. This focus on populations over territories places less emphasis initially on territory and more on the practical influence of authority in both securing and ordering populations, both through and within particular types of spaces – be they towns, camps or even bodies. Each approach evokes similar themes yet offers nuanced differences in emphasis, thus creating critically different approaches to the form and process of legitimate rule.

The conceptual re-reading offered here offers a critical reflection on the connections and disjunctions between Schmitt's nomic understanding of sovereignty and law, with Foucault's genealogy of security, territory and population. It is hoped that this will draw out the interplay between order, territory and security as more than themes of discussion but as variables of analysis, and thus enhance our reflection on the challenges to social and spatial ordering over time. This temporal twist emphasises the importance of an analysis that looks betwixt and between the discrete layers of process, suggesting that change itself is an ongoing 'interplay' between variables; and it is study of this interplay that allows us to get to the root of nomic and ethical principles that underpin the creation of a secure spatial order in everyday life. This can also contribute to 'going beyond' traditional readings of politically realist, historically materialist and even dialectically materialist approaches to the growth and development of the state and sovereign power in a (re)constitutive way. The underpinning values of a nomic order may be seen to in fact complement operable political actions as akin to practices of governmentality. If we suggest that nomos and everyday life inform each other, they can be seen to some extent as creating each other, thus becoming the foundation upon which actions taken to secure a given order are made legitimate or illegal, ethical or unethical, right or wrong. This becomes an analysis of the 'internal war' of adversarial relationships implicit in the conduct of everyday life, and security thus becomes securing the order inherent in our perpetual war. That is securing the conduct of struggle itself. Even though the politico-geographical context at the time that Foucault was writing appears much more stable than that of Schmitt, perhaps with the exception of Algiers, there is in his earlier lectures a distinct emphasis on adversarial relations that is sublated within a more abstract appreciation of the 'counter-conduct' inherent in civil society and populations and, thus, in everyday life.

Both 'nomos' and the 'counter-conduct' of everyday life as concepts evoke a sense of processual ordering of experience in different ways, examples of readings that broaden the exceptional beyond the juridical are beginning to emerge from analytical interpretations of Schmitt and Agamben, and the work on exception is a larger part of the contemporary surge in interest in Schmitt (see Minca in this volume). Alongside this the historical geographies of nomos give a political applicability to the major themes in relation to debates in international relations (Odysseos and Petito, 2007) but there is room for a thematic appraisal as well, and I have sought to develop here an appreciation of these themes that evokes the adversarial qualities of order itself. The theoretical appraisal of order, security, territory and population forms a backdrop for a related, but distinct, contribution to work on security, emergency planning, disaster management and the looming threat of natural disaster and bio-terrorism, and while we do not develop these issues of research in depth here there is much to gain from thinking critically about the nomic ordering of ethical government in the identification of the adversary, the ordering of adversarial relations and the orderly struggle of everyday life through the themes of order, territory and security.

A larger part of this critique of Schmitt has suggested that the juridical is over-emphasised at the expense of the experiences of power identified in Foucault; this creates some problems for the perceived shift into ever more decentralised administrative distinctions on how such appropriations, distributions and productions of resources from land are made legal and placed at the centre of understanding every social and economic order, as discussed in the concluding corollaries (Schmitt, 2003 [1950]: 324–55). In justifying his juridical emphasis Schmitt returns to the logical structure of creating social order through overly disciplinary doctrines:

> Unlike philologists, jurists and historians usually translate nomos as 'law' or, to distinguish it from written law, as 'tradition' or 'custom'. I prefer the simplest approach, since we are interested in determining the structure of various social orders and doctrines in all the specialised disciplines, and in finding the proper formulation of the questions with respect to the core of their ethic and their view of history.
> (Schmitt, 2003 [1950]: 325–6)

This is an interesting point, and it suggests that the question of a new nomos – that is never entirely answered by Schmitt in *The* Nomos *of the Earth* – is perhaps an attempt to problematise the decline of an ethical everyday life immanent within, and at the core of, the concrete spatial order of *Jus Publicum Europaeum*. In securing this emergent nomic spatial order we can develop Schmitt in particular cases of international relations, but in terms of assessing the everyday life of a broader modernity we must look elsewhere as others have, to offer a new and refined reconstitution of Schmitt and Foucault for a more holistic analysis of how the adversarial ordering of populations is to be secured in future.

Notes

1. For some more detailed attempts to do so refer to the work of Prozorov (2004) that charts links between Foucault, Schmitt and Kundera in regard to ethical descisionism; Levinson (2005) that offers a comparative focus on the convergence of themes between Foucault, Schmitt and Baudrillard on relations of power as duopolies; and Hannah (in this volume) regarding pastoral power in more depth.
2. Given that our focus is here on the specifically spatial aspects of Schmitt we do not go into great depth on this, but for more detail refer to the *Concept of the Political* (Schmitt, 1996 [1932]: 26–34).
3. This should not be confused as a tie between the creation of global linear thinking, and the creation of new international law through the contestation of amity lines as emerging from the shift towards a new global thinking post-1492; this is directly related to the shift from the authority of the Pope to that of regionalised monarchies as moral as well as administrative orders in their own right in the sixteenth and seventeenth centuries.
4. To some extent this may be framed also as to the extent by which the enemy is defined as 'other', though this distinction is by no means straightforward (see Legg in this volume).
5. While neither Schmitt nor Foucault use these explicit periodisations – Schmitt refers to the Middle Ages, renaissance and nomic periods, whereas Foucault emphasises

the classical and enlightenment, for example, they are used here for the sake of brevity and consistency.
6 This is specifically the case in the shift from a medieval framework to *Jus Publicum Europaeum*, less central to the emergence of the new nomos of the Earth, of which Schmitt was intensely critical.
7 Importantly for Schmitt the population of the territory, in particular the relations of individuals with each other, and as a collective, are addressed through his work on the concept of the political, political theology and in the distinctions between 'friend' and 'enemy', less a theme in *The* Nomos *of the Earth*, which is the most spatial of his works.

References

Deuber-Manowski, A. (2008) 'Nothing is Political, Everything can be Politicised: On the Concept of the Political in Michel Foucault and Carl Schmitt', *Telos*, 142: 135–62.

Foucault, M. (2003) *Society Must be Defended: Lectures at the Collège du France 1975–1976*, London, Palgrave, trans. D. Masey.

Foucault, M. (2004) *Security, Territory, Population: Lectures at the Collège du France 1977–1978*, London, Palgrave, trans. G. Burchill.

Levinson, B. (2005) 'The Coming Nomos; or, the Decline of Other Orders in Schmitt', *The South Atlantic Quarterly*, 104 (2): 205–15.

Mouffe, C. (2007) 'Carl Schmitt's Warning of a Unipolar World' in Odysseos, L. & Petito, F. (eds) (2007) *The International Political Thought of Carl Schmitt: Terror, Liberal War and the Crisis of Global Order*, London, Routledge: 148–53.

Odysseos, L. and Petito, F. (eds) (2007) *The International Political Thought of Carl Schmitt: Terror, Liberal War and the Crisis of Global Order*, London, Routledge.

Poggi, G. (1990) *The State: Its Nature, Development and Prospects*, Stanford, CA, Stanford University Press.

Prozorov, S. (2004) 'Three Theses on "Governance" and the Political', *Journal of International Relations and Development*, 7 (3): 267–93.

Schmitt, C. (1996 [1932]) *The Concept of the Political*, Chicago, University of Chicago Press, trans. George Schwab.

Schmitt, C (2003 [1950]) *The Nomos of the Earth: In the International Law of the Jus Publicum Europaeum*, New York, Telos, trans. G.L. Ulman.

Zarmanian, T. (2006) 'Carl Schmitt and the Problem of Legal Order: From Domestic to International', *Leiden Journal of International Law*, 19: 41–67.

Part IV

Responses to the *Nomos*

12 Remembering Nazi intellectuals

David Atkinson

One problem with reading Schmitt, Dean notes limpidly, is that for many contemporary scholars the Nazi concentration camps '... haunt every word Schmitt writes, no matter how illuminating [they might be]' (Dean 2006: 12). Like Heidegger, here is a thinker compromised by the stain of Nazi associations. The long shadow of National Socialism darkens his reputation as it does with other intellectuals who were affiliated to the regime. Indeed, as Moses points out, twenty-first century Germany still witnesses left-leaning thinkers such as Jurgen Habermas and Gunter Grass interrogated over their slender connections to Nazism when young (Moses 2007). Schmitt by contrast, and despite his undulating influence in the higher reaches of the regime, remained an enduring supporter of Nazism and, after 1945, refused to be de-Nazified. Neither was he typical of the European intellectuals drawn to 'the seductions of unreason', the apparent glamour and 'the intellectual romance of fascism' – in Wolin's (2004) terms – because he was too significant politically. His work as an advisor to Papen and Schleicher under the Weimar Republic, plus his later associations with Göring and his drafting of key early legislation for the Nazis, lent him influence well beyond mere fascist sympathisers such as Paul de Man, T.S. Eliot, Ezra Pound or, Wolin adds, George Bataille (Cristi 1998; Moses 2007; Stirk 1999; Wolin 2004). Consequently, his politics tarnish his work due to a mass of (often understandable) preconceptions and reservations about the man and his oeuvre. Some critics worry about the responsibility of exploring and unleashing these ideas; others saw Schmitt more plainly as a moral pollutant (Dean 2006). Many writing about him seem to respond to an affective requirement to condemn Schmitt's politics. Indeed, so conspicuous are these disconcerting, discomforting Nazi associations that Balakrishnan opens his biography by stating that 'In the English-speaking world [Schmitt] is terra incognita, a name redolent of Nazism [whose work comes] to us from a disturbing place and time' (Balakrishnan 2000: 1).

A disturbing place indeed: as Judt writes, the twentieth century was 'uniquely horrible [and] in many ways a truly awful era, an age of brutality and mass-suffering perhaps unequalled in the historic record' (2009: 4). Consequently, remembering twentieth-century fascisms is a troubling, worrying business that agitated some corners of post-war academia relentlessly. Remembering Nazism is more difficult still, due to the bleak magnitude of the regime's crimes and the destruction it wrought. Remembering and exploring intellectuals who allied willingly with National Socialism is one of the more minor, but still thorny, challenges within these fields – particularly as any potential insight these thinkers offer are thereafter tainted by these woeful political associations. This essay outlines briefly the broad contours of how some European academic debates have ignored and, later, remembered the connections between National Socialism and German intellectuals across the post-war period (although it also addresses other interwar fascisms tangentially when post-1945 commentators conflated Nazism with them). It thus helps to contextualise how we have remembered, and how we should recall, thinkers such as Schmitt with their problematic politics.

Abjecting National Socialism and its intellectuals after the war

The trauma and terror of the Second World War convulsed societies for much of the subsequent decades. In Europe, this second total war in a short period further transformed how people interpreted warfare, ideology, patriotism and the state. For modern warfare affected civilian lives too – particularly for continental Europeans who were often scarred by occupation and oppression, and the constant risks of forced dislocation, disease, poverty and famine. Consequently, given these raw, recent memories and the continuing issues of reconciliation and retribution that still coursed through daily lives, the war was never far from public memories in the early post-war period. Further, as the realisation of the intent and extent of the Holocaust and associated Nazi crimes filtered into Western imaginations in the 1950s–60s, such was the additional enormity of these events that the Nazi episode cast a lengthy pall over European civil society thereafter. To some, it seemed that this particularly epochal event had changed European civilisation forever: as Theodore Adorno claimed in 1949, 'to write poetry after Auschwitz is barbaric' (Adorno 1967, 19; Rothberg 2000).

Indeed, such was the trauma of this episode that a tendency emerged to demonise, abject and distance Nazism from modern, 'civilised' society. So dreadful were Nazi crimes that it was easier to see the regime as an aberration – as separate and other, as abhorrent and alien, as an isolated calamity when a nation was led astray by a criminal minority (Dawidowicz 1991; Eley 1988; Gubar 2003). In (West) Germany, the post-war social democracy was based upon a repentant and confessional ethos fuelled by shame and guilt (Moses 2007). Some work suggests that Germany's public atonement was mirrored by a more subdued but persistent metaphor of the 'catastrophe' of Nazism that had befallen Germany (Lüdtke 1993). Likewise, in 1959 Adorno broadcast a lecture entitled *What does coming to terms with the past mean?*, which identified various forms of erasure, repression and wilful forgetting among many (West) Germans (Lüdtke 1993). While this elision of the past allowed a measure of self-respect to Germans (Eley 1988; Evans 1989), these displacement strategies were ways of coping (Moses 2007).

A further coping mechanism – that I focus upon from here onwards – was disavowing the notion that the Nazis produced, used and celebrated ideas, culture, scholarship and learning. Wolin (2004) suggests that in the immediate post-war years it was often comforting to portray Nazism (and fascisms more generally) as anti-intellectual and generally suspicious of ideas and independent thinkers. This approach allowed fascisms to be circumscribed and *contained* as evil and barbarous, as unique events from beyond modern, civilised European societies. This strategy filtered into academic approaches too (Hamilton 1971). Amid the varied and numerous attempts to explain the phenomenon of Nazism, many writers persisted with the blanket assertion that the regime was devoid of thinkers, ideas and ideology. This stance proved to be curiously durable.

Marxist commentators of the interwar years and the 1950s, for example, reiterated that no legitimate thinking could emerge from Nazi Germany. They interpreted European fascisms as reactionary movements responding to a crisis of capitalism, but also as projects that rendered the mass media an instrument of tyranny intended to brainwash and divert an unthinking population (Paxton 2004). Their approach ignored the possibility of human choice and the mass appeal of the regime, but it also failed to address the possibility that ideas or ideology might have existed within fascisms, or that these ideas might have earned consensus. This omission was echoed by the mass-psychology theories of fascisms that argued that the uneducated (and undifferentiated) masses were attracted by the order promised by fascist regimes and beguiled by charismatic leaders (Nathan 1943; Reich 1946). Despite the furore that surrounded him, Daniel Goldhagen (1996) is simply the latest to argue that the German people were hard-wired to respond to clear orders and leadership. But again, in all these traditions, the role of ideas and rational, measured intellectual choices was not seen as part of the decision to support, or acquiesce, to the regime's agenda. Rather, it was usual to dismiss fascist ideologies as ad hoc, partial or simply non-existent (Griffin 1998: 6); again, such explanations sidelined any thinkers, ideas or intellectual content that were involved in fascisms' support because such an eventuality was inconceivable to many commentators.

The theories of totalitarianism that developed in the 1950s did see a creeping acceptance that ideas and ideologies might inform fascisms. In 1945 Hannah Arendt prophesised that totalitarianism and the question of evil would dominate intellectual debate in post-war Europe. In 1951's *The Origins of Totalitarianism* she therefore insisted that we should engage with regimes' ideologies – although she focused upon the banal, everyday reproduction of evil (Arendt 1951). Likewise, Friedrich and Brzezinski's influential analysis of totalitarianism admitted that fascisms contained 'official ideologies' (Gregor 1997 [1974]: 222) – although this concession was perhaps prompted by a Cold War requirement to label the Soviet Union, with its clear ideology, as totalitarian (Friedrich and Brzezinski 1956). Similarly, later work on fascism by Weber (1964) and Nolte (1965) also began to take fascist ideologies and their genealogies more seriously, and by the mid-1970s Gregor (1997 [1974]) and Sternhell (1976) could talk more openly about fascist ideas and their lineage – although each admitted this would not have been possible a few years earlier (Eatwell 1992; Griffin 1998); indeed, Gregor claimed that even after half a century, the number of competent works on the ideology of Italian fascism could still be counted on one hand (1997 [1974]). Although fascist ideas were being acknowledged by some, there remained a stubborn tendency to deny that there was any intellectual content in these regimes.

For example, post-war orthodoxy held that many who ascended Nazi hierarchies successfully were 'opportunists' driven by the desire for power and favour; few, it was implied, offered any learning or philosophy to the regime. Yet this erasure of ideas and intellectuals from Nazism seems to have been a luxury that only academics enjoyed, and only after the event. For those charged with the practical business of de-Nazifying the defeated state it was clear that intellectuals had worked for the regime. This was hardly surprising: many of the 'opportunists' were well educated, not least as early twentieth-century Germany was perhaps the most modern, efficient state in Europe (Eley 1988). It was thus myopic of subsequent commentators to excise ideology from Nazism and its public appeal: many educated Germans were either sympathetic to the regime's initial aims and rhetoric, assented to its rise, or actively supported the Nazis (Wolin 2004). Others were drawn within the regime's purview once it attained power over the state apparatus in 1933; many more found it expedient to cooperate thereafter (given the intolerance of political opposition).

The business of de-Nazification, therefore, had to address the infusion of Nazi ideas and cultures into numerous corners of German society. The 're-education' of Germans involved asserting that they were *all* guilty for the crimes of the regime (Marcuse 2001), but some quarters of society received particular attention. University academics closely connected to the regime were often purged, as were individuals from other branches of education and the public services. Schmitt was interned and questioned by the Allies. His refusal to engage with de-Nazification cost him his Chair at Berlin University and he was excluded from post-war academic life, although his high-profile reputation as the key legal theorist of the regime also contributed to his eviction (Bendersky 1983; Preuss 1999). Likewise, de-Nazification did not always progress as planned elsewhere. In the Western zones at least, it became a bureaucratic behemoth that confirmed self-pity and notions of victimhood among the 95 per cent of Germans categorised as 'fellow travellers'. Further, many of those purged in 1945–6 were reinstated between 1948 and 1951 as the US administration started to rebuild local government urgently so that it might function in response to emerging Cold War threats (Lüdtke 1993). Meanwhile Schmitt, while exiled from academic institutions, continued to write and publish – including *The* Nomos *of the Earth*. On its own terms then, de-Nazification and re-education failed to stop us debating Schmitt today.

In sum, although an understandable attempt to contain and deal with the enormity of the Nazi past, the various efforts of the post-war years to separate the regime from its contexts floundered. The urge to disavow the cultural and intellectual elements of National Socialism was similarly futile. By contrast, recent attempts to reassess German fascism are more critical of these simplistic positions and the structuralist urges that drive them. Moreover, according to Wolin, we also enjoy a new perspective upon '... the relationship between German scholarship and National Socialism. Intellectual collaboration, once thought to be the exception, has turned out to be the rule' (2004: 92). In this final section I will discuss how these newer approaches open up the field of state-intellectual engagements for further study, and more specifically, how they help us to better contextualise Schmitt by exploring academic knowledge production under the Nazi regime.

Reappraising academics and the state in Nazi Germany

As the second half of the twentieth century developed, so did our understandings of the Nazi regime. For instance, although useful and employed widely in initial attempts to comprehend the Holocaust academically, reductionist ontological categories such as 'victims', 'perpetrators' and 'bystanders' started to appear rather lumpen for useful application to Germany's interwar history (Hilberg 1961; Moses 2007). Likewise, 'guilt' is too lax a concept for the entangled, tortured memories and emotions that erupt around the Nazi past. Equally, dualistic categories (remembering/forgetting; good/bad, etc.) are also too blunt to assess these histories (Moses 2007). And a figure such as Schmitt – an intellectual with a clear enthusiasm for the regime and a post-war reluctance to apologise – also blurs the simplistic binary distinctions that characterised many initial attempts to understand the regime and its consensus. By contrast, more recent research allows us to situate the roles of academics and intellectuals and their tangled relations with the regime more productively.

As Szöllösi-Janze points out in her comprehensive survey of science under Nazism, well into the 1970s historians reproduced the story that National Socialism was fundamentally anti-scientific: at once in thrall to 'distorted pseudo-sciences' while established German science was 'misused, severely damaged and finally destroyed' as genuine scholars were persecuted or exiled on political grounds (Szöllösi-Janze 2001: 4). Likewise, the 1950s theories of totalitarianism often read science as *legitimising* these regimes: from this perspective, science was simultaneously politicised and compromised. For sure, formal academic production was hindered by some Nazi strategies. Fifteen per cent of university academics were excluded by the first racial laws in April 1933 for example (which Schmitt failed to protest), and critics argue that long-term damage was done to scientific education and research (Dawidowicz 1991). Meanwhile, the regime prompted some academics to retreat into 'internal exile' whereby they withdrew from academic organisations, publishing and any other public roles. Others, like Schmitt, embraced Nazism. He joined the party in

May 1933 and soon became increasingly enmeshed in the regime's institutions and ever more public in his support of Nazi projects, including its anti-semitism (Bendersky 1983). This was an open and conscious commitment (Stirk 2005). He elected to provide a theoretical underpinning for the regime's initial legal manoeuvres, while positions such as head of the Nazi law professors' guild required his active collaboration. Schmitt, it seems, was making his way through the various interest-groups of Nazi Germany.

By the 1980s the impacts of contextualised, situated studies of science in society allowed more nuanced interpretations of how thinkers like Schmitt might flourish (or falter) under such circumstances. Subsequent research explored the interdependence between political structures and knowledge production under fascisms (Szöllösi-Janze 2001). This reassessment allowed some aspects of Nazi science to be embedded within their wider, international contexts. 'Racial hygiene science', for example, could be connected to international eugenics debates rather than being held apart as unique and discrete. The utilitarian and technocratic nature of the Nazi state – with its increasing number of research institutes and 'experts' – was also acknowledged increasingly (Herf 1984). This entailed understanding how the comparatively early scientisation of German society from the 1880s and the subsequent emergence of technocrats (especially the rise of social scientists who modelled and monitored society) is also part of this story. This early development of a knowledge economy in Germany – a 'scientific society' to Szöllösi-Janze, with significant investment in research and development – became more militarised under the Weimar Republic, and further still under Nazism. For example, the spatial planners of the regime won funding for research centres and found clear applications in the *Ostforschung* – the planning of Eastern Europe as a colonial domain (Burleigh 1988). Further, the 'intellectual justifications for German political hegemony, far from being of exclusively Nazi provenance, were widely purveyed by nationalistically inclined German scholars of varying political persuasions' (Wolin 2004: 90). These willing academics also spanned the sciences and humanities.

Indeed, for all the irrational mysticism and esoteric racial theory that we remember from some quarters of Nazism, the more mundane, rational, natural and physical sciences continued to function normally under the regime. Many academics in aeronautics, medicine, engineering and biology and, less immediately, in physics and chemistry, were promoted by the Nazi state as long as they could adapt to these new working contexts (Szöllösi-Janze 2001). In turn, the regime promoted, funded and applied the knowledge that emerged. Geography, for example, found support for exploration, for surveys of territories coveted by the Nazi hierarchy, and also contributed to the *Ostforschung* initiative; other geographers taught younger Germans about their fatherland and its expansionist requirements, while the geopolitical theorists surrounding Karl Haushofer's *Zeitschrift für Geopolitik* sought to diffuse expansionist theorising to a wider, popular audience (Fahlbusch *et al.* 1989; Heske 1986; Ó Tuathail 1996; Sandner and Rossler 1994). And as with other high-profile ideas from Nazi Germany, the subsequent notoriety of geopolitics caused a post-war hiatus in the study of political geography (Atkinson and Dodds 2000).

The humanities also chased the regime's attention and favour – not least to keep in touch with their scientific peers. Historians, for example, found roles in preparing for Eastern colonisation and in the Reich's 'Institute for the History of the New Germany' (Dawidowicz 1991; Wolin 2004). Other subjects that had less obvious practical applications survived and developed. Sociology established itself as a subject of use in researching border studies, migration, employment issues and marginal groups – all of which was deemed useful knowledge by the expansionist state. Even psychology and psychotherapy (once purged of what the Nazis perceived as Jewish practitioners and 'influence') emerged in this period and were gradually institutionalised as recognised academic pursuits (Szöllösi-Janze 2001).

Finally, these new portraits of science and the state were rendered more complex by the realisation that the Nazi state was not as monolithic and totalitarian as previous interpretations suggested. Leading Nazis and the ministries or organisations they headed vied for Hitler's attention, approval and patronage; they also pursued a range of ideologically driven pet projects, some of which seeped into higher education and research. These various centres of power meant that intellectuals had to navigate within and across the spaces of this sometimes chaotic polycratic state to access influence and patronage (Mason 1995). This shifting matrix of power hindered some thinkers, and provided opportunities for others at different times. Schmitt, for example, despite his prominence and utility to the regime, encountered intermittent opposition: he was once warned about articulating ideas that Hitler was also claiming as his own (Stirk 1999), and in 1936 he was excluded from further serious influence in Nazism when his work prompted negative press coverage from elements of the SS (Neocleous 1996). Göring protected Schmitt, however, who continued to write in support of Nazism and its ends (Stirk 2005).

Again, the initial post-war blanket recollections of 'good science' and 'bad science' that preponderated in some quarters did not reflect the complexities of interwar Germany. There were many more grey areas than these interpretations allowed. Further, as Szöllösi-Janze (2001) emphasises, although there were some marked changes to the university system, other elements of academia simply continued under Nazism and, indeed, through into the post-war period. Journals continued to publish and universities continued to function; again, it is clear that Nazi Germany was not a land without intellectuals.

Conclusion: putting Schmitt in his place

Such are our contemporary understandings of early-twentieth-century Germany, and this is where we should situate Carl Schmitt and his work. We may understand why earlier commentators did not wish to acknowledge the roles of science, ideas and intellectuals under Nazism and fascist regimes. We can also recognise why the demonisation of Nazism as an abject, alien eruption in modern European history was an attractive option to some (although this position fails to acknowledge how the regime and its terror were produced and enabled by European modernity (Bauman 1989)). Nevertheless, Weimar and Nazi Germany and their applied intellectual cultures provide one of Schmitt's contexts – however uncomfortable this may be for contemporary reassessments of his insight. The second context I will note is the evolving debates over how we remember Nazism and its thinkers. Again, we may not be comfortable with the number of interwar thinkers who were drawn to fascisms, but their numbers demonstrate that we cannot ignore them or the appeal of fascist regimes. The aftermath of National Socialism still swirls through German society in particular and many branches of the academy are tentatively excavating their roles under Nazism. As more twenty-first-century scholars adapt Schmitt's ideas across a range of different scenarios, we also need to remain attuned to the various debates about how he and his ilk should be remembered.

References

Adorno, T.W. (1967) Cultural Criticism and Society, in his *Prisms* (trans. Samuel and Shierry Weber), Cambridge, MA: MIT Press.

Arendt, H. (1951) *The Origins of Totalitarianism*, New York: Harcourt.

Atkinson, D. and K. Dodds (2000) Geopolitical Traditions: Critical Histories of a Century of Geopolitical Thought, in K. Dodds and D. Atkinson (eds) *Geopolitical Traditions: A Century of Geopolitical Thought*, London: Routledge, 1–24.

Balakrishnan, G. (2000) *The Enemy: An Intellectual Portrait of Carl Schmitt*, London: Verso.

Bauman, Z. (1989) *Modernity and the Holocaust*, Cambridge: Polity Press.

Bendersky, J.W. (1983) *Carl Schmitt: Theorist for the Reich*, Princeton, NJ: Princeton University Press.

Burleigh, M. (1988) *Germany Turns Eastwards: A Study of Ostforschung in the Third Reich*, Cambridge: Cambridge University Press.

Cristi, R. (1998) *Carl Schmitt and Authoritarian Liberalism*, Cardiff: University of Wales Press.

Dawidowicz, L.S. (1991) *The Holocaust and the Historians*, Cambridge, MA: Harvard University Press.

Dean, M. (2006) A Political Mythology of World Order: Carl Schmitt's Nomos, *Theory, Culture and Society*, 23: 1–22.

Eatwell, R. (1992) Towards a New Model of Generic Fascism, *Journal of Theoretical Politics*, 4: 174–85.

Eley, G. (1988) Nazism, Politics and the Image of the Past: Thoughts on the West German Historikerstreit 1986–1987, *Past and Present*, 121: 171–208.

Evans, R. (1989) *In Hitler's Shadow: West German Historians and the Attempt to Escape the Nazi Past*, New York: Pantheon.

Fahlbusch, M., M. Rossler and D. Siegrist (1989) Conservatism, Ideology and Geography in Germany 1920–1950, *Political Geography Quarterly*, 8: 353–67.

Friedrich, C.J. and Z.K. Brzezinski (1956) *Totalitarian Dictatorship and Autocracy*, Cambridge, MA: Harvard University Press.
Goldhagen, D.J. (1996) *Hitler's Willing Executioners. Ordinary Germans and the Holocaust*, New York: Alfred Knopf.
Gregor, A.J. (1997; 1st edn. 1974) *Interpretations of Fascism*, London: Transaction Publishers.
Griffin, R. (1998) 'Introduction', in R. Griffin (ed.) *International Fascism: Theories, Causes and the New Consensus*, London: Arnold, 1–20.
Gubar, S. (2003) *Poetry After Auschwitz: Remembering What One Never Knew*, Bloomington: Indiana University Press.
Hamilton, A. (1971) *The Appeal of Fascism: A Study of Intellectuals and Fascism, 1919–1945*, London: Anthony Blond.
Herf, J. (1984) *Reactionary Modernism*, Cambridge: Cambridge University Press.
Heske, H. (1986) German Geographical Research in the Nazi Period: A Content Analysis of the Major Geography Journals, 1925–1945, *Political Geography Quarterly*, 5: 267–81.
Hilberg, R. (1961) *The Destruction of the European Jews*, New York: Holmes & Meier.
Judt, T. (2009) *Reappraisals: Reflections on the Forgotten Twentieth Century*, London: Vintage.
Kalyvas, A. (2008) *Democracy and the Politics of the Extraordinary. Max Weber, Carl Schmitt, and Hannah Arendt*, Cambridge: Cambridge University Press.
Lüdtke, A. (1993) 'Coming to Terms with the Past': Illusion of Remembering, Ways of Forgetting Nazism in West Germany', *Journal of Modern History*, 65: 542–72.
Marcuse, H. (2001) *Legacies of Dachau: The Uses and Abuses of a Concentration Camp, 1933–2001*, Cambridge: Cambridge University Press.
Mason, T. (1995) *Nazism, Fascism and the World Class: Essays by Tim Mason*, edited by J. Caplan, Cambridge: Cambridge University Press.
Moses, A.D. (2007) *German Intellectuals and the Nazi Past*, Cambridge: Cambridge University Press.
Nathan, P. (1943) *The Psychology of Fascism*, London: Faber & Faber.
Neocleous, M. (1996) 'Friend or Enemy? Reading Schmitt Politically', *Radical Philosophy*, 79: 13–23.
Nolte, E. (1965) *Three Faces of Fascism: Action Française, Italian Fascism, National Socialism*, London: Wiedenfield & Nicholson.
Ó Tuathail, G. (1996) *Critical Geopolitics*, London: Routledge.
Paxton, R. (2004) *The Anatomy of Fascism*, London: Penguin.
Preuss, U. (1999) Political Order and Democracy: Carl Schmitt and His Influence, in C. Mouffe, *The Challenge of Carl Schmitt*, London: Verso, 155–79.
Reich, W. (1946) *The Mass Psychology of Fascism*, New York: Orgone Institute Press.
Rothberg, M. (2000) *Traumatic Realism: The Demands of Holocaust Representation*, Minneapolis: University of Minnesota Press.
Sandner, G. and M. Rossler (1994) 'Geography and empire in Germany, 1871–1945', in A. Godlewska and N. Smith (eds) *Geography and Empire*, Oxford: Blackwell, 115–29.
Sternhell, Z. (1976) 'Fascist Ideology', in W. Laqueur (ed.) *Fascism: A Reader's Guide*, London: Wildwood House, 315–76.
Stirk, P. (1999) 'Carl Schmitt's *Völkerrechtliche Grossraumordnung*', *History of Political Thought*, 20: 357–74.

Stirk, P. (2005) *Carl Schmitt, Crown Jurist of the Third Reich. On Preemptive War, Military Occupation, and World Empire*, Lampeter: Edwin Mellen Press.

Szöllösi-Janze, M. (2001) 'National Socialism and the Sciences: Reflections, Conclusions and Historical Perspectives', in M. Szöllösi-Janze (ed.) *Science in the Third Reich*, Oxford: Berg, 1–35.

Weber, E. (1964) *Varieties of Fascism*, New York: Van Nostrand.

Wolin, R. (2004) *The Seduction of Unreason: The Intellectual Romance with Fascism from Nietzsche to Postmodernism*, Oxford: Princeton University Press.

13 Partisan space

Daniel Clayton

Introduction

Carl Schmitt's authoritarian and existential political thought was rooted in the distinction between friend and enemy, and attached conceptual and concrete significance to matters of soil, territory, spatial order and geographical division. The grounding of the friend–enemy distinction in law and the state is central to Schmitt's 1932 *Concept of the Political*. This distinction is also evident in much of Schmitt's 1950 *The Nomos of the Earth*, but it is more muted and tied more directly to the appropriation, distribution and production of space. I seek here to remark briefly on how Schmitt came to articulate 'space' and 'the political' anew in his 1963 *Theory of the Partisan* (*Theorie des Partisanen*), a short book that stemmed from two lectures he gave at the Universities of Pamplona and Zaragoza in Franco's Spain in the spring of 1962; on how Schmitt used this work to address some of the shortcomings in his previous attempts to relate the idea of nomos to the question of friend and enemy; and on how Schmitt's attempt to construe a theory of partisanship (one with glimmerings of a new nomos of the Earth) from the history of the partisan as he told it (in Eurocentric terms and with strong Prussian inflections) coincides with the 1950s and 60s guerrilla wars (principally in Malaya, Kenya, Cuba and Vietnam). These were dubbed 'hot wars' of the Cold War and decolonisation because many of them were located in the tropical world.

Tensions between 'the political' and 'the nomos of the Earth'

In the wake of the Great War and from the vantage point of a crisis-ridden Weimar Germany, Schmitt suggested in *Concept of the Political*, the modern state seemed increasingly unable to undertake what Thomas Hobbes had identified as its prime function and *raison d'etre*: to protect its people from violence and conflict, and draw the line between war and peace, in return for their acquiescence to its norms. What Schmitt (2003 [1950]: 140–3, 351–5) later delineated as his second 'nomos of the Earth' and principle of 'order and orientation' (*Ordnung und Ortung*) – the *Jus Publicum Europaeum*, a 'Eurocentric spatial order', he called it, dating from the Age of Discovery (sixteenth century) and founded on the 'bracketing of war' (limiting of enmity) and 'dual balance' (of land and sea power, and of land powers) in the European inter-state system – was on the wane, and a barer political life was coming into view. Much of Schmitt's *The* Nomos *of the Earth* is concerned with how the *Jus Publicum Europaeum* (the bedrock of this 'bracketing' and 'the spatial order of European consciousness') revolved around the division of the world, chiefly through the binary of civilisation and savagery, with an ordered European legal-spatial domain articulated with 'uncivilised' peoples and spaces outside Europe, a constitutive outside 'beyond the line' that was deemed free for colonisation and became 'a theatre of ruthless struggle among Europeans' (Schmitt 2003 [1950]: 82–8; 219). Always seeking to reconnect political thought to concrete historical experience and change (or what he usually simply called 'reality'), Schmitt (1996: 26) famously argued in *Concept of the Political* that as the European inter-state system became fractured from the late nineteenth century onwards, and (what in his *Nomos* work he termed) a new 'spaceless universalism' increasing the threat of civil and global war began to take its place, the

> specific distinction to which political actions and motives can be reduced is that between friend and enemy ... [This distinction, rather than that between freedom and oppression] denotes the utmost degree of intensity of a union or separation, of an association or dissociation.

One of Schmitt's aims in *The* Nomos *of the Earth* is to further historicise this conception of the political and point to the dangers that stemmed from the absence (as he saw it) of a new nomos of the Earth to replace the *Jus Publicum Europaeum*. Commentators observe that his ideas of 'nomos' and 'the political' are underpinned by a theological conviction: that on account of Original Sin, the capacity for friendship and peace are unthinkable without the possibility of enmity and war (Hooker 2009: 158; Schmitt 1996: 65; Slomp 2009: 17–19). The purpose of nomic thinking and history was (for him) to account for the workings of the *katechon* – of showing that while enmity is an inherent feature of the human condition, there have been periods in history when it has been tempered.

Yet Schmitt's combining of the nomos with the principle of friend and enemy creates manifold tensions. A core political-ontological one, Alberto Moreiras (2005: 578) suggests, revolves around whether the nomos of the Earth 'rules over politics' (over the friend–enemy distinction that makes the political 'sovereign'), working as 'the ultimate ... organizer and distributor of political power and political defeat', and with 'nomic antithesis' both 'generat[ing]' and 'stand[ing] above' the friend–enemy division and its concrete groupings, as Schmitt seems to argue in *The* Nomos *of the Earth*; or whether (particularly in periods when nomic ordering seems strained) it should be regarded as 'simply a manifestation of politics' and thus subordinate to the friend–enemy distinction. If the former holds, then as Moreiras (2005: 580–4) and others ask, we need to recognise that 'the nomos secrets its own enmity' through friendship, and that from the perspective of those 'beyond the line' (i.e. non-European people 'without nomos', so to speak) its spatiality is inherently colonising because it 'always already regulates, and subsumes, its externality' (cf. Hooker 2009: 106–8; Toscano 2008: 419). Externality (or enemy-making) is both produced by, and integral to the supposed existence of, nomic order. On this account, Moreiras (2005: 583–5) concludes, it is friends who always ultimately 'split the order of friendship to fight discriminatory wars' and who can only ever make those located 'beyond the line', 'potential enemies . . . inasmuch as they are also potential friends'.

On the other hand, if the principle of friend and enemy is sovereign and operates independently of nomic antimonies, as Schmitt seemingly argues in *Concept of the Political* (1996: 39), then the universality of the nomos is fractured and we are left with the question of whether the existence or legitimacy of nomic authority is recognised as such. As Moreiras (2005: 583–4) observes in connection with Schmitt's vexed discussion in *The Nomos of the Earth* (2003 [1950]: 168–71) of Kant's formulation of the 'unjust enemy':

> if the notion of the just enemy is an impossibility – that is, if the enemy, in virtue of his very justice, is always already a friend – then all enemies, to be enemies, must be unjust. If all enemies are unjust, then every single enemy stands outside the jurisdiction of the nomos. The nomos then has effective jurisdiction only over friends, and it loses its universality.

What is more, if all enemies are unjust enemies, and thus weaken the nomos as a stable or credible political concept, then 'there is no end and no limitation to war'; war becomes total war, for both friends and enemies.

Enmity, nomos and *The Theory of the Partisan*

It was this incompatibility between 'the political' and 'the nomos of the Earth' – or what Moreiras (2005: 584) and others (Hooker 2009; Knüfer 2007; Scheuerman 2006; Toscano 2008) see as the 'untheorisable space' between them – that Schmitt took up in his work on the partisan. Gabriella Slomp (2009: 79–81) notes that in 1963 Schmitt re-issued *Concept of the Political* with a new preface explaining that some of the misunderstandings surrounding his work could be put down to the fact that he had not theorised enmity as carefully as he had friendship. Schmitt saw *Theory of the Partisan* as an attempt, in part, to fill this lacuna, subtitling this work a *Commentary/Remark on the Concept of the Political*, and investing the partisan with both historical and ontological significance. As Jan-Werner Müller (2003: 144) neatly observes:

> The figure of the partisan allowed Schmitt to reiterate his theses about the end of modern European statehood and the international legal system of the *jus publicum Europaeum*, while at the same time reinserting the

possibility of the political into what [post-1945] threatened to become Kojève's universal homogenous state.

The latter is a nihilistic 'world order' shaped by Cold War antimonies and machine-like bureaucratic states.

Schmitt begins his historical narrative of partisanship with the Spanish guerrilla war (waged largely by peasants) against Napoleon's army (1808–13), and does so, Slomp (2009: 79–83) and William Hooker (2009: 158–61) urge, in order to argue that the partisan's identity and political status rests on three criteria: first, and foremost, on her/his 'irregularity'; second, on the way 'irregularity' depends on an antithetical realm of 'regularity'; and third, on the historical recognition that it is only with Napoleon, the modern state, and the development of regular armies and mass warfare potentially involving whole populations and targeting entire state territories (and thus surpassing the medieval model of the duel) that the partisan comes into being as a characteristically modern figure. Schmitt also views the guerrillas who fought Napoleon in Spain, the Tyrol and Russia as profoundly traditional and defensive – 'telluric' and 'autochthonous' – figures bent on the defence of home, soil and life-world, yet notes that, in this sense (from this 'orientation'), they were concomitantly modern, in that they were symptomatic of the erosion of the *Jus Publicum Europaeum*. In short, the time and space of the partisan constituted an internal rupture in the nomos, in what counted as normal, legal and legitimate inter-state interaction and combat, and spatial order and balance.

It is in this latter regard that, for Schmitt (2004: 13), the partisan also starts her/his life, albeit fleetingly, as an ontological figure – as 'one of the last sentries of the earth', by which he meant a true bearer of 'the political' at a historical moment when there was no consolidated European inter-state stand (or declaration of enmity) against Napoleon's expansionist and universalist ambitions. While Schmitt (2004: 7–8) is interested in how the Congress of Vienna (1814–15) re-solidified the *Jus Publicum Europaeum* by codifying 'war between states conducted by one regular state army against another' as the legal norm, and concomitantly criminalised the partisan and obscured the legal status of civil and colonial wars, he saw in Napoleon and the partisan reaction to his occupying armies a means of looking past a vexed nomic order and into a more dissolute twentieth-century world. He finds in the history of partisanship a 'turn away from the conventional enmity of contained war' and towards 'an other – real – enmity that rises through terror and counter-terror, up to annihilation', a form of enmity that blurs distinctions between war and peace, combatant and non-combatant, legitimate enemy and criminal, foreign and domestic enemy, and legal and illegal conflict (Schmitt 2004: 7–14, 50–2).

Schmitt (2004: 50–2, 63–7) sees 'real enmity' as an instinctual (or spontaneous) realm where the declaration of friend and enemy is made apart from the state – a realm that resists 'normative regulation'; one that, in drawing friend and enemy into its own irregular and disjunctive field (Schmitt says in a 'contagious' fashion), and in ways that are not caught in the nomic paradox of friendship identified by Moreiras, might serve as a different harbinger of 'the political', with partisan struggle (and the growth of the partisan band into an army, a party and even statehood) restoring the connection between protection and obedience in an age when the modern nation-state's monopoly on naming the enemy is threatened; a political realm working from the outside in that might eschew the universalism of a United States-dominated nomos that so concerned Schmitt.

However, Schmitt (2004: 63–74) is acutely concerned with how partisanship became expedited as 'absolute enmity' – as a realm driven by 'moral compulsion', one which removes spatial fetters on enmity (and thus is set against the very idea of nomos), and that he traces from Napoleon, to Lenin's global class enemy, to the case of Raoul Salan (the French general who, in 1961, founded the Organisation d'Armée Sècrete in Algeria, which terrorised both Algerians and French settlers and opposed anti-colonialism in general, seeking to undermine the 1962 Evian Peace Accords – he was tried for treason) (see Toscano 2008: 425). Schmitt sees the partisan's 'real enmity' as a purposive response to the political undecidability that has insinuated itself into the nomic orientation captured by Susan Buck-Morss (2008: 156) thus: that 'The right . . . to order the world in a certain way is the claim of sovereign power that embodies and *enacts* legitimacy, preceding and 'nourishing' the laws that follow it.' On the flip side, however, Schmitt uses Napoleon, Lenin and Salan to register the concern that if 'real enmity' becomes 'absolute enmity' and sees only enemies and loses sight of friends, 'the political' is compromised (he bypasses Hitler's absolute enmity) (Slomp 2009: 115).

According to Schmitt (2004: 32–53), the partisan has four generic attributes, two main variants and two modalities of spatial (scalar) articulation. The partisan is defined by her/his 'irregularity', 'mobility', 'political commitment' and 'tellurian character'. Partisan warfare was comprised of a combination of surprise attack and rapid retreat, camouflage and concealment, a zealous dedication to cause, attachment to the local population, and a detailed knowledge of the enemy and the environment of war. Schmitt drew a series of distinctions between the 'earthly' or 'tellurian partisan', whose enmity is 'relative' (defensive and spatially contained), and the 'global partisan' whose enmity is 'absolute' (or aggressive and unlimited). He also identified 'third parties' (outside/distant backers) and technology (the thoroughgoing mechanisation of war since the nineteenth century) as key to partisan success, the scope of partisan enmity, and the way partisanship disrupts the pretence of democratic progress (its absorption of externality), by finding and exploiting a fluid space of shifting allegiances and hostilities.

Each of these attributes, forms and modalities could be unpacked in more detail. Schmitt (2004: 36) notes that the four attributes are interrelated and together call into question 'not just the military line but the whole edifice of political and social order'. However, they do not serve identical purposes in his study. As Hooker (2009: 161–8) and Slomp (2009: 86–93) pinpoint, the first two attributes are what make Schmitt's partisan an internal and disruptive pressure on the modern state and regular warfare on European soil, whereas the second two serve more as theoretical crucibles in which Schmitt tries to think past the idea of the state as the 'conventional' (if by 1963 crisis-ridden) locus of war and friendship/enmity, with the terrestrial and politically committed partisan emerging in a theoretical capacity as primordial and visceral (albeit still fringe) bearer of the political.

Schmitt traces the partisan's modern constitution through to the 1960s with a qualified appreciation of the telluric partisan's 'real enmity', and a corresponding disdain for a spatially un-moored partisanship that constructs a global enemy and purveys a limitless hostility. As Slomp (2009: 91–3) surmises, the global partisan's 'degree of intensity of a union or separation' is no more or less intense than that of the telluric partisan defending the intimacies of family, home and land; rather, the difference between these two archetypes lies in the target of their enmity, and Schmitt tends to reduce partisanship to a binary between limited and unlimited (and balanced and unbalanced) enmity. The telluric partisan provides a challenge to the nomic order (seeking to set itself up in the place of the state) whereas the global partisan, in declaring a boundless enmity, sets itself against nomic order as such. While Schmitt 'sympathesize[s] with the telluric partisan who ignores the *jus publicum europaeum*', Slomp (2009: 92) suggests, and sees 'real enmity' as an existential condition of the twentieth-century world of anti-colonial and revolutionary war, such sympathy is conditional upon the spatial limit that the 'telluric character' of partisanship places on real enmity, and is fettered by the concern that 'real enmity' breeds 'absolute enmity'. In short, the partisan served as a conceptual cipher for the 'union and disunion' of 'nomos' and 'the political' in a troubling age of nomic dissolution.

Post-war partisanship and irregular warfare

Theory of the Partisan is idiosyncratic, schematic and difficult to fathom without a familiarity with Schmitt's previous work. He did not intend it to be an exhaustive global history of partisan struggle, and did not try to offer a systematic theory of the partisan. His arguments left a deep impression on both the radical left and radical right in Germany and other parts of Europe through to the 1970s (Müller 2003: 152–5; Schickel 1970). More recently, and in the light of the so-called 'war on terror', his partisan work has been re-read for what it says about 'the existence of a mismatch between the existing rules of war and the political realities of modern terrorism' – a space in which 'the legal regulation of irregular combatants constitutes a legal black hole in which executive discretion is necessarily at its apex' (Scheuerman 2006: 120–1). But let me end this piece with the complaint made by commentators with postcolonial sensibilities that Schmitt's study is convened, quite resolutely, on European soil, and skips too glibly and dismissively over the anti-colonial 'orientation' of guerrilla and civil warfare during the 1960s.

Schmitt registered his admiration for Fidel Castro's Cuban Revolution and the Vietnamese guerrillas (dubbed the 'Vietcong') who fought the Americans, and dwelt on how Mao Zedong's unique fusion of telluric and global partisanship hinted at a new *Großraum* or system of 'great spaces' (Schmitt 2004: 41). However, Alberto Toscano (2008: 426) is surely right to observe that in *The Nomos of the Earth* Schmitt describes the non-European regions of the global order installed through his favoured nomos in 'brutal' and unforgiving language, and that the flagging of this spatial order (hastened after the Second World War) 'is depicted as a more-or-less endogenous [Western] process – rather than one caused by external resistance'. *Theory of the Partisan* appeared during a remarkable period in the history and theory of guerrilla insurgency, but suffers from this Eurocentrism. Ernesto 'Che' Guevara's (1985 [1961]) and Vo Nguyen Giap's (1962) celebrated manuals on 'guerrilla warfare' and 'people's war', Bob Taber's (1965) and Robert Thompson's (1966) important works on communist insurgency and western counter-insurgency in Southeast Asia, appeared within a few years of Schmitt's text, and by 1961 American analysts were writing of 'irregular warfare' (Garder 2009). However, the literature on guerrilla warfare from this period and through to Regis Debray's 1970s lament *A Critique of Arms* pays scant attention to Schmitt, and Schmitt in turn did not subject this literature to detailed scrutiny. Yet there are obvious and still largely unexplored affinities between them (see Harkavy and Neuman 2001).

In spite of the dismissive manner in which Schmitt surveyed forces of decolonisation, he helps us to sharpen understanding of guerrilla theory and practice in its anti-colonial mode, and some of its weaknesses. Guevara (1985: 12–24, 52) and Giap (1962: 13–26, 42) both underscored the 'telluric' quality of their 'irregular' endeavours (without using the term) – how 'relation to the soil . . . [attachment to] the autochthonous population and the geographical specificity of the country – mountains, forest, jungle, desert', as Schmitt (2004: 13–15) put it, was fundamental to the partisan's intense commitment – or what Taber (1965: 22) termed 'the people's will' – to overthrowing American imperial aggression. Guevara's famous 'foco' model of guerrilla warfare, and Giap's 'protracted war' and 'synthesised strategy' (modelled on Mao's three-stage revolutionary strategy – see Duiker 2007) homed in on the tactical exploitation of environmental conditions to enhance mobility and irregularity.

The Vietnam War, and particularly the jungle environment in which it was set, fractured the idea that the 'normal' – regular or conventional – way of waging war was in a temperate environment, ideally on an isotropic plain, through the heavy deployment of military materiel and regular combatants (see Krepenivich 1986: 4–5, 75–80, 165–8). American military leaders and troops struggled to distinguish Vietnamese friend from enemy, and the Vietcong's sophisticated use of camouflage made a mockery of General William Westmorland's bullish 1966 pronouncement in *Time Magazine* that the Americans were 'going to out-guerrilla the guerrilla and out-ambush the ambush' (cited in Hamilton 1998: 5). The Americans did not find a 'normal' enemy in Vietnam, or a 'conventional' landscape of war; and as Schmitt (2004: 49) helps us to see, the Vietcong successfully mounted its defence of homeland by 'forcing his enemy into another space . . . a darker dimension, a dimension of depth'. Guevara (1985: 208) said something similar: that 'get[ting] the enemy out of its natural environment, and forc[ing] it to fight in regions where its own life and habits will clash with existing reality' was central to forging 'a new scale of values'. And as Francis FitzGerald (1972: 178) wryly remarked, in simply firebombing Vietnamese villages on their 'search and destroy' missions to 'flush the enemy out', and failing to discern the Vietcong's maze of tunnels beneath the villages, American marines literally 'walked over the political and economic design of the Vietnamese revolution'.

At the same time, had Guevara read Schmitt he would have found a stark warning about the need for the partisan to not lose sight of his relation to the soil (Slomp has suggested to me that Schmitt regarded the partisan as a profoundly masculine figure). While Schmitt eulogised the telluric partisan for 'political' reasons, Debray later claimed that Guevara's downfall, in Bolivia in 1967, stemmed from his attempt to build a tri-continental guerrilla project that had lost touch with 'the people' and 'the soil'. Guevara had 'painted a canvas [of enmity, trained on the USA] whose vast scope', Debray (1977: 223) remarked, was so 'ludicrously out of proportion to the precariousness of the situation'. A kind of partisan overstretch that animates debates about the relationship between 'irregular warfare' and the 'scale of enmity' that continue to this day.

References

Buck-Morss, S. (2008) 'Sovereign Right and the Global Left' *Cultural Critique* 69: 145–71.
Debray, R. (1977) *A Critique of Arms* Vol. 1, trans. R. Sheed, Baltimore, MD and Harmondsworth: Penguin.
Duiker, W. (2007) 'Ho Chi Minh and the Strategy of People's War', in M. Lawrence and F. Logevall (eds), *The First Vietnam War: Colonial Conflict and Cold War Crisis*, Cambridge, MA: Harvard University Press, 152–74.
Garder, L. (2009) 'Irregular Warfare: A Selected Bibliography' US Army War College. Online. Available at www.scribd.com/doc/23393666/Irregular-Warfare (accessed 17 November 2009).
Giap, V. (1962) *People's War, People's Army*, New York: Praeger.
Guevara, E. (1985) *Guerrilla Warfare* [orig. pub. 1961 as *La Guerra de Guerrillas*], Lincoln: University of Nebraska Press.
FitzGerald, F. (1972) *Fire in the Lake: The Vietnamese and the Americans in Vietnam*, New York: Vintage Books.
Hamilton, D. (1998) *The Art of Insurgency: American Military Policy and the Failure of Strategy in Southeast Asia*, Westport, CN: Praeger.
Harkavy, R. and Neuman, S. (2001) *Warfare in the Third World*, New York: Palgrave Macmillan.
Hooker, W. (2009) *Carl Schmitt's International Thought*, Cambridge: Cambridge University Press.

Knüfer, A. (2007) 'Mobilité et caractère tellurique: l'espace des partisans et le nouveau, 'nomos de la terre', Lampe-Tempête 1. Online. www.lampe-tempete.fr/Mobilite.html (accessed 15 May 2010).

Krepinevich, A. (1986) *The Army in Vietnam*, Baltimore and London: The Johns Hopkins University Press.

Moreiras, A. (2005) 'Beyond the Line: On Infinite Decolonization' *American Literary History* 17: 575–94.

Müller, J.-W. (2003) *A Dangerous Mind: Carl Schmitt in Post-War European Thought*, New Haven and London: Yale University Press.

Scheuerman, W. (2006) 'Carl Schmitt and the Road to Abu Ghraib' *Constellations* 13: 108–24.

Schickel, J. (1970) *Guerilleros, Partisanen: Theorie und Praxis*, Munich: Hanser.

Schmitt, C. (1996) *The Concept of the Political*, trans. G. Schwab, Chicago: University of Chicago Press.

—— (2003 [1950]) *The Nomos of the Earth in the International Law of the Jus Publicum Europaeum*, trans. G. L. Ulmen, New York: Telos Press Publishing.

—— (2004) 'The Theory of the Partisan: A Commentary/Remark on the Concept of the Political', trans. A.C. Goodson. *CR: The New Centennial Review* 4: 1–78.

Slomp, G. (2009) *Carl Schmitt and the Politics of Hostility, Violence and Terror*, London: Palgrave Macmillan.

Taber, R. (1965) *The War of the Flea: A Study of Guerrilla Warfare Theory and Practice*, New York: The Citadel Press.

Thompson, R. (1966) *Defeating Communist Insurgency: The Lessons of Malaya and Vietnam*, New York: F.A. Praeger.

Toscano, A. (2008) 'Carl Schmitt in Beijing: Partisanship, Geopolitics and the Demolition of the Eurocentric World', *Postcolonial Studies* 11: 417–33.

14 The virtual nomos?

François Debrix

Carl Schmitt's *The* Nomos *of the Earth* (2006a) is famous for its abundance of physical inscriptions, its earth/soil/land metaphors, and its images and terms derived from the idea of a natural material rootedness of human existence. Schmitt's thought about order and humanity has been described as 'telluric' (Dean 2007: 246). For Schmitt, the Greek word *nomos* refers first and foremost to a 'concrete enclosed location (*Ortung*) on the surface of the earth' (Ojakangas 2009: 35). Commentators have written that 'Schmitt time and again stresses that the true law has an intimate relationship with soil (*Boden*) and land (*Land*). It is always bound to the earth (*Erde*)' (Ojakangas 2009: 35). The inscription of a concrete order into the earth and the derivation of human law from the soil explain why *delineation* (of terrains, territories and fields, or what topography really amounts to for Schmitt) and *appropriation* (of uncultivated lands, states and resources, or what one might suggest political geography should be for Schmitt) are two crucial concepts. In *The* Nomos *of the Earth*, Schmitt affirms that '[s]oil that is cleared and worked by human hands manifests firm lines, whereby definite divisions become apparent' (2006a: 42). He adds that 'land-appropriation precedes the order that follows from it. It constitutes the original spatial order, the source of all further concrete order and all further law' (2006a: 48). Thus, it appears that there can be little doubt that Schmitt wants to insist on the fundamentally geophysical character of legal order and political organisation. What could be called (with Mika Ojakangas's assistance) Schmitt's mode of geopolitical 'primevalism' determines (grounds and bounds) anything, any object, any condition of possibility, any life and any meaning that come next.

But what if Schmitt's nomos were to be read as a blueprint for a theorisation of the virtual, or better yet for what might be called virtual territorialisation? Put differently, what if Schmitt's nomos opens up the possibility for a geopolitical thought that entertains – perhaps requires – the presence of virtual spaces and places? Could Schmitt, despite his apparent geopolitical 'primevalism', actually be considered to be a precursor to those theories and theorists of the virtual in (geo)politics? And how can we (or dare we) suggest that Schmitt's nomos opens the door for a conceptualisation of virtual territoriality when his writings about the order of human affairs are supposedly so closely tied to a 'mythology of the earth', as Mitchell Dean (2007) puts it?

I would like to argue in this essay that Schmitt's texts do offer some openings that, at times, take him (and us, his critical geopolitical commentators) away from what would appear to be a foreclosed geophysical 'primevalism'. I want to suggest that the condition of possibility for the virtual (or virtual territoriality, or a virtual nomos) is present in Schmitt's *The Nomos of the Earth*, particularly in passages that, quickly read, may appear to be only additions, supplements or mere clarifications of some of Schmitt's major concepts as they relate to an Earth-bound encasement of order and space. Two key passages that point to an understanding of space as/through virtuality are considered in this essay. Both passages are hinted at in the main text of *Nomos* but, more crucially, become the object of a special reflection by Schmitt in the supplementary essay 'Nomos–*Nahme*–Name' (Schmitt 2006b). One key passage deals with the issue of nomadism and its relationship to land. Schmitt insists that the nomad has his/her own nomos, his/her own way of delineating and appropriating open land and space, even if it is a rather primitive or incomplete one, at least when compared with the modern inter-state legal order of the *Jus Publicum Europaeum*. The second passage under scrutiny here deals with the notion of the *Ausland*, or the 'space of the outside', a notion that turns out to be crucial to Schmitt's overall desire to fend off any form of universalisation or uniformisation of the Earth, space and political order by ideologies and political powers (championing such ideologies) that claim to wish to end all wars and to resolve conflicts between friends and enemies, selves and others, and insiders and outsiders. I turn to the issue of the nomad first.

The nomad, Schmitt believes, is not free to roam the Earth boundlessly and cannot escape the material conditions of the soil/land. The nomad occupies a space and inscribes his/her order onto a territory, the territory where s/he travels. At the same time, Schmitt recognises that the nomad does not cultivate the land. The nomad is like a shepherd (*nomeus* is the Latin term that Schmitt translates as 'shepherd') who 'tends to' or 'looks after' (2006b: 340). Moreover, the space of the nomad constantly shifts. As Dean writes, Schmitt's nomad 'wanders in search of pasture' (2007: 244). This leads Schmitt to state that the land appropriations of the nomad are 'perennially provisional appropriations and divisions' (2006b: 341). While the nomad moves on and throughout the Earth, the territory 'marked' by the nomad has expandable limits. Schmitt speaks of a nomadic nomos, but this is clearly a transitional one, or a 'prelude' to modern territoriality (Dean 2007: 244). Containment and location, grounding and fixing are anathema to nomadic life. By contrast, travel, movement and displacement are conditions of possibility for the nomad not only to survive, but also to be in space, itinerant and shifting as this space may be. As Gilles Deleuze and Felix Guattari have famously stated, nomadism is about making use of and proliferating through one's actions and motions 'smooth space' (1987: 380). It is not about fixing oneself into the static and 'striated' space of the law and centralised power.

Clearly, Schmitt wants to recognise that the nomad has a nomos, and perhaps an infinite expanse of the Earth's territory to occupy or capture.[1] But it is not clear how this mode of occupation of land or space would be the equivalent of the type of sedentary occupation/appropriation of soil-based places and activities that Schmitt takes to be the foundation of the mostly European and modern geopolitical nomos. Schmitt is forced to admit that the nomad's occupations or appropriations are not based on cultivation since cultivation requires fixity. Moreover, the dimension of delineation of the nomad's nomos is unclear. What lines do the nomad's wanderings trace? Can they be clearly established, respected and defended? Perhaps, as Deleuze and Guattari have intimated, we should think of the nomad's tracings onto the Earth as 'rhizomatic' (as opposed to arborescent, or tree-like) (Deleuze and Guattari 1987: 8). The lines of the nomad are not the early modern Spanish and Portuguese *rayas* or the modern European states' boundary lines that Schmitt highlights in the *Nomos*. It is not even obvious that they could count as precursors to those lines and divisions. Rather, they are markings or footsteps that both follow and precede the nomad's movements and displacements. They have no apparent beginning or end point. They do not easily delineate a here and a there, an inside and an outside.[2]

I would suggest that, to the extent that Schmitt's nomad does have a nomos, it is a virtual one; it is a nomos premised upon the possibility of virtual territoriality. However, the lines in the ground that, Schmitt affirms, are necessary foundations for any proper land-law order and for any organisation of a human community, are not imaginary in the case of the nomad. These lines exist, but they are different. And it may not be enough to refer to them as 'provisional', as Schmitt does (as if those nomadic markings were dotted lines whose blank spaces early modern *rayas* and sovereign boundary lines would later fill). Indeed, these lines are trajectories that may or may not successfully connect the daily meanderings of nomadic existence. More than lines in the soil, markings onto the surface of the Earth, they are memorisations (and their narrations) of past travels as well as anticipations about future journeys that may or may not chart a territory ahead. These tracings or footsteps that follow and precede the nomad and his/her ceaseless movements are lines that do visualise and virtualise a space: the space of nomadic life. Yet, they lack the traditionally Earth-bound reference points or representational markers that normally (and normatively) delineate geopolitical territories, at least according to a modern understanding of space.[3] Only as virtual then (already passed through and not yet arrived at) is the territory of the nomad realised. More crucially perhaps, only through the passing of time or by way of travel and displacement can lines and appropriations be said to be meaningful to the so-called nomadic nomos. But those nomadic lines and appropriations that may have more relevance with regards to time (seasons, natural cycles, etc.) than with space are always in a condition of virtuality vis-à-vis the Earth-bound territory of Schmitt's preferred modern and European geopolitical nomos that, allegedly, enables the existence of distinct sovereign nation-states.

An additional dimension of Schmitt's concept of the nomos that seems to encourage the possibility of virtual territoriality is the idea of the *Ausland*, or the 'space of the outside'. Ojakangas (2007) has intimated that Schmitt's notion of appropriation as a basis for the creation of any concrete geopolitical order actually depends on what Schmitt, once again in the 'Nomos–*Nahme*–Name' supplement, refers to as the 'space of the outside' or 'exterior space' (Schmitt 1988: 37; Ojakangas 2007: 206). The *Ausland* is a space that must always remain separate from the inside (the state, the nation), but also, and perhaps more critically, must stay 'open and fluid' or 'fixed yet not ossified', as Schmitt puts it (2006a: 78). Thus, this *Ausland* is not just an 'outside territory' (one that would be opposed to an inside, or to what is contained within fixed boundaries). Rather, this 'space of the outside' is *the* condition of possibility for any inside/outside division. It is a space or, better yet, a spatial potentiality that enables any inside/outside antagonism to make geopolitical sense.

The need for this *Ausland*, according to Schmitt, is intimately linked to his fear about the crisis of the modern European nomos in the early twentieth century and, in particular, his anxiety about the dangers of a unification of the world into a single dominant religious, ideological or political system (on this topic, see Odysseos 2007). The possibility that the geopolitical pluralism of the modern nomos (multiple sovereign states with their own territories safeguarded by borders) could give way to a new ungrounded and universalising way of envisioning international political space is indeed a terrifying prospect. As Schmitt already stated in *The Concept of the Political*, 'the political world is a pluriverse, not a universe' (Schmitt 1996: 53). The transformation of a pluriverse of sovereign states into a universal order dominated by one vision of humanity may well be the consecration of cosmopolitan or liberal politics on a global scale. But, for Schmitt, it is also the certainty that wars without end will be waged on behalf of the defence of humanity. Ironically, inhumanity will result from this desire to unify and defend humanity at all costs. Schmitt famously argued that two major consequences are to be expected from this imposition of universalism (or, at least, from this semblance of universality often masking the political, economic and cultural designs of some hegemonic or imperial power) and from the imposition of this new de-territorialising nomos. First, the bracketing of war that was a characteristic of the modern *Jus Publicum Europaeum* – wars take place between sovereign states, but in a limited and regulated fashion, or on the outside of the inter-state system (colonial wars, for example) – now gives way to a total prohibition of war, to worldwide pacification (Schmitt 2006a: 246 and 270). Outlawing war, casting it out of the nomos, actually ensures that endless dehumanising 'wars to end all wars' will take place, thus rendering humanity ever more insecure. Second, the concept of the enemy as a concrete public opponent disappears in favour of the figure of the absolute enemy, a totally terrorising outlaw whose very presence becomes the mark of inhumanity or even evil itself (Schmitt 2007: 321). The principle of recognition of the 'just enemy' is thus sacrificed to the requirement of the implementation of 'just wars' fought on behalf of the defence and integrity of a liberal and supposedly democratic global order (from *justus hostis* to *bellum justum*).

Schmitt fears that, ultimately, it is the notion of land appropriation (*Landnahme*) that gets to be totally excluded from what unfolds as a new universal nomos. What is there to appropriate, cultivate, mark in the ground or make one's own when the world is unified and the law is designed to preserve a system of uniformisation of the Earth and political order (for example, by condemning the recourse to war by individual states to sort out disputes and, instead, devising an international system of collective security – with global institutions and international courts – that will transcend such individual and selfish actions)?[4] The removal of land appropriation is, according to Schmitt, the prerequisite for the establishment of a universal order. Thus, as Ojakangas further notes, if the nomos of the Earth is to remain pluralistic for Schmitt (or be restored as a pluriverse), the 'real possibility of appropriation' must be rediscovered (Ojakangas 2007: 215). Maintaining at all costs a system of appropriation by multiple land-based political entities (preferably nation-states) is the only safeguard against the risk of imposition of a universal order. And to keep open or revive the possibility of appropriation, a 'space of the outside' must be preserved or recreated. In other words, there always must be an uncharted zone that lies beyond, or remains in excess of, any delineations and possessions by political entities (even beyond the inside/outside divide, as indicated above). Otherwise, a total saturation of space, a world unity, will take over.

But the crucial problem faced by Schmitt in the early twentieth century is to rediscover or recreate the *Ausland*, to ensure that territories and lands will remain open for capture, at a time when all lands have been colonised and are occupied (and thus potentially find themselves under the dominion of one global order). It is precisely at this point, I would suggest, that virtual territoriality comes to the rescue of Schmitt's theory of the nomos again. In another passage from the 'Nomos–*Nahme*–Name' essay, Schmitt writes:

> Allegedly no longer is anything taken... An important representative of political science at a leading university in the United States recently wrote me: 'Land-appropriation is over and done with.' I replied it has become even more serious with the appropriation of space. We have no right to close our eyes on the problem of appropriation, and to refuse to think any more about it, because what one today calls world history in the West and the East is the history of the development in the objects, means, and forms of appropriation interpreted as progress. This development proceeds from the *land-appropriations* of nomadic and agrarian-feudal times to the *sea-appropriations* of the 16th to the 19th century, over the *industry-appropriations* of the industrial-technical age ..., and, finally, to the *air-appropriations* and *space-appropriations* of the present.
> (Schmitt's original emphases, 2006b: 347)

Rather unexpectedly, land appropriation is suddenly expanded by Schmitt to include other seemingly equivalent forms of appropriations. These new appropriations, while they are supposed to be extensions of the land-based model of human possession of the soil/earth, are surprisingly ungrounded, detached from 'mother Earth', non-telluric. In fact, not only sea and air appropriations are now acceptable for Schmitt, but even what he calls 'industry-appropriations' and 'outer space-appropriations' can count as valid territorial captures and modalities of spatial delineation. In an era when a universal order of the Earth is about to prevail (if it does not already), these non-terrestrial spatialities must be urgently recruited. Otherwise, the 'free space of action' that is guaranteed by the presence of the *Ausland* will forever disappear (Ojakangas 2007: 215). But this *Ausland* now made visible and rendered meaningful thanks to industrial or even celestial appropriations is only virtually comparable to the *Ausland*, the exterior space, of the old terrestrial nomos. Or perhaps, and more centrally for Schmitt's theory of the nomos, we may have to reconsider whether Schmitt's notion of the 'space of the outside' was not always already intended to be in excess of land, in excess of physical territoriality, and virtually telluric. This *Ausland* that guarantees the boundless possibility of territorial capture was perhaps always supposed to function as a virtual construct in Schmitt's work, a geographical construct that, virtually, would enable the continuation of appropriations and delineations by humankind irrespective of whether there are any unoccupied, open or free lands and soils to be discovered anymore.

As I have shown in this essay, it may not be exaggerated to suggest that, similar to Schmitt's notion of the nomad discussed above, the always possible extension of the *Ausland* by way of appropriations that are the product of eminently de-territorial human activities gives birth to a virtual nomos, to an ordering of space and an organisation of human societies that conceptually turn to models and forms of virtual territoriality in order to remain concrete. In fact, such a virtual but concrete ordering of space and people may present itself as the only remaining challenge to the otherwise unstoppable universalisation of the Earth and political order. As Schmitt puts it: 'what would be terrifying is a world in which there no longer existed an exterior (*Ausland*), but only a homeland (*Inland*)' (1988: 37). The virtuality of space is thus for Schmitt a crucial way to fend off both conceptually and politically such a terrifying prospect. Virtually appropriated territories, following a model of occupation or delineation of space already introduced by nomadic displacements, make sure that the nomos of the Earth (old or new) is continuously re-territorialised.

Notes

1   In this way, Schmitt's nomad appears to be quite different from the characteristics of groundlessness and absence of attachment to place that Schmitt attributes to the Jewish diaspora. As Anthony Carty notes, according to Schmitt, 'it is a particular characteristic of Jewish existence that any "natural relationship with Land/ground" is missing' (Carty 2001: 36).

2 There may be an interesting parallel here with another figure that emerges in some of Schmitt's later works, that of the non-autochtonous political partisan (my thanks to Stephen Legg for pointing this out to me). As Schmitt affirms, '[f]lexibility, speed, and the ability to switch from attack to retreat, i.e., increased mobility, remains today characteristic of the partisan' (Schmitt 2007: 16). Interestingly, two 'nomadic' figures characterised by a virtual connection to space/land appear to bracket the modern *Nomos* of the *Jus Publicum Europaeum*. And one of the key elements that enable this (virtually) mobile or flexible connection to space/land/political order for the partisan is technology, or what Schmitt refers to (in *Theory of the Partisan*) as 'technicisation'. I will address below this technical way of apprehending space that emerges in some of Schmitt's writings.
3 For a critical reading of modern conceptualisations of space, see Soja 1989 or Agnew 1998.
4 Here, we are reminded of Schmitt's critical reading of the League of Nations (Schmitt 2006a: 240–58).

References

Agnew, John. (1998) *Geopolitics: Re-visioning World Politics*, London: Routledge.
Carty, Anthony. (2001) 'Carl Schmitt's Critique of Liberal International Order between 1933 and 1945', *Leiden Journal of International Law*, 14: 25–76.
Dean, Mitchell. (2007) '*Nomos*: Word and Myth', in L. Odysseos and F. Petito (eds), *The International Political Thought of Carl Schmitt*, London: Routledge, 242–58.
Deleuze, Gilles and Felix Guattari. (1987) *A Thousand Plateaus: Capitalism and Schizophrenia*, Minneapolis: University of Minnesota Press.
Odysseos, Louiza. (2007) 'Crossing the Line? Carl Schmitt on the "Spaceless Universalism" of Cosmopolitanism and the War on Terror', in L. Odysseos and F. Petito (eds), *The International Political Thought of Carl Schmitt*, London: Routledge, 124–43.
Ojakangas, Mika. (2007) 'A Terrifying World without an Exterior', in L. Odysseos and F. Petito (eds), *The International Political Thought of Carl Schmitt*, London: Routledge, 205–21.
Ojakangas, Mika. (2009) 'Carl Schmitt and the Sacred Origins of Law', *Telos*, 157: 34–54.
Schmitt, Carl. (1988) *Glossarium – Aufziechnunger des Jahre 1947–1951*, Berlin: Duncker & Humblot.
Schmitt, Carl. (1996) *The Concept of the Political*, Chicago: University of Chicago Press.
Schmitt, Carl. (2006a) *The* Nomos *of the Earth in the International Law of the* Jus Publicum Europaeum, New York: Telos Press.
Schmitt, Carl. (2006b) '*Nomos–Nahme–*Name', in C. Schmitt, *The* Nomos *of the Earth*, New York: Telos Press, 336–50.
Schmitt, Carl. (2007) *Theory of the Partisan*, New York: Telos Press.
Soja, Edward. (1989) *Postmodern Geographies: The Reassertion of Space in Critical Social Theory*, London: Verso.

15 Pastoral power

Matthew Hannah

Themes surface throughout Carl Schmitt's complex 1950 work that appear to suggest a broad range of connections to Foucault's notion of biopower and to various developments of the concept by others. Lacking space for any sort of overall assessment of these affinities, I will merely identify some passages that seem to offer the possibility of fruitful discussion. These passages concern the respective treatments by Schmitt and Foucault of the relations between 'pastoral power', 'economy' and the origins of modern political order. I will suggest that Schmitt recognized quasi-biopolitical dimensions of political order, though his analysis of their significance moved in different directions to that of Foucault. The divergences as well as the convergences, however, may help us see more clearly some of the questions left unanswered by a broadly Foucauldian approach to biopower. Given the limited length of these 'reactions', it will be necessary simply to bracket some very important issues to do with the 'materialization' or 'concretization' of any potential links between Foucauldian and Schmittian approaches to biopolitical questions. In particular, issues of the 'scale' of political relations are unavoidably raised by the basic fact that Schmitt focuses upon global orderings while Foucault concerns himself chiefly with 'national'-level biopower. However, scale will be unceremoniously left aside here in favour of a somewhat old-fashioned conceptual comparison of textual passages. If the conceptual argument holds any water, then it may be worth pursuing issues such as that of scale further.

Pastoral power, nomos and biopower

In a broad sense, there is already something quasi-biopolitical in Schmitt's approving assessment of the *Jus Publicum Europaeum*, the nomos that forms the chief subject of his book (Schmitt 2003, 140). Schmitt hails as a major achievement the legal discourses and practices by which Europeans were able, from the sixteenth to the late nineteenth centuries, to reduce war *within* Europe to an activity 'somewhat analogous to a duel' (Schmitt 2003, 141). 'When war becomes a struggle between purely state entities', he writes, 'then everything that is non-state – in particular, the economy, trade and the whole sphere of civil society – is left undisturbed' (Schmitt 2003, 203). This is of course a programmatic, not an empirical, statement, but in any event there is clearly a link for Schmitt between 'nomos' and the support of life. To get a more detailed sense of what this link involves, and the extent to which it overlaps or at least crosses paths with Foucault's notion of biopower, it is worth delving more deeply into what Schmitt means by 'nomos'. 'Nomos', as other contributions to this volume make plain, is a complex, multi-layered concept that can be made to resonate with a number of current discourses in political theory. In one of many definitions, Schmitt characterizes nomos as:

> the immediate form in which the political and social order of a people becomes spatially visible – the initial measure and division of pastureland, i.e., the land-appropriation as well as the concrete order contained in it and following from it. [. . .] *Nomos* is the *measure* by which the land in a particular order is divided and situated; it is also the form of political, social and religious order determined by this process. Here, measure, order and form constitute a spatially concrete unity.
>
> (Schmitt 2003, 70)

Here nomos seems in substantive terms to encompass a territorially concretized articulation of sovereignty and biopower, a spatial-cum-social order, but with a developmental dimension as well as aspects of a broadly calculative discourse ('measure'). The invocation of pastureland here and elsewhere additionally associates this order with 'provision', and in so doing suggests links to Foucault's discussions of pastoral power. But here already we see an important divergence. For Schmitt, pasturage is never separable from the founding moment of 'taking' or 'laying claim to' land before it is offered to a herd or flock as pasture. Schmitt's strong emphasis throughout the book upon this appropriative moment is one of its most potentially useful features. In my view it can offer us tools for connecting biopower more firmly to sovereignty, and for a critique of neoliberal, globalized capitalism and property relations that converges more with that of Harvey (2003), Blomley (2005, 2007) or Klein (2007) than with the 'spongier', centreless account of Hardt and Negri (2000, 2004). The processes of 'enclosure' and 'appropriation by dispossession' (Harvey 2003, 137–82; Blomley 2007) continue to be central to the (re-)production of the global order, and continue to involve coercion. Foucault, in his lectures on pastoral power, scrupulously avoids identifying any independent, territorial source of authority on the basis of which pasturage can be offered to flocks, and thus is able to avoid attributing to the shepherd any ulterior motive other than potentially self-sacrificing care (Foucault 2007, 125–32, 163–90). This is chiefly a result of his interest in distinguishing pastoral power as sharply as possible from the more familiar, territorially understood forms of sovereignty. But it is fundamentally a truncated account of pastoral power. Although I must simply leave this assertion hanging, it is important to complete our sense of what is involved in biopower in part by recognizing the inherence of 'possession', 'taking' or 'laying claim to' as a condition of possibility for 'providing'.

The passages in Schmitt most strongly suggestive of possible links between nomos and biopower are to be found in the three short appendices originally published in 1953, 1957 and 1955, respectively, and tacked onto the *Nomos* as 'corollaries'.[1] In the first of these, 'Appropriation/Distribution/Production: An Attempt to Determine from *Nomos* the Basic Questions of Every Social and Economic Order', Schmitt explores the etymology of nomos, deriving the term from the Greek verb *nemein*, which means at the same time to take or appropriate, to divide or distribute, and finally, '*weiden*', a German term narrowly definable as 'to pasture', but interpreted more broadly by Schmitt to indicate 'the productive work that normally occurs with ownership' (Schmitt 2003, 326–7). *Nemein* is thus in this third sense 'to pasture, to run a household, to use, to produce' (Schmitt 2003, 327). The suggestive connection of nomos with pasturing in this definition as well as in the 1953 etymology is augmented by a remarkable, if brief, section in the second of the three appendices, a short chapter entitled 'Nomos–*Nahme*–Name' (Schmitt 2003). Here, although Schmitt continues to see 'pasturage' as a *semantic* element of all *nomoi* up to the present, pastoral power in the more literal sense as a technology of rule is consigned to the dustbin of history, having been superseded by 'economy'. Foucault, in contrast, sees pastoral care and economy as themes that separate into different institutional settings between ancient and early modern times, at which point they begin a process of rearticulation as part of the broader process of the 'governmentalization of the state' (Foucault 2007, 109).

These contrasting historical judgements can be traced in their respective treatments of the significance of Plato's rejection of the figure of the shepherd as a model for the statesman in his late eponymous work *Statesman* (Schmitt 2003, 340; Foucault 2007, 140–7). Foucault takes Plato's contrast between the rule of the shepherd and the rule of the statesman as paradigmatic, not for the obsolescence of pastoral rule, but rather for the fact that discussions of the shepherd–flock model of government made only brief appearances in ancient Greek political philosophy before developing for many centuries chiefly in discourses and practices associated with the Christian pastorate. Schmitt, more focused on spatial aspects of rule and more narrowly concerned than Foucault with forms of rule *by states*, sees Plato's dismissal of the shepherd's rule as symptomatic of a wider epochal transition that renders pastoral power historically obsolete:

> In *Statesman*, Plato distinguishes the shepherd from the statesman: the *nemein* of the shepherd is concerned with the nourishment (*trophe*) of his flock, and the shepherd is a kind of god in relation to the animals he herds. In contrast, the statesman does not stand as far above the people he governs as does the shepherd above his flock. [...] The statesman does not nourish; he only tends to, provides for, looks after, takes care of.
> (Schmitt 2003, 340)

> The most important period was the transition from the nomadic age to the fixed household: the *oikos*. This transition presupposed a land-appropriation which, by its finality, distinguished itself from the perennially provisional appropriations and divisions of the nomads.
>
> (Schmitt 2003, 341)

In the first of these passages, Schmitt, like Foucault, notices that pastoral power, despite its seemingly beneficent character, at the same time demands from those under its sway a more absolute submission or 'pure obedience' than do other forms of rule (cf. Foucault 2007, 174). Most intriguingly, Schmitt introduces a distinction not found explicitly in Foucault between 'nourishment' and 'care'. For Foucault (2007, 127), 'the shepherd is someone who feeds and who feeds directly, or at any rate, he is someone who feeds the flock first by leading it to good pastures, and then by making sure that the animals eat and are properly fed. Pastoral power is a power of care.' Foucault is rather casual here about the difference between 'feeding directly' and 'making sure the animals eat', but this distinction is arguably an important one in liberal thought. At any rate, Schmitt's emphasis on the distinction seems to anticipate better than Foucault does the rhetoric of post-welfare state neoliberalism.

Schmitt's etymological way of proceeding in these appendices allows him to notice further points of contemporary interest. While Greek-derived terms for power with the suffixes '-*archy*' and '-*cracy*' ('monarchy', 'democracy') refer to the bearers or forms of power, Schmitt observes that the suffix *–nomy* most often characterizes power in terms of the object or material of rule. Like Foucault, Schmitt zeroes in on 'economy' as a particularly pregnant concept in the history of power, noting that in connection with economy, 'a special relation exists between *nomos* and what today we call *Daseinsvorsorge* [cradle-to-grave social welfare]' (Schmitt 2003, 339). There then follows a very interesting passage:

> The *nomy* ... apparently belonged more to the *oikos* than to the *polis*. Strangely enough, even after further developments, when spaces and measures were expanded, the word *oikos* was retained. At the end of the 18th century, a new scholarly discipline arose in Europe, a kind of science of economics, which was called either 'national economy' or 'political economy.' How extraordinary that, in the expansion of *nomos* from the house to the *polis*, it retained its linguistic relation to the old 'house' – it was not called national- or polito-nomy but eco-nomy.
>
> (Schmitt 2003, 339)

Foucault famously poses this problem of the transferability of the arts of government between the household, the individual and the principality in his lecture of 1 February 1978, the watershed lecture in which he changes tack in his genealogy of biopower from an account of 'apparatuses of security' to a longer historical narrative of the development of techniques of 'governmentality' (Foucault 2007, 94). In his view the model of the family household was not the surviving touchstone of modern rule but in fact a 'blockage' that had to be overcome on the way to the modern recognition of 'the population' as the proper object of biopolitical rule (Foucault 2007, 105). To see how this recognition emerged, Foucault rewinds from the early modern period to focus in his next few lectures upon pastoral power, the power of the shepherd over a flock, as understood in the ancient Hebrew, Greek and Christian traditions. This review of pastoral power reveals the basic logic of care of a collection of individuals as a form of power. Pastoral power, mediated through the long arc of institutional Christian church history, is for Foucault the 'embryonic point' of techniques that would eventually issue in the modern 'care of life' (Foucault 2007, 165). 'In fact', he writes, 'pastoral power in its typology, organization, and mode of functioning, pastoral power exercised as power, is doubtless something from which we still have not freed ourselves' (Foucault 2007, 148). In subsequent lectures he moves on to early modern discourses around 'reasons of state', and it is at this stage that he offers an account of precisely how the model of the family is overcome, in part through the 'depersonalization' of rule during the European sixteenth and seventeenth centuries (Foucault 2007, 294–5). But it is important to keep in mind that, for Foucault unlike for Schmitt, some features of pastoral power (most obviously, solicitousness and beneficence toward the objects of government) remained perfectly compatible with aspects of household government as both were later *aufgehoben* (taken up and transformed) into modern biopolitical rationalities.

Among the many points of contact between Schmitt and Foucault it is also worth noting the emphasis both place upon the notion of 'balance' in the emergence of the modern state system. Yet Foucault takes up the theme as somewhat of a side-note, admitting, in effect, that his narrative of the crystallization of 'something like a political technology' in sixteenth- and seventeenth-century writings on reasons of state would not be convincing without acknowledgement of 'a historical reality' for which this technology served as 'the principle of intelligibility' (Foucault 2007, 290). This historical reality is the nascent Westphalian system, in the absence of which abstract, comparable and de-theologized units called 'states' could not easily have been ascribed general 'reasons'. The lecture of 22 March 1978 is thus devoted to sketching the historical framework for the competitive relation between states that would make husbanding and augmenting the 'forces' of the state a rational enterprise. But having laid out this basic framework, Foucault then returns in the remainder of his lecture course to the genealogy of arts of government.

For Schmitt, by contrast, inter-state balance was crucial to the first modern nomos (the *Jus Publicum Europaeum*) and must remain so for any viable successors to it (Schmitt 2003, 140, 145, 161, 354–5). What interests Schmitt above all as a condition for the support of the life of peoples is, again, *the provision of a stable, inherently spatial political framework*. This frame of reference is above all spatial in the sense that it is a broadly accepted and understood ordering of *who may do what where*. Social and economic life, consisting as it does inescapably of specific activities in specific places, will run more smoothly under such a generally accepted spatial ordering. A nomos, then, or more accurately the modern *nomoi* of the nineteenth and twentieth centuries, might usefully be thought of as Schmitt's rough parallel to the 'apparatuses of security' Foucault discusses in the first three lectures of his 1977–8 course (Foucault 2007, 1–86).

This moves us unavoidably from the level of semantic or conceptual affinities and tensions between nomos and biopower to concrete, historical constructions of political scale. Foucault had little to say about the possible relevance of his ideas on biopower to international relations. But writers such as Agamben and Hardt and Negri have made this transfer (Agamben 1998, 2005; Hardt and Negri 2000, 2004). Schmitt was already thinking, in the mid-1950s, about the range of different potential configurations of the post-Cold War nomos of the Earth. In the last of the three appendices to the book, he stresses that the Cold War division into (as Schmitt notes, longitudinally arbitrary) 'East' and 'West' was still premised on a qualitative difference between land and sea as media for the projection and maintenance of power. With the rise and consolidation of air power, Schmitt sees the erosion of a stable basis for such a split. In the newly uncertain configuration, he contemplates three shapes an emerging nomos might take: (1) outright victory for one side in the Cold War (he clearly assumes this will be the USA), followed by the consolidation of unipolar global rule under the sign of technocracy; (2) a new, redrawn balance, with the United States taking over an enhanced version of the British role, guaranteeing global geopolitical balance with sea and air power; and (3) 'a combination of several independent *Großräume* or blocs', also a matter of balance, but balance without a single hegemonic power. Writing in 1955, Schmitt considered the second of these three possibilities most likely, but the third 'rational' (Schmitt 2003, 354–5).

Hardt and Negri's construction of Empire would constitute a fourth possibility, one that moves beyond the 'container' model of global space still so central to Schmitt's thinking and conceives global power relations in terms of assemblages and networks (Hardt and Negri 2000). But, as indicated above, Schmitt's steady emphasis on sovereign power would insist more strongly on the practices and agencies that continue to enforce this Empire. He was certainly aware of the tendencies already at work in the 1950s for networks to transcend state boundaries, as can be seen for example in his observation that '[t]oday, many believe that the whole world, our planet, is now only a landing field or an airport, a storehouse for raw materials, and a mothership for travel in outer space' (Schmitt 2003, 354). Landing fields and airports are nodes in the new apparatuses of security. But whose security, what 'life', do they serve, and in what ongoing appropriations must they be complicit in order to serve it?

Note

1 Another important difference between Schmitt and Foucault is of course in the area of method. Schmitt's penchant for etymological analysis, which comes through strongly in these three appendices, is at least two major steps removed from Foucault's genealogical approach (etymology – discursive formations – non-discursive power relations). However, this difference will simply be set aside here in the interest of exploring conceptual overlaps and divergences.

References

Agamben, G. (1998), Homo Sacer: *Sovereign Power and Bare Life*, trans. D. Heller-Roazen. Princeton, NJ: Princeton University Press.
Agamben, G. (2005), *State of Exception*, trans. K. Attell. Chicago: University of Chicago Press.
Blomley, N. (2005), 'Remember property?', *Progress in Human Geography* 29(2): 125–7.
Blomley, N. (2007), 'Making private property: enclosure, common right, and the work of hedges', *Rural History* 18(1): 1–21.
Foucault, M. (2007), *Security, Territory, Population: Lectures at the Collège de France, 1977–1978*, trans. G. Burchell. Basingstoke: Palgrave Macmillan.
Klein, N. (2007), *The Shock Doctrine*. London: Penguin.
Hardt, M. and Negri, A. (2000), *Empire*. Cambridge, MA: Harvard University Press.
Hardt, M. and Negri, A. (2004), *Multitude: War and Democracy in the Age of Empire*. New York: Penguin.
Harvey, D. (2003), *The New Imperialism*. Oxford: Oxford University Press.
Schmitt, C. (2003), *The Nomos of the Earth in the International Law of the Jus Publicum Europaeum*, trans. G. Ulmen. New York: Telos Press.

16 Mapping Schmitt

Michael Heffernan

The recent revival of interest in the writings of Carl Schmitt suggests a frustration with liberal democracy, at least among those legal philosophers, political scientists and scholars of international relations who have been in the vanguard of his reassessment. Their anxieties are in one sense understandable. In the smoothed out, globalised world of the early twenty-first century, where wars and conflicts should more easily be controlled, the 'international community' that Schmitt so deplored has manifestly failed to resolve political and economic problems previously attributed to the brutal divisions of the Cold War. Meanwhile, ostensibly democratic states act exactly like nineteenth-century empires, justifying disastrous military interventions in Iraq, Afghanistan and elsewhere by reference to supposedly universal humanitarian values, another of Schmitt's favourite targets. In these messy and tragic circumstances, is it any wonder that some are drawn to an anti-liberal, anti-democratic thinker such as Schmitt who, despite his unappealing political views, offers prescient and perceptive observations that speak directly to the ironies and dilemmas that have beset the post Cold War world, particularly since 9/11?

And yet the rehabilitation of Schmitt (for that is what is at stake here) is a troubling manoeuvre. One's sense of unease is not readily assuaged by the assertions that his complex writings defy simple right–left ideological categorisation, or that his views changed significantly over the course of his life, although there is a germ of truth in both these claims. The younger, more impassioned writer of the interwar period was certainly the less appealing character, railing against the injustices of the Versailles Treaty, the failings of the Weimar Republic, and the Jews, while advocating a deeply reactionary 'political theology' based on a fusion of the religious and the secular, ideas he explored with undeniable brilliance in *Political Theology: Four Chapters on the Concept of Sovereignty* (1922), *The Crisis of Parliamentary Democracy* (1923), *The Idea of Representation* (1923), *Roman Catholicism and Political Form* (1923) and *The Concept of the Political* (1927), the milestones on a personal odyssey that ended with his membership of the Nazi Party in 1933 and spirited legal defences of Hitler's regime (Bates 2006). The mature post-war Schmitt presented a rather different image, writing with less passion but more assurance in an intriguing spatial vocabulary about the history of the world political order in *The Nomos of the Earth* (1950), *Land and Sea* (1954) and *The Theory of the Partisan* (1963). This distinction would be perfectly reasonable but for the fact that Schmitt's earlier works have provoked most of the recent commentaries, both critical and sympathetic, while a close reading of his later 'geographical' works highlight the continuities, rather than the differences, between the younger and the older writer.

It's equally problematic to claim, as some have, that Schmitt's work has remained largely unread in the Anglophone world prior to the last decade or so, and is therefore ripe for reinterpretation freed from the censorial constraints of the immediate post-war period when his Nazi past prevented a balanced assessment. While it is true that few, if any, of Schmitt's writings were translated from the original German before his death in 1985, and that post-war German scholars were understandably reluctant to consider such a controversial figure, his influence was significant among German émigré intellectuals, though this connection has admittedly only recently been explored. His critics within that constituency included fellow conservatives whose opposition was expressed in well-known texts published in English many years ago. The work of the German Jewish historian Ernst Kantorowicz is an excellent example, particularly his classic book *The King's Two Bodies: A Study in Medieval Political Theology* (1997 [1957]). This extraordinary text, which traces the origins of the idea of the king sovereign as simultaneously a corporeal, human presence and an embodiment of the wider political community of the realm, was initially interpreted by historians as a kind of homage to Schmitt, revealed partly by Kantorowicz's use of the term 'political theology' in his sub-title but also because the young historian shared the same political values as the young Schmitt, seven years his junior. A conservative, nationalist firebrand before and during the First World War, Kantorowicz spent 1919 battling against Spartacists in Berlin and socialists in Munich, before joining the far-right, elitist circle of young mystics associated with Stefan George in Heidelberg during the 1920s, influences all too evident in his first book, an unreadable defence of absolutism in the form of a hagiographic, mythologising biography of the Emperor Frederick II (Ruehl 1977). Kantorowicz's deeply conservative instincts never wavered, sparking controversy among the next generation of medieval historians (Cantor 1991, 79–117), but three decades after his first book, having fled the Nazis and found employment first at Berkeley (which he left following his principled refusal to sign the oath of loyalty imposed on all faculty at the height of the McCarthy purges) and then at Princeton, he finally completed his magnum opus on the intermingling of religious and secular values in medieval and early-modern state formation. Recent readings of *The King's Two Bodies*, prompted by its influence on Foucault and the apparent connection to Schmitt, have revealed that this most erudite of texts is, in fact, a subtle but damning critique of Schmitt's views and a defence of English-style evolutionary constitutionalism against the tyrannical theorising of continental European legal scholars such as Schmitt. The *King's Two*

Bodies is a warning against any attempt to convert politics into a quasi-religious sensibility, a strategy Kantorowicz believed was deployed by all twentieth-century totalitarianisms, fascist and communist (Halpern 2009; Kahn 2009; and more generally Boureau 2001 [1990]; Landauer 1994). The point to emphasise here is that Schmitt cannot be presented as a previously ignored but original thinker whose time has come. He has always been with us and for the most part has functioned as an appropriate foil against which to defend liberal democratic ideals, even from writers on the conservative right such as Kantorowicz, whose personal journey meant that he knew better than most the disturbing implications of Schmitt's ideas.

It can be argued, of course, that Schmitt should be subjected to the same dispassionate scrutiny that students of philosophy bring to the study of Heidegger, for example, whose Nazi party membership has also been widely discussed. But Schmitt, unlike Heidegger, was an overtly political writer, a legal philosopher who consistently espoused authoritarian convictions broadly consistent with those developed by the Nazis. Schmitt's arguments are important for that very reason, of course, but they should not be removed from their historical context, though that is precisely the danger we confront when seeking to interrogate Schmitt's continuing relevance. This inevitably runs the risk of converting a writer whose views reflected currents of thought in Weimar and Nazi Germany into a transcendent guru whose ideas can be cherry-picked without reference to the multitude of p's – period, place, personal politics – with which they were so consistently implicated. You do not have to be a Marxist to note the perplexing irony here. We appear to live in a political and intellectual climate in which Marx is now read (insofar as he is read at all) as a figure whose writings were shaped by his times, whereas Schmitt is paraded as a prophetic voice of direct relevance to current problems and therefore worthy of deep and serious consideration.

So what advantage is to be gained from a new geographical reading of Schmitt? It is certainly no surprise that geographers should take an interest in Schmitt given his consistent use of geographical and spatial language, particularly in his later works *The* Nomos *of the Earth* and *Land and Sea*, but it is important to sound another note of caution against interpreting Schmitt as an original, profound or imaginative geographical commentator, even as a crypto-geographer himself (Hooker 2009, 196). Although Schmitt discourses at length about the 'spatial orders' and 'spatial transformations' of the geo-political formations he describes in *The* Nomos *of the Earth*, from the medieval *Respublica Christiana* through the early-modern *Jus Publicum Europaeum* to the new nomos of the twentieth century, the spatial phrases are deployed in an essentially rhetorical manner, and are often startlingly devoid of content, geographical or otherwise. Schmitt's geographical language is intriguing, to be sure, but it remains primarily a style of writing about the fundamental questions – legal, political and philosophical – that lie at the core of his detailed discussions. Schmitt's language is important, of course, but it is only one aspect of his work and while he undoubtedly has interesting things to say about the concepts of 'land' and 'territory' in *The* Nomos *of the Earth* and about the relationship between the two elemental categories discussed in *Land and Sea*, his assessments of these categories are scarcely unheralded. His discussion of 'land appropriation', in particular, draws directly on John Locke, and his linear spatiality theme owes a great deal to the familiar legal debates that took place before and after the international agreement to adopt the Greenwich prime meridian in 1884. His method, moreover, is essentially historical rather than geographical, *The* Nomos *of the Earth* proceeding in a broadly chronological fashion, describing the kinds of historical characters and earlier jurists that shaped the different phases in what is essentially a global legal history.

There are at least two reasons why Schmitt's geographies have only a rhetorical, abstract register. First, he says little about the world's physical environments and therefore cannot comment on the material relationships between environments and human populations, the central concern not only of professional geographers throughout the nineteenth and twentieth centuries, but also of other global theorists with whom Schmitt might more readily be compared, notably Oswald Spengler and Arnold Toynbee. Schmitt's reluctance to be drawn on the influences of the physical environment reflects his suspicion of deterministic reasoning, but the corollary is that his sense of the physical environment lacks depth and his geographies are consequently drained of content and curiously free-floating. Second, the spaces Schmitt invokes are expressed in resolutely textual terms, rather than in cartographic or visual representations. While he repeatedly discusses how the spaces of the globe are surveyed and mapped, he provides no visual content to flesh out the geographical imaginations and sensibilities he suggests are created by these processes. It is revealing (but not in the way that Schmitt might have anticipated) that the single visual image included in *The* Nomos *of the Earth* is not a map but an abstract 'global diagram' of the *Jus Publicum Europaeum* (Schmitt 2003 [1950], 184).

These absences were deliberate choices rather than unacknowledged failings, which reinforces the sense that Schmitt's priorities were essentially legal and political and his geographies essentially rhetorical. This is made abundantly clear in the oblique and infrequent references Schmitt makes to an earlier generation of late nineteenth- and early twentieth-century professional geographers, specifically Friedrich Ratzel whose organic, Darwinian theory of the state is mentioned and dismissed in *The* Nomos *of the Earth* (Schmitt 2003 [1950], 88 and 283) and, perhaps more surprisingly, the historical geographer and historian of technology Ernst Kapp whose observations on maritime navigation inform the interesting discussion of the 'spiritual' significance of the compass in *Land and Sea* (Schmitt 1997 [1954], 11). Schmitt's most explicit comment about the discipline of geography is made in the foreword to *The* Nomos *of the Earth* where he expresses his debt to Halford Mackinder, an observation immediately qualified by a passage (quoted in the introduction to this volume) that geographers interested in Schmitt would do well to heed: '. . . a juridical way of thinking is far different from geography. Jurists have not learned their science of matter and soil, reality and territoriality from geographers. The concept of sea-appropriation has the stamp of a jurist, not a geopolitician' (Schmitt 2003 [1950], 37). Schmitt, the self-professed jurist, had no interest in geography as a formal disciplinary project, and still less with the geopolitical movement that formed such a significant part of the wider German geographical project between the wars. This was not because he rejected the arguments developed by Karl Haushofer and his fellow geo-politicians for there was no single, coherent perspective to be opposed here. Haushofer's *Zeitschrift für Geopolitik* included a remarkable range of opinions, including articles penned by such cosily liberal individuals as the British geographer Dudley Stamp (Hepple 2008). Rather, Schmitt saw no need to concern himself with the discipline of geography, including the geopolitical movement, because he rejected its form of argument and style of exposition, specifically the traditional geographical concern with human–environment relations and the reliance on the map, whether viewed as heuristic, explanatory device or as technique of persuasion and propaganda. These elements bore the disciplinary 'stamp' of the geographer rather than the jurist.

This is a significant omission, however, because the history of German geography both challenges and supports a central component of Schmitt's argument – his insistence that universalism serves the political and economic interests of Anglo-American capitalism by disqualifying alternative world-views, specifically those developed within German *Kultur*, from operating at the global scale. Geography challenges Schmitt because the relationship between the national and the international was an important (arguably the most important) motivating force in German geographical writings from the end of the eighteenth century, inspired in large measure by Kantian idealism, the primary source of cosmopolitan universalism through the opening decades of the nineteenth century (Tang 2008). Schmitt was well aware of this, of course, but his criticism of Kant in *The* Nomos *of the Earth*, for example, focuses exclusively on arcane legal questions associated with the notion of the 'unjust enemy' rather than the relationship between Kant's sense of geography and his understanding of the universal (see also Harvey 2000, 2009). Schmitt's indifference to geography as a science and a discipline also meant that he felt no need to ponder the implications of a figure such as von Humboldt, for example, whose celebrated life and works exemplify more than any other nineteenth-century scientist how the modern idea of Germany reflected the kind of fusion of the national and the international that Schmitt rejected.

And yet Schmitt's argument is also at least partially endorsed by the later history of German geography in the years before and after the First World War. This can be demonstrated by reference to one of the most remarkable German geographical projects of this period – the plan to construct an international 1:1,000,000 map of the entire terrestrial globe based on uniform conventions to emphasise physical landscape features rather than political divisions, a perfect exemplification of the spatial universalism Schmitt so despised. The earliest advocate of an international *Weltkarte* was Albrecht Penck, a pioneering coastal and glacial geomorphologist and oceanographer based initially at the University of Vienna and later at the University of Berlin, where he would succeed Max Planck as Rector during the First World War. Penck's initial proposal was issued as a challenge to the assembled geographers at the 1891 Berne International Geographical Congress using arguments that foreshadowed those subsequently developed by American and British 'closed space' theorists such as Frederick Jackson Turner and Halford Mackinder (Kearns 2009). The exploration, mapping and delineation of the globe was more or less complete, argued Penck, and the last remaining areas of unmapped space, the ever diminishing patches of *terra nullius*, would soon be absorbed into the mapped world. This process had arisen from an invigorating national competition between rival European states but this meant that the existing cartographic archive was bewilderingly complex and effectively unusable because it reflected different national and imperial styles, conventions and geographical priorities. The Earth as an integrated whole, a global common equally available to all its inhabitants, could not be conceptualised or analysed systematically using existing maps and atlases. A familiar British world map, displayed on the Mercator projection with the empire coloured proudly in red, was not an image of the world, implied Penck, but a representation of Britain's dominance of the world, and the same argument could be made with respect to French, American or German maps and atlases (see, however, Biltcliffe 2005; Driver 2010; Heffernan 2009).

According to Penck, a more scientifically rational image of the world was urgently required to educate the coming generation about the Earth's potential. Put simply, a globalised twentieth century required a radically different approach to space, and a collaborative, international map of the whole Earth was a modest but significant statement about the values destined to shape the new age, a fitting geographical monument to mark the opening of the new century. The *Weltkarte* could be readily compiled from existing national maps, Penck reasoned, but would necessitate new surveys in more remote, previously unmapped areas. The millionth scale neatly conformed to the metre, the standard, universal unit of length derived from the configuration of the Earth itself, one ten millionth the distance from the pole to the equator. To cover the entire terrestrial globe, Penck suggested a numbered grid of c.2,700 map sheets, each covering an area six degrees of longitude by four degrees of latitude, irrespective of political borders. A single map sheet would fit easily on an ordinary-sized table, and an entire continent could be displayed in an average school playground. International agreement decreed Greenwich as prime meridian but the map would use a simple polyconic projection, devised in the 1820s by the Swiss-American surveyor Ferdinand Rudolph Hassler, selected in preference to the outdated, irredeemably imperialist Mercator projection. The existing national cartographic agencies would carry out the work, of course, each taking responsibility for their own national and imperial territories, but each map sheet would use the same symbols, colours and other conventions, the idea being to produce different editions in the major languages.

Expressed in these terms, Penck's *Weltkarte* suggests the utopian, pacifist universalism of the radical left, represented in the discipline of geography by anarchist writers such as Elisée Reclus and Petr Kropotkin. But Penck was no starry-eyed advocate of universal peace and harmony. He was, rather, a patriotic German realist, though he clearly detected no contradiction between his conventional nationalist convictions and the internationalism he so passionately espoused in his scientific work. In Penck's view, international science was an arena in which German cultural values would naturally triumph, an argument no doubt shaped by his intimate knowledge of the successful hegemony that German scientists had developed in the epoch-defining discipline of physics.

By downplaying existing geopolitical divisions and emphasising natural landscape features, Penck intended that the *Weltkarte* would reveal the world's 'natural regions' more clearly than ever before, unimpeded by 'unnatural' political divisions and borders. The idea of the 'natural region' was the 'Holy Grail' of late nineteenth-century geography, a fundamental, immanent spatial unit that acquired an almost mystical significance in some geographical writings. Penck, like many other geographers within and beyond Germany, believed 'natural regions' should be the building blocks of a new, more rational world geopolitical order. The 'one-worldism' of Penck's *Weltkarte* was, therefore, merely a first step, a representational strategy that removed the old spatial order while emphasising the need for a new one. This implication was not lost on some of the British, French and American critics of Penck's proposal, who interpreted the *Weltkarte* in precisely these geopolitical terms, as a German plot to reinforce its international technical hegemony in the field of map and atlas production while creating an international image of the Earth that suggested that its 'closed' spaces were still 'up for grabs' and should be reconfigured, based perhaps on new pan-regional configurations like the one that had already emerged in the Americas where an ostensibly non-imperialist United States had successfully carved out its own *Großraum* in Latin America by excluding rival powers.

Penck tirelessly promoted the *Weltkarte*, with the support of other leading German geographers, and eventually convinced an initially sceptical international geographical community. Two international conferences were organised, in London in 1909 and Paris in 1913, to finalise the legal arrangements between the leading cartographic agencies and carry the project forward, the latter event establishing, among other things, an official headquarters for what was by then known as the International Map of the World (IMW) not in Germany, the project's spiritual home, but in the offices of the British Ordnance Survey. It is important to note, however, that the United States formally withdrew from the project on the eve of the Paris conference, to the dismay of some leading American geographers.

The First World War dramatically changed the nature of the IMW project, and effectively undermined the liberal internationalism that had originally inspired Penck. British and French cartographic agencies brought forward their own versions of million-scale map sheets during the war, and the project was revived after 1918, with limited support from the League of Nations, but the initial German impetus collapsed after 1918. Penck, humiliated by the British in London at the outbreak of war where he received the Gold Medal of the Royal Geographical Society and was then promptly arrested as an enemy alien (Heffernan 2000), became an increasingly embittered figure, spending much of the interwar period attacking the ethnographic maps that had been used at the Paris Peace Conferences to justify the dismemberment of the Austro-Hungarian Empire and the creation of Poland. German cartographic agencies continued to produce million-scale map series of different parts of the world throughout the Weimar and Nazi periods, including some explicitly designated as IMW map sheets, but the motivation behind these programmes was often aggressively nationalist and imperialist, notably in the Wehrmacht's 1:1 million series covering Europe, central Asia, the Middle East and Africa, compiled between 1939 and 1941. The American Geographical Society in New York, operating outside the IMW programme but respecting its conventions, also compiled its stunning Map of Hispanic America on the millionth scale through the 1920s and 1930s, perhaps the defining legacy of early twentieth-century million-scale mapping and an eloquent commentary on how late nineteenth-century idealism and internationalism was converted into twentieth-century imperialism (Heffernan and Pearson 2009). The IMW project limped on after 1945, and was eventually absorbed into the United Nations scientific and technical programme in the 1950s, before finally fizzling out in the 1970s, a victim of the many twentieth-century technological changes, not least the rise of aerial reconnaissance, that had long since rendered a laboriously compiled map on this scale an irrelevance (Pearson *et al.* 2006).

The story of Penck's *Weltkarte* complicates Schmitt's spatial reasoning about the nature of universalism. It challenges Schmitt's argument to the extent that Penck's original proposal suggests that he, and those who supported his project, made precisely the opposite calculation to Schmitt prior to the First World War, namely that liberal, scientific internationalism worked against the established geopolitical order and in favour of restless new powers such as Germany that had most to gain from a radically re-imagined world. It endorses Schmitt to the extent that the First World War, a war fought to realise Germany's global ambitions, ended up converting universalism and internationalism into a more defensive, even conservative rhetoric, one that served to protect and preserve the geopolitical order (re)created by the Allied powers in Paris in 1919. In so doing, a much earlier, quintessentially geographical and cosmopolitan internationalism, rooted in eighteenth- and nineteenth-century German cultural and scientific achievement and exemplified by figures such as Kant and von Humboldt, was eradicated for at least a generation, with disastrous consequences for the entire world (for an excellent analysis of the collapse of German cosmopolitanism in the 1920s, see Lipton 1978).

There are many obvious reasons why Schmitt has had less influence, even in his own field of international law, than more accessible and less cerebral global theorists such as Mackinder (Kearns 2009). But the fact that his important writings have not received the critical reading they undoubtedly deserve does not mean that they have a transcendent political or intellectual value. His later works, notably *The Nomos of the Earth*, have a consistent geographical 'flavour' but I am sceptical whether these provide anything more than an intriguing, occasionally dazzling extension of German interwar geopolitical writing into the post-war period. At the very least, Schmitt's more overtly geographical texts reinforce the need for more research on the politics and tangled interconnections of German geography in the middle decades of the twentieth century.

References

Bates, David (2006) Political theology and the Nazi state: Carl Schmitt's concept of the institution, *Modern Intellectual History* 3: 415–42.

Biltcliffe, Pippa (2005) Walter Crane and The Imperial Federation Map Showing the Extent of the British Empire, *Imago Mundi* 52, 1: 63–9.

Boureau, Alain (2001 [1990]) *Kantorowicz: Stories of a Historian* (Baltimore, MD: Johns Hopkins University Press).

Cantor, Norman F. (1991) *Inventing the Middle Ages: The Lives, Works and Ideas of the Great Medievalists of the Twentieth Century* (New York: William Morrow & Co.).

Driver, Felix (2010) In search of the imperial map: Walter Crane and the image of empire, *History Workshop Journal* 69, 1: 146–57.

Halpern, Richard (2009) The King's two buckets: Kantorowicz, Richard II, and fiscal *Trauerspeil*, *Representations* 106: 67–76.

Harvey, David (2000) Cosmopolitanism and the banality of geographical evil, *Public Culture* 12, 2: 529–64.

Harvey, David (2009) *Cosmopolitanism and the Geographies of Freedom* (New York: Columbia University Press).

Heffernan, Michael (2000) Professor Penck's bluff: geography, espionage and hysteria in World War I, *Scottish Geographical Journal* 116, 4: 267–82.

Heffernan, Michael (2009) The cartography of the Fourth Estate: mapping the new imperialism in British and French newspapers, 1875–1925, in Akerman, James (ed.) *The Imperial Map: Cartography and the Mastery of Empire* (Chicago: University of Chicago Press) 261–300.

Heffernan, Michael and Pearson, Alastair (2009) The American Geographical Society's Map of Hispanic America: million scale mapping between the wars, *Imago Mundi* 6, 2: 1–29.

Hepple, Leslie (2008) Dudley Stamp and the Zeitschrift für Geopolitik, *Geopolitics* 13, 2: 386–95.

Hooker, William (2009) *Carl Schmitt's International Thought: Order and Orientation* (Cambridge: Cambridge University Press).

Kahn, Victoria (2009) Political theology and fiction in *The King's Two Bodies*, *Representations* 106: 77–101.
Kantorowicz, Ernst H. (1997 [1957]) *The King's Two Bodies: A Study in Mediaeval Political Theology* (Princeton, NJ: Princeton University Press).
Kearns, Gerry (2009) *Geopolitics and Empire: The Legacy of Halford Mackinder* (Oxford: Oxford University Press).
Landauer, Carl (1994) Ernst Kantorowicz and the sacralization of the past, *Central European History* 27, 1: 1–25.
Lipton, David R. (1978) *Ernst Cassirer: The Dilemma of a Liberal Intellectual in Germany, 1914–1933* (Toronto: University of Toronto Press).
Pearson, Alastair, Taylor, D. R., Kline, K. D. and Heffernan, Michael (2006) Cartographic ideals and geopolitical realities: international maps of the world from the 1890s to the present, *Canadian Geographer* 50, 2: 149–76.
Ruehl, Martin (2000) 'In this time without emperors': the politics of Ernst Kantorowicz's *Kaiser Friedrich des Zweite* reconsidered, *Journal of the Warburg and Courtauld Institutes* 63: 187–242.
Schmitt, Carl (1997 [1954]) *Land and Sea* (trans. S. Draghici; first edition 1942) (Washington, DC: Plutarch Press).
Schmitt, Carl (2003 [1950]) *The Nomos of the Earth in the International Law of the Jus Publicum Europaeum* (New York: Telos Press).
Tang, Chenxi (2008) *The Geographic Imagination of Modernity: Geography, Literature and Philosophy in German Romanticism* (Stanford, CA: Stanford University Press).

17 Air power

Nasser Hussain

The Nomos *of the Earth in the International Law of the* Jus Publicum Europaeum is a work of astonishing breadth and prescience. It combines Schmitt's particular understanding of a legal order with a global focus that is at once juridical, geographical and historical. The book is also a nostalgic elegy of sorts. Published in 1950, *Nomos* is as much a lament for the irretrievable passing of a European public law as it is a document of its operation. For Schmitt, from the seventeenth to the twentieth century a distinct European public law regulated relations of war and peace not only between the European sovereign states but also, if only by negative exclusion, between Europe and the 'free' space of the new world and the colonies. This law was based on a concrete spatial order in Europe and organized the world with Europe as its centre: 'this European core determined the nomos of the rest of the Earth' (Schmitt 2006: 126–7). This public law conceived of war as a conflict of interests between mutually equal and sovereign states – *justus hostis* as opposed to rebels or criminals – and as a result produced a crucial bracketing of war, whereby it became possible to no longer consider prisoners as objects of vengeance or as slaves, and private property as booty (Schmitt 2006: 308–9). For Schmitt, the crucial bracketing of war that took place within Europe from the seventeenth to the early twentieth century involved the observation of certain basic rules. But paradoxically such a rule-based warfare comes about not because war is brought into the domain of law but precisely because it is removed from theological and juridical conceptions of justice and placed firmly in the domain of political conflict between sovereigns: 'the formal reference point for determining just war no longer was the Church's authority in international law, but rather the equal sovereignty of states. Instead of *justa causa*, international law among states was based on *justus hostis*' (Schmitt 2006: 121). For Schmitt then the central and defining elements of the nomos were both the stable definition of war, and the concrete political and spatial order of European states. Indeed, the bracketing he speaks of applied only to war between Europeans on European soil and not to non-Europeans or their lands. From the seventeenth to the twentieth century, Europe expanded its colonial acquisitions both through the discovery of the new world to the west and through the adventures of the great trading companies to the east.

The wars that marked this expansion both between the competing European powers and between these powers and the indigenous people they encountered were distinctly outside the *Jus Publicum Europaeum*, and, in fact, by being 'beyond the line' constituted the nomos of the Earth as a whole. Schmitt repeatedly utilizes the concept of 'beyond the line' – a distinction that he makes clear was not just conceptual but physical, marked along longitudes in secret agreements between the Portuguese and Spanish or the English and the French – to explain the difference in warfare within the constitutive European core and that which lay beyond it: 'everything that occurred 'beyond the line' remained outside the legal, moral, and political values recognized on this side of the line' (Schmitt 2006: 94).

By the twentieth century, however, first in 1919 with the Treaty of Paris and the League of Nations, and later with the decisive entry of air power, this very concrete and bounded spatial order gave way to a 'spaceless universalism', (Schmitt 2006: 192) with a lack of a central (that is for Schmitt a Eurocentric) orientation and was hence lost forever.

It is the introduction of air power that combines at a historical moment specific spatial transformations within a global nomos with changes in the technology of weaponry. Schmitt is both insistent and persuasive about the fact that bombing campaigns cannot be assimilated into existing notions of warfare proper to the *Nomos*. This is because first of all air war upsets any sense of the *territorial demarcations* of war, converting, for example, entire stretches of land and open sea into a battleground. Second, the object of a bombing campaign can be neither seizure nor occupation, nor even a blockade, but simply destruction. Certainly as Schmitt recognizes land war may also be based on a principle of destruction both as an offensive and defensive manoeuvre – consider the scorched earth policy – but that is not its only and immediate purpose. Land wars often involve occupation, and even temporary occupation involves some emphasis on order and utility. By contrast, as Schmitt repeatedly insists, 'the only purpose and meaning of an air raid is destruction' (Schmitt 2006: 316). The rule created to contain that destruction to objects of 'military necessity' has turned out, as Schmitt astutely predicted, 'only a problematic formulation, not a precise rule' (Schmitt 2006: 316).

But Schmitt's account of air power is also limited by certain omissions and inaccuracies. For example, when he insists that air power is 'purely destructive', he neglects a whole theory and practice of strategic bombing that seeks to exert political pressure through the select targeting of key nodes. This sort of bombing is, as Schmitt claims for all bombing, certainly destructive, but what is important here is the choice of what is being destroyed, the way that such a theory attempts to shape the exertion of power by emphasizing selectivity and precision. It is this type of morale bombing that informed the project of air power from the very beginning, both in Europe and in the colonial air control programmes of the interwar years, such as in Iraq, where the air force replaced ground troops in the occupation and maintenance of the mandate. No matter how tortured its shape, morale bombing was used, contra

Schmitt, to maintain occupations. Moreover, while Schmitt is certainly correct that the rule restricting bombing to targets of 'military necessity' (Article 147 of the Fourth Geneva Convention) is notoriously imprecise, he sometimes assumes a reductionist approach to the complexity of how rules work. Thus since Schmitt, even the thin doctrinal prohibition of indiscriminate bombings of civilians has taken on a more global and normative weight. This has, however, not prevented states from using the so-called dual exception of the laws of war, which permits the incidental targeting of civilian objects if the purpose of the attack is one of military necessity. Thus, on the one hand, prohibitions against civilian targets have been internalized in the air forces of modern democracies; on the other hand, neither legal nor ethical restraint has managed to curb the destructive effects of bombing on civilians. Indeed, such bombing campaigns *have been facilitated by the rules themselves*, with the dual use exception coupled with claims of ever increasing technological precision offering powerful justification. Such claims no matter how strained in practice importantly inform the conceptual project of air power, from the colonial air control programmes of the interwar years to more recently the air war in Kosovo. Any contemporary theorizing of air power that turns to *Nomos* will have to accommodate Schmitt's neglect of these and other claims. Indeed, given how pivotal the role of air power is in Schmitt's account of the passing of the nomos, it is a bit startling how little detail Schmitt offers on what such a power entails. Absent are not just any detailed accounts of bombing campaigns, but even more importantly, any consideration of the important modernist theorists of air war, such as the Italian Giulio Douhet or the Englishman Hugh Trenchard. Douhet's absence from the stunning range of *Nomos*' 'Name Index' is particularly perplexing, given that his 1921 work, *Il Domino dell Aria* (The Command of the Sky) had a profound impact on military thought throughout Europe (Douhet 1983). Prior to Schmitt, Douhet also argued that air power had transformed the space of war, effectively cancelling out any distinction between the front and the interior, and between soldiers and civilians. For Douhet unlike for Schmitt this did not pose a problem: air power could and should be used to attack the 'vital centres' of the enemy, thereby effectively bringing any conflict to a quick and decisive conclusion. Later theorists such as J.F.C. Fuller, Liddell Hart and Hugh Trenchard would modify Douhet's call for attacks on population centres, concentrating more on targets that would produce a profound 'dislocation' rather than an outright destruction – an idea that was to become the cornerstone of air policing in the colonies (Linqvist 2001: 43–4; Meilinger 1996; Salmond 1922). But even these more 'humane' theorists of bombing shared Douhet's central insight that with air attacks 'the psychological effects of bombardment would be more pronounced than the physical effects' (Meilinger 2000: 472).

In order then to explicate Schmitt on air power fully, to parse his omissions along with his enduring insights, one needs to consider, I would suggest, even if very briefly, the question of what sort of critical posture one should adopt to *Nomos* as a whole? Kenneth Surin notes that part of the confusion arises because Schmitt was deeply indebted to Weberian ideal types (which in a sense the *Nomos* certainly is) and yet gives the *Nomos* an 'ontological solidity' so that it is not clear when it is an 'ideal type masquerading as a real type' (Surin 2005: 189). This leads to historiographic difficulties because, as Surin also notes, 'Schmitt was always a scholar of philosophical jurisprudence, and despite his formidable learning no expert in historical sociology'. And yet Surin insists, and I would agree, that the correct response here is not some 'no-nonsense' factual history but a parsing of Schmitt's fundamental insights, which no single detail can obscure. In the case of air power I would argue that such an approach bypasses any singular pronouncement or omission and returns us to Schmitt's central organizing themes of the *Jus Publicum*: the definition of the enemy as *justus hostis* as opposed to a criminal, and the definition of war as analogous to a duel.

Schmitt saw with clarity that air war would not only create an 'intensification of the technical means of destruction' and the 'disorientation of space', but that these factors would themselves in turn intensify *the problem of unequal sides* thereby accelerating the process by which the enemy is labelled a criminal. One can certainly imagine air war as aerial dog fights between equally powerful states, but Schmitt understood that air power was just as likely if not more so to create a world where those who commanded the sky could police and punish those who do not. For Schmitt, this widening gap is both the cause and result of a juridification of war, a shift towards conceptualizing war as a policing activity of criminals. It is worth quoting Schmitt on air power here in full:

> Both sides have a specific relation to the types of weapon. If the weapons are conspicuously unequal, then the mutual concept of war conceived of in terms of an equal plane is lacking. To war on both sides belongs a certain chance of victory. Once that ceases to be the case, the opponent becomes nothing more than an object of violent measures. Then the antithesis between the warring parties is increased exponentially. From the distinction between power and law, the vanquished are displaced into a *bellum intestinum* (internal war). The victors consider their superiority in weaponry to be an indication of their *justa causa* and declare the enemy to be a criminal because it no longer is possible to realize the concept of *justus hostis*.
>
> (Schmitt 2006: 320–321)

Here Schmitt offers us a tantalizing glimpse of a different approach to the question of what constitutes the *justus hostis*? Earlier I emphasized that for Schmitt the *justis hostis* of the *Nomos* were European sovereigns enclosed within a rationally ordered centre. Everything outside the centre was free space, where actions were unfettered by the rules of warfare that obtained within the *Jus Publicum Europaeum*. In short, it was 'beyond the line'. What is it that discounts these lands, peoples and governments from the status of *justus hostis* accorded to European states? At different points in the book, Schmitt offers us a reasonably standard explanation that emphasizes the cultural and political 'deficits' of non-Europeans. These people do not and cannot share in the civilization of rationalism and commerce, and their governments do not deserve the title of full sovereignty, either because they are nomadic or despotic (Schmitt 2006: 216). So far, so standard colonialist rhetoric, but Schmitt also offers us another, more intriguing reason why non-Europeans cannot be offered the status of the proper enemy. This has to do with the technological capability, or lack thereof, to conduct a war in which both sides have a more or less equal capability. Aerial bombing over those who have no chance to reply in kind then is by definition not a war but an unequal contest – asymmetric conflict is the currently popular term – which by its very nature accelerates the process by which war becomes a policing action and the adversary becomes a criminal or a mere object of violent reprisal. As Schmitt makes clear in the quote above, such policing actions both begin and end with the criminalization of the enemy. Schmitt thus offers us a conceptual framework for productively analysing *current* deployments of air power, from the 'humanitarian' air war in Kosovo to the drone attacks that are shaping the Americans' war on terror.

NATO's March 1999 war in Kosovo against the Milošević regime was purely an air war, with the avowed intention from the very beginning of avoiding ground troops. What initially was meant to be a two-day airstrike stretched on for 78 days. The story is a complex one and opinion remains divided to this day over key questions leading up to the war. Was the war a response to a budding humanitarian crisis or was it a geostrategic move to emphasize the dominance of NATO? Was the failure of diplomacy at Rambouillet predictable given NATO's demands? Even if the war was a genuine humanitarian intervention, when and should force be used in the pursuit of human rights (Ignatieff 2000)? The last question in particular, posed as a novel issue for a post Cold War world, has absorbed so much interest that it has almost eclipsed the *form* of the war itself. Despite all its claims of technological prowess and global humanitarianism, or to follow Schmitt's logic *because* of these claims, the Kosovo war is perhaps closer to the logic and structure of colonial air control and air policing. Even prior to Kosovo, as early as 1993, the Clinton Administration had explored similar plans to use air strikes (without ground troops) in Bosnia. As David Parsons notes,

> since these strikes had little chance of destroying all of the Serbian artillery positions and were not going to be coordinated with any ground operations, they would have amounted to little more than punitive attacks. The concept of using aircraft based on the periphery of an isolated conflict to bring peace by meting out punishment when and where it is deserved is the essence of air control.
>
> (Parsons 1994: 7)

In Kosovo, if we follow Schmitt's conceptual framework, we are able to see how claims of Milosevic's crimes against humanity (regardless of the full veracity of such claims, which were obviously to some extent true), claims of humanitarian intervention, *and* the accelerating and widening scope of the bombing targets to include vital civilian infrastructure, *are not contradictory but perfectly consistent* when war between the *justus hostis* of the *Nomos* has given way to the aerial policing action of criminals in a global *bellum intestinum*.

Similarly with the increasing use of Unarmed Aerial Vehicles, more popularly known as drones, Schmitt's argument about how air power destabilizes the definition of war, converting it into a policing and punitive action against criminals, has enduring relevance. It has, of course, become a truism to say that the war on terror is a different and unprecedented kind of war. Everyone from Slavoj Zizek to George W. Bush himself has made that claim (Bush 2001; Zizek 2002). The war has been described as global, asymmetric, hybrid, perpetual. In retrospect while Bush was actually quite accurate in his description of the hybrid nature of the war, as well as its particular temporality, he perhaps exaggerated its unprecedented quality. In fact, it would be more accurate to claim that the war on terror has rendered explicit and global, trends in conflict that had been emerging for many decades. These claims are evident in the use of drones to carry out targeted killings of terror suspects, far from the conventional battlefields of Iraq and Afghanistan, in Somalia, Yemen and the tribal areas of Pakistan (Bergen and Tiedermann 2009: 2; Dworkin 2002: Mayer 2009; Moore 2009). Once we move past a simple fascination with the fact that the piloting of these aircraft is done remotely, it is clear that drones, despite the technological changes in the delivery, remain very much within the imaginary of aerial bombing and air control. This is a condition which, following Schmitt's argument, one could describe as the violent reprisals against criminals in a global *bellum intestinum*. It is a condition that is both made possible by and itself adds to the dissolution of any stable definition of war. The legality of drones for targeted killings is said to be based on the fact that they are part of an ongoing 'armed conflict', that is to say a war (Koh 2010). And yet the more the drone programme expands as a global 'policing' programme of potential terrorists, scattered around the world, the more difficult it will be to slot into existing laws of war categories of 'armed conflict'. Thus inconsistencies in legal justifications of drone attacks actually reflect the hybrid nature of the practice itself.

Obviously there is more to these examples, just as there is more to Schmitt's book than my brief synopsis covers, but my intervention here has been to try to cover some of the limitations and possibilities of Schmitt's analysis of air power in *Nomos*. Thus we see how, despite a lack of detail about the theory and practice of airpower, Schmitt's central argument still has deep conceptual relevance for analysing contemporary forms – a testament to the uncannily prescient quality of *The* Nomos *of the Earth*.

References

Bergen, P. and Tiedermann, K. (2009) 'Revenge of the Drones. An Analysis of Drone Strikes in Pakistan', New America Foundation (19 October). Available at: www.newamerica.net/publications/policy/revenge_of_the_drones (accessed 22 June 2010).

Bush, G.W. (2001) Address to a Joint Session of Congress, 20 September. Available at: http://archives.cnn.com/2001/US/09/20/gen.bush.transcript/ (accessed 22 June 2010).

Douhet, G. (1983) *The Command of the Air*, trans. Dino Ferrari, Washington, DC: USAF.

Dworkin, A. (2002) 'The Yemen Strike: The War On Terrorism Goes Global', Crimes of War Project (14 November). Available at: www.crimesofwar.org/onnews/news-yemen.html (accessed 22 June 2010).

Ignatieff, M. (2000) *Virtual War: Kosovo and Beyond*, New York: Henry Holt.

Koh, H. (2010) Legal Adviser, Department of State, 'The Obama Administration and International Law', Keynote Address at the Annual Meeting of the American Society of International Law (25 March). Available at: www.state.gov/s/l/releases/remarks/139119.htm (accessed 22 June 2010).

Lindqvist, S. (2001) *A History of Bombing*, trans. Linda Haverty Rugg, New York: The New Press.

Mayer, J. (2009) 'The Predator War', *The New Yorker* (26 October).

Meilinger, P.S. (1996) 'Trenchard and "Morale Bombing": The Evolution of Royal Air Force Doctrine Before World War II', *The Journal of Military History* 60.

Meilinger, P.S. (2000) 'The Historiography of Air Power: Theory and Doctrine', *The Journal of Military History* 64(2): 467–501.

Moore, M.S. (2009) 'What Are Those Warships Doing Off Somalia' *Miller-McCune* (18 November). Available at: www.miller-mccune.com/politics/what-are-those-warships-doing-off-somalia-5046/ (accessed 22 June 2010).

Parsons, D.W. (1994) 'British Air Control: A Model for the Application of Air Power in Low-Intensity Conflict?' *Air Power Journal* (Summer). Available at: www.Airpower.maxwell.af.mil/airchronicles/apj/apj94/sum94 (accessed 22 June 2010).

Salmond, J. (1922) 'Statement by Air Marshall Sir John Salmond of his views upon the principles governing the use of Air Power in Iraq', Air Staff Memo no. 16, p. 7. National Archives, London: AIR 5/338.

Schmitt, C. (2006) *The Nomos of the Earth in the International Law of the Jus Publicum Europaeum*, trans. G.L. Ulmen, New York: Telos.

Surin, K. (2005) 'World Ordering', *The South Atlantic Quarterly* 104: 2.

Zizek, S. (2002) *Welcome to the Desert of the Real*, London: Verso.

18 Postcolonialism

Julia Lossau

The following response to *The* Nomos *of the Earth* engages with Carl Schmitt's book from a postcolonial perspective. It is written from the personal viewpoint of a political geographer who first encountered Schmitt in German and who, therefore, cannot help but take the German edition of the book, i.e. *Der Nomos der Erde im Völkerrecht des Jus Publicum Europaeum*, as a point of departure. Against such a background, questions of language will inevitably play a role in this response. Instead of thinking about translation in terms of originality, however, I will draw upon postcolonial ideas of transference or circulation, discussing the specific qualities of the *Nomos* as a travelling theory (Edward Said). Moreover, my response will critically engage with some of the arguments and historical interpretations developed by Schmitt in the *Nomos*. Given the postcolonial rationale of this response, I will focus on the second part of the book entitled 'The Land-Appropriation of a New World'. Finally, I am intrigued by the peculiar usage of spatial terminology in Schmitt's writings. Drawing upon a book on the German tradition of *Geopolitik* by Rainer Sprengel, I will elaborate on Schmitt's spatiality, ultimately contrasting the latter with spatialities conveyed by postcolonial theorists.

When I was first asked to participate in a collection devoted to the discussion of a book of Carl Schmitt's, the idea sent cold shivers up and down my spine. For the majority of German(-speaking) social and cultural theorists, Schmitt is still an author who is to be avoided due to his involvement with Nazi thought and politics, which 'raise fundamental questions about how we should read and appropriate his writings today' (Dean 2006, 3). When I realised, however, that the editors of the collection were known for their critical theoretical positions and that there was, moreover, a whole 'Schmitt revival' (Chandler 2008, 47) among critical theorists, especially in the Anglo-American world, I was tempted to accept the invitation. I recalled that Chantal Mouffe (2005) drew prominently upon Schmitt in her reflections on the political – a theoretical choice that had puzzled me when I first read her book. According to Mouffe, there is much we can learn from Carl Schmitt, given that he was:

> very critical of liberal universalism with its pretence of offering the true and only legitimate political system. He criticised the liberals for

using the concept of '*humanity*' as an ideological weapon of imperialist expansion and he saw humanitarian ethics as a vehicle of economic imperialism.

(Mouffe 2005, 78, original emphasis)

After having reread Mouffe, my temptation to participate had further grown: What is it that makes Schmitt interesting for various strands of critical theory, from post-structuralism to (critical) cosmopolitanism? What insights does the *Nomos* provide for a postcolonial perspective in particular? Does the notorious 'crown jurist of the Third Reich' not represent an antipode to critical thinking, given, among others, his views on the superiority of the Europeans as expressed, for instance, in the following passage from the *Nomos*:

From the standpoint of the discovered, discovery as such was never legal. [. . .] Discoveries were made without prior permission of the discovered. Thus, legal title to discoveries lay in higher legitimacy. They could be made only by peoples intellectually and historically advanced enough to apprehend the discovered by superior knowledge and consciousness. To paraphrase one of Bruno Bauer's Hegelian aphorisms: a discoverer is one who knows his prey better than the prey knows himself, and is able to subjugate him by means of superior education and knowledge.

(Schmitt 2003 [1950] 131–132)

Here they were again, these shivers down my spine. . . In the meantime, however, I had begun my own critical engagement with Schmitt's work, and I had found my 'entry' into what, to me, is most striking about the *Nomos*: the peculiar spatiality conveyed by Schmitt.

Oppositional spatialities

In his *Kritik der Geopolitik. Ein deutscher Diskurs 1914–1944*, Rainer Sprengel (1996) points out that, during the revitalisation of the geopolitical arguments of the 1990s, Carl Schmitt and Fernand Braudel have been rediscovered. According to Sprengel, the two authors mark two extremes of the geopolitical discussions of their time. While Schmitt had given attention to the spatial in and of itself – '*das Räumliche an und für sich*' (Sprengel 1996, 51), Braudel had focused on the concrete, virtually tangible spatiality of the Earth: 'Schmitt argued as a political philosopher of space and history, Braudel as a subject specific geohistorian' (Sprengel 1996, 51, trans. JL).

It is striking, indeed, how little interest Schmitt shows in the physical materiality of the Earth, at least in a traditional geographical sense. Despite his frequent hints to 'the telluric', his usage of spatial terminology differs greatly from the conceptualisations of space and spatiality we know from political geographers of the pre- and interwar period. Traditional political geography used to speak of space in a concrete, non-representational sense that tended to be deterministic in that the development of society (be it in terms of cultural traditions, political boundaries or the economy) was thought to causally depend on the qualities of the material substrate. Ideas of concrete, earthly space figure prominently, for instance, in the writings of Friedrich Ratzel, whose *Anthropogeographie* entails the idea of 'natural lands' (*Länder*) that, in turn, represent the demarcated territories of (supposedly) socially homogenous entities or nation-states (see Lossau 2009a). The idea of a 'natural land' feeds into Ratzel's definition of the state as an organic whole which, for him, developed out of the interaction between a specific group of people and the discrete territory the group occupies – *ein Stück Menschheit und ein Stück Boden*, as he famously wrote (Ratzel 1903, 4).

Schmitt's work, in contrast, seems to go without the idea of concrete space of matter and land. In the author's foreword in the *Nomos*, Schmitt distances himself from geographical thinking and identifies his approach as juridical. At the same time, it is precisely the idea of the nomos that makes Schmitt a spatial thinker par excellence. The nomos – described by Schmitt as the combination or unity of order (*Ordnung*) and spatial orientation (*Ortung*) – represents a 'fence-word' (Schmitt 2003 [1950], 75) that gives birth to territories, delineates dwelling places or households and produces paturages. It does so according to the content of the Greek verb *nemein*, which comprises, according to Schmitt, not only the meaning of the German verb *nehmen* (to take or appropriate), but also of *teilen* (to distribute or divide) and of *weiden* (to graze or pasture). For Schmitt, the appropriation of telluric space is of pivotal importance for human history, marking the source of the political as well as of economic development. As Sprengel writes, 'the appropriation of land conveys the constitution of a self which differs from another self. The process of distribution/division shapes this self [*gibt diesem Selbst eine Form*], the grazing reproduces the self in a material sense' (Sprengel 1996, 54, trans. JL).

As a consequence, it is by land appropriation that the abstract notion of humanity is confronted with concrete, empirical differences. As is generally known, Schmitt thinks of political communities as hostile entities, and the Schmittian rationale of the political is the battle for the finite space of the Earth:

> The political world is a pluriverse, not a universe. [...] Intrinsically, political unity cannot be universal in the sense of a unit comprising the whole of humanity and the Earth. [...] Humanity as such can not wage war because it has no enemy, at least not on this planet.
> (Schmitt 1963 [1932], 54, trans. JL)

Coming back to questions of space, it can be argued that the world-as-pluriverse poses a general threat. This threat is due to the fact that there is no assignable cause of the allocation of communities over the Earth's surface. Put differently, there is no compulsive reason why a given community has appropriated a particular space (and not another one) – and why this community should content itself with that space. As Sprengel writes, it is 'the memory of the *arbitrariness* of the original and any subsequent land-appropriation that is threatening' (Sprengel 1996, 55; trans. JL, emphasis added). While the arbitrariness cannot be avoided, the related thread can be contained by the nomos – i.e. a political and legal order of mutually binding rules that orchestrate the conduct of external affairs. This does not mean, however, that war and further land appropriation was no longer possible. The nomos's significance lies rather in its ability to foster (in German, Schmitt speaks of *hegen* which is usually translated as 'bracket') armed conflicts related to the appropriation of land, to give them a form and thus to rationalise them.

At this point, the difference between the grasp of spatial terminology in the *Nomos*, on the one hand, and in the geopolitical tradition, on the other hand, becomes manifest: while for the geopolitical tradition, the proper place of a community is determined by geography – a highly political move that supposedly negates the political by subordinating politics under nature – Schmitt underlines the contingent, arbitrary character of the *where* of appropriation. While Schmitt, therefore, can be said to rely on a more deliberate and, of course, explicit notion of the political, the question remains whether his approach, which is surprisingly contingent in terms of its non-naturalised understanding of the human relationship with nature, can be fruitfully connected with postcolonial perspectives.

Eurocentrism and the dialectics of humanity

The nomos, as has just been outlined, represents a geopolitical order that, albeit being based on the process of appropriation, balances power by providing the legal frame in which sovereign political communities negotiate their interests. Given the nomos's ability to 'foster war', wars were no longer aimed at annihilating the other but were waged as tests of strength between enemies that mutually accepted each other as individuals of the same kind (see Sprengel 1996, 54). It is interesting to note that the nomos of the *Jus Publicum Europaeum* – 'in a balance of land and sea' (Schmitt 2003 [1950], 172) – comprises not only a continental order but also an order of the sea, ultimately concerning 'the entire globe, including the oceans' (Schmitt 2003 [1950], 172). Nevertheless, the nomos is Eurocentric insofar as it guarantees the 'fostering of war' for Europe exclusively.

This contradiction is explained by the fact that the two orders, i.e. the continental order and the order of the sea, have a counterpart on which the nomos is virtually based. This counterpart is the 'new world' 'as *free space*, as an area open to European occupation and expansion' (Schmitt 2003 [1950], 87, original emphasis): 'The ordered enmity that pervaded Europe under the *Jus Publicum Europaeum*', Alberto Toscano writes, 'was enabled for Schmitt by the radical asymmetry between the European space of regulated conflict and the extra-European space of conquest' (Toscano 2008, 425–426). This asymmetry was provided by a 'global linear thinking', i.e. a strategic division of the globe along global lines among which Schmitt emphasises the 'amity lines':

The significance of amity lines in 16th and 17th century international law was that great areas of freedom were designated as conflict zones in the struggle over the distribution of a new world. As a practical justification, one could argue that the designation of a conflict zone at once freed the area on this side of the line – a sphere of peace and order ruled by European public law – from the immediate threat of those events 'beyond the line', which would not have been the case had there been no such zones. The designation of a conflict zone outside Europe contributed also to the bracketing of European wars, which is its meaning and its justification in international law.

(Schmitt 2003 [1950], 97–98)

Regarding the justification of the European occupation of the New World, 'the justice or injustice of the *conquista*' (Schmitt 2003 [1950], 101), Schmitt discusses the famous *relectiones* of Francisco de Vitoria. Contrary to the Aristotelian argument that 'the natives' were not humans but barbarians and, as 'slaves by nature', legitimate prey, Vitoria held that the Amerindians were 'no less human than are the European land-appropriators' (Schmitt 2003 [1950], 102). That the *conquista* is nevertheless justified by Vitoria is explained by Schmitt by the fact that the former's 'lack of presuppositions, his objectivity and neutrality, have their limits, and do not go so far as to disregard the distinction between Christians and non-believers':

On the contrary: the practical conclusion is completely consistent with Vitoria's Christian convictions, which found their true justification in Christian mission. It never occurred to the Spanish monk that non-believers should have the same rights of propaganda and intervention for idolatry and religious fallacies as Spanish Christians had for their Christian missions.

(Schmitt 2003 [1950], 113)

It can be argued, therefore, that it is precisely 'the stated inherent potential in all humans, even barbarians, to know the truth [i.e. to affirm the truth of the Gospel] that gave European Christians their irresistible and irreversible legal wedge' (Rasch 2003, 132).

Against such a background, William Rasch has made the point that, by challenging Vitoria, Schmitt had pointed out Christendom's and modernity's central and inescapable asymmetry: 'Schmitt tries to grasp something both disturbing and elusive about the modern world – namely, the apparent fact that the liberal and humanitarian attempt to construct a world of universal friendship produces, as if by internal necessity, ever new enemies' (Rasch 2003, 135). While this seems to me quite a generalised interpretation, a drive to criticise the concept of humanity is undeniable in Schmitt's writings. The 'idea of humanity', Schmitt states in the *Nomos*, 'is two-sided and often lends itself to a surprising dialectic' (Schmitt 2003 [1950], 103):

> Only when man appeared to be the embodiment of absolute humanity did the other side of this concept appear in the form of a new enemy: the *inhuman*. The expulsion of the inhuman from the human was followed in the 19th century by an even deeper division, between the *superhuman* and the *subhuman*. Just as the human presupposes the inhuman, so, with dialectical necessity, the superhuman entered history with its hostile twin: the subhuman.
>
> (Schmitt 2003 [1950], 104, original emphases)

A similar critique of humanity is characteristic of the postmodern/poststructuralist debate. While the dialectics of humanity also represent an integral part of the postcolonial critique, the argument here has been developed further towards a critique of the 'universalising panoptic eye of the Enlightenment' (Hall 1996, 252) under which 'all forms of human life were brought . . . within the universal scope of a single order of being'. Despite such selective parallels, however, Schmitt hardly qualifies as a warrantor for postcolonial thinking. Although he 'forces us to consider the history of land appropriation, territorial expansions, war and colonialism' (Dean 2006, 8), he seems to valorise 'a Eurocentrism disturbingly stripped of pastoral, paternalistic or liberal-imperialist justifications' (Toscano 2008, 426). By nonchalantly representing non-European space as being 'without masters, uncivilised or only semi-civilised', he reduces the colonies to 'the spatial element upon which European law is founded' (Schmitt 1991 [1941], quoted in Toscano 2008, 427). At the same time, the nomos is praised as 'the strongest possible rationalisation and humanisation of war' (Schmitt 2003 [1950], 142), providing 'the highest form of order within the scope of human power' (Schmitt 2003 [1950], 187).

Travelling *Nomos*

'Like people and schools of criticism', Edward Said writes, 'ideas and theories travel – from person to person, from situation to situation, from one period to another' (Said 1983, 226). While such movement is described as 'both a fact of life and a usefully enabling condition of intellectual activity', Said urges us to 'specify the kinds of movement that are possible . . . and whether a theory in one historical period and national culture becomes altogether different for another period or situation' (Said 1983, 226). Thinking of the *Nomos* as a travelling theory, it seems to me that it represents quite a remarkable example in that it somehow fits better to its current embeddings than to the circumstances when it first entered discourse. With its current embeddings, I mean the *Nomos*' significance in the (supposedly) international academic discourse that has English as its *lingua franca* and that greatly differs from the rather localised academic and political discourse of immediate post-war Germany.

In the context where the *Nomos* was first published, there was not much research into ambiguity, heterodoxy or ambivalences – qualities for which the

Nomos is hailed today. Louiza Odysseos and Fabio Petito, for instance, praise 'the polysemic nature of the Nomos' and 'the *heterodox* international thought of Schmitt' which, due to its ambiguity and not easily classifiable nature, 'renders it of such interest and particular relevance to IR in the present condition of crisis in international order and epoch-making changes in the normative structures of international society' (Odysseos and Petito 2008, 466; original emphasis). It is only fair to add that, in post-war Germany, bold discussions on international order were no more popular than stark criticism of liberalism or rationalism.

Maybe the legacy of this reluctance is another reason why, in Germany, Schmitt still meets with a refusal, whereas he is positively referenced in the English-speaking literature. Chantal Mouffe, who has already been mentioned in the introduction to this response, describes Schmitt 'as one of the most brilliant and intransigent opponents of liberalism' (Mouffe 2005, 5). To her:

> one of Schmitt's central insights is his thesis that political identities consist in a certain type of we/they relation, the relation friend/enemy which can emerge out of very diverse forms of social relations. By bringing to the fore the relational nature of political identities, he anticipates several currents of thought, such as post-structuralism, that will later stress the relational character of all identities.
>
> (Mouffe 2005, 14–15)

In fact, Mouffe problematises her decision to conduct her arguments 'under the aegis of such a controversial thinker as Carl Schmitt' (Mouffe 2005, 4). At the same time, however, she believes 'that it is the intellectual force of theorists, not their moral qualities, that should be the decisive criteria in deciding whether or not we need to establish a dialogue with their work' (Mouffe 2005, 4–5).

I am not entirely convinced by this argument, although I understand that there might be a danger in conflating the theoretical with the political or the moral. More importantly, however, I would like to argue that one does not really need Schmitt in order to think through the relational nature of political identities. Especially from a postcolonial perspective, scholars have theorised the implications of antagonistic we/they, same/different or equal/unequal relations for decades. What differentiates the postcolonial critique from Schmitt's work, though, is the emphasis that is put on the problems inherent in dualistic reasoning.

It is by thinking about space differently that these problems are supposed to be addressed (see Lossau 2009b). Doreen Massey, for instance, has argued that a spatialised perspective holds open the possibility of the existence of alternatives in that the spatial is 'the sphere of juxtaposition, or co-existence, of distinct narratives, [. . .] the product of power-filled social relations' (Massey 1999, 21). In a similar vein, Homi K. Bhabha is interested in hybridity as 'the "third space" which enables other positions to emerge' (Bhabha 1990, 211), while bell hooks has conceptualised the margin as 'a space of radical openness [...] – a profound edge' (hooks 1990, 149), which 'gives us a new location from which to articulate our sense of the world' (hooks 1990, 153).

Compared to the different alterity and hybridity allowed for in the spatialities of postcolonial critique, the ontological spatiality of the *Nomos* seems to me rather ponderous, if not deadlocked. Against such a background, I am somewhat reluctant to establish a deeper dialogue with Schmitt's work, and while Mouffe proposes to think 'with Schmitt against Schmitt' (Mouffe 2005, 14), I prefer, at the end of the day, to think without Schmitt.

References

Bhabha, H.K. (1990) 'The Third Space' in J. Rutherford (ed.) *Identity, Community, Culture, Difference*, London: Lawrence and Wishart, 207–221.

Chandler, D. (2008) The revival of Carl Schmitt in International Relations: the last refuge of critical theorists? *Millennium – Journal of International Studies* 37: 27–48.

Dean, M. (2006) A political mythology of world order. Carl Schmitt's *Nomos*. *Theory, Culture & Society*, 23: 1–22.

Hall, S. (1996) 'When was "the postcolonial"? Thinking at the limit', in I. Chambers and L. Curti (eds) *The Postcolonial Question: Common Skies, Divided Horizons*, London, New York: Routledge, 242–260.

hooks, b. (1990) *Yearnings*, Boston, MA: South End Press.

Lossau, J. (2009a) 'Anthropogeography (After Ratzel)', in R. Kitchen and N. Thrift (eds) *The International Encyclopedia of Human Geography*, Amsterdam, London: Elsevier, 140–147.

Lossau, J. (2009b) 'Pitfalls of (third) space: rethinking the ambivalent logic of spatial semantics', in K. Ikas and G. Wagner (eds) *Communicating in the Third Space*. New York, London: Routledge, 62–78.

Massey, D. (1999) *Power-Geometries and the Politics of Space-Time*, Heidelberg: Department of Geography, University of Heidelberg.

Mouffe, C. (2005) *On the Political*, London, New York: Routledge.

Odysseos, L. and Petito, F. (2008) 'Vagaries of interpretation. A rejoinder to David Chandler's reductionist reading of Carl Schmitt'. *Millennium – Journal of International Studies* 37: 463–475.

Rasch, W. (2003) Human rights as geopolitics. *Cultural Critique* 54: 120–147.

Ratzel, F. (1903) *Politische Geographie*. 2nd edition. Munich, Berlin: Oldenbourg.

Said, E. (1983) *The World, the Text, and the Critic*, Cambridge, MA: Harvard University Press.

Schmitt, C. (1952) Die Einheit der Welt. *Merkur* 6: 1–11.

Schmitt, C. (1963 [1932]) *Der Begriff des Politischen. Text von 1932 mit einem Vorwort und drei Corollarien*, Berlin: Duncker & Humblot.

Schmitt, C. (2003 [1950]) *The Nomos of the Earth in the International Law of the Jus Publicum Europaeum*. Annotated and trans. G.L. Ulmen, New York: Telos Press.

Schmitt, C. (1991 [1941]) *Völkerrechtliche Großraumordnung mit Interventionsverbot für raumfremde Mächte. Ein Beitrag zum Reichsbegriff im Völkerrecht*, 4. Ausgabe, Berlin: Duncker & Humblot.

Sprengel, R. (1996) *Kritik der Geopolitik. Ein deutscher Diskurs 1914–1944*, Berlin: Akademie-Verlag.
Toscano, A. (2008) Carl Schmitt in Bejing: partisanship, geopolitics and the demolition of the Eurocentric world. *Postcolonial Studies* 14: 417–433.

19 *Land and Sea*

Eduardo Mendieta

Carl Schmitt's *Land und Meer: Eine weltgeschichtliche Betrachtung* (2001 [1942]) (*Land and Sea: A Consideration on World History*) has not received the attention that it merits. Written in 1942, during a period in which Germany was at war on several fronts, and Schmitt himself having withdrawn from the public limelight due to the attacks by the SS that threatened his life,[1] the book could be read as an act of resistance, even as a veiled critique of the Nazi regime.[2] It can also be read as the register of a major paradigm change in Schmitt's own thinking, and as the testament to what Nicolaus Sombart called a 'intellectual and moral *midlife-crisis*' (Sombart, 1984, 251, original emphasis). *Land and Sea*, at the very least, has to be read as a conceptual bridge between his *The Leviathan in the State Theory of Thomas Hobbes: Meaning and Failure of a Political Symbol* (2008 [1938]) and his *The* Nomos *of the Earth in the International Law of* Jus Publicum Europaeum (2003 [1950]). While the central ideas of the *Nomos* book are all anticipated, although not fully developed, in *Land and Sea*, this book takes up where the Hobbes book leaves off, namely on the 'meaning and failure of a political symbol'. It can be said that *Land and Sea* is Schmitt's answer to his own assessment of Hobbes' failure to see through and beyond his own evocative political symbol of the leviathan (Nowak, 2008). In contrast to these two other books, which are circumscribed and specialized, *Land and Sea* is wide-ranging, encyclopaedic, poetic and philosophically provocative. If there is a book that contains Schmitt's philosophy, it is this. Additionally, thoughtful consideration of this book will also reveal that Schmitt's thought had undergone a major theoretical shift between 1938 and 1942. In a very general sense it can be said that from the 1920s through to the late 1930s Schmitt's theoretical position had to do with 'the political' and the relationship between the sovereign, the state and the law. This general period can be labelled the 'decisionist' phase of his thinking, which is captured in the phrase: 'The specific political distinction to which political actions and motives can be reduced is that between friend and enemy' (Schmitt, 2007 [1927], 26). This formulation could be rephrased in the following way, paraphrasing Schmitt himself (2007 [1927], 52): The decision as to who is a friend and who is an enemy is the ground of the sovereignty of the state. Thus, '*protego ergo obligo* is the *cogito ergo sum* of the state'. From 1938 through 1942, Schmitt would shift his concern from state sovereignty and the political towards what he calls the spatial order that is the ground of all law [*Raumordnung*].³ The central pivot of Schmitt's new thinking is expressed in the formulation '*Jede Grundordnung is eine Raumordnung*' [Every fundamental order is a spatial order] (2001 [1942], 71). Nomos, law, to use its most approximate translation, is no longer conceived as emanating from the decision of a sovereign, but from an original 'appropriation, distribution, production' that establishes a new spatial order (2003 [1950], 324). Law is now conceived spatially (Palaver, 1996). It could be said, then, that the new *cogito ergo sum* of the state, as a spatial ordering that grounds the law, would be *ego conquiro ergo obligo* (Dussel, 1985, 3). For this reason, the exclusive focus on Schmitt's *Concept of the Political* that has marked the reception and rediscovery of Schmitt in contemporary political theory is a distortion of Schmitt's own intellectual itinerary and what he in fact contributed to the understanding of law, politics and the history of political philosophy. At the same time, we must be critical of the uses that can be made of Schmitt in international law and contemporary geopolitics (see Elden in this volume).

Land and Sea is a remarkable book and it is difficult to give it a proper characterization. As its subtitle indicates, it is a *consideration on world history*, but it is more than a reflection on the meaning of world history. The book is in fact a combination of mytho-poesis, philosophical speculation and political mythology (Dean, 2006). Hans Blumemberg's term of metaphorology (1997 [1960]) would be apt to use with respect to what Schmitt is doing in this text, for he is deciphering the rational meanings of key metaphors in the history of Western political thought. The book is made up of twenty sections, each no longer than three pages. Dedicated to his daughter, Anima, it is written as if a series of parables were being told. In fact, the dedication says: 'narrated to my daughter Anima'. At times, Schmitt interjects to remind his reader that this is being addressed to his daughter. I have identified at least seven key themes that make this a compendium of Schmitt's philosophy and also the point of departure for his new thinking on law.

- First, it is a mythopoetic analysis of the fundamental elements in nature. As Schmitt notes in section two, we can understand human history as humanity's transit through and contenting with the four elements: earth, water, air and fire. To each spatial order there corresponds the control of one of these elements. World history can be understood poetically as the supremacy of one of these elements over the others.
- The second theme is thus already announced, namely that to the supremacy of each element there corresponds a political symbol, which has its corresponding mythology. Schmitt in fact develops what can be called a political bestiary. Thus, the leviathan is to water, what the behemoth is to earth, what the griffin is to air, what the sphinx is to fire.
- Third, then, we have also a philosophy of war, or rather a world historical analysis of the different ways in which war has been waged. World

history, as he writes in section three, is 'the history of the struggle of sea powers against land powers, and of land powers against sea powers' (2001 [1942], 16). Each form of power, or control, engages in a particular type of war, which has different consequences for how it relates to its enemy. Each power also wages war on the grounds or use of a different element. The history of war is the history of different theatres of war and elements made into weapons.

- Fourth, each form of power (land power, sea power, airpower, etc.) relates to law differently, or rather because its relationship to the state is different, its fundamental order is going to be different. Schmitt shows how a certain legal order depends on whether a sea or a land power has been hegemonic. To each imperial ordering corresponds a legal regime, a way of conceiving law and the relationship between sovereign and ruled. For this reason *Land and Sea* should be read as a genealogy of law. All law, nomos, emanates from a land appropriation that orders space. This appropriation is evidently the result of war. Law is thus grounded in the war that orders space. As Schmitt puts it: 'War, said Heraclitus, brings together, and law is conflict' (2001 [1942], 75). Schmitt also realizes that every peace corresponds to its proper spatial order. Indeed, peace has to be the inauguration of a new spatial order. As he put in an essay from 1940:

> The sense of every not meaningless war lies in peace, which ends the war. The essence of peace does not reside in that now the canons cease to fire, the bombers do not drop any more bombs, and the diplomats sit talking around the peace banquet, which we know about from Geneva. For then peace would be merely not-war ... In the great history of humanity every true peace is true only once. Peace, which truly ends a war of spatial ordering [*Raumordnungskrieg*], can only be a peace of spatial ordering [*Raumordnungfrieden*].
>
> (Schmitt, 1995, 389)

Schmitt, thus, is not simply a philosopher of war, but also a philosopher of peace, who is trying to understand what secures a lasting peace (Schmitt 2010 [1950]). In *Land and Sea*, in fact, Schmitt also tracks the ways in which when a spatial order is challenged by another, war overflows the controls of the established spatial order. Section seven of the book is a meditation of the role of pirates and whale hunters that discerns in them a form of lawless violence. Schmitt is not simply concerned with the way in which war may originate a new order, but also on how to control it, how to bind it within a certain legal order. In contrast to the position he held in the late 1920s, 'To the state as an essentially political entity belongs the *jus belli*, i.e. the real possibility of deciding on a concrete situation upon the enemy and the ability to fight him with the power emanating from the entity' (2007 [1927], 45), now Schmitt holds that war irrupts from without to challenge the state.

- Fifth, the book is a philosophy of spatiality, of the production of space by war and the conquest of one element over the others. The book is permeated by reflections on spatial orders, and the ways in which to each form of Empire there corresponds a spatial paradigm. The book therefore could be summarized in one question: 'what is a spatial revolution?' (2001 [1942], 55). One can in fact compare *Land and Sea* to Henri Lefebvre's *The Production of Space* (1991). At the centre of Schmitt's philosophy of spatiality is an appropriation of Martin Heidegger's view on spatiality. In fact, Schmitt quotes Heidegger without directly naming him:

    > Today, for the first time, it is possible for us to think something that in other epochs had been impossible and that a contemporary German philosopher has expressed thusly: the world is not in space, instead space is in the world.
    >
    > (2001 [1942], 106)

    Schmitt is here paraphrasing Heidegger's statement in *Being and Time*: '*Space is neither in the subject nor is the world in space*. Rather, space is "in" the world since the being-in-the-world constitutive for Da-sein has disclosed space' (Heidegger, 1996, 105/111, original emphasis).[4] Indeed, for Schmitt, the spatiality of the world is always disclosed by founding moments of taking and distributing (see Minca in this volume).[5]

- A sixth theme is one that links technology to space and to law. *Land and Sea* is suffused with remarks on the ways in which different technological breakthroughs have reconfigured our relationship to space. So, section six of the book discusses the revolutionary impact that the different types of naval ships had on both inter-state relationships, but also war waging. The history of war is the history of different theatres of war, with their respective types of technological materiel. These reflections culminate in chapter seven of *The Nomos of the Earth*, in which Schmitt raises the problem of how, under the new conditions of air war, just war theory is made either obsolete or redundant (see Hussain in this volume, as well as Ruschi, 2008).

- Finally, and seventh, *Land and Sea* is the development of Schmitt's own brand of philosophical anthropology, that is a philosophical speculation about how the fundamental structure of the human being results in certain social orderings. For Schmitt, as for Heidegger, the human being is a spatializing creature, who worlds, who fashions worlds, by arranging or conflagrating the basic elements. While the human being is a terrestrial creature, and most of his fundamental metaphors and myths are grounded in the earth, he is also one that can transverse all the other elements. The human being is exocentric. While his feet may be planted on the earth, he can also become sea fearing and air dwelling. He can make his own dwelling on the abode of his choosing:

    > But now the essence of the human is not to be absorbed by his environment. He has the power to conquer historically his being

[Dasein] and consciousness. He knows not only birth, but also the possibility of rebirth. In many difficulties and dangers in which animals and plants helplessly succumb, can he save himself to a new existence by virtue of his intelligence, his unerring observation, capacity for logical thinking, and decision. He has a playroom for his power and historical potentiality. He can select, and in determinate moments even chose through his own action and effort the element through which he can give himself a new total form of historical existence.

(2001 [1942], 14)

The book concludes with the provocative note that the attentive reader should read *Land and Sea* as an attempt to develop paragraph 247 of Hegel's *Philosophy of Right*, in a parallel way to how Marxism was an attempt to develop paragraphs 243–6. Paragraph 247 reads: 'The condition of the principle of family life is the earth, the firm and solid ground. Similarly, the natural element for industry, animating its outward movement, is the *sea*' (Hegel, 2008, 222, original emphasis). This attempt culminates in Schmitt's own philosophy of law *The Nomos of the Earth*.

Nicolaus Sombart, the son of the famous German sociologist, and with whom Schmitt spent a lot of time during his Berlin years, noted in his memoir of his youth during the war that *Land and Sea* was Schmitt's 'most beautiful, most important book, because it contains *in nuce* the quintessence of his Gnostic philosophy of history' (Sombart, 1984, 255). Whether this is a Gnostic philosophy of history is not as important as the judgement by someone who knew Schmitt intimately during the period when it was drafted, namely that this was his most beautiful and most important. It is indeed a beautifully written book that is full of flashes of brilliance and inchoate hypotheses. From the themes I identified, however, I want to foreground four hermeneutical keys that make it an indispensable point of reference for any proper understanding of Schmitt's thought.

Land and Sea has to be read as a commentary of political symbols. It is a political metaphorology, to appropriate Blumemberg's useful terminology. As was suggested, this book takes up where the Hobbes book left. In this Schmitt claims: 'In the long history of political theories, a history exceedingly rich in colourful images and symbols, icons and idols, paradigms and phantasms, emblems and allegories, this leviathan is the strongest and most powerful image' (2008 [1938], 5). The history of political philosophy is partially the history of the attempts to decipher the meanings of some of its key symbols and allegories. If we can say that the history of Western philosophy is an attempt to decipher the many meanings of Plato's allegory of the cave in his *Republic*, Schmitt argues that the history of political philosophy is the ceaseless task of deciphering the meaning of the two mythical beasts of the behemoth and the leviathan. Here a key passage from his book *Political Romanticism* can be informative:

When the subject lacks real aesthetic – in other words, lyrical-musical – productivity, an argument develops out of historical, philosophical, theological, or some other scientific material, an intellectual music for a political program. This is not the irrationality of myth. That is because the creation of a political or a historical myth arises from political activity, and the fabric of reasons, which myth cannot forgo either, is the emanation of a political energy.

(1986, 160)

Sections three and twenty of *Land and Sea* are direct engagements with what I called a political bestiary (Mendieta, 2010). To the world historical struggle between land and sea powers, metonymically expressed in the struggles between the behemoth and leviathan, Schmitt now adds that of a great bird, which he does not name here, but does in a text from 1943 as the griffin. We also know from his correspondence with Ernst Jünger during the years he is writing this book that he also considered the phoenix, and the dragon. Section twenty, which closes the book, announces that with the introduction of air war, and air weapons, a new element in the history of humanity appears to ascend to hegemony: air or perhaps even fire. With this ascent, 'Disappear the fundaments of the English conquest of the sea, and with them the *nomos* that has until now existed on the earth' (2001 [1942], 106). *Land and Sea* postulated two great planetary spatial revolutions. The first revolution took place in the sixteenth century when the oceans were opened up, the Earth was circumnavigated, and America was discovered, taken, portioned and made productive by the Europeans. The second was just dawning, as Berlin, and Schmitt with it, crouched in bomb shelters listening, as he put it in a letter from this period to Jünger, to: 'the furious roar of behemoth as it greets the great bird Ziz' (Jünger and Schmitt, 1999, 107). This book, second, has to be read as anticipating the spatial turn in social theory that is going to be expressed by thinkers such as Henri Lefebvre, and later David Harvey and Edward Soja. Every social order is fundamentally an ordering of space, to which correspond different ways of visualizing, representing and living space. To paraphrase Heidegger, humans produce worlds by ordering space. Space as such is produced through violent acts of appropriating, dividing and distributing the world. What is important for Schmitt is that in the age of 'neutralizations' brought on by the imposition of a spaceless ordering, humans deceived themselves that we have entered an age in which everything is mere production and consumption, in which 'man can *give* without *taking*' (2003 [1950], 347, original emphasis).

While many have read Schmitt as a bellicose, war-mongering philosopher, the truth is that Schmitt was far more preoccupied with the interplay between 'limitation' of war and its 'dehumanization' through moralization. Every planetary spatial revolution presupposed a period of pirate war, lawless violence or guerrilla warfare that unsettles and disorders some established spatial order. The negotiated peace would arise from the limitation of war through the development of a new legal regime. What Schmitt was concerned with since the early 1940s was precisely the interplay between the dawning new nomos and the rise of total war that entailed the criminalization and demonization of the enemy. Thus a third theme of this particular period but also of most of his work during the 1940s was the limitation of war (Schmitt, 2010 [1950]).

Finally, *Land and Sea* can be read as a cautionary fable about wielding properly or improperly certain elements and their respective forces. One can read section twenty as a veiled critique of the Nazi failure to properly wield the weapons of war corresponding to this new type of war. At the very least, it can be read as announcing the demise of the Nazi empire because it has been caught between two beasts, one which now is being assisted by a third: the beast of the air. With the destruction of the old European nomos that Schmitt anticipated in his book, there begins to emerge a new one:

> a new *nomos* of our planet emerges unopposed and inevitably. The new relations among men, and the new and old elements call this forth; the change in the dimension and conditions of human existence imposes it. Many will only see death and destruction in it. Some believed the end of the world had arrived. In reality we are living only the end of the relation between land and sea that ruled until now.
>
> (2001 [1942], 81)

Notes

1. For information on this critical period in Schmitt's life, I have relied on Joseph W. Bendersky (1983, 1987), as well as Nicolaus Sombart (1984), who used to go walking with Schmitt during these particular years.
2. Gopal Balakrishnan has argued that Schmitt's Hobbes book can be read as either expressing disappointment in the Nazi regime or in fact as an indirect critique of the Nazi failure to create a properly unified state (2000, p. 214). I agree with Balakrishnan's assessment. I would add that the same critical attitude can be discerned in *Land and Sea*.
3. There is a series of articles Schmitt wrote from 1938 through 1942 that must also be considered when trying to understand the nature of this shift. They are now collected in Carl Schmitt *Staat, Großraum, Nomos: Arbeiten aus den Jahren 1916–1969*, edited and annotated by Günther Maschke (Berlin: Duncker & Humblot, 1995). The third part, entitled 'Großraum und Völkerrecht', contains the relevant essays. For a critical and thorough analysis of this shift in Schmitt's thinking, see Schmoeckel, 1994.
4. I am quoting from Joan Stambaugh's translation. The second number refers to the German pagination.
5. There is in fact a fascinating triangle among Heidegger, Jünger and Schmitt that deserves careful study and consideration. We know that Heidegger was deeply influenced by Jünger's *Der Arbeiter*, and that Schmitt read avidly his work as well, mentioning him quite often, especially in his *Excaptivate salus* (Schmitt 2010 [1950]). Schmitt's and Jünger's correspondence has been published (Jünger and Schmitt, 1999). See the dated but still informative study by Christian Graf von Krockow (1958). See also Mendieta (2006).

References

Balakrishnan, G. (2000) *The Enemy. An Intellectual Portrait of Carl Schmitt*. Verso: London.
Bendersky, J.W. (1983) *Carl Schmitt: Theorist for the Reich*. Princeton University Press: Princeton, NJ.
—— (1987) 'Carl Schmitt at Nuremberg' *Telos* 72 (Summer), 91–6.
Blumemberg, H. (1997 [1960]) *Paradigmen zu einer Metaphorologie*. Suhrkamp: Frankfurt am Main.
Dean, M. (2006) 'A Political Mythology of World Order: Carl Schmitt's Nomos' *Theory, Culture & Society*, Vol. 23, No. 5, 1–22.
Dussel, E. (1985) *Philosophy of Liberation*. Orbis Books: Maryknoll, NY.
Graf von Krockow, C. (1958) *Die Entscheidung: Eine Untersuchung über Ernst Jünger, Carl Schmitt, Martin Heidegger*. Stuttgart: Ferdinand Enke Verlag.
Hegel, G.W.F. (2008) *Outlines of the Philosophy of Right*, trans. T.M. Knox. Oxford University Press: Oxford.
Heidegger, M. (1996) *Being and Time*, trans. Joan Stambaugh. SUNY Press: Albany.
Jünger, E. and Schmitt, C. (1999) *Briefe, 1930–1983*. Stuttgart: Klett-Cotta.
Lefebvre, H. (1991) *The Production of Space*, trans. D. Nicholson-Smith. Blackwell: Oxford.
Mendieta, E. (2006) 'War the School of Space: The Space of War and the War for Space' *Ethics, Place and Environment*, Vol. 9, No. 2 (June), 207–29.
—— (2010) 'Political Bestiary: On the Uses of Violence' *Insights* Vol. 3, No. 5. Available online at: www.dur.ac.uk/ias/insights/volume3/article5/. Last accessed 13 January 2011.
Nowak, P. (2008) 'Incarnations of Leviathan,' 285–300, in Minkov, S. and Nowak, P. *Man and his Enemies: Essays on Carl Schmitt*. Bialystok: University of Bialystok.
Palaver, W. (1996) 'Carl Schmitt on Nomos and Space' *Telos* (Winter), 105–27.
Ruschi, F. (2008) 'Space, Law and Power in Carl Schmitt' in *Jura Gentium: Journal of International Law and Global Politics*, IV, available online at: www.juragentium.unifi.it/en/surveys/thil/nomos.htm. Last accessed 12 January 2011.
Schmitt, C. (1986 [1919]) *Political Romanticism*. MIT Press: Cambridge.
—— (1995) *Staat, Großraum, Nomos: Arbeiten aus den Jahren 1916–1969*, edited and annotated by Günther Maschke: Duncker & Humblot: Berlin.
—— (2001 [1942]) *Land und Meer: Eine weltgeschichtliche Betrachtung*. Klett-Cotta: Stuttgart.
—— (2003 [1950]) *The Nomos of the Earth in the International Law of the Jus Publicum Europaeum*. Telos Press: New York.
—— (2007 [1927]) *The Concept of the Political*. University of Chicago Press: Chicago.
—— (2008 [1938]) *The Leviathan in the State Theory of Thomas Hobbes: Meaning and Failure of a Political Symbol*. University of Chicago Press: Chicago.
—— (2010 [1950]) *Excaptivitate salus. Experiencias de la época 1945–1947*. Madrid: Minima Trotta.
Schmoeckel, M. (1994) *Die Großraumtheorie: Ein Beitrag zur Geschichte der Völkerrechtswissenschaft im Dritten Reich, insbesondere der Kreigszeit*. Duncker & Humblot: Berlin.
Sombart, N. (1984) *Jugend in Berlin 1933–1943. Ein Bericht*. Hanser: Munich.

20 Free sea

Philip E. Steinberg

A space without geography

There are few concepts more problematic in international law than that of the "free sea."[1] In 1608, Hugo Grotius (1916) coined the principle of *mare liberum* to justify the United Provinces' (The Netherlands') right to seize a Portuguese ship in Southeast Asia. In a later era, the United Kingdom used the principle to justify the interdiction of ships engaged in the slave trade. And today, it is being used to discipline Somali maritime robbers, enforcing an order that state authorities are not willing or able to exercise on land. Clearly, this is a very specific kind of "freedom" that is being implemented in the ocean, and one that is not so "free" for those caught on the wrong side of its self-appointed guardians.

Since Schmitt is suspicious of all legal principles and platitudes, especially as they might be used to support a liberal, universalist ideal that diverges from the actual power relations that predominate between state actors, it should come as no surprise that he is wary of using the concept of "free sea" to guide state action. As Schmitt notes, the version of "free sea" that has prevailed in a specific time and space has been less a consistent application of an absolute principle than "a matter of differently assessed constructions and of the free play of forces" (Schmitt 2003: 99). The principle has been used to justify everything from "a zone free for booty... [where] there [are] no limits, no boundaries, no consecrated sites, no sacred orientations, no law, and no property" (Schmitt 2003: 43) ... "a desolate chaos of mutual destruction" (Schmitt 2003: 99), to the present day where it is being used to assert just the opposite: a "free" space for commerce "designated for agonal tests of strength" (Schmitt 2003: 99) and where state powers are "free" to suppress those who would challenge the established rules governing "free" trade. Schmitt notes that historically there has been so much variation in the principle's application that, like all legal principles, it is useless as a positive guide to action. Thus, for instance, it seems certain that Schmitt would have little patience for neo-Wilsonian idealists who have suggested that the principle of *mare liberum* be a model for a new world order in which the universal desire for freedom in the marine global commons be used to inspire a world of peaceful coexistence (e.g. Borgese 1998, 1999; Pacem in Maribus 1992).

While Schmitt is cautious about making any statements about freedom as an overriding concept that transcends its application to specific historical contexts, substantive freedoms, or political agendas, he is less circumspect about asserting a constant *space* with which that concept of freedom is associated. Schmitt recognizes a "historical and structural relation between such spatial concepts of free sea, free trade, and free world economy, and the idea of a free space in which to pursue free competition and free exploitation" (Schmitt 2003: 99) that has remained consistent throughout what he terms the "industrial" era. This, in turn, leads one to ask: Why the sea? What is it about the ocean that has made it such an attractive environment for applying the legal trope of freedom, notwithstanding its radically varying substantive content?

Schmitt approaches these questions directly, and his responses, in addition to being nuanced, reveal much about his thoughts regarding the relation between the planet's geophysicality and its system of geopolitical order. On the one hand, Schmitt rejects environmental determinist explanations that appeal to the physical differences between land and sea to justify the different levels of political control found in the two domains. Such explanations "steer attention too much away from international law, and to either a geographical-scientific or an elemental-mythological approach" (Schmitt 2003: 37). The sea, for Schmitt, is anything but a place without history.

But the history that emerges on the sea is very different than the history that prevails on land. Land, writes Schmitt, has three central characteristics that link it with law, order, and control. First, investments in a specific parcel of land yield value, providing unity to a cycle that, in its materialization, fixes in place and stretches across time the concept of property. Second, the very act of engaging in this cycle on land transforms the land in a manner that is visible to any onlooker. Thus the spatialization of property is communicated. Third (and closely related to the second point), the physicality of land facilitates further modifications that communicate boundedness, division, ownership, and control, fixed in space and continuous across time. Thus, social actors on land construct fences, buildings, and neighborhoods that convey class divisions and other power relations, drawing lines and producing territories.

The sea, Schmitt argues, has none of these characteristics. The investments that one makes in the ocean and the value that one reaps from those investments are not fixed in space, in contrast with the spatialization that occurs when one, for instance, ploughs a specific field. Even when investments do occur at specific points in ocean space, the visible character of those points is not changed, in contrast with what occurs when a field is sown. And furthermore, even if individuals find ways to invest in and transform parts of the ocean into territory, there is no way for them to add features like fences and walls to communicate the limits of that territory. Thus, concludes Schmitt, "The sea has no *character*, in the original sense of the word, which comes from the Greek *charassein*, meaning to engrave, to scratch, to imprint. The sea is free" (Schmitt 2003: 42–43), a statement that closely parallels Roland

Barthes' depiction of the sea as a "non-signifying field [that] bears no message" (quoted in Connery 2001: 177). In short, Schmitt's sea may not be a space without history, but it is a space beyond inscription—quite literally a space without geography.[2]

Schmitt's "postoceanism"

Schmitt's perspective is thus "postoceanic," a term that Connery (2001) uses to describe Schmitt's reference to an era in which the essential divide between land and sea has been superseded by technology. My usage of this term, while overlapping with Connery's, is somewhat different: Schmitt's world is not only one in which technology has obliterated the land–sea distinction; it is also one in which the ocean is fundamentally without substance.[3] Schmitt writes, "On the waves, there is nothing but waves" (Schmitt 2003: 42–43). Schmitt's ocean, deprived of all matter, is reduced to a series of vectors that cycle in endless monotony. Schmitt's ocean not only has no geography; it has no future.

Schmitt's "postoceanic" perspective is problematic for a number of reasons. Geophysically, the ocean is anything but an undifferentiated, two-dimensional surface, even if some of its "places" are themselves dynamic and mobile (e.g. the paths of currents). Indeed, historically the social construction of the ocean has involved a series of attempts to know and name its points, as they vary across space and time, in three dimensions, and this linkage of state power with naval science continues to this day. Attempts by the United Kingdom, and later the United States, to construct the ocean as a functionally frictionless surface, an empty (or "free") space across which commercial and military ships can move in contrapuntal opposition to the bounded and ordered territories that fundamentally define land, have themselves been dependent on efforts to "know" the sea (Hamblin 2005; Reidy 2008; Rozwadowski 2005). As early as the Papal Bulls of 1492, European powers have been drawing lines in the ocean in an effort to construct a world in which (certain) European powers could expand without obstacles. The preservation of the ocean as a "free" space has been facilitated by investments in navigational aids, navies, and scientific research, and each of these investments has added value to the ocean as a material entity with distinct spaces and natures, requiring and facilitating a conceptualization of the ocean that is very different from its idealization as a geophysical vortex where there is "nothing but waves." Even as naval powers have asserted that the sea is a fundamentally placeless void immune from social power, they have eagerly applied their resources to understanding and, when possible, controlling the forces (whether human, oceanographic, or meteorological) that might impinge on its idealization as an empty surface for movement. As Deleuze and Guattari (1988) note, the construction of the ocean as a smooth space necessarily involves continual efforts at striation.

In part, then, the ongoing involvement of state (and non-state) actors in the construction of the ocean as a set of places is due to the practical problems inherent in mobilizing resources in and across a relatively inaccessible and physically hostile environment. Freedom requires policing and mobility requires fixity, and both of these activities require continual efforts to striate the ideally smooth ocean. There is, however, another, more profound reason for the long history of actors asserting power in the ocean in the name of freedom, and this can be traced to a dialectic *within* the idealization of the ocean as a "free" space of commerce. The ocean emerges as a favored space for facilitating commercial and territorial expansion because it is a representation of pure distance, and thus it is idealized as a space that can be annihilated by putatively footloose capital that has freed itself from the bonds of materiality. From pre-Biblical texts, through Hegel, and on through nineteenth-century maps, Mackinder, Schmitt, and the fantasies of twenty-first-century finance capital, the ideal ocean is an absent ocean (Connery 1996, 2001, 2006; Steinberg 1999, 2001, 2009). This idealized annihilation of the ocean might hypothetically be attainable if the sea truly were "nothing but waves," but if it ever were to happen a crisis would ensue. After all, the annihilation of the ocean would also mean the annihilation of distance, and this, in turn, would deprive capital of the means to realize value through movement. In other words, the ideal of the "free" sea is highly problematic. True "freedom" would reveal systemic contradictions, and this presumably would lead to a new desire to striate ocean-space and rematerialize distance, so that value once again could be generated by crossing its expanse or extracting its resources.

Both of these subtleties—the practical need for marine freedom to involve exertions of power and the dialectic within the very idea of marine freedom—are lost on Schmitt. Even as Schmitt rejects a simple environmental determinist explanation of the division between land and sea, he subscribes to one in which the two surfaces are on singular but divergent historical paths. The physical binary of environmental determinist thought is replaced with a social binary that is no less rigid: Land is the space of territorialization while the sea is the space of deterritorialization. The division of space into fixed categories is thus naturalized, establishing a foundation for classical geopolitical thinking, whether it be the thallocentric perspective of Mahan or the 'postoceanic' perspective of Schmitt and Mackinder.

Freed by the sea

How, then, can one move beyond Schmitt to consider the complex ways in which the sea historically has been idealized as a "free" space and how this idealization, with all of its contradictory elements, has been implemented in practice? One route would be to consider the complex intersection between ideals of freedom and control in a variety of spaces and institutional-legal frameworks, but without the starting point of a land–sea binary. Lauren Benton's (2010) work is exemplary in this regard, as she demonstrates how European empires constructed an array of spaces, with varying degrees of "freedom" and control, on land and at sea. The functional division of spaces that is key to Schmitt's argument is preserved, but rather than there being a fixed binary of spatial categories of spaces, the world's surface is arrayed in endless variety and characterized by imperial powers' *unwillingness* to assign stable categories.

This approach could well be effective (and, indeed, it is for Benton), but here I propose a different route. Like Schmitt, I begin by considering the fluid geophysicality of the sea, but, rather than understanding the sea as a space *without* geography, the sea is understood as a space with a *different* geography. Schmitt's assertion that "on the waves, there is nothing but waves" arguably is accurate, but those waves themselves consist of movement *and* matter, forces *and* substance. Just because the ocean is a space that is in constant motion—*mobilis in mobile*, to quote Professor Aronnax in *20,000 Leagues Under the Sea* (Verne 1962)—does not mean that it does not have distinct places and natures. However these are different kinds of places and natures than those typically identified on land, because there is no static background against which this geography of mobility can be "located." The ocean is not a world of stable places that are impacted by moving forces. Rather, in the ocean, moving matter *constitutes* places, and these places are specifically mobile.

The challenge, then, is to develop an alternative geography that can interpret this fluvial world. Here it is useful to turn away from social theorists and maritime-legal historians and instead engage the work of oceanographers. Oceanographers, unencumbered by the mercantilist concept of a "free" (and therefore ideally immaterial) sea but recognizing that the sea is essentially a space of movement, have long sought to construct such an alternative geography. They are well aware that the ocean, even if consisting of "nothing but waves," is a complex system that defies simple explanation.

To be sure, much oceanographic research adopts a spatial ontology not that different from Schmitt's. Many oceanographers work from what is known as a Eulerian perspective wherein they measure and model fluid dynamics by recording the forces that act on stable buoys. Eulerian researchers compare the presence and characteristics of these forces at different points in an effort to identify general patterns across space and time. Eulerian research remains dominant in oceanography, perhaps because it mimics the terrestrial spatial ontology wherein points are fixed in space and mobile forces are external to and act on those points, or perhaps because the alternative is both costlier and mathematically more complex (Davis 1991). From the Eulerian perspective, as in the spatial ontology adopted by Schmitt, matter exists logically prior to movement. The fixed points of geography, represented in the world of Eulerian oceanography by buoys, would persist even in the absence of the forces of movement that cross the "free" space between and beyond these points.

The alternative is to adopt a Langrangian perspective wherein movement, instead of being subsequent to geography, *is* geography. Oceanographers working from this perspective trace the paths of "floaters" that travel in three-dimensional space, with each floater representing a particle, the fundamental unit in Lagrangian fluid dynamics. Movement is defined by the displacement across space of material characteristics within mobile packages, not abstract forces, and these characteristics are known only through their mobility (Bennett 2006). In other words, objects come into being as they move (or unfold) through space. Conversely, space ceases to be a stable background but a part of the unfolding. The world is constituted by mobility without reference to any stable grid of places or coordinates. From this perspective, movement is the foundation of geography. Hence there can be no basis for conceiving of a "free" (marine) space of movement *beyond* geography.

Although not specifically referencing oceanographic research, Manuel DeLanda (2002) elaborates on the conceptual links between, on the one hand, Deleuzian philosophy and, on the other hand, the Riemannian differential geometry that forms the mathematical basis for Lagrangian fluid dynamics. In both cases, there is an "absence of a supplementary (higher) dimension imposing an extrinsic coordinatization, and hence, *an extrinsically defined unity*" (DeLanda 2002: 12, original emphasis). Space, from this perspective, is less a thing or a stationary framework than a medium that is constantly being made by its dynamic, constitutive elements. It does not, like Schmitt's ocean, *defy* inscription; rather it is *constituted* by its inscription, and its continual reinscription, thus pluralizing the basis—while dispersing the territorial biases—of the classical understanding of geopolitics.[4]

Beyond "freedom" and "order"

According to his translator, Schmitt defines a nomos as a "concrete order," in contradistinction to the abstract orders that are derived from law (Ulmen 2003). And yet, even for Schmitt, the sea is neither concrete nor ordered. Its "freedom" has little substantive content across specific contexts, and, as a space that defies inscription that fixes meaning in space and time, it can never be a repository of order, notwithstanding the perpetual desire to order it.

This chapter has suggested, *contra* Schmitt, that the power of the sea does not lie in its function as a "free" space within the modern world. Such "freedom," as Schmitt himself acknowledges, has always been variable and may be put to any number of different ends and applications. Rather, the power of the "free sea" concept lies in its ability to "free" the way that we think about world order. When one considers the sea's physicality, order becomes something that is dynamic and continually reconstituted, as moving forces construct unstable spaces that are continually transformed through new acts of movement. This is a nomos far removed from any envisioned by Schmitt, but it may be the sea's most profound contribution to the nomos that will characterize the postmodern era.

Notes

1 I am grateful to Baerbel Bischof and Mauro Caraccioli for comments on an earlier draft of this reflection.
2 Here I refer to the literal definition of geography as "earth writing" or "earth inscription."

3 My use of the term "postoceanic" parallels the way in which postcolonial theorists use the term "postcolonial." Like postcolonial theorists, I use "postoceanic" to refer not simply to an era *after* the "oceanic" era (which is how Connery uses the term) but to a socio-cultural system in which the norms of oceanism (like the norms of colonialism) simultaneously are affirmed, transformed, and negated by new, "postoceanic" relations.

4 My appeal to Lagrangian thought to destabilize the idea of place as a static concept that exists in opposition to movement and time closely parallels Doreen Massey's (2005, 2006) appeal to plate tectonics. The Lagrangian metaphor is preferable, however, both because the continual transformation of place is more complete in the ocean (after all, plates remain constant over time, even as their locations shift) and because the ocean is an actual experienced place of contemporary mobilities while geologic time occurs at a scale well beyond that of human experience.

References

Bennett, A. (2006) *Lagrangian Fluid Dynamics*, Cambridge: Cambridge University Press.

Benton, L. (2010) *A Search for Sovereignty: Law and Geography in European Empires, 1400–1900*, New York: Cambridge University Press.

Borgese, E. M. (1998) *The Oceanic Circle: Governing the Seas as a Global Resource*, Tokyo: United Nations University Press.

—— (1999) "Global civil society: lessons from ocean governance," *Futures* 31: 983–991.

Connery, C. L. (1996) "The oceanic feeling and the regional imaginary," in W. Dissanayake and R. Wilson (Eds.), *Global/Local: Cultural Production and the Transnational Imaginary*, Durham, NC: Duke University Press.

—— (2001) "Ideologies of land and sea: Alfred Thayer Mahan, Carl Schmitt, and the shaping of global myth elements," *Boundary 2* 28: 173–201.

—— (2006) "There was no more sea: the supersession of the ocean, from the bible to cyberspace," *Journal of Historical Geography* 32: 494–511.

Davis, R. (1991) "Lagrangian ocean studies," *Annual Review of Fluid Mechanics* 23: 43–64.

DeLanda, M. (2002) *Intensive Science and Virtual Philosophy*, London: Continuum.

Deleuze, G. and Guattari, F. (1988) *A Thousand Plateaus: Capitalism and Schizophrenia*, trans. Brian Massumi, London: Athlone.

Grotius, H. (1916 [1608]) *The Freedom of the Seas, or the Right Which Belongs to the Dutch to Take Part in the East Indian Trade*, trans. Ralph Van Deman Magoffin, New York: Oxford University Press.

Hamblin, J. D. (2005) *Oceanographers and the Cold War: Disciples of Marine Science*, Seattle: University of Washington Press.

Massey, D. (2005) *For Space*. Thousand Oaks: Sage.

—— (2006) "Landscape as a provocation: reflections on moving mountains," *Journal of Material Culture* 11: 33–48.

Pacem in Maribus (1992) "Ocean governance: a model for global governance in the 21st century?" Background paper prepared for Pacem in Maribus XX, 1–5 November, Valetta, Malta.

Reidy, M. S. (2008) *Tides of History: Ocean Science and Her Majesty's Navy*, Chicago: University of Chicago Press.

Rozwadowski, H. M. (2005) *Fathoming the Ocean: The Discovery and Exploration of the Deep Sea*, Cambridge: Belknap.
Schmitt, C. (2003 [1950/1974]) *The* Nomos *of the Earth in the International Law of the* Jus Publicum Europaeum, trans. G. L. Ulmen, New York: Telos.
Steinberg, P. E. (1999) "The maritime mystique: sustainable development, capital mobility, and nostalgia in the world-ocean," *Environment and Planning D: Society & Space* 17: 403–426.
—— (2001) *The Social Construction of the Ocean*, Cambridge: Cambridge University Press.
—— (2009) "Sovereignty, territory, and the mapping of mobility: a view from the outside," *Annals of the Association of American Geographers* 99: 467–495.
Ulmen, G. L. (2003) "Translator's introduction," in C. Schmitt, *The* Nomos *of the Earth in the* Jus Publicum Europaeum, New York: Telos.
Verne, J. (1962 [1870]) *20,000 Leagues Under the Sea*, trans. Anthony Bonner, Toronto: Bantam.

21 No peace beyond the line

Peter Stirk

In *The Nomos of the Earth* Carl Schmitt gives a striking account of the significance of the discovery of the Americas. It is an account of the simultaneous appropriation of a new world and a division of the world on a global scale. In part it is an account of the justification of this appropriation of an entire continent: a process that aroused controversy at the time and still continues to elicit new interpretations (see, for example, Vitoria 1991; Tuck 1999; MacMillan 2006). It is, even more so, an account of the legal significance of these appropriations: in the language of Schmitt's subheading, of 'Land-Appropriation as a Constitutive Process of International Law' (Schmitt 2003 [1950]: 80). According to Schmitt this appropriation inaugurated a new epoch of international law that had come to an end only during Schmitt's own lifetime.[1] Immediately after announcing the epochal significance of these events Schmitt turned to what he called 'global linear thinking':

> No sooner had the contours of the earth emerged as a real globe – not just sensed as myth but apprehensible as fact and measurable as space – than there arose a wholly new and hitherto unimaginable problem: the spatial ordering of the earth in terms of international law.
> (Schmitt 2003 [1950]: 86)

The following comments focus on the political connotations of this idea of 'global linear thinking'.

In *The Nomos of the Earth* Schmitt discussed several examples of this thinking in relation to the Americas. The first manifestation was said to be the *rayas* dividing the new world, and indeed the globe, between Spain and Portugal, beginning with Pope Alexander VI's bull of 4 May 1494 and consolidated by the Treaty of Tordesillas between Spain and Portugal of the same year and the later Treaty of Saragossa of 1526 (Schmitt 2003 [1950]: 88–9). Schmitt noted that these '*rayas* were not global lines separating Christian from non-Christian territories, but were internal divisions between two land-appropriating Christian princes within the framework of one and the same spatial order ... whereby there was no distinction between land- and sea-appropriation' (Schmitt 2003 [1950]: 92).[2]

The second manifestation, more important for Schmitt's subsequent argument, was the amity lines that he traced back to 'a secret clause in the treaty of Cateau-Cambrésis' of 1559 between Spain and France. In addition to this Schmitt mentioned only a French declaration drafted by Richelieu on 1 July 1634 confirming these amity lines and the English–Spanish Treaty of 15 November 1630 disavowing them. His other reference points were a handful of jurists and political theorists. The significance he ascribed to these amity lines was, however, enormous:

> At this 'line' Europe ended and the 'New World' began. At any rate, European law, i.e., 'European public law', ended here. Consequently, so too, did the bracketing of war achieved by traditional European international law ... Beyond the line was an 'overseas' zone in which, for want of any legal limits to war, only the law of the stronger applied.
> (Schmitt 2003 [1950]: 93–4)

Initially he dealt only generally with a third manifestation, namely the *'Western Hemisphere'*, describing it as 'the first counterattack of the New World against the Old' but insisting that it was conceptually linked to the preceding lines (Schmitt 2003 [1950]: 99). When he returned to the theme of the western hemisphere he specified that this line was enshrined in the Monroe Doctrine of 1823. He paused to discuss a later variant, namely the Panama Declaration of 3 October 1939 whereby the American states asserted a neutral security zone 300 miles wide on either side of the coast of the Americas. In *The Nomos of the Earth* he gave it rather cursory treatment 'because the presupposed neutrality of the American states vanished' (Schmitt 2003 [1950]: 282), though he had accorded it more significance in earlier works, both before and after the United States entered the war (Schmitt 1995a: 256–7; 1995c: 442–3). He then stated that the Monroe Doctrine 'is the most important example of what we have called the *global linear thinking* of Occidental rationalism' (Schmitt 2003 [1950]: 286). It was, however, very different from the previous lines, being 'a line of self-isolation' rather than a line of distribution (the *rayas*) or an 'agonal' line (the amity lines), though this was the prelude to a critique of the transformation of the Monroe Doctrine into a justification of intervention based on the moral superiority of the United States.

The potential attractions of Schmitt's account are not difficult to discern, especially in relation to what he says about the old amity lines and the dilemma he ascribed to the pattern of thought associated with the Monroe Doctrine. In relation to commentary on recent developments his account provides an image of a distinction between a zone of peace and a zone of war or a distinction between a zone in which conflict is regulated by some sense of justice and is restrained by traditional laws of war and a zone in which no rules apply. The linkage to the rhetoric and practices of the war on terror is obvious. Similarly his account provides an image of a nation imbued with a sense of moral superiority but torn between an inclination to hold itself apart from a morally inferior and chaotic outside world and an increasingly strong inclination to intervene in that outside world in the cause of a civilizing mission. The two images coincide when intervention is seen as being accompanied by the lack of restraint beyond the line conjured up in the first image. The attraction is evident in a recent article that is in other respects critical of Schmittian accounts of the United States. There it is claimed Schmitt's 'global linear thinking . . . captures the kind of normative framework that imposed restraint on war between the "civilized" states of *Jus Publicum Europaeum* but released these same states from any restraint when they fought against "uncivilized" communities beyond the society of states' (Ralph 2009: 633). A second commentator notes the primary role ascribed to the United States, pausing to add: 'Here, too one could say that everything begins in 1492' (Anidjar 2004: 56). A third concedes that 'the practice of the "lines" seems outdated today' but promptly adds that 'Schmitt's work does not deserve to be relegated to the archives of the history of internationalist theory' (Ruschi 2008). All three accept Schmitt's account of linear thinking including his assessment of the amity lines.

There are, indeed, reasons for doing so. Schmitt explicitly drew on the work of other scholars in offering his account of linear thinking. He paid special attention to the work of the German Adolf Rhein and the American Frances Gardiner Davenport. He referred to the 'outstanding description' in Rhein's work on several occasions (Schmitt 1995a: 242; 1995b: 312; 2003 [1950]: 90) and generously conceded that in respect of the amity lines it was Davenport and Rhein who 'clarified their significance for colonial history' (Schmitt 2003 [1950]: 90). It was Davenport whom Schmitt cited when he traced the beginning of the amity lines back to the secret agreement at Cateau-Cambrésis (Schmitt 2003 [1950]: 92). It is not necessary to have recourse to Carl Schmitt to come to conclusions similar to his about the significance of amity lines and a division of the world into different zones of law or even that later American foreign policy, especially in the shape of the Monroe Doctrine, stands in some relationship of continuity with fifteenth- and sixteenth-century international history and law. Thus Eliga Gould, under the title 'Zones of Law, Zones of Violence', with no allusion to Schmitt, refers to 'so-called lines of amity' establishing a 'system of licensed violence' that did not disrupt the peace in Europe. Gould duly notes the distant origins of this system in the Treaty of Tordesillas and the secret agreement at Cateau-Cambrésis (Gould 2003: 479–80). Prominent among Gould's sources is, however, Davenport, supported this time by the American historian Max Savelle rather than Adolf Rhein. Savelle in turn made fulsome acknowledgement of Davenport's work, describing it as 'the only significant work on the subject in existence' (Savelle 1967: xii).

It is worth pausing here to make clear the connotations of this summary of these arguments. First, although Davenport, Rhein, Savelle and Schmitt figure prominently it is not claimed that they invented all the arguments or slogans associated with the so-called amity lines. For example, the slogan 'no peace beyond the line' in that precise formulation may have been used first by Walter Scott (cited in Mattingly 1963: 158, 161; Fisch 1984: 144). Second, the authors mentioned above were scarcely the only ones to use that slogan. As Mattingly put it, after the first decade of the twentieth century 'everyone writes as if everybody had always known this saying and it is a slender book about English overseas activity which does not have in its index the heading "no peace beyond the Line" anywhere from two or three to a dozen citations' (Mattingly 1963: 161). Third, that slogan and an acceptance of the account of the amity lines including their origins in Cateau-Cambrésis, or sometimes with another provenance such as the Treaty of Vervins of 1598 can appear in quite diverse contexts without the associations ascribed to them especially by Rhein and Schmitt and Savelle (for example Williamson 1949: 46 and Blake 1977, 160). Fourth, there is considerable divergence between the authors discussed above in terms of the use to which they put the material where they are in agreement; Gould being the most distinct. Fifth, despite these differences, they all agree upon the existence of amity lines, the idea that they constituted an institution of international law and that they are of enduring significance. It is precisely this that makes the account presented in Schmitt's *The* Nomos *of the Earth* so apparently compelling.

There are, however, some dissenters who question both the historical accuracy and the legal significance of the claims made by Davenport, Rhein and Schmitt and to varying degrees the host of those who have followed them or held analogous views without reference to them. Pre-eminent among these dissenters are Garrett Mattingly, an American historian of early modern Europe, and Jörg Fisch, a contemporary German historian of international law and international relations. Mattingly's scepticism, evident in the title of his brief article, 'No Peace Beyond What Line?' (1962), was focused primarily on Davenport and shows no awareness of the arguments of Schmitt or Rhein whereas the substantial and detailed volume by Fisch has Schmitt and Rhein as some of its prime targets. Both, however, deal with the evidence and type of claim illustrated above.

On the matter of evidence Mattingly noted the paucity of the sources cited by Davenport regarding the secret agreement at Cateau-Cambrésis, adding that the Spanish negotiator Granvelle, a prime source for Davenport, 'had advised his sovereign that, in his opinion, it would be unwise to let so small a point postpone indefinitely a peace which both sides desired', though he also conceded that there was evidence of some agreement on where peace would be observed and where not, but no clarity about what the dividing lines were to be (Mattingly 1963: 146–7). Be that as it may, his main point is that he could find no evidence of Englishmen using such language before 1625 (Mattingly 1963: 160). Although he does not make the point, even if Mattingly had found Englishmen saying such things it would not amount to recognition of them as statements of international law, especially a law agreeing that there was a zone of violence, a law-free zone beyond the line. There was no need for such a resort in order to justify English action against Spaniards in the

Caribbean. English action could be justified, as it seems to have been in the famous case of the Spanish protest against Drake's predations: 'The Spaniards have brought these evils on themselves by their injustice towards the English, whom, *contra ius gentium*, they have excluded from commerce with the West Indies' (Cheyney 1905: 660). Something of that sentiment was still evident in 1664 when the language of the line was used in the response of the English ambassador to Spanish protests against depredations despite peace between the two countries: 'we have told him . . . that if we had Peace with *Spain* beyond the Line, we should also have liberty of Trade and use of their Ports' (Fanshaw 1702: 112).

Fisch was even more suspicious of the claims relating to Cateau-Cambrésis, finding it odd that there would be reliance on an oral agreement at a time when treaties were negotiated primarily in writing (Fisch 1984: 60). Fisch's main concern though was with the simple paucity of reference to what was supposed to be the central agreement: there being little beyond an allusion to the treaty of 1559 in a letter of 1604 from Henry IV of France that justified French retaliation because the Spanish persisted in treating the French as enemies 'beyond the line' (Fisch 1984: 115; for the letter, see Davenport 1917: 221). The Spanish unilaterally asserted a monopoly and a right to police the Caribbean and the French and increasingly the English rejected this right. Indeed Fisch argued that there is not even a clear assertion of a zone of mutual rights and an absence of law until two letters by Marie de Medici in 1610–11 to the English asserting the validity of a French prize taken from Spain and that even here the allusion to an oral agreement came only in the second letter that followed a year after the first (Fisch 1984: 115–16). Mattingly also identified this as the 'first French definition I have found of 'lines of amity' (Mattingly 1963: 148). Here Marie wrote:

> The Spanish Ambassador has no right to reclaim property taken by my son's subjects beyond the line, since there has never been any kind of peace between the subjects of the two crowns in those waters, as can be verified by all the treaties since the time of Francis I. And no matter how many times negotiators from both sides have met, they have never found any resolution of this particular difficulty, except to agree verbally and by word of mouth that, however many hostile acts occur beyond the meridian of the Azores to the west, and the Tropic of Cancer to the south, there shall be no occasion for complaints and claims for damages, but whoever proves the stronger shall be taken for the lord.
> (Mattingly 1963: 149)[3]

It is upon such slender bases that Schmitt and others constructed a 'constitutive process of international law' (Schmitt 2003 [1950]: 80).

The question that remains is why Rhein, Schmitt and Savelle should have snatched at such slender evidence. There is no single answer. The discovery of a new world, in which its strange inhabitants might conveniently be perceived as 'slaves by nature' or as dwelling in a state of nature, provided an enduring image that readily lends credence to such constructions. Yet, from the outset such characterisations were disputed. The complexity and ambiguity of European attitudes to this new world is well known and still evident in the widely divergent interpretations of the most famous commentator on the appropriation of the new world, Francisco de Vitoria (Vitoria 1991; Pagden 1995; Todorov 1999). Even the bleaker assessments would suggest, however, that Europeans asserted an iniquitous title to be lords of this world: not that they held this world to be a zone of violence in which the right of the stronger was the only right they would accept from each other. Nevertheless, the simple fact of the new world probably played a role. So too did the fact that, as Mattingly put it in relation to the dogma of no peace beyond the line, 'everyone writes as if everybody had always known this saying' (Mattingly 1963: 161); though that begs the question of why they should have suddenly done so.

At least for Rhein, Schmitt and Savelle there is a more precise answer: namely the debate surrounding the role of the United States in the world, especially in relation to the Monroe Doctrine. That two Germans should have been fascinated and troubled by this is obvious, for they lived with the prospect of 'the world hegemony of the Anglo-Saxon powers . . . a *pax anglo-saxonica*' (Meinecke 1998: 431–2).[4] Ironically, Americans too exhibited renewed enthusiasm for the Monroe Doctrine after the First World War despite the fact that there was then less reason than ever before to fear the European intervention in the Americas that was the root cause of that doctrine (Perkins: 314–15). Indeed one commentator was induced to produce an assessment under the title 'The Recrudescence of the Monroe Doctrine' (Garner 1930). There Garner noted the unprecedented insistence on the insertion of clauses 'safeguarding' the Monroe Doctrine in bilateral arbitration treaties, numbering 24 treaties between 1928 and the date of his article, but also that the United States 'apparently does not desire that the doctrine should be considered as a principle of international law and probably would not admit it to be such in case it were so regarded by other nations' (Garner 1930: 249). That of course was precisely what fascinated and terrified Carl Schmitt in his 'Forms of Modern Imperialism in International Law' (see Chapter 2 of this volume). In his account of the division of the world, of the *rayas*, the amity lines and the original Monroe Doctrine and its vicissitudes Schmitt searched for the roots of the power of this 'ruler over grammar' and also for formulations that would constrain it. He projected back into the history of early modern Europe and its encounter with the new world his fears and even more so his hopes and regrets. In doing so he ascribed to Spanish monarchs and a French queen regent a degree of authority in shaping international law that they would have dearly loved to attain but had no realistic hope of. At the same time he provided a significant contribution to the perpetuation of a myth. It is a myth we can understand but we are not obliged to subscribe to it.

Notes

1. On Schmitt's periodisation of international law, see Stirk (2009).
2. It is doubtful that the Papal bulls had quite the significance claimed for them by Schmitt. See Steinberg (1999).
3. The text of both letters can be found in Asseline (1874: 149–53).
4. Although it can be argued that Schmitt saw the United States as his enemy (Stirk 2003) it is worth recalling the ambiguity of attitudes to America, especially in what was regarded as the most Americanised of European countries, Germany (Berg 1963).

References

Anidjar, Gil (2004), 'Terror Right', *The New Centennial Review*, 4(3): 35–69.
Asseline, David (1874), *Antiquitez et chroniques de la ville de Dieppe*. Dieppe: Marais.
Berg, Peter (1963), *Deutschland und Amerika 1918–1929*. Lübeck: Matthiesen.
Blake, John W. (1977), *West Africa. Quest for God and Gold 1454–1578*. London: Curzon.
Cheyney, Edward (1905), 'International Law under Queen Elizabeth', *The English Historical Review*, 80: 659–72.
Davenport, Frances Gardiner (1917), *European Treaties bearing on the History of the United States and its Dependancies to 1648*. Washington, DC: Carnegie.
Fanshaw, Richard (1702), *Original Letters of his Excellency Sir Richard Fanshaw*. London: n.p.
Fisch, Jörg (1984), *Die europäische Expansion und das Völkerrecht*. Stuttgart: Steiner.
Garner, James (1930), 'The Recrudescence of the Monroe Doctrine', *Political Science Quarterly*, 45: 231–58.
Gould, Eliga (2003), 'Zones of Law, Zones of Violence: The Legal Geography of the British Atlantic, circa 1772', *William and Mary Quarterly*, 40: 471–510.
MacMillan, Ken (2006), *Sovereignty and Possession in the English New World*. Cambridge: Cambridge University Press.
Mattingly, Garrett (1963), 'No Peace Beyond What Line?', *Transactions of the Royal Historical Society*, 13: 145–62.
Meinecke, Friedrich (1998), *Machiavellism*. New Brunswick, NJ: Transaction.
Pagden, Anthony (1995), *Lords of all the World*. New Haven, CT: Yale University Press.
Perkins, Dexter (1967), *A History of the Monroe Doctrine*. Boston: Little, Brown & Company.
Ralph, Jason (2009), 'The Laws of War and the State of the Exception', *Review of International Studies*, 35: 631–49.
Rasch, William (2003), 'Human Rights as Geopolitics', *Cultural Critique*, 54: 120–47.
Ruschi, Filippo (2008), 'Space, Law and Power in Carl Schmitt', *Jura Gentium Online*. Available at: http://juragentium.unifi.it/en/surveys/thil/nomos.htm. Last accessed 1 January 2010.
Savelle, Max (1967), *The Origins of American Diplomacy*. London: Macmillan.
Schmitt, Carl (1995a [1940]), 'Raum und Großraum im Völkerrecht', in Carl Schmitt, *Staat, Großraum, Nomos*. Berlin: Duncker & Humblot.
Schmitt, Carl (1995b [1941]), 'Völkerrechtliche Grossraumordnung', in Carl Schmitt, *Staat, Großraum, Nomos*. Berlin: Duncker & Humblot.

Schmitt, Carl (1995b [1943]), 'Die letzte globale Linie', in Carl Schmitt, *Staat, Großraum, Nomos*. Berlin: Duncker & Humblot.
Schmitt, Carl (2003 [1950]), *The Nomos of the Earth*. New York: Telos Press.
Steinberg, Philip (1999), 'Lines of Division, Lines of Connection', *Geographical Review*, 89: 254–64.
Stirk, Peter (2003), 'Carl Schmitt's Enemy and the Rhetoric of Anti-Interventionism', *The European Legacy*, 8: 21–36.
Stirk, Peter (2009), 'Et l'ére de l'État touché á sa fin', *Revue Études internationals*, 40: 37–54.
Todorov, Tzvetan (1999), *The Conquest of America*. Norman: University of Oklahoma Press.
Tuck, Richard (1999), *The Rights of War and Peace*. Oxford: Oxford University Press.
Vitoria, Francisco de (1991), *Vitoria. Political Writings*. Cambridge: Cambridge University Press.
Williamson, James A. (1949), *Hawkins of Plymouth*. London: Adam & Charles Black.

22 The border

Nick Vaughan-Williams

> The enclosing ring—the fence formed by men's bodies, the man-ring—is a primeval form of ritual, legal, and political cohabitation.
>
> (Schmitt 2003: 74)

This short response reads Carl Schmitt's *The* Nomos *of the Earth* (2003 [1950]) (hereafter *Nomos*) through the lens of the border. The aim is to identify and examine the work that the concept of the border does in his account of the trajectory of the development of the spatial underpinnings of law. This concept is not 'defined' by Schmitt as such, but appears in different ways at various junctures within that account. I will argue that the very idea of nomos is intimately bound up with border-making practices and that it is through these practices that the nature of the relation between order and orientation of a given historical epoch finds expression. Moreover, I want to make the case that Schmitt's tantalising discussions of the possibility of the existence of a new nomos suggests a shift in his own geopolitical thinking beyond the horizon of the state and its borders within which he had been arguably hitherto shackled. In contrast with certain accounts of globalisation today, however, Schmitt does not predict the straightforward obsolescence of borders in global politics, but rather hints at their movement, mutation, and technological transformation.

The figure of the border is pivotal in Schmitt's attempt to 'understand the normative order of the earth' (Schmitt 2003: 39). In the opening discussion of *Nomos* Schmitt draws attention to the way in which humans establish and maintain lines of division via the demarcation of fields, pastures, and forests in their working of the land (Schmitt 2003: 42). Indeed, he argues that it is through the making of 'fences, enclosures, boundaries, walls, houses, and other constraints' that the nature of the relation between order and orientation in social life is manifested. Moreover, these borders both constitute and render visible the otherwise hidden link between the earth and law: the delineation of the former is, on Schmitt's formulation, a condition of possibility of the latter.

It is precisely this division of the earth and the juridical-political order it determines that Schmitt seeks to grasp using the central concept of nomos. If

Michel Foucault sought to investigate the 'how' of power then, according to Mitchell Dean, Schmitt's exercise was to explore the 'where' of law (Dean 2006). As is detailed elsewhere in this volume, this concept is a derivation of the Greek word *nemein* meaning 'to take or appropriate' (Schmitt 2003: 67). In German *nemein* translates as *nehmen*, which, in turn, is linked to the verbs *teilen* (to divide or distribute) and *weiden* (to pasture) (Schmitt 2003: 344–5). The idea of nomos, then, encompasses these three dimensions – the appropriation, division, and cultivation of land – as the 'primal processes of human history, three acts of the primal drama' (Schmitt 2003: 351). A form of spatial consciousness, Schmitt refers to nomos as a 'fence-word' because 'like a wall it is based on sacred orientations' (Schmitt 2003: 70).

In Schmitt's view, while the nature of the relation between order and orientation varies according to historical and cultural context, nomos is nevertheless afforded the status of a fundamental and constant structure in human social life: 'Every new age and every new epoch in the coexistence of peoples, empires, and countries, of rulers and power formulations of every sort, is founded on new spatial divisions, new enclosures, and new spatial orders of the earth' (Schmitt 2003: 79). In this way, *Nomos* offers a history of the spatial consciousness of the earth – and its relation with law – via an investigation of various types of borders.

The three epochs Schmitt identifies as having a distinctive nomos are each characterised by what might be called different border logics. Up until the 'age of discoveries' of the late fifteenth and sixteenth centuries, he argues, there was no concept of the planet as we think of it today. While notions of 'heaven' and 'earth' existed, the idea of the globe as a unit of measurement did not. As such, there was no nomos 'of the *earth*' at this time, though *respublica Christiana* was a spatial order reliant upon divisions between the soils of the medieval West, the soils of the heathens, and the soils of Islamic empires. Every people, according to Schmitt, thought of themselves as the centre of the Earth and conceived of the 'outside' as a chaotic and barbaric zone: 'practically, this meant that in the outer world and with good conscience, one could conquer and plunder to a certain boundary' (Schmitt 2003: 352).

With the circumnavigation of the globe, however, came the opening up of the seas, new cartographic representations, and the advent of what Schmitt refers to as 'global linear thinking' (Schmitt 2003: 87). The 'discovery' of the American continent in 1492 created free space for the appropriation, division, and cultivation of colonial lands by Europeans. In turn, this posed the need for new global spatial ordering, which stimulated the emergence of a second nomos: the *Jus Publicum Europaeum* ('European Public Law'). Examples of the first 'global lines' include Pope Alexander VI's *inter caetera divinae* in 1494 (a pole-to-pole line that granted lands in America to Spain), the *partition del mar Océano* of the same year (a carving up of the Atlantic between Spain and Portugal), and the later Anglo-French 'amity lines' of 1559. The latter were of particular significance in the emergence of European international law, according to Schmitt. These borders demarcated the ending of European soil and the beginning of the 'New World'. The effect of this partitioning was to contain or 'bracket' war outside Europe where 'only the law of the stronger applied' (Schmitt 2003: 94).

The *Jus Publicum Europaeum* went hand in hand not only with a central division between European and non-European spaces, but also with a juridical-political order based upon centralised, spatially self-contained, sovereign states. At the heart of this new European spatial order was the concept of the border of the state, which, at least in Schmitt's presentation, provided for political unity, an end to civil wars, and clear demarcations between jurisdictions: 'The core of the *nomos* lay in the division of European soil into state territories with firm borders, which immediately initiated an important distinction, namely that this soil of recognized European states and their land had a special status in international law' (Schmitt 2003: 148). In this way, the medieval order predicated on messy and overlapping ties of personal loyalty was transformed into a modern centralised system of sovereign states bound together by a mutual recognition of equality and other 'substantive and calculable norms' (Schmitt 2003: 201).

While the Eurocentric spatial order remained hegemonic for over three centuries, Schmitt argues that this nomos fell into a period of terminal decline between 1890 and 1918. Again it is via an analysis of the changing nature of borders – through which the spatial consciousness of the Earth is manifested – that his account of these seismic changes unfolds. First and foremost the dissolution of the *Jus Publicum Europaeum* was set in motion as a result of the increasing juridical insignificance of the categories of 'civilised', 'half-civilised (barbaric)' and 'wild peoples (savages)' (Schmitt, 2003: 234). Whereas these categories had previously accompanied firm distinctions between European and non-European zones of juridical-political order, Schmitt claims that the European motherland and overseas colony became increasingly blurred. As a result of this blurring, Schmitt points to the emergence of a new global universalism alongside the ascendancy of liberal economic thinking and commercialism, free trade and labour, and the absence of an overarching spatial sense: 'In short: over, under, and beside the state-political borders of what appeared to be a purely political international law between states spread a free, i.e. non-state sphere of economy permeating everything: a global economy' (Schmitt 2003: 235).

Unsurprisingly, Schmitt laments the dissolution of the *Jus Publicum Europaeum*, which he sees as reaching its nadir during the Paris Peace Conferences of 1918–19. Writing thirty or so years later, and with political preferences known all too well, his assessment of the League of Nations is that it ultimately failed to offer a viable alternative to the previous nomos. Indeed, he criticises the architects of the League for their lack of awareness of the importance of – and therefore the ability to achieve – a coherent spatial order. The chief problem, on Schmitt's view, was that the League aimed to be universal, which meant that it could no longer contain war in the non-European sphere: 'Instead of bracketing war, a net of intentionally vague, formal compromises and cautiously worked stylized norms was assembled, and, in turn, was subjected to an ostensibly purely juridical interpretation' (Schmitt 2003: 243). What followed, therefore, was the emergence of profound global *dis*order, which became reproduced by the very universalist norms and institutions that sought to overcome these problems.

Again, the question of borders occupies a central place in Schmitt's critique of what he considered to be the vapid spaceless universalism of interwar idealism. As Louiza Odysseos has pointed out, the problem with such universalism, from a Schmittian perspective, is that it is perceived to be 'unable and unwilling to draw lines and spatial distinctions' (Odysseos 2007: 125). In many ways this refusal stands in radical contrast with the hallmark of Schmitt's political philosophy with its typical emphasis on the importance of borders. Indeed, in Schmitt's earlier works, notably *The Concept of the Political* (1927) and *Political Theology: Four Chapters on the Concept of Sovereignty* (1922), an approach to politics was staked out in terms of a series of line-drawing practices. Most notably, this is reflected in his paradigmatic definitions of the political in terms of the friend–enemy distinction (Schmitt 1996) and sovereignty as the decision on the exception (Schmitt 2005).

What is also distinctive about these texts is that they take the modern, sovereign, territorially bordered state as the tacit ground on which Schmitt's geopolitical imagination rests (Vaughan-Williams 2008). While Schmitt is notoriously unclear about whether sovereignty resides in the person of the Head of State, the government, or a particular regime as a whole, for example, we are left in little doubt that his analysis of sovereignty in *Political Theology* privileges the state as the supreme political entity. Thus, Hidemi Suganami writes:

> In short, the state, when it functions and qualifies as a sovereign political entity, is the supreme authority in the sense of the authoritative-entity-in-decisive-cases that makes decisions to resort to war against its enemy, internal or external, when it judges it necessary to do so.
> (Suganami 2007: 517)

The result of this privileging is that in his earlier work Schmitt reads the notion of 'juridical-political order' as synonymous with the state. Interestingly, however, Schmitt's speculations about the possibility of the emergence of a new spatial consciousness towards the end of *Nomos* imply a shift in his thinking.

As well as the growth of a world economy, Schmitt identifies several other symptoms of the coming of a new global nomos following the end of the Second World War and the planetary division between East and West. One is the dawn of a new technical-industrial era, which facilitated not only warfare on land and sea but also *air* as 'the force-field of human power and activity' (Schmitt 2003: 354). Another related symptom is the growing political, legal (as well as economic) influence of the US beyond its territorial delimitations as conventionally understood. While Schmitt concedes that 'every true empire around the world has claimed [...] a sphere of spatial sovereignty beyond its borders', he argues that the extension in the 1930s of the US security zone up to 300 miles from its shores constituted a *Großraum* of new proportions (Schmitt 2003: 281–2).

Whereas the assumption in *The Concept of the Political* and *Political Theology* had been that the limits of sovereignty, law, and territory were necessarily and straightforwardly coterminous, Schmitt's analysis towards the end of *Nomos* challenges this starting point. Indeed, he implies that a logic of 'inside/outside' (Walker 1993), upon which the entire juridical-political edifice of the *Jus Publicum Europaeum* had rested, was no longer apposite to the contemporary world (dis)order. Rather, Schmitt problematises the image of the border of the state as a sharp delimitation of sovereign power and neat container and expression of order and orientation. Instead, he introduces a more complex topology of 'magnetic power fields of human energy and work' to attempt to characterise the new *nomos* (Ulmen 2003: 30). This alternative topology implies a 'messiness' of overlapping influences, jurisdictions, and loyalties akin to that of the medieval period, but while it is proffered as an alternative to the inside/outside frame it is ultimately left under-explored in Schmitt's largest published work.

On the one hand, what is common among the symptoms of a new global nomos identified by Schmitt is a supposed erasure of borders of sovereign nation-states and concomitant logics of inside/outside, internal/external, domestic/foreign, and so on. Indeed, *prima facie*, *Nomos* appears to prefigure much of the pro-globalisation literature of the 1990s, which heralded the end of the Westphalian system of sovereign states and the rise of the so-called 'borderless' world. According to this by-now somewhat hackneyed account, the growth of a 24-hour global market economy was accompanied by the development of global governance structures at once below and above the 'level' of the state. On the other hand, however, Schmitt's treatment of the new nomos is more sophisticated in its refusal to get caught in the familiar trap of a zero-sum binary between either the obsolescence of state borders or their continued importance in global political relations. Significantly, Schmitt warns that although the old Eurocentric order had unmistakably come to an end this did not automatically imply the demise of the fundamental principles of the need for planetary division: 'The new nomos of our planet is growing irresistibly [...] To be sure, the old *nomos* has collapsed, and with it a whole system of accepted measures, concepts, and customs. But what is coming is ... not boundlessness or a nothingness hostile to *nomos*' (Schmitt 2003: 355). Instead, the possible scenarios of a new nomos painted by Schmitt are all characterised by distinctive border logics. In each case, the figure of the border is not simply abandoned, but transformed.

The first image of the future offered at the end of *Nomos* is one that predicts the victory of one of the superpowers resulting in the coronation of a new planetary sovereign: 'he would appropriate the whole earth—land, sea, and air—and would divide and manage it in accord with his plans and ideas' (Schmitt 2003: 354). Importantly, as this extract highlights, the victor of the Cold War is presented as reigning over a global space striated as a result of lines drawn unilaterally rather than some kind of borderless world. The second future imagined by Schmitt is one whereby the victor administers and/or guarantees the balanced structure of the previous nomos, as in the case of *pax Britannica* in the nineteenth century. Here borders are not elided, but predicted to operate like 'magnetic fields' of energy and influence that stretch beyond the physical territorial limits of the state. Again, this problematises the inside/outside logic of the modern state-system without envisaging the elimination of the fundamental activity of line-drawing. Third, Schmitt presents a final option that involves the combination of several independent power blocs or *Großraüme* constituting future world order: one where the state has been displaced by greater spaces vying for the ability to control planetary division.

Irrespective of the historical efficacy of these scenarios, what is interesting and significant from the point of view of this response essay is Schmitt's insistence on the continued importance of line-drawing as a fundamental activity, albeit one that, under certain circumstances, may not occur within the horizons of the modern sovereign bordered state. Thus, gesturing to the implications of *Nomos* for critical reflections on the supposed antithesis today between cosmopolitanism and the global war on terror, Odysseos rightly argues that Schmitt offers a

> reminder that the transgression of lines evoked by the political discourse of universal humanity is not an assured path to a modernity without violence; rather, seeing to end war has historically led not to its limitation and humanisation, but to its ever more intensified and violent occurrence.
> (Odysseos 2007: 140)

In conclusion, Schmitt's account of the appropriation, division, and management of the entire Earth from the Middle Ages through the *Jus Publicum Europaeum* to the Cold War is a highly contestable grand narrative. Moreover, as illustrated by his mourning of the Eurocentric nomos, vehement critique of liberal universalism symbolised by the League, and desire to see the reinstatement of a strong spatial consciousness, *Nomos* is unmistakably infused with Schmitt's own politics. Beyond these problems, however, the text presents a unique history and future theorisation of global world (dis)order via an appreciation of the centrality of the concept of the border in the way humans organise themselves politically, socially, and economically. What is unusual about Schmitt's account is that it takes the nature and location of 'the border' as an object of analysis in its own right – as the symptom of deeper structural shifts in the spatial consciousness of the Earth – rather than as a form of background noise. On this basis, while *Nomos* is, for sure, a 'hidden classic' in international relations (IR) (Odysseos and Petito 2007), it is also one of the most provocative yet under-utilised sources in the inter-disciplinary field of border studies.

References

Dean, Mitchell (2006) 'A Political Mythology of World Order: Carl Schmitt's *Nomos* Theory', *Culture and Society*, 23(5): 1–22.

Odysseos, Louiza (2007) 'Crossing the Line? Carl Schmitt on the "Spaceless Universalism" of Cosmopolitanism and the War on Terror', in L. Odysseos and F. Petito (eds) *The International Political Thought of Carl Schmitt: Terror, Liberal War, and the Crisis of Global Order* (Abingdon and New York: Routledge).

Odysseos, Louiza and Fabio Petito (eds) (2007) *The International Political Thought of Carl Schmitt: Terror, Liberal War, and the Crisis of Global Order* (Abingdon and New York: Routledge).

Schmitt, Carl (1996 [1927]) *The Concept of the Political*, trans. G. Schwab (Chicago, IL and London: The University of Chicago Press).

Schmitt, Carl (2003 [1950]) *The* Nomos *of the Earth in the International Law of the* Jus Publicum Europaeum, trans. G. Ulmen (New York: Telos Press).

Schmitt, Carl (2005 [1922]) *Political Theology: Four Chapters on the Concept of Sovereignty*, trans. G. Schwab, 3rd edition (Chicago, IL and London: The University of Chicago Press).

Suganami, Hidemi (2007) 'Understanding Sovereignty through Kelson/Schmitt', *Review of International Studies*, 33(3): 511–30.

Ulmen, Gary (2003) 'Translator's Introduction', in Schmitt, Carl (2003 [1950]) *The* Nomos *of the Earth in the International Law of the* Jus Publicum Europaeum, trans. G. Ulmen (New York: Telos Press).

Vaughan-Williams, Nick (2008) 'Borders, Territory, Law', *International Political Sociology*, 2: 322–38.

Walker, R.B.J. (1993) *Inside/Outside: International Relations as Political Theory* (Cambridge: Cambridge University Press).

23 *Ordnung* und *Ortung*/ order and localisation

Thalin Zarmanian

In influential branches of political science, political geography and international relations the assumption persists that stable political formations organize themselves territorially by claiming and exercising effective authority over a defined portion of the Earth. Many such theories treat political units as universes, i.e. communities based upon some sort of fundamental political covenant or identity principle which, on one hand, binds all their members, preventing the units from dissolving and, on the other, marks their distinctiveness, preventing their fusion with others. The Earth is therefore partitioned in distinct, internally pacified, uniform units, orderly coexisting next to each other and entertaining more or less conflictual relationships.

But how and why do these territorially organized units emerge in the first place? What is the nexus between geographical space and the political? How do single political formations emerge out of a context of multiple individuals or socio-anthropological formations competing for scarce resources? And, most importantly, how do these political units manage to persist despite the centripetal forces and incentives encouraging their members to try and subvert the internal equilibrium/distribution by taking advantage of available external resources or siding with external actors?

Mainstream political theory or international relations approaches do not usually focus on these questions, that is, they fail to thoroughly contemplate collapse, political chaos and widespread, unorganized, violence: many, quite simply, lack a theory of order. In contrast, Carl Schmitt's work is entirely focused on and informed by the concept of (legal) order, which he strives to define and explain (Zarmanian, 2006).

Contrary to mainstream approaches, Schmitt does not regard the emergence – and, most importantly, the persistence – of any political order as necessary or given. Rather, he assumes that any order is constantly exposed to the centripetal forces of plurality, that push individuals and groups back to a Hobbesian state of nature and that therefore the combination of plurality within a political unit, let alone the coexistence of more than one such unit – in his words a stable coexistence of *pluriverse* and *universe* – is something exceptional that deserves an explanation.

In his early writing Schmitt focused on explaining order at the domestic level. According to him, order can emerge to the extent that any potential bearer of disorder – individual and group – is given a possibility to fulfil its *Lebensmöglichkeit*, meaning both 'opportunity of life' and 'way of life' (Schmidt, 1963), and is therefore given its own place, in the sense of soil, status, rules and liberties.

Schmitt defined as *sovereign* any instance, not necessarily a person, but also a principle, organization or institution capable of producing such legal order. The sovereign, later identified with the catholic concept of *kat'echon*, is therefore *he who keeps* (*auf-halten*) chaos out, and prevents it from taking over (Schmitt, 1950, 28). In his later writings Schmitt brought his legal and political theory to completion by identifying the central role played in any legal order (Zarmanian, 2006; Odysseos and Petito, 2007) by its spatial component, the *Ortung* (here in the sense of 'orientation'), and on the way it combines with the juridical one, the *Ordnung*.

In *The Nomos of the Earth* Schmitt describes the emergence of any order, domestic or international, as a unitary process consisting of three fundamental actions: appropriating (*nehmen*), i.e. defining a determined space as the sphere of action of a particular legal-political principle; distributing (*teilen*), i.e. further organizing space by defining the terms of use and a system to securely determine the property (or any alternative system of resource distribution) of each area and resource within the common space; and exploiting (*weiden*), i.e. defining the rules of use and circulation of generated resources. Appropriation, distribution and exploitation are the earliest meanings of the Greek word 'nomos', which Schmitt therefore uses to convey the concrete profound co-implication of sovereignty and space and to extend it to the 'international' level.

In his book Schmitt goes beyond merely stating that any political order is spatially defined and must have a spatial reference: he defined the nomos as a 'structuring combination of *Ordnung* and *Ortung*' (Schmitt, 1950, 48), i.e. as the result of a *specific*, complex interaction between ideal/legal and geographic/material elements. By identifying and describing them and the way in which they combine to produce order, he constructed a comprehensive, trans-epochal, theory of the political (Galli, 1996, 877) which effectively explains both the emergence of individual units and their stable coexistence within a complex 'international' order.

The first pre-condition for the formation of a political unit is the encounter of two or more groups concretely competing for the same territory or resources. The simplest form of nomos – which in his earlier 'internationalist' writings Schmitt referred to with the term *Großraum*, which he later abandoned because of the Nazi connotation it gained during that period – is created to the extent that a sovereign, as defined above, emerges and establishes a legal order.

This happens through the creation of some sort of *commonality* based on a *radical title*, from which *all* the members of a *Großraum* derive their right on a particular part of its soil or resources, and which therefore also contains a principle of distribution and exploitation. Whether the establishment of this commonality gives rise to a hierarchic system in which multiple political units, perceived as distinct, are subject to one, or to an anarchic system in which the role of *kat'echon* is exercised in common, is irrelevant.

Schmitt developed the nomos theory due to the insufficiency of the *Großraum* theory in explaining order at a *global* level. According to him a full-fledged nomos only emerges when some of the members of a *Großraum* gain access to external spaces and resources: Schmitt defines the sudden availability of a new space – including the possibility to exploit previously unexploited elements such as the high seas, the airspace and later outer space – as *spatial revolutions*. According to him therefore the first full-fledged nomos of the (whole) Earth only emerged after new portions of the Earth, including the oceans and the high seas, became *concretely* available for Europeans to appropriate, distribute and exploit.

This kind of systemic shock, unfolded by material, concrete changes in technology and economy, reveals the fundamental problem of the coexistence of universe and pluriverse to the fullest: first, it creates a conflict among the members of a *Großraum* as to how to distribute and exploit the new spaces; second, it creates an opportunity for some of them not only to take advantage of the new resources or to side with external actors to alter the *internal distribution or the principles of exploitation* of the *Großraum* but also offers them an incentive to try and subvert its very foundation, i.e. the *radical title* on which the commonality, and therefore the order derived by it, ultimately rests.

In order to accommodate a spatial revolution a more complex combination of *Ordnung* and *Ortung* is necessary. The creation of a nomos capable of containing these pressures cannot merely consist in extending the *Ordnung* of *one particular Großraum* to include a wider space. Whereas the nature and basic features of any *Ordnung* remain the same, a global nomos requires a specific *kind* of *Ortung*, based on a very sophisticated geographical thought and spatial awareness.

As said, the potential for chaos and indiscriminate violence generated by a spatial revolution can in fact only be overcome to the extent that all those who are capable of waging war or bringing violence and disorder within a particular space regard such space – and of course its *Ordnung* – as *essential* to their *Lebensmöglichkeit* and therefore abstain from disrupting it and they actively intervene whenever one of its members or an external actor tries to do so. This means that they regard themselves, and are perceived by others, as *stakeholders* (*die Beteiligte*) in a particular space and *Ordnung*.

This allegiance towards a particular space and *Ordnung* is, in turn, possible to the extent that, first, within one's *Großraum* indiscriminate violence is limited and that the means capable of generating chaos and widespread disorder are excluded. Second, it requires that the questions regarding the acquisition, distribution and exploitation of beyond-the-line land and resources are considered *secondary* to the conservation of the *Großraum* and its internal order. Finally, both these conditions imply that the members of a *Großraum* do not regard each other as enemies to be vanquished (or criminals to be punished) but rather as bearers of a legitimate title over their land or resources.

Within a global nomos, *Ortung* is therefore first a *localisation*, the creation of a *qualitative differentiation* among spaces – including the high seas (and, later, the air and outer space) – and the *bonding* of political units to one particular *Großraum*. Second, it consists of an *orientation*, i.e. in dictating their relative status and their relationship to each other.

According to Schmitt this is achieved through a specific kind of geographical thought based on what he calls *global linear thinking* (*globales Liniendenken*) (Schmitt, 1950, 55), which is essential to any possible order resulting from the coexistence of pluriverse and universe. Global lines are not, as Schmitt writes, 'pure geographical concepts' (Schmitt, 1950, 150), rather they result from a combination of material/geographical and ideal/juridical elements.

In *The Nomos of the Earth*, Schmitt discusses how the rise and development of the first global nomos, regulated by the *Jus Publicum Europaeum* and centred on its cardinal institution, the state, depended on the ultimate coherence between the normative concepts that prevailed over a long series of European crises, and the profound features of European society and economy during the epoch of the *Jus Publicum Europaeum*.

The most fundamental quality of this nomos is that it was Eurocentric: since those who were capable of waging war in all of the earthly spaces all belonged to the same *Großraum* they were able to unilaterally dictate the nomos of the whole Earth and to structure it around *one* space, the European soil. This was defined in opposition to the other spaces – namely non-state, extra-European land and the high seas – as the only area where violence and disorder were radically limited. The limitation of war was threefold: within European soil only states could wage war; they were bound to respect the limitations of time, space and means of the European law of war; all wars concerning non-European soil were banned from it and should only be fought on extra-European land or by sea.

As stated, this was made possible by the emergence of a specifically modern and European institution, the state. Its fundamental feature, according to Schmitt, is that it was an agent of neutralization and de-politicization of conflicts within the European common space. Until the end of the nineteenth century the *modern, European* state did not claim an absolute authority to dictate the law and it did not side (or should not have sided) with internal or external agents to try and impose *one political principle over all Europe*. Rather, each state was a grantor, within its territory, of an *Ordnung* common to the whole European space, which in turn was based on plurality. The state actually used its power to grant public order, a neutral public sphere in which individuals and groups were free to pursue their own ends.

The respective spheres of action of the state and the individual/group were clearly defined through oppositions (Schmitt, 1934) – a way that once again reflected the global linear thought – shared by all members of the system:

public-private, religious-secular, legal-moral and political-economic. It was the existence, at the very base of European international society of this common law and shared system of geographical and juridical thought, that ultimately bound the European actors to their particular space and made the limitation of war within Europe and the emergence of a shared and stable nomos of the whole Earth possible.

In particular, the fact that the whole European soil was subject to one *meta-Ordnung* incorporating local laws and practices made it theoretically governable by any European state. The fact that European sovereigns were bound to respect, and actually to enforce, the local laws (the law of the land) also provided the system with the necessary flexibility to adjust its internal distribution by exchanging territories without provoking disorder and rebellion on behalf of the population. This circularity of European territory, in turn, made it valuable for any sovereign, and provided sovereigns with an incentive not to resort to indiscriminate and destructive violence but rather to promote the economy and protect the rights even of temporarily occupied lands, from which they derived their taxes and levies.

All these factors, in turn, were made possible by the most profound features of modern European society and economy. States were able to win the allegiance of the population by, first, monopolizing military force and thus preventing all other actors from bringing chaos and disorder within their territories and, second, by building an efficient, non-personal, bureaucracy.

The concrete order of *The* Nomos *of the Earth* is neither a *taxis* (i.e. a totally artificial order) based on pure normative elements, nor a *kosmos* (i.e. a natural order) necessarily emerging from material conditions.

In his book, however, Schmitt ultimately describes the demise of The Nomos of the *Jus Publicum Europaeum* – and the consequent re-emergence of absolute war within Europe – as the result of mostly normative and ideal factors: the loss of spatial awareness and the demise of global linear thinking; the dissolution of the *Jus Publicum Europaeum* in an empty normativism developed after the First World War along Kelsenian lines; the growing *Politisierung* of the state and international relations, i.e. the involvement of the state and its organization in the growing conflict within society and/or transnational relations, which resulted during the nineteenth and twentieth century in latent or explicit civil wars and therefore in the demise of its neutralizing role and in the dissolution of the clear distinctions on which the *Jus Publicum Europaeum* rested (Colombo, 2006). Schmitt only attributes a secondary role to material factors as the spatial revolution of air warfare and calls for a new nomos and a new limitation of war based on new global lines.

The world since the 1950s is, of course, much altered, especially through profound changes in society and economy. Post-Fordism, globalization – the emergence of widespread economic, social and commercial networks – and technological development, have broken the nexus between population density, territorial extension, government revenues and the need for government action in the world as a whole. The effects of these changes are less dramatic and visible in the West: after the Second World War, the Western world was able to rebuild a common economic order, and despite the prevailing normativism and universalism, to form a spatially oriented security community based on a democratic *Ordnung* (Colombo, 2010). Even though it is easy to see how imperfect this embryonic new Western nomos is, the *longue durée* of Western civilization prevents the consequences of these epochal changes from exploding.

There are, nonetheless, some areas of the Earth that have not followed the logics on which *modern* European states were based. Especially in those places where the state is relatively new, the overlapping of globalization, pre-industrial economies and availability of natural resources have generated so-called 'looting economies'. They are based on the exploitation of resources that are generated irrespective of both the size of labour and the action of government. Contrary to what happens in agricultural and industrial societies, their power and wealth is inversely proportional to the number of people they control and they consequently share an incentive to exclude rather than include, and have different conceptions of order within a territory. Within these systems key players can profit by spreading violence and displacing 'unnecessary' populations. In many cases, they need only to secure the allegiance of a sufficient number of people to seize the resources or the government controlling them. Hence, in these areas societies and the political are extremely fragmented and a trusted central government capable of guaranteeing security fails to emerge. Thanks to the fact that never before has mass destruction been so easily achievable and to the growing availability of easy-to-operate and mobile arms, the number of those capable of bringing about disorder and insecurity (including the spread of genocidal drives) has grown dramatically.

This scenario is more similar to Schmitt's description of the sea and of maritime warfare than to the terrestrial nomos. The fundamental question for a twenty-first-century nomos then is whether the maritimization of large portions of the Earth can be sustained and whether a new equilibrium of spaces can emerge.

Whatever the answer, it is clear that no nomos can emerge out of an uncritical transposition of an abstract set of rules that was developed in a particular and specific historical and, most importantly, geographical context, onto others. In particular, to the extent that contemporary international law, in the name of effectivity or, worse, in the name of democracy, allows the forces who control the state – possibly after they have used brutal violence or intimidation to alter the numeric balance or the fragmented populations within a region in order to win 'democratic elections' – to use its resources as instruments of repression, terror and disorder, it cannot qualify as *Ordnung*. The challenge then is to give international law an authentic localization, creating incentives for the most fundamental logics of human interaction to generate a new war-limiting nomos.

References

Colombo, A. (2006) *La Guerra ineguale*. Il Mulino, Bologna.
Colombo, A. (2010) *La Disunità del Mondo. Dopo il secolo globale*. Feltrinelli, Milano.
Galli, C. (1996) *Genealogia della politica: Carl Schmitt e la crisi del pensiero politico moderno*. Il Mulino, Bologna.
Galli, C. (2001) *Spazi politici. L'età moderna e l'età globale*. Il Mulino, Bologna.
Odysseos, L. and Petito, F. (eds) (2007) *The International Political Thought of Carl Schmitt: Terror, Liberal War and the Crisis of Global Order*, Routledge, London.
Schmidt, H. (1963) Der Nomosbegriff bei Carl Schmitt. *Der Staat*, 1, 81.
Schmitt, C. (1934) *Über die Drei Arten des rechtswissenschaftlichen Denkens*. Hanseatische Verlagsanstalt, Hamburg.
Schmitt, C. (1940) Über die Zwei Grossen 'Dualismen' des heutigen Rechtssyste. In *Positionen und Begriffe*, Duncker & Humblot, Berlin, p. 261.
Schmitt, C. (1950) *Der Nomos der Erde im Volkerrecht des Jus Publicum Europaeum*. Duncker & Humblot, Berlin.
Schmitt, C. (1963) *Theorie des Partisanen. Zwischenbemerkung zum Begriff des Politischen*. Duncker & Humblot, Berlin.
Zarmanian, T. (2006) Carl Schmitt and the Problem of Legal Order: From Domestic to International. *Leiden Journal of International Law*, 19, 41–67.

Index

Unless otherwise stated, any listed works are by Carl Schmitt. Spellings and the presentation of terms follow the majority usage. The letters *n* or *nn* in a page reference indicate a note or notes.

Afghanistan 100–1
Africa 69, 110–11, 117, 134
Agamben, Giorgio 11, 13–15, 130–2, 133, 151, 159*n*11, 169–70, 171, 174–5, 176, 177
Age of Leviathan 82, 178
air power 245–9
Americas 28, 32, 35, 39, 41, 47, 69, 113–14; discovery/appropriation of 80–1, 186–7, 276–81, 285–6; *see also* Monroe Doctrine
amity lines 3, 60, 62, 107, 132, 254–5, 277, 278–9, 280, 285–6
anarchism 83
anomie 154
anomos of the Earth 65, 70, 72
anthropogenesis 174–5
Anthropogeographie (Ratzel) 253
anthropological archaeology 188
anthropological machine 171, 175
anthropology: philosophical 263–4; political 147, 174
anti-immanence 159*n*13
anti-liberalism 5–6, 7–8, 17, 77, 82–4, 115, 135–7; *see also* liberalism
anti-Semitism 4–5, 77, 83, 85
anti-universalism 159*n*13, 223–4, 286–7
appropriation *see* land appropriation
'Appropriation/Distribution/Production' 229
Aradau, Claudia 11
arcanum 177–8, 178–9
Arendt, Hannah 95, 203
Asia 48–51, 69

asylum seekers, Glasgow 155–6, 157, 159*n*14, 160*nn*15–16
Ausland 221, 222–5
Austrian/German customs union 37, 46
authoritarianism 76, 84, 86, 129, 133, 236

Balakrishnan, Gopal 76–7, 201
'balance', inter-state 231–2
Benjamin, Walter 2
Benton, Lauren 10, 271–2
'beyond the line' concept 212, 213, 245, 247–8, 255, 277, 278–80
Bible 87
Bielefeldt, Heiner 84
biopolitics 17, 165–6, 173–4, 178, 189–90
biopower 227–32
Blair, Tony 1, 101
Blakeslee, George H. 50
Bolivia/Paraguay conflict 41
bombing 245–9
border concept 16, 284–90; *see also* amity lines
Bosnia 248
bracketing of war 5, 8, 79, 112, 132, 188, 212, 223, 244–5
Braudel, Fernand 252
Britain *see* Great Britain
British Empire 109, 239
Brzezinski, Zbigniew 203–4
Buddhist civilization 69
Bush, George W. 1, 2, 64, 74, 75, 249

capitalism 66–7
Caribbean 279–80

Carr, E. H. 120
cartography: Earth as globe 96–7; Huntington 68–9, 72; lack of in Schmitt's work 237; Map of Hispanic America 241; Schmitt's metacartography 130–2; *Weltkarte* 238–41
Cateau-Cambrésis agreement 277–80
Catholicism 2–3, 86, 86–8, 178
Cavalletti, Andrea 163, 165–6, 167, 172–4, 179n1
Central America 36–9, 40
Chandler, David 11
China 48, 49–51, 53n8
Christianity 30, 86–8, 109, 177, 255; Catholicism 2–3, 86, 86–8, 178
civilizations 145; 'clash of civilizations' thesis 62–4, 69–70, 72; as *Großräume* 67–70, 72; Huntington's cartography 68–9
civilized–uncivilized distinction 30–1, 113, 212, 255–6, 278, 286
civil war 132, 133, 135
'clash of civilizations' thesis 62–4, 69–70, 72
Cold War 11, 68, 129, 211, 232, 289
colonialism 2–3, 10, 107–9, 111
'colonial war' 129, 132–4, 137
colonies 30, 36, 78, 109, 118, 256
colony–protectorate distinction 30
Concept of the Political 5, 7–8, 66, 67, 95, 108, 114, 135, 136, 152, 261, 287–8; *see also* 'political, the'
Congo 110, 134
conquista, justification for 255
constituent and constituted power 150–6, 157, 169; and space 143–4, 150, 155
Constitutional Theory 152
constitutive disorder 154
corruption 67
cosmopolitanism 68, 85, 178, 238, 241–2, 289
'counter-conduct' concept 195
Covenant *see* League of Nations
creditor- versus debtor-peoples 31
Crisis of Parliamentary Democracy 135
Cromwell, Oliver 87
Cuba 36–8, 110
cultural identities 145–6

Davenport, Frances Gardiner 278–9
'Davos Culture' 68
Dean, Mitchell 157, 169–70
death, taking life 84–6
Debrix, François 14
decisionism/decisions 1, 6–7, 8, 11–12, 127, 131, 132–3, 260, 261–2, 287
DeLanda, Manuel 273
de La Pradelle, Albert 51
Deleuze, Gilles 221, 222
delineation *see* land delineation
de Medici, Marie 280
democracy 48, 49, 50, 77, 83–4, 114, 149
democratic politics of space 155–6, 157, 157–8
demography *see* population
de-Nazification 204
depoliticization 66–7, 114–15, 148–9
deterritorialization of geopolitics 128–9, 137, 140–1
dictatorship 131
difference, ontology of 147
disarmament treaties 41–2
disciplinary mechanisms 189–90
discipline 194
'dollar diplomacy' 47, 110, 112
domestic versus international domains 139, 140–1
dominium–imperium distinction 95
Douhet, Giulio 246
drones (Unarmed Aerial Vehicles) 249
Dugin, Alexander 158n4
Dyzenhaus, David 85

Earth as globe 96–7
East Asian Monroe Doctrine 48–51
economics 29–30, 66–7, 100, 115, 286
'economy', and power 230
Elden, Stuart 164–5, 168–9
elements, symbols of 261
Empire (Hardt and Negri) 11, 232
empires (*Reiche*) 80, 94, 96, 100, 109, 113, 167, 177, 239, 271
England *see* Great Britain
enmity 60, 62, 127–8, 137, 139, 254–5, 255–6; 'absolute enemy' 223; 'political enmity' 183; *Theory of the Partisan* 92, 129, 211, 213–18; 'unjust enemy' 213; *see also* bracketing of war; friend–enemy distinction
ethics 115
Ethiopia 117
etymology 233n1; nomos concept 95, 229, 253, 285, 292; *see also* terminology

300 *Index*

Eulerian perspective 272
Eurocentrism 217, 254–6, 294
Europe 3, 10, 11–12, 30–1, 80, 82, 106, 109, 111, 117, 132, 277, 244, 286, 294–5; 'beyond the line' 212, 213, 245, 247–8, 255, 277, 278–80; German-dominated *Mitteleuropa* 93–4; as Old World 61–2; *see also* Germany; *Jus Publicum Europaeum*
exceptionalism/exceptions 1–2, 6–7, 8, 10, 11–12, 13–15, 83, 130–2, 133, 168, 170; England as 'state of exception' 109; '*nomos* of exception' 14; USA as 'state of exception' 58, 59, 60, 64–5

'failed states' 59, 60–1, 65
family household model 230–1
fascism 91, 201, 203–4, 205; *see also* National Socialism
First World War 39–40, 79, 241
Fisch, Jörg 279, 280
force, Schmitt's advocacy of 84–6
'Forms of modern imperialism in international law' 9, 29–45, 78, 113
Foucault, Michel 17, 65, 101, 120–1, 133, 182, 188–90, 190–3, 194, 195, 227–32
'founding rupture 151–2, 153–4, 157, 159nn10–11, 169
'fragile states' 59, 65, 66
France, Cateau-Cambrésis agreement 277–80
'free sea' concept 9, 268–73
'free' world market 48
Friedrich, Carl 203–4
friend–enemy distinction 2, 7, 59, 85–6, 147, 174, 179n4, 212–13; *amis/ ennemis politiques* 139; Foucault versus Schmitt 191; and the League of Nations 114; scriptural authority 87; us–them and self–other 63, 71, 107–8, 184, 187, 193; *see also* 'political, the'

Galli, Carlo 6, 11, 111–12
Garner, James 281
geography 12–13, 206–7; Germany and the *Weltkarte* 238–41; movement as 272–3; Schmitt's indifference 236–8, 252–3; sea as space without geography 269–70
geopolitics 128, 133, 135–7, 220–1; context of Schmitt's writings 76–80, 91–102; deterritorialization of 137,

140–1; multipolar global order 143–4, 144–50, 157; *see also Ortung* und *Ordnung* 97
Germany 5, 31, 33, 44–5, 76, 81, 82, 94, 116, 206–7; denial of state status 112–13; geography and the *Weltkarte* 238–41; *Mitteleuropa* 93–4; post-war guilt/reparation 115, 202–3, 204, 205; right to wage war 78–9; Weimar republic 7, 8, 78, 135; *see also* National Socialism
Giap, Vo Nguyen 217
Gilroy, Paul 10
Glasgow 155–6, 159n14, 160nn15–16
global economy 286
global identity crisis 71
globalization 66
'global linear thinking' 276–81, 285, 294
'global lines' 2–3
global *nomos* 287–8, 293, 294
global recession 58–9, 63–4
globe, Earth as 96–7
Glossarium 86
Goldhagen, Daniel 203
Gould, Eliga 278–9
'governmentalized' states 190
governmentalities 5–6, 67, 121, 121–2, 192, 231
governments, recognition by US 39
Great Britain 79, 82, 111, 239; English action in Caribbean 279–80; English sea-based imperialism 9, 12, 80–2, 109
Gregor, A. James 204
Gregory, Derek 14
Großraum concept 8–9, 15–16, 52, 52n1, 58, 93, 94, 101–2, 159n13, 217, 292–4; civilizations as *Großräume* 67–70, 72; Huntington's groupings 62–3; and multipolar world order 144, 146–9, 157; and 'new world order' 99–101; *Völkerrechtliche Großraumordnung* 16, 92–3, 116
'*Großraum* versus universalism' 9, 46–52, 78, 116
Gross, Raphael 4, 82
Guattari, Felix 221, 222
guerrillas/partisans 213–18, 226n2
Guevara, Ernesto 'Che' 217, 218

Habermas, Jürgen 84
Hardt, Michael 11, 232
Haushofer, Karl 238

Hegel, G. W. F. 81, 264
hegemony 146, 149; United States 35–6, 39, 39–40, 68, 110–11, 144–5, 158*n*3
Heidegger, Martin 97, 171, 263, 266*n*5
Hitler, Adolf 51–2, 79, 85–6, 92, 94
Holocaust 5, 202
Holy Alliance 32
Hooker, William 11, 91
horror vacui 175–9
household government 230–1
human beings, structure 263–4
humanisation 174
humanism 5, 8
humanitarianism 114
humanities, Nazi Germany 207
humanity 174–5, 191, 255–6
Huntington, Samuel 58, 62–4, 67–9, 71, 75

identities: cultural/religious 145–6; global identity crisis 71; 'identity of state and society' 136; national 84–6
ideologies, fascist 203–4
Il Domino dell Aria (Douhet) 246
imperialism 3, 10, 68, 113–14, 109, 117; 'Forms of modern imperialism in international law' 9, 29–45, 78, 113; and the Monroe Doctrine 47, 49; sea-based 9, 12, 80–2, 109; *see also* Great Britain; United States
'independence' concept 37–8
indeterminacy 150–1, 152
India 118
individualism 66, 77, 78, 115
international/domestic domains 139, 140–1
internationalism 6, 110–12, 117, 241–2
international law 97–8, 111, 114, 116–17; and the Monroe Doctrine 34–5; private property as 'sacred' 39; US/Cuban intervention treaty 36–8; *see also Jus Publicum Europaeum*
International Map of the World (IMW) *see Weltkarte*
international relations theorists 11, 101, 127, 138–41
inter-state relations 127–9, 137–40, 188, 231–2
intervention treaties, US 36–9
Iraq war 64, 100–1
Italian theorists 10–11
Italy 165

Japan 53*n*8
Japanese Monroe Doctrine 48–51

Jewish people 77, 78, 82, 83, 85–6, 87, 178; anti-Semitism 4–5, 77, 83, 85
Jünger, Ernst 266*n*5
jus belli (the right to war) 129, 262
Jus Publicum Europaeum ('European Public Law') 15, 81, 110–11, 130, 132, 186, 187–8, 212, 214, 254, 286, 294, 295; *see also* Nomos *of the Earth in the International Law of the Jus Publicum Europaeum, The*
justa causa problem 12
justis hostis 244, 247–8
'just war' concept 87, 134, 187, 223

Kalyvas 159*n*12
Kant, Immanuel 95, 238
Kantorowicz, Ernst 235–6
Kaplan, Robert 74
Kapp, Ernst 127
katechon 7, 87, 109, 148, 158*n*7, 177, 212, 292–3
Kellogg-Briand Pact 38, 41–4
King's Two Bodies, The (Kantorowicz) 235–6
Kingsway estate, Glasgow 155–6, 157, 159*n*14, 160*nn*15–16
Kosovo, air war 248, 249
Kritik der Geopolitik (Sprengel) 252

Land and Sea 9, 82, 109, 170–1, 172, 177, 260–6
land appropriation 153–5, 157, 167–8, 169, 184, 220, 224–5, 253–4; legal war concept 185–6; in the New World 80–1, 186–7, 276–81, 285–6; and the nomad 221–2, 225*n*1; and pasturage 228–30
land characteristics 269
land delineation 220, 221; border concept 16, 284–90; and the nomad 222, 226*n*2
land law 93–4
land power versus sea power 81–2
land–sea distinction 159*n*9, 271, 271–2; 'postoceanism' 270–1, 274*n*3
Langrangian perspective 272–3, 274*n*4
Latin America, Huntington's cartography 69
law 7, 30, 261, 262; Foucault versus Schmitt 193–4; land law 93–4; legal positivism 48, 53*n*7, 133, 139; 'legal war' concept 185–6; 'legal world revolution' 136; threefold roots of 183–5; and violence 131–4, 262;

see also international law; *Jus Publicum Europaeum*
League of Nations 8, 27–8, 30–1, 34–5, 38–9, 40–1, 43, 44, 46, 78–9, 106, 111–12, 286; challenging Schmitt's reading 117–22; Schmitt's loathing for 112–17
League of Nations and the Rule of Law, 1918–1935, The (Zimmern) 119–20
Lebensmöglichkeit 292, 293
Lebensraum 173
Lebensrecht 50
Lefebvre, Henri 101
Legality and Legitimacy 129, 131, 135
legal positivism 48, 53*n*7, 133, 139
'legal war' concept 185–6
'legal world revolution' 136
legitimacy principle 32, 85, 135
Leviathan, Age of 82, 178
Leviathan in the State Theory of Thomas Hobbes, The 135
Lewis, Bernard 74–5
Leydet, Dominique 84
liberal democracy 48, 49, 50
liberal internationalism 6
liberalism 5, 82–4, 115; liberal geopolitics 135–7; *see also* anti-liberalism
'limited war' 79–1, 265–6, 294
Locke, John 93, 95
London Charter (1945) 100
Long, Johnson 51
'looting economies' 296

Mackinder, Halford 101
maps *see* cartography
mare liberum ('free sea') 268–73
Marxism 10, 83, 203, 236
Mattingly, Garrett 279, 281
Mehring, Reinhard 84
metaphorology 261, 264–5
Mitteleuropa 93–4
modernism, reactionary 179*n*4
Molotov–Ribbentrop pact 94
Monroe Doctrine 9, 15, 31–6, 44, 46–8, 51–2, 109–11, 114, 146, 277–8, 281; Asian 48–51; and the League of Nations 40, 41, 78–9
Moreiras, Alberto 212–13
Morgenthau, Hans J. 127, 138–41
Mouffe, Chantal 144–50, 153, 155, 251–2, 257
movement as geography 272–3
Müller, Jan-Werner 213–14

multipolar global order 143–50, 157, 159*n*13

Napoleon 214, 215
national identities 71, 84–6
nationalism 77–8, 187
National Socialism 91, 94–5, 201–2, 202–5, 266; Nazi Just State 85–6; role of academics 4, 205–7, 207–8; Schmitt's association 3–5, 7, 76–7, 80, 92, 129, 201–2, 207, 236; *see also* Hitler, Adolf
nation-states *see* sovereign states
nativity 169–70
NATO, Kosovo 248, 249
'natural regions/lands' 240, 253
naval power *see* sea-based imperialism
naval wars 79
Nazism *see* National Socialism
Negri, Antonio 11, 232
New World 254–5; discovery/appropriation of 80–1, 186–7, 276–81, 285–6; versus Old World 132
'New World Order' 2, 58, 61–2, 99–101; Huntington 69
nomadism 221–2, 225*n*1, 226*n*2
nomic orders 154, 193, 195; and enmity/partisanship 213–16
nomos concept 57, 65, 80, 167, 168, 169; and biopower/pastoral power 227–32; and border concept 16, 284–90; and colonialism 107–9; criticism of 18; etymology of 95, 229, 253, 285, 292; as Eurocentric 254–6; and everyday life 193–6; and 'founding rupture' 153–4, 157; global nomos 287–8, 293, 294; and internationalism 110–12; Pope as point of reference 80; as spatial order 183–5; tension with 'the political' 211–13; virtual nomos 221–5; *see also* law; *Nomos of the Earth in the International Law of the* Jus Publicum Europaeum, *The*
'Nomos–*Nahme*–Name' 221, 223, 224, 229
'*nomos* of exception' 14
Nomos of the Earth in the International Law of the Jus Publicum Europaeum, *The* 2, 3, 9–12, 18–19; analytical geographies 130, 133, 143–4, 150–1, 153–5, 157–8, 164–5, 183, 187; historical geographies 57–8, 60, 61,

62, 72, 82, 91, 92–5, 96–8, 99–102, 112, 116–17; responses to 220, 244, 247, 251, 252, 253, 254, 255, 256–8; *see also Jus Publicum Europaeum*; nomos concept
non-intervention principle 32, 36
'no peace beyond the line' 278–80
Notion du 'Politique', La (Morgenthau) 138

Obama, Barack 70–1
Obereigentum/Landesherrschaft distinction 95
oceanographers 272
Odysseos, Louiza 11, 287, 289
oiknomia 11
Ojakangas, Mika 151–2, 159*nn*10–11, 223, 224
Old Diplomacy 119
Old World versus New World 132
ontological indeterminacy 150–1, 152
ontology, spatial 16–17, 163, 167–9, 170, 172–3, 176–8, 178
order–disorder tension 151–2, 154, 159*n*13
order/ordering: nomic orders 154, 193, 195, 213–16; political order 135; of populations 188–90; of the sea 254; and security of everyday life 190–3; *signatura* 'order' 176; social order 182, 191, 192, 194, 196, 228, 263, 265; space as ground for 148–9, 150, 153, 154–5, 169; of territory 193–4; *see also* spatial order
Ordnung und *Ortung* 14, 15, 97, 167, 168–9, 178, 211–12, 291–7
'original spatialisation' 170, 172–5
Ostforschung initiative 206
ownership rights 183–5

Panama/US relations 38–9, 277
Paraguay/Bolivia conflict 41
parliamentarism 83–4
Parsons, David 248
partisans/guerrillas 213–18, 226*n*2
pastoral power 227–32
PATRIOT Act 70, 71
peace 41–2, 43–4, 65, 114, 262, 277
Peace of Westphalia 80
Penck, Albrecht 239–41
people, relation with space 156
performance, spaces of 16
Petito, Fabio 11, 144–50, 153, 155
philosophical anthropology 263–4

Plato 229
Platt Amendment 36
pluralism 145, 147–8, 149
Poland 94
poles *see* multipolar global order
police 193
'political, the' 27, 76, 92, 128, 163, 164, 173, 174, 193, 253; *Concept of the Political* 5, 7–8, 66, 67, 95, 108, 114, 135, 136, 152, 261, 287–8; and E. H. Carr 120; Foucault versus Schmitt 121; Morgenthau's conception 139–41; multipolar readings 147–9, 157; and partisanship 216; tension with the nomos 211–13; *Theory of the Partisan* 92, 129, 211, 213–18; *see also* friend–enemy distinction
political anthropology 147, 174
'political enmity' 183
political metaphorology 261, 264–5
political order 135
Political Romanticism 264–5
political theology 86–8, 97; *katechon* 7, 87, 109, 148, 158*n*7, 177, 212, 292–3
Political Theology 5, 6–7, 83, 96, 129, 135, 152, 287–8
Political Theology II 92
Politics Among Nations (Morgenthau) 139–40
politics 7, 8, 120, 139, 140; biopolitics 17, 165–6, 173–4, 178, 189–90; democratic politics of space 155–6, 157, 157–8; depoliticization 66–7, 114–15, 148–9; domestic versus international domains 139, 140–1; relationship with space 149–50, 155; versus trade 29–30 *see also* geopolitics; 'political, the'
Pope 80, 100
population concept 173; space–population/density 173–4
populations: nomos and everyday life 192, 193–6; order and security of 188–90
Portugal 2, 97, 285; *rayas* 2–3, 276, 281
Positionen und Begriffe 9, 78–9
positivism 48, 53*n*7
postcolonialism 254, 256, 256–8
postmodernism 256
'postoceanism' 270–1, 274*n*3
poststructuralism 256
power 60, 139, 230, 262; air power 245–9; biopower/pastoral power 227–32; constituent and constituted

143–4, 150–6, 157, 169; disciplinary forms of 189–90; Foucault versus Schmitt 191–2; land versus sea 81–2; Morgenthau versus Schmitt 140–1; spiritual/earthly 187
presidential decisionism 131
'primary spatialisation' 172–5
'primevalism', geopolitical 220–1
'proper', logic of the 148–9
protectorates 30, 36, 38, 78, 109
Protestantism 86

quantitative total state 129

Rasch, William 10, 11, 130
Ratzel, Friedrich 101, 173, 237, 253
Raumhoheit 99
Raumordnung see spatial order
Raumordnungskrieg 94
rayas, Spain/Portugal 2–3, 276, 281
reactionary modernism 179n4
realism 127–8, 139
Reiche see empires
religion 86, 100, 177; Christianity/ Catholicism 2–3, 30, 86–8, 109, 177, 178, 255; and Huntington's cartography 68–9; *see also* Jewish people; political theology
religious identities 145–6
religious wars, Europe 80
Respublica Christiana 186, 187, 285
Rhein, Adolf 278–9, 280–1
Rhineland territory 113
rights of ownership 183–5
romanticism 83
Roosevelt, Franklin D. 48
Roosevelt, Theodore 47, 48, 49

Said, Edward 107–8, 256
Salan, Raoul 215
Savelle, Max 278–9, 280–1
science, Nazi Germany 205, 206
sea: 'free sea' concept 9, 268–73; *Land and Sea* 9, 82, 109, 170–1, 172, 177, 260–6; land–sea distinction 159n9, 271, 271–2; order of 254; 'postoceanism' 270–1, 274n3
sea-based imperialism 9, 12, 80–2, 109
Second World War 79–80, 94, 202–3
security 193, 194; of everyday life 190–3; of territory/populations 185–90; US responses to (in)security 70–2
self-defence measures 43

self/other distinction 107–8
September 11 (9/11) 2, 13, 75; post 9/11 US anxiety 64–5
Sermon on the Mount 87
shepherd–flock government 229–30, 231
signatura 'order' 176
social order 182, 191, 192, 194, 196, 228, 263, 265
social welfare 230
sociological reality 139
Sombart, Nicolaus 264
'sovereign', conception/definition 6–7, 152, 292
sovereign states 12, 36, 38–9, 78, 100, 169–70, 173, 174–5, 176, 179n4, 185–9, 223, 253; and deterritorialization 128–9, 137; European 244, 286, 294–5; Foucault versus Schmitt 190, 192, 194; and global nomos 288; quantitative total state 129
sovereignty: Foucault versus Schmitt 120–1; order–disorder tension 151–2, 154, 159n13; 'paradox of sovereignty' 13–14; versus liberalism 5; *see also* decisionism/decisions; exceptionalism/exceptions
sovereign violence 131–4, 293
space 166–70; and constituent power 143–4, 150, 155; as ground for order 148–9, 150, 153, 154–5, 169; *horror vacui* 175–9; relation to order 154; relation to people 156; relation to politics 149–50, 155; state control of 99–100; as/through virtuality 221–5; *see also* order/ordering
space–population/density concepts 173–4
spaces of exception *see* exceptionalism/exceptions
spaces of performance 16
Spain 2, 97, 276–80, 285; *rayas* 2–3, 276, 281
Spanish guerrilla war 214
spatialisation, original/primary 172–5
spatial ontology 16–17, 163, 167–9, 170, 172–3, 176–8, 178
spatial order 3, 9–10, 11, 61, 93, 96–7, 183–5, 261, 265; and *Land and Sea* 263; and the League of Nations 116–17, 118; *Raumordnungskrieg* 94; and security of territory 185–90; *see also* order/ordering; *Ordnung* und *Ortung*

'spatial revolution' 109, 176, 263, 265, 293
Sprengel, Rainer 252, 253
state control of space 99–100
state of exception *see* exceptionalism/exceptions
state/politics dissociation 7
state power 60
states *see* sovereign states
Statesman (Plato) 229
Stimson Doctrine 48, 53*n*8
Strauss, Leo 76
Suganami, Hidemi 287
Surin, Kenneth 246
Szöllösi-Janze, Margit 205, 206

'technical work', League of Nations 118–19, 119
technology 263
telluric partisans 214–18
terminology: Americas/US/Western Hemisphere 28; imperialistic 44–5; suffixes denoting 'power' 230; 'territory' 98; translation of terms 93; *see also* etymology
territorial integrity 100–1, 137
territory 95–9, 101–2; Foucault versus Schmitt 192–3; and 'New World Order' 99–101; ordering 193–4; and 'political enmity' 183; rights of ownership 183–5; security of 185–90; virtual territoriality 221–5
terrorism 59–60, 71, 249; post 9/11 US anxiety 64–5; September 11 (9/11) 2, 13, 75; 'war on terror' 10, 13, 71, 75, 249, 277
theology *see* political theology; religion
'theory of the League' 119, 120
Theory of the Partisan, The 92, 129, 211, 213–18
totalitarianism 203, 205
'total war' 79–80, 82, 134, 202–3
trade versus politics 29–30
travelling theory, Nomos *of the Earth* as 256–8
Treaty of Tordesillas 2, 97, 276
Treaty of Versailles 8, 92, 111, 117

unipolar world order 144–5
United States 1, 3, 10, 28, 61–2, 74–5, 100–1, 109, 177, 248, 287–8; civilizational imperatives 70; and Cold War 68, 232; hegemony 35–6, 39–40, 68, 110–11, 144–5, 158*n*3; Huntington's cartography 69; imperialism 29–45, 47, 49, 81, 110–11; intervention treaties, Central America 36–9; and the League of Nations 113–14; Panama/US relations 38–9, 277; recognition of 'legal' governments 39; responses to (in)security 70–2; September 11 (9/11) 2, 13, 64–5, 75; as 'state of exception' 58, 59, 60, 64–5; Vietnam war 217–18; *see also* Monroe Doctrine
universalism 6, 78, 111–12, 114, 116, 178, 223–4, 238, 286–7; '*Großraum* versus universalism' 9, 46–52, 78, 116; *Weltkarte* 238–41; of Western values 67–8
'unjust enemy' 213

Valli, Luigi 174
Vaughan-Williams, Nick 14
Vietnam War 217–18
violence 131–4, 262, 293
virtual nomos 221–5
Vitoria, Francisco de 255, 281
vocabulary *see* etymology; terminology
'Völkerrechtliche Formen des modernen Imperialismus' 9, 29–45, 78, 113
Völkerrechtliche Großraumordnung 16, 92–3, 116
von Humboldt, Alexander 238

war 114, 129, 147, 261–2, 263, 265–6; air power 245–9; bracketing of 5, 8, 79, 112, 132, 188, 212, 223, 244–5; civil war 132, 133, 135; 'colonial war' 129, 132–4, 137; as duel 227–8; Foucault versus Schmitt 191–2; 'just war' 87, 134, 187, 223; 'legal war' 185–6; 'limited war' 79–1, 265–6, 294; partisans/guerrillas 213–18, 226*n*2; *Raumordnungskrieg* 94; Schmitt's justification of 78–9; 'total war' 79–80, 82, 134, 202–3; versus 'peaceful occupation' 43–4; violence 131–4, 262; zones of war and peace 277
'war on terror' 10, 13, 71, 75, 249, 277
wars: Bosnia 248; Eurocentric 254–5; First World War 39–40, 79, 241; Iraq 64, 100–1; and the League of Nations 115, 117; religious wars, Europe 80; Second World War 79–80, 94, 202–3; Spanish guerrilla war 214; Vietnam 217–18
Washington Accord 41

Wehberg, Hans 43
Weimar republic 7, 8, 78, 135
Weltkarte 238–41
'The West' and 'The Rest' 62–7, 68, 69;
  universalism of Western values 67–8
Western Hemisphere 28, 277; *see also*
  Americas; Monroe Doctrine
Westphalian system 231
Who Are We? (Huntington) 71
Willoughby, Westel W. 49–50
Wilson, Woodrow 40–1, 47–8, 64, 112

Yoo, John 75
Young, C. Walter 50

Zarmanian, Thalin 151–2
Zimmern, Alfred 119–20
Ziz 172
Zolo, Danilo 144–50, 153, 155
zones of clash 62–4, 69–70, 72
'Zones of Law, Zones of Violence'
  (Gould) 278
zones of war and peace 277